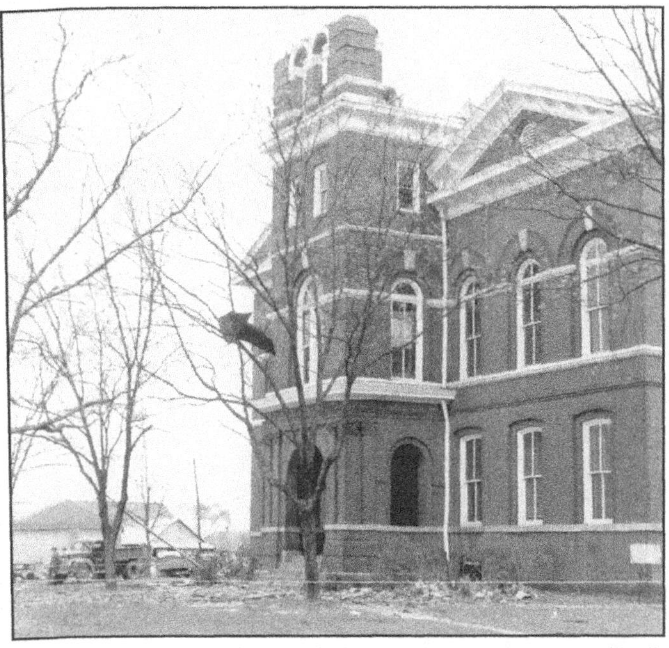

Pike County Courthouse, 1949 tornado damage. Courtesy of Kenneth Caldwell.

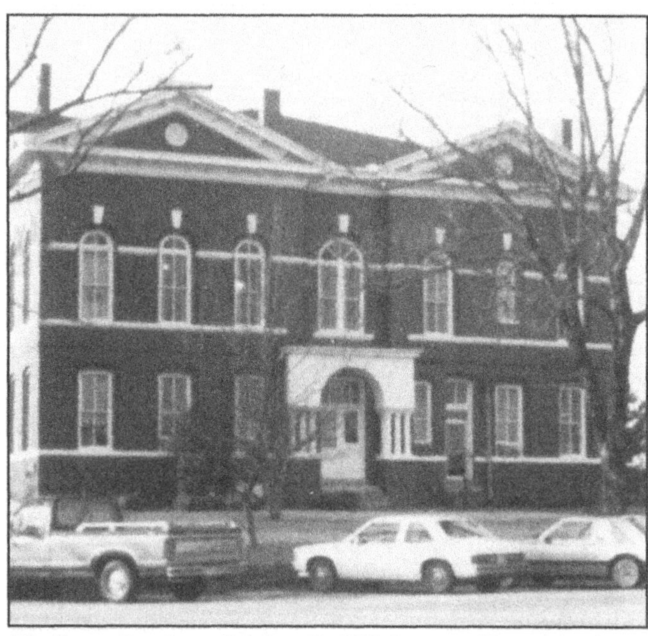

Pike County Courthouse, Zebulon, GA, 1986. Courtesy of Lynwood and Anita Johnson.

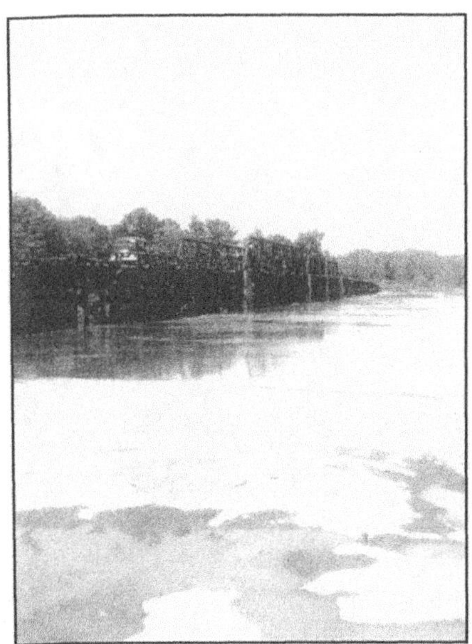

Old Bridge at Flat Shoals. Courtesy of Joann Fenley.

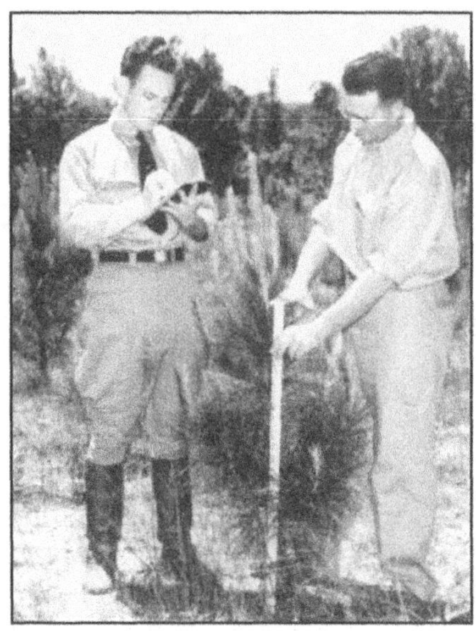

The county agent makes a visit to the farm to check the progress of the pine seedlings. Courtesy of Rachel McClelland.

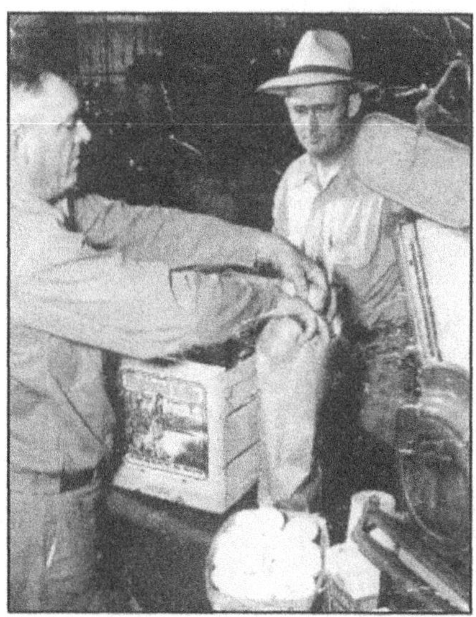

Mr. Julius McGee barter oranges and other citrus fruit for farm eggs from farmer Holloway Norris. Citrus fruit was one of the few foods not raised on the farm. Courtesy of Rachel McClelland.

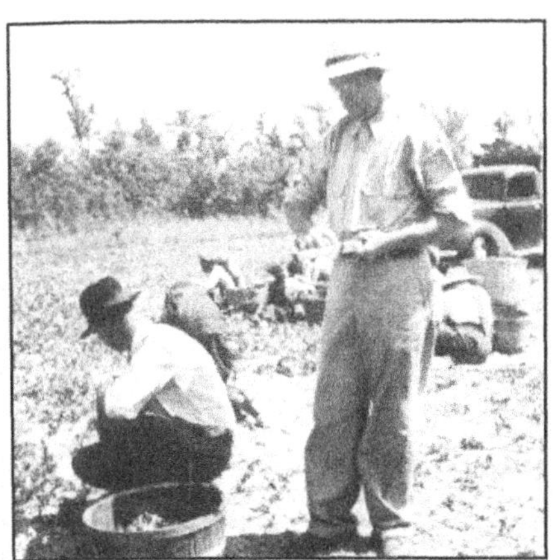

Holloway Norris sharpens knives for cutting turnip greens for cannery. Courtesy of Rachel McClelland.

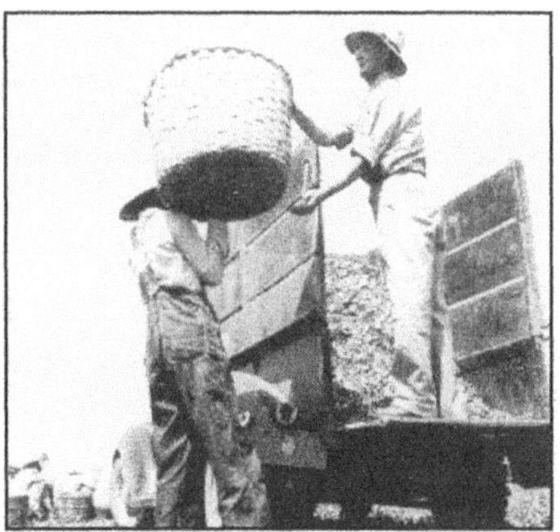

Harvesting turnip greens for canning at Pomona Products Company. Courtesy of Rachel McClelland.

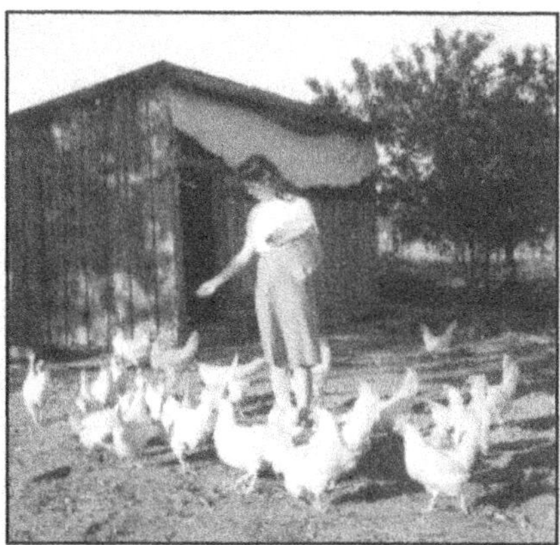

Virginia Norris feeds the chickens near chicken house in background. Courtesy of Rachel McClelland.

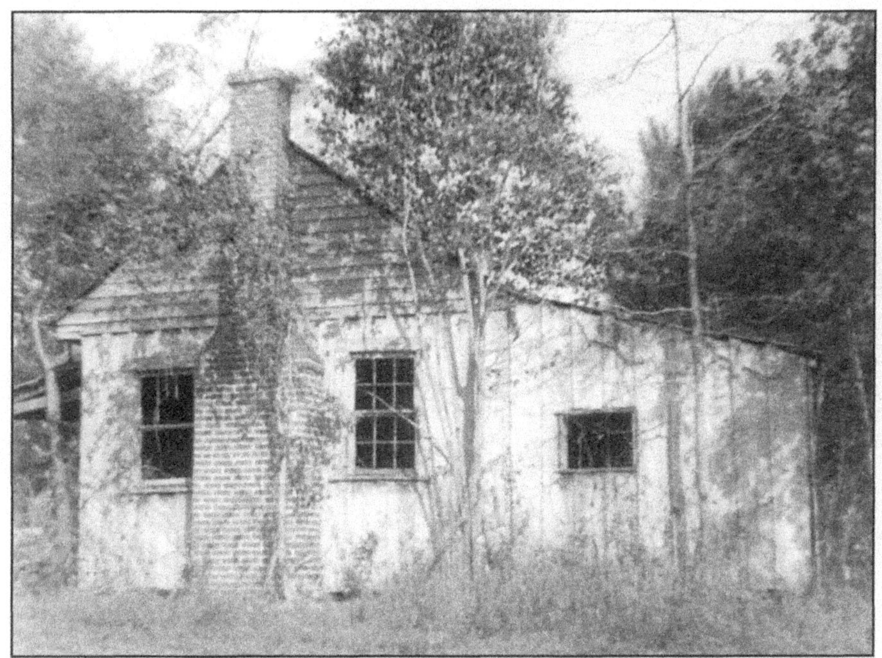

Last Camp house at Lifsey Springs. Courtesy of Rosalee King.

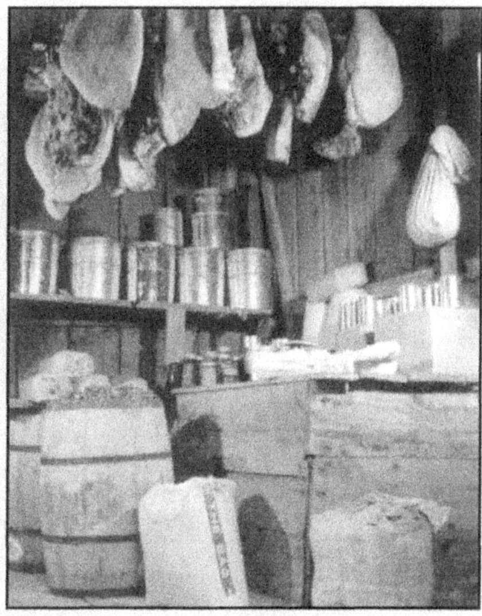

The family smokehouse filled with larder for the winter. Hanging are cured hams. Lard and cracklings, syrup, etc. are in cans. Shown also are saltboxes where other meat was preserved and pecans and meal and flour sacks on lower shelf. Courtesy of Rachel McClelland.

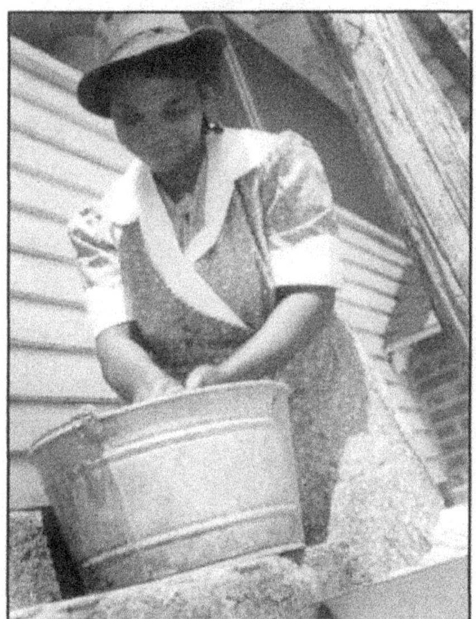

Washing was a big chore on the farm in the 1940's. Courtesy of Rachel McClelland.

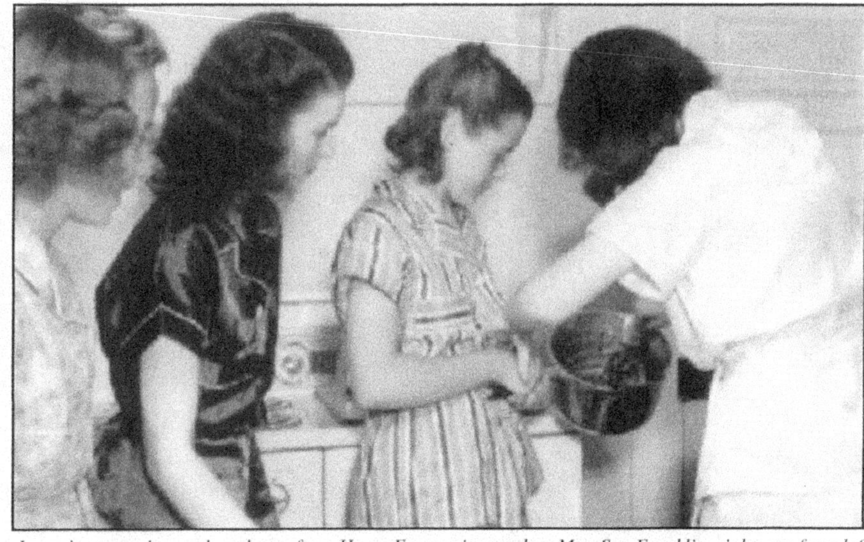

Learning to make candy at home from Home Economics teacher, Mrs. Sue Franklin, right, are from left, Thelma Wilson Sullivan, Iris Salter Jimmerson and Willaminta Norris Hight. Courtesy of Rachel McClelland.

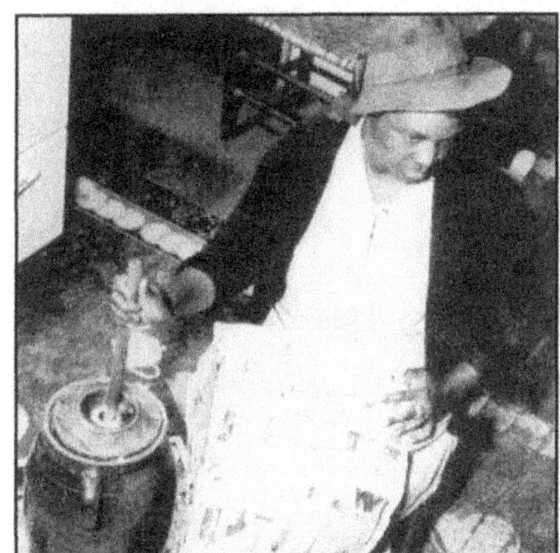

Churning the clabbered milk to make buttermilk and butter was a regular weekly chore at the farm home. Courtesy of Rachel McClelland.

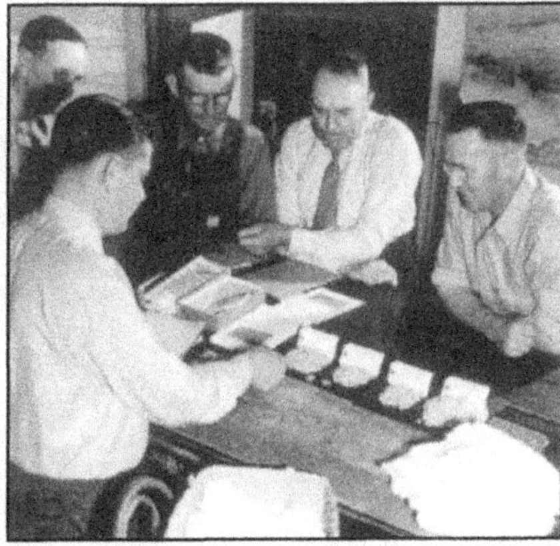

W.H. Means, J.S. Slade, W.J. McDaniels and W.H. Norris examine seed samples at Zebulon Ginning and Fertilizer company Meansville Office. Courtesy of Rachel McClelland.

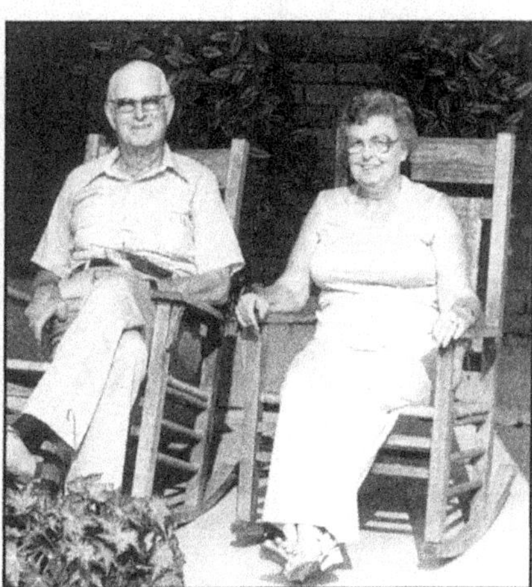

Render and Doris Lawrence, 1981. Courtesy of Billy Lawrence.

PIKE COUNTY, GEORGIA

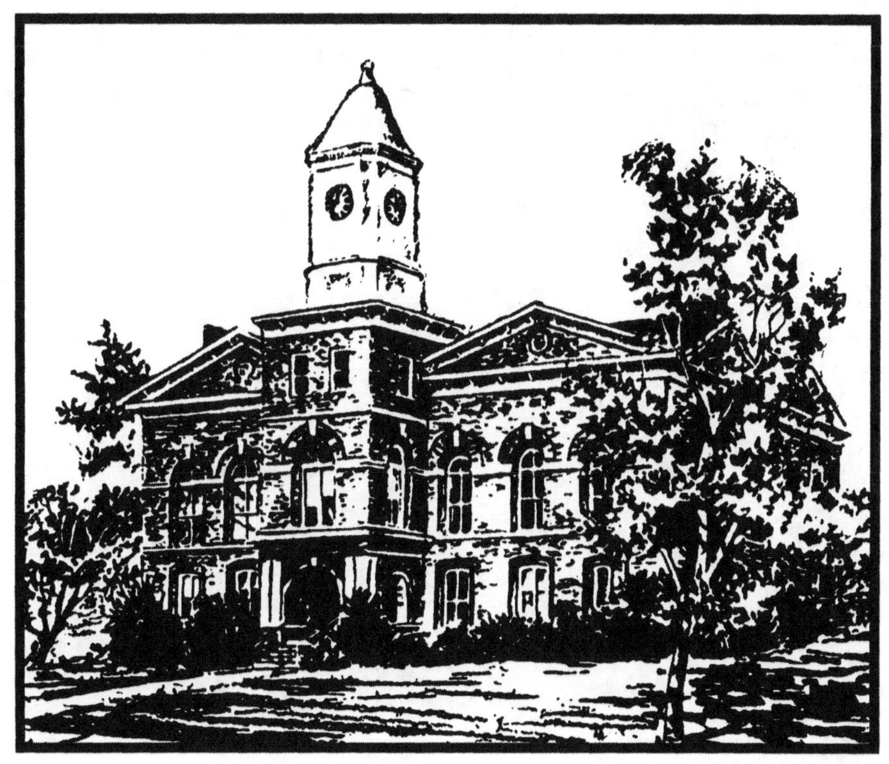

Pictorial History 1822 – 2004

TURNER PUBLISHING COMPANY
Nashville, Tennessee

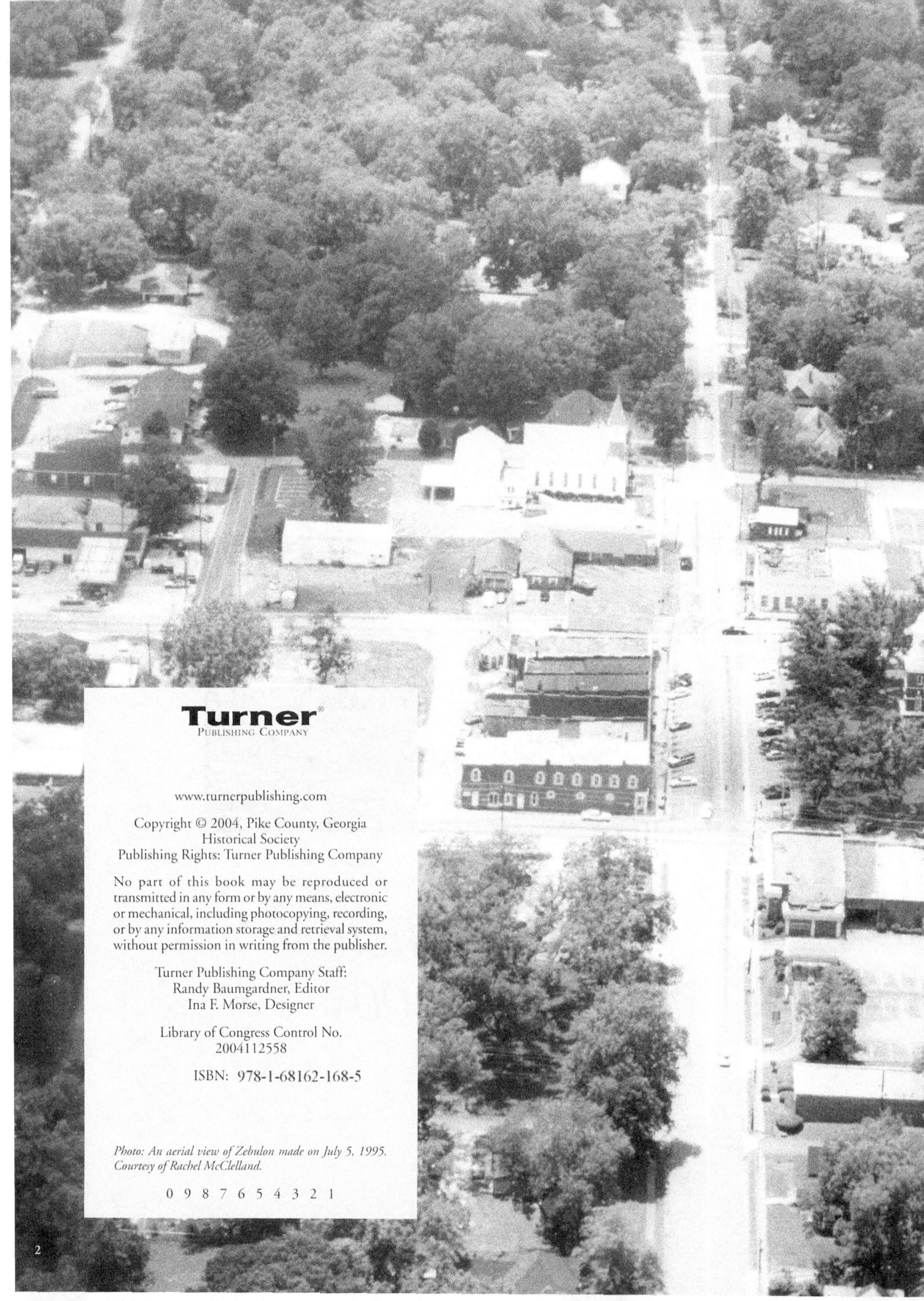

Turner®
PUBLISHING COMPANY

www.turnerpublishing.com

Turner Publishing Company Staff:
Randy Baumgardner, Editor
Ina F. Morse, Designer

Library of Congress Control No.
2004112558

ISBN: 978-1-68162-168-5

Photo: An aerial view of Zebulon made on July 5, 1995. Courtesy of Rachel McClelland.

0 9 8 7 6 5 4 3 2 1

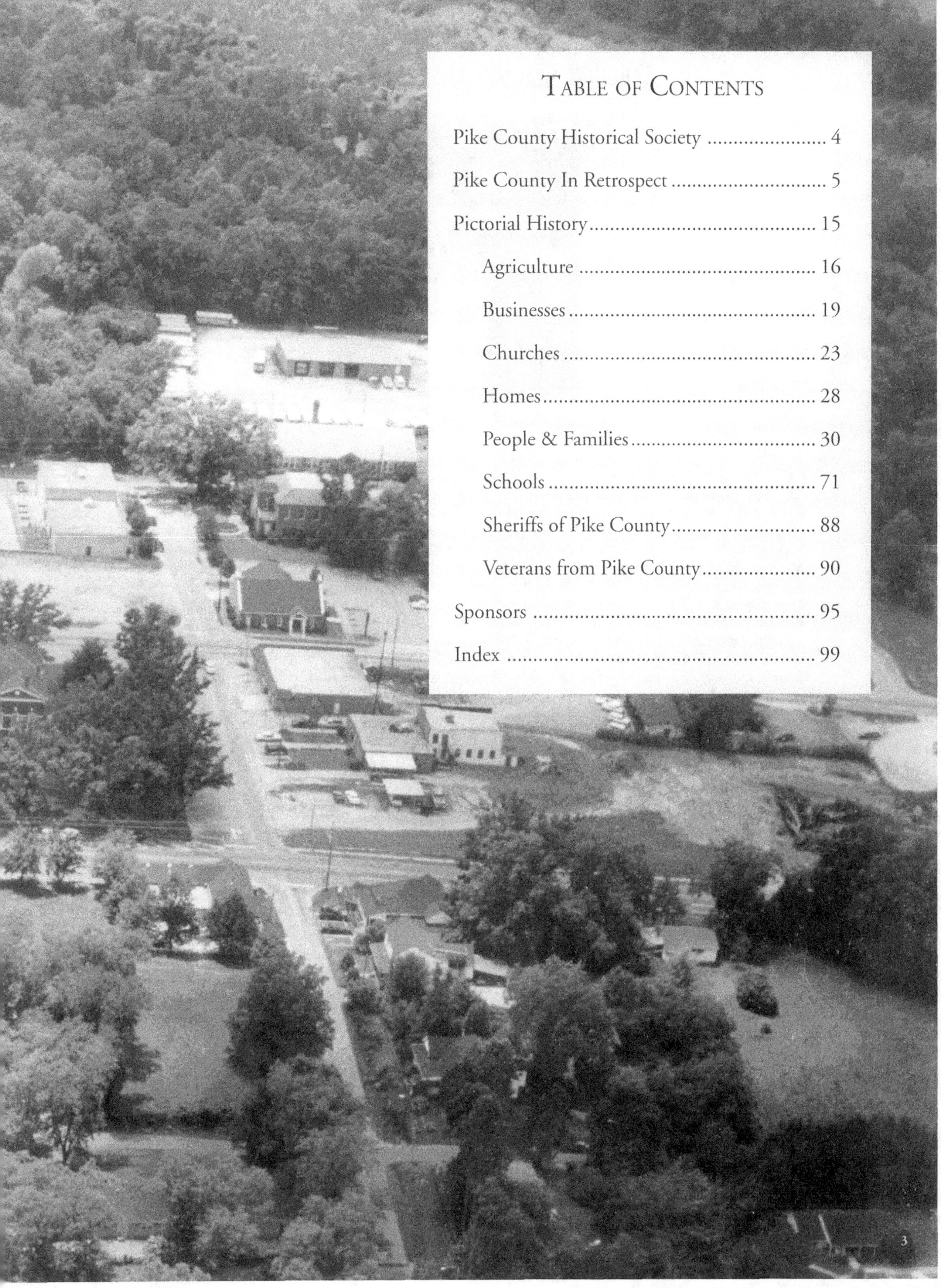

Table of Contents

Brief History of
The Pike County Historical Society

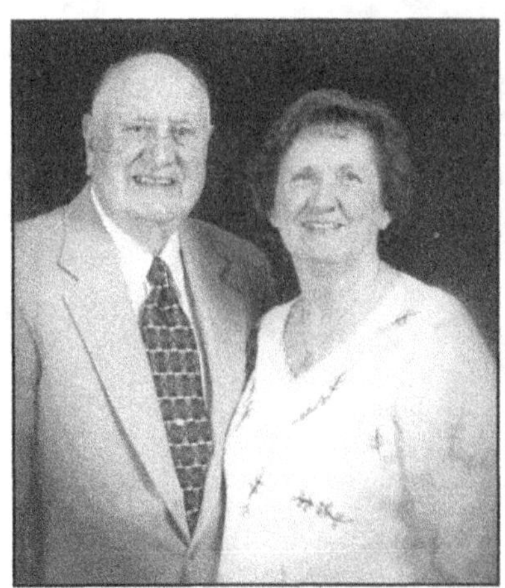

Tom and Sonya Morton

Tom & Sonya Morton founded and incorporated the Pike County Historical Society on October 25, 1999. At their invitation, ten interested citizens of Pike County volunteered to form an initial steering committee. As a result of this effort, the first general membership organizational meeting was held on October 25, 1999 at the Lions Club Railroad Depot in Zebulon, Georgia. Approximately 73 members signed the original Charter of the Society. The first year membership totaled approximately 120 members. The first officers of the Society were: Tom Morton, Founder and President; Bob Williamson, 1st Vice President; Kelly Barrow, 2nd Vice President; Geneva Sanders, Treasurer; Carolyn Holladay, Secretary; Amanda Hollar, Correspondence Secretary; and Robert Morton, Legal Counsel. The initial board of directors included: Gina Fry, Carol Barton, Larry Lynch, Geneva Woods, Richard Beckham, Virginia Oglesby, Dr. E.L. Jones, Stephanie Bradley, Jack Park and Loretta Snowden.

Since its inception, the Society has been extremely active, publishing a quarterly newsletter and annual status letters; an annual banquet held each April; two outdoor bar-b-ques; staffing a booth at the Concord Annual Jubilee; and staging several historical field trips. The Quilt Committee has made two quilts that have been very successful fundraisers.

The Society is presently seeking to establish a permanent home and recently established a building fund. The Society is also currently working on a Pike County Historical Map, and one member is updating data on the cemeteries in Pike County. Each year the Society has made a "Historian of the Year" Award. Both the Board of Directors and the General Membership meet on a quarterly basis. The Society has 15 members serving on the Board of Directors; its colors are peach and green.

The Society has been approved by the IRS as a non-profit organization and is exempt from federal income taxes.

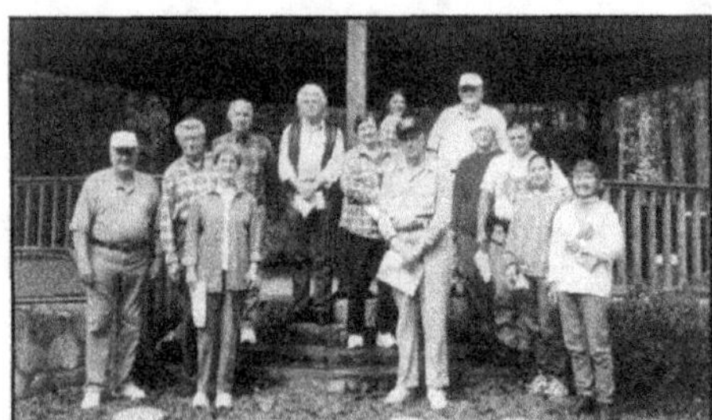

Pike County Historical Society Field Trip. Courtesy of Tom Morton.

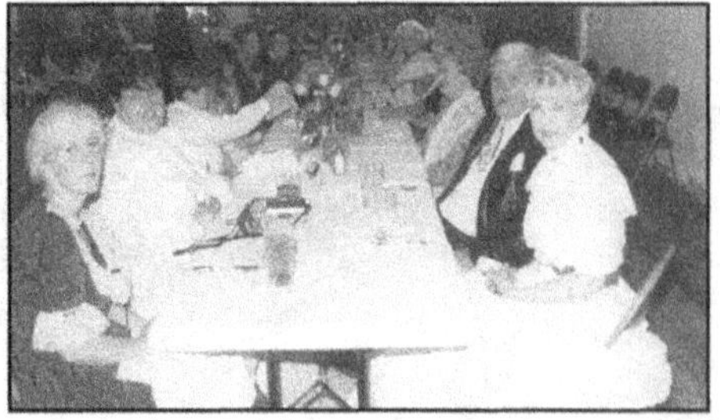

Scenes from the Pike County Historical Banquet held by the Society on April 27, 2002. Courtesy of Teri Totten.

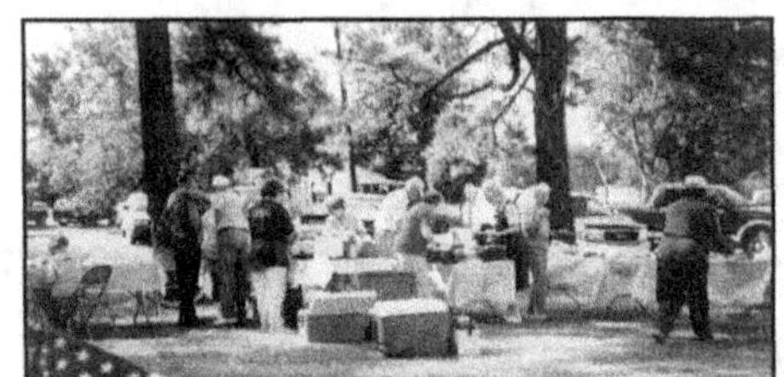

Pike County Historical Society Bar-B-Que. Courtesy of Tom Morton.

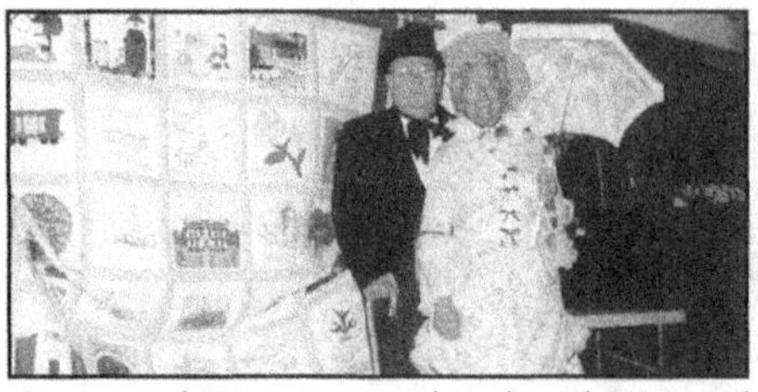

Courtney and Nancy Austin with quilt at the Historical Banquet, April 27, 2002. Courtesy of Teri Totten.

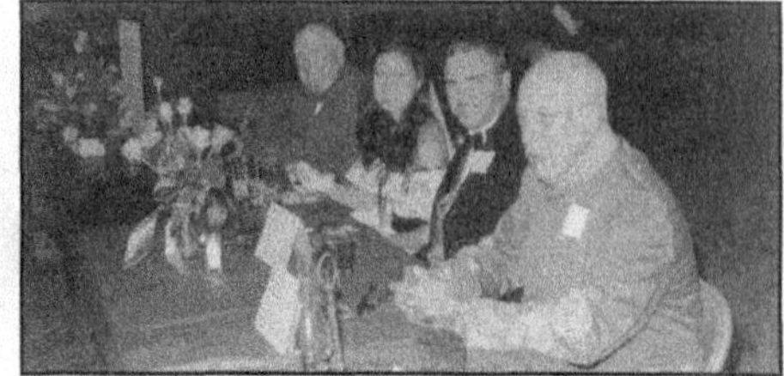

Tom Morton, Gina Fry, Steve Fry and Jim Totten at the Historical Banquet, April 27, 2002.

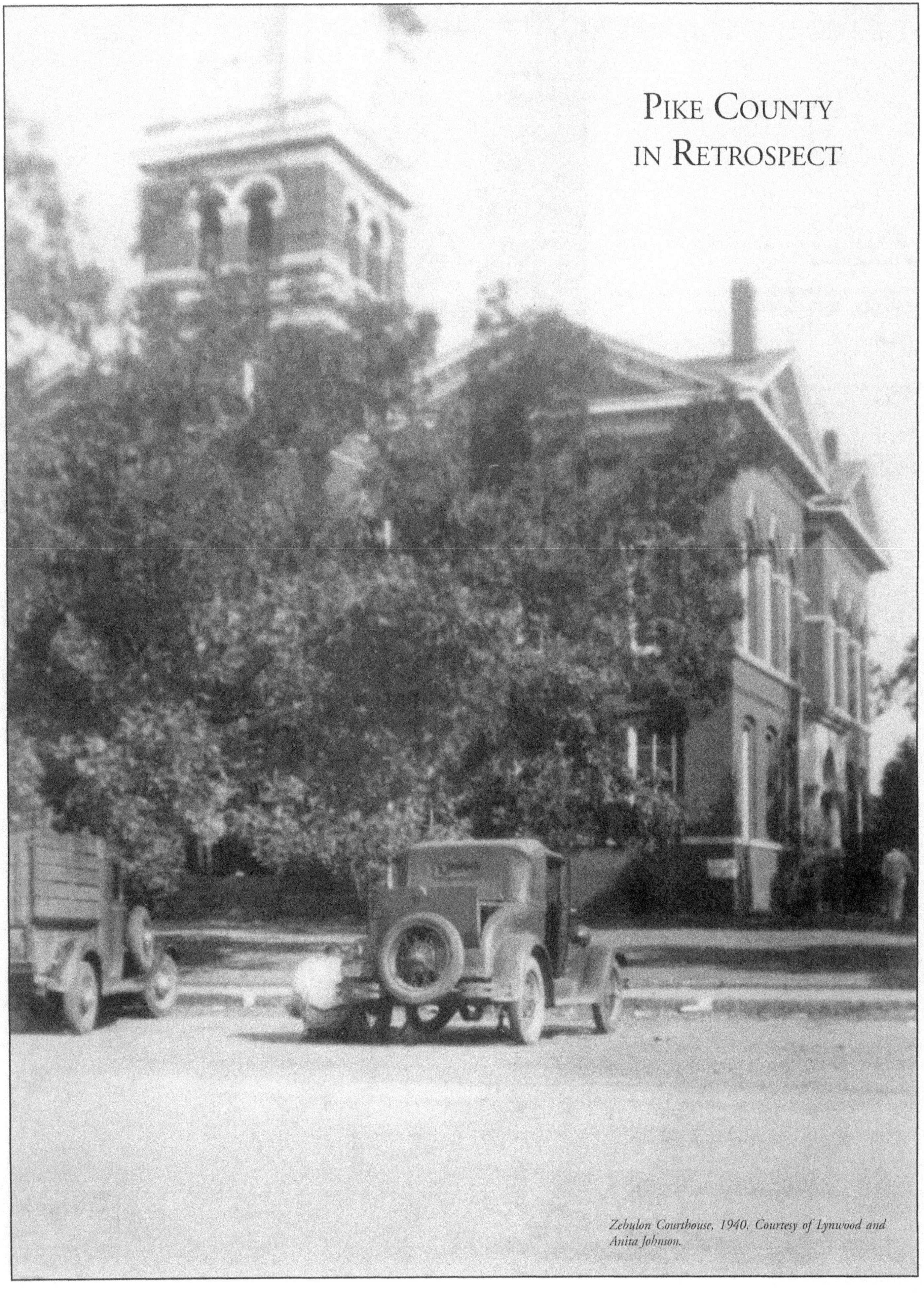

Pike County in Retrospect

Zebulon Courthouse, 1940. Courtesy of Lynwood and Anita Johnson.

Top: *Zebulon, looking west in September of 1940. Courtesy of Lynwood Johnson.*

Center left: Last Courthouse of Lifsey Springs which stood on Lifsey Spring Rd. Courtesy of Rosalee King.

Center right: Lifsey Springs in its early years. Courtesy of Rosalee King.

Bottom: Aerial view of Pike County Courthouse made on July 13, 1995. Courtesy of Rachel McClelland.

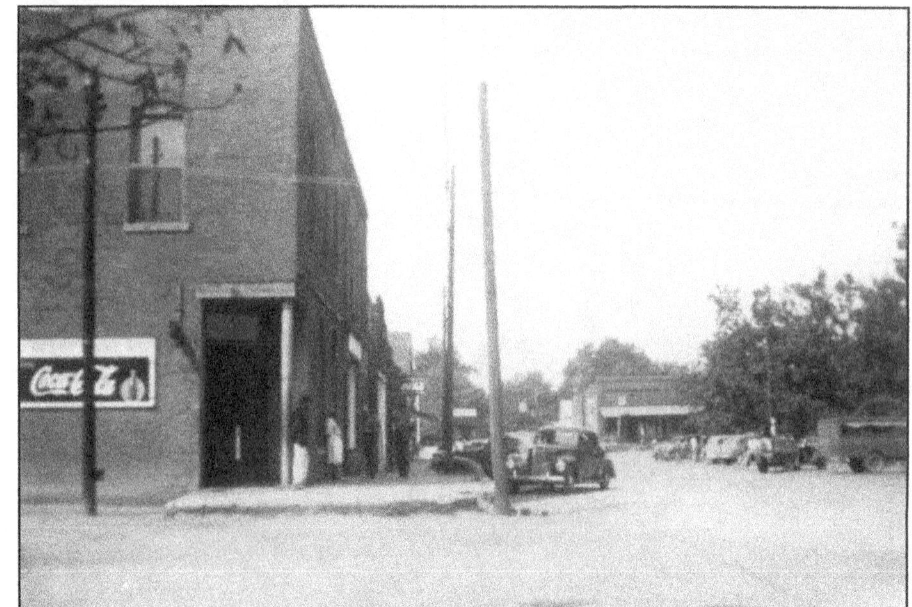

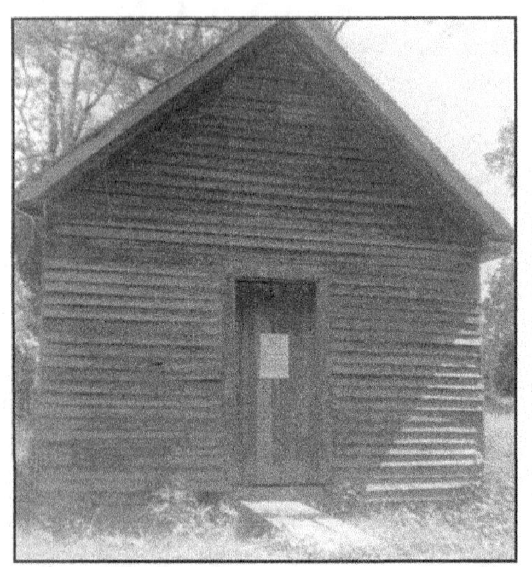

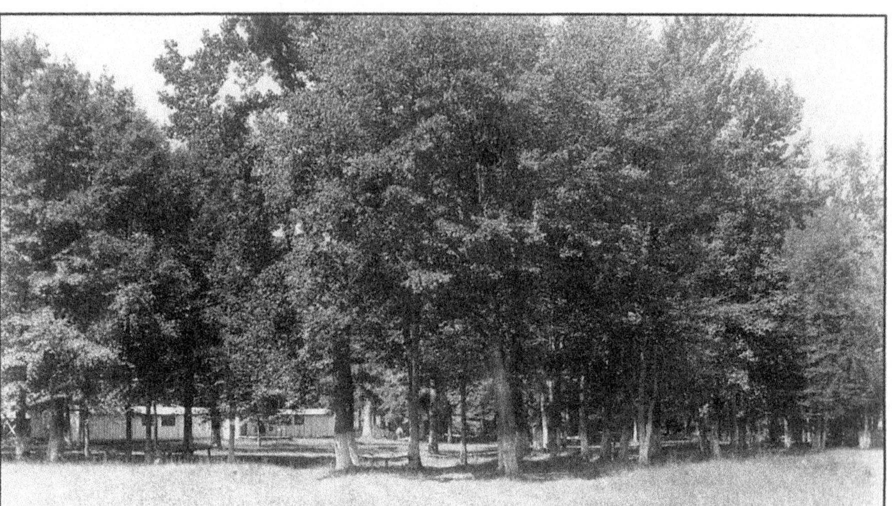

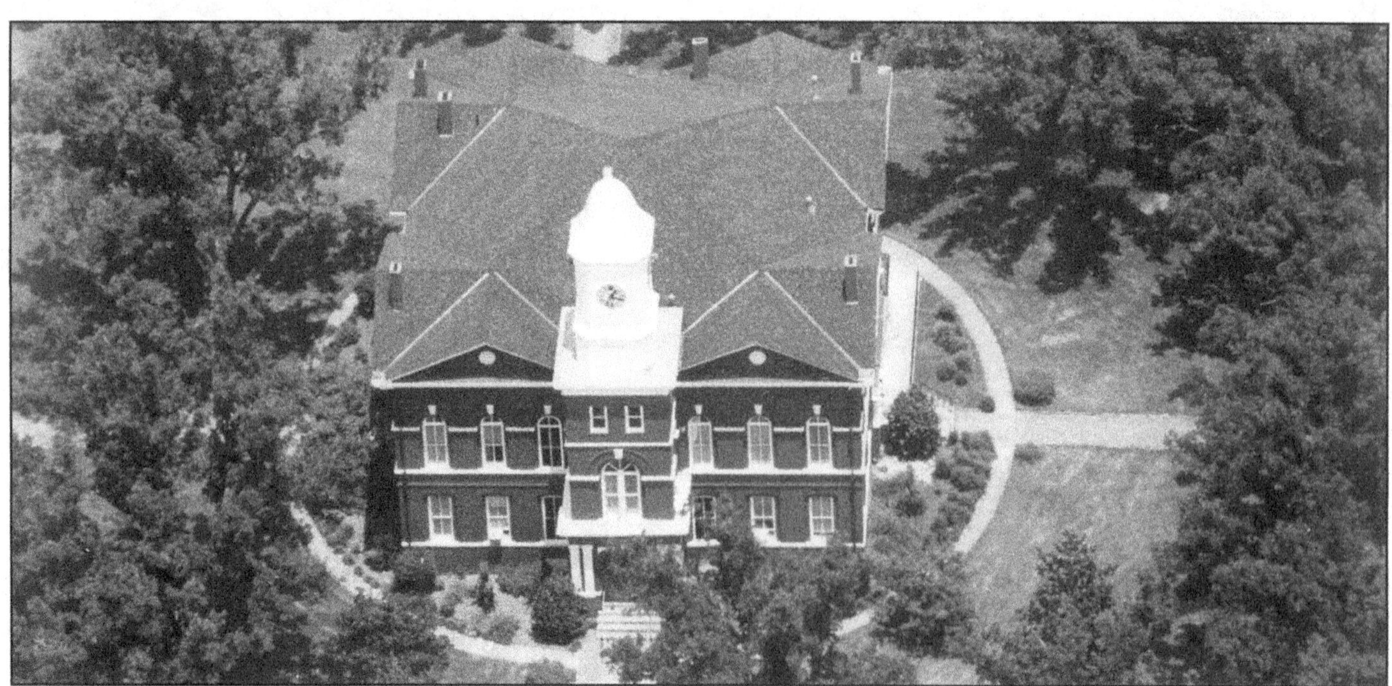

Introduction

A pictorial history of Pike County will be enhanced by first presenting a brief, but adequate, textual framework of the County's history. This should provide a meaningful context for the pictorial presentation which follows.

This treatment deserves qualification and delimitation at the outset so that it does not fall short of the reader's expectations in terms of scope and comprehensiveness. Those familiar with Pike County's history should recall the premier scholarly history of the County by the venerable educator, Lizzie Mitchell, first published in the 1930's, the more limited historical reminiscences of the Rev. R. W. Rogers in 1920, and the voluminous history published in 1989 which included within it reprints of the two previously mentioned. To assume that the limited textual coverage here could in any way replicate, expand or amplify these previous treatments would be a vast misconception of the purpose of this text.

Rather, the treatment here, to provide the textual basis for the pictorial presentation, will draw from these previously done histories as a broad source base, gleaning from them quite selectively along with other sources to develop a pertinent historical record for this presentation.

The Broader Geographical Setting

Important to its history and character is the fact that Pike County is situated in Georgia's Lower Piedmont Area, which includes thirty-five counties forming a band across the entire State, east to west. This band of counties comprises the southerly flank of Georgia's share of the Piedmont plateau, a broad band of rolling-to-hilly terrain which separates the mountainous regions from the coastal plains. This geographical phenomenon, through its impact on agriculture, types of resources, and transportation, as well as other factors, has profoundly affected the history and character of the region and that of Pike County per se.

In fact, Pike is one of only five counties in Georgia's entire fifty-two county Piedmont Plateau that share the scenic beauty of the Pine Mountain range, extending east-west and spanning most of the distance between the Ocmulgee and the Chattahoochee Rivers. The Pine Mountains have the distinction of being the most southerly mountain range in the southeastern United States (east of the Mississippi River). This mountainous terrain, paralleling Pike's southern boundary, has had its impact on Pike's history and character, as will be noted further in this treatment.

While thoroughly agrarian from the time of its earliest settlement, Pike County never fit the stereotype of the plantation society in a slave economy. Rather, it was populated from the outset by a yeoman class of independent small farmers predominantly of sturdy Scots-Irish stock who benefited from the virtually free distribution of lands in the hilly Piedmont section, considered less desirable for expansive plantation culture. These settlers were not typically the landed aristocracy nor were they the poor whites. They were, rather, a large middle class, which was perhaps most characteristic of the bulk of the Southern Piedmont and which one social historian has described as a society of "common men."

With few exceptions, Pike's settlers were typically small landowners who owned relatively few slaves and practiced their agriculture intensively. The census of 1850 for Pike County, which was near the peak of the development of the South's slave economy, showed a total population of 11,933 with 4,721, or forty percent of the population, being slaves. Even more revealing is the fact that there were 1,210 white households to which these 4,721 slaves were attached, or an average of less than four slaves per household. This compares with approximately six slaves per farm throughout most of the slaveholding South in 1850. This means that relatively few of Pike County's antebellum farmers could be considered as members of a "planter" class, as those who owned twenty or more slaves were termed.

The Beginnings

Pike County was created by an act of the Georgia legislature in December, 1822. It was carved out of Monroe, an original county acquired by treaty with the Lower Creek Indian Nation on January 8,1821. Monroe originally extended from the Ocmulgee River on its eastern boundary to the Flint River on its western boundary. The new county of Pike was created from Monroe's western portion and was bounded on the west by the Flint River, which in 1822 represented central Georgia's western frontier. Thus, at the time of Pike's earliest settlement, Creek Indians continued to occupy lands on the western side of the Flint River.

According to Mitchell's history, the legislative act that created the county also appointed five managers for the sole purpose of holding an election and organizing the new county's government. Consequently, these five managers—Willis Whatley, Neal Erquet, John Hammel, William Towers, and Jonathan Bonner—met with the responding residents at the County's first "courthouse," a crude

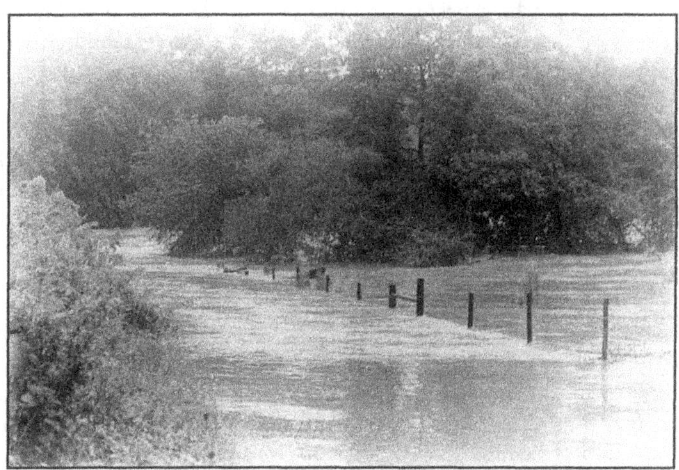

Flint river during the flood of 1993. Courtesy of Rosalee King.

log cabin with a dirt floor located just west of Potato Creek near what was later to become the Piedmont community (now in Lamar County). This election resulted in the selection of five justices of the Inferior Court, viz.: Samuel Black, Lewis Winn, William Duke, Thomas Lewis, and William Mitchell. In addition, W. Whatley was elected sheriff; J. H. Broadnax, clerk of the Superior Court; William Myrick, clerk of the Inferior Court; and Joel Moore, Coroner.

The role and significance of the Inferior Court as an institution of that era in county government should not be underestimated. This panel of officers elected from the County's citizenry served a multi-function role as a court with both civil and criminal jurisdiction and as the administrator of all county operations. In the context of today's county government, the responsibilities of this five-man panel of officers would parallel that of county commission board, county manager, and probate judge. Those considered worthy of election to this office were expected to be, not only persons of integrity, but also capable and discreet. To be elected to serve as judge of the Inferior Court was considered a high honor, and those who served did so without fee, salary or any monetary compensation. This court was abolished in 1868 with its decidedly judicial function assumed by the Court of Ordinary (now Probate Court) and its administrative function assumed by the county commissioner(s) or a county manager

In 1823, Pike's first five Inferior Court justices chose Land Lot No. 202 as the site of the county seat. This site was located at what today is the junction of Georgia Highway 109 and the Zebulon-Meansville Road. This particular site was selected because it represented the approximate geographical center of original Pike County. This lot was laid out into town lots and named Newnan in honor of General Daniel Newnan of Revolutionary War fame.

The location of this first county seat, though near the County's geographic center, was not without "considerable contention" and dissatisfaction among a contingent of its citizens. This stemmed from the fact that the Pine Mountains divided the county east-to-west and a location north of the mountains created a disadvantage for those traveling to the county seat from south of the mountains. This discontent precipitated a move to create a new county which would include most of that portion of Pike County south of the Pine Mountains. Thus, Upson County was created by an act of the General Assembly on December 15, 1824, with its county seat of Thomaston.

Faced with the handicap that the Pine Mountain chain imposed on those traveling from one side of the mountains to the other, travelers sought the most naturally accessible points for crossing. Perhaps, the best known and most commonly used of such crossing points was a natural gap in the mountains some two miles or less south from the town of Meansville. Mitchell records that those first settlers from north of the mountains traveling by horseback to the point near Potato Creek to participate in the first election and the organization of the County crossed the mountains at or near this natural gap.

As might be expected, this gap became the crossing point for one of the first primitive thoroughfares from the County's southeastern section to the county seat north of the mountains. It afforded the added attraction of a fresh-water spring which provided refreshment for those traveling on foot, wagon or horseback.

This site became known in the County's annals as Mountain Gap. It was a part of the land holdings of early settler Isaac Jones. In 1878, his widow, Mary Jones, deeded the site for the location of a "school and courthouse." Some forty years later it was acquired by the Mountain Gap Church and became the site of the Mountain Gap Church and the Mountain Gap Camp Meeting, and continues so at this writing.

Now the necessity to conform to the law requiring the county seat to be as near the center of the county as possible prompted a search for a new county seat for Pike. This search resulted in the selection of Land Lot No. 227, about four miles north of Newnan, the original county seat. It was early in 1825 that this new site was

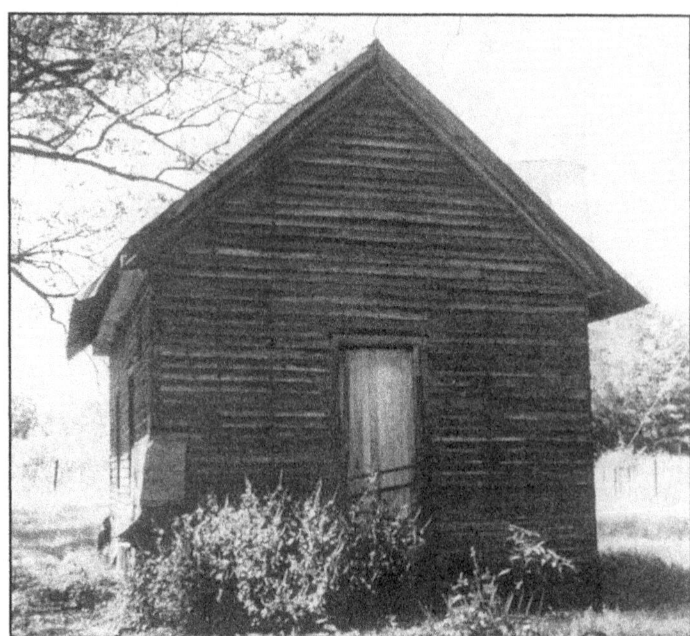

Old "Courthouse" at Meansville, used as voting station and Justice of the Peace court. It was abandoned in the 1940's. Courtesy of James W. Adams.

laid out and named in honor of Zebulon M. Pike, famed explorer and military officer, for whom the County was also named. By 1826, the new town of Zebulon was growing rapidly with several manufacturing and retail establishments already in operation. The town of Newnan was soon abandoned with some of its merchants moving to Zebulon and some to Thomaston.

Roads, Railroads and Economic Development

Being situated some distance from a sea coast or a commercially navigable stream, Pike County was subject to both the capabilities and the limitations of land transportation. This fact has exerted its distinct impact upon the historical development of the County. Obviously, when the County was formed in 1822 and opened for settlement, it was a virtual wilderness, having been sparsely occupied by Creek Indians. The Creeks tended to locate their villages along the banks of the major streams such as the Flint and the Chattahoochee Rivers. These villages were connected with well-worn trails, which became the basic routes followed by the first settlers, some of whom had entered the County as squatters on Indian territory before the land was acquired by treaty from the Creeks. Often, portions of these trails could only be traversed by foot or on horseback, necessitating modifications by the settlers to accommodate their wagons and other primitive conveyances.

Two such trails penetrated the wilderness that became Pike County and became the first crude thoroughfares across its territory. The Oakfuskee trail entered the County near its northeastern corner in what is now Spalding County and exited at Flat Shoals on the Flint River to continue on westward into Alabama to the Great Oakfuskee Town of the Upper Creek Indians on the Tallapoosa River near Dadeville, Alabama. The other trail entered Pike County's eastern boundary (now in Lamar County) at a point near Liberty Hill and continued southwesterly across the County to exit it at the Flint River only a short distance below the Spewrell Bluff State Park in Upson County. Both of these routes were used by the stream of settlers wending their way along a common path of movement from the already-settled Georgia counties to the east as well as directly from the Carolinas. Stage coaches began operating over both these routes sometime during the 1820s, carrying both passengers and mail.

It was the latter of these two lines that became the more prominent thoroughfare through the County and along which the first significant core of settlement and activity developed within its original boundaries. It became a stage line, operating between Augusta, Georgia, through Pike County on through Columbus, Georgia, on the Chattahoochee River and ultimately on to Natchez and New Orleans. This route became known in its day as the Alabama Road, and portions of it are preserved today in the area's local roads. A number of the country's notables, such as President Martin Van Buren, Henry Clay, James K. Polk, General LaFayette, General Andrew Jackson and others, traveled this road by stage coach in the 1820s and 1830s. There were tavern-type accommodations for travelers at appropriate intervals along it and horse-team relay points at about every fifteen miles.

Due largely to the impact of this thoroughfare, the areas along and in close proximity to the Alabama Road reflected some more rapid development over the early decades of the County's settlement. As a result of the formation of Lamar County from a portion of Pike County in 1920, a span of only some three or four miles of the Alabama Road remains within the bounds of Pike County, cutting across the tip of its southeastern corner.

One of the ironies of Pike's history is the transformation in its residential development now spreading from its northern boundary, largely the impact of Griffin's urban spread, which itself is being driven by Greater Atlanta's metropolitan sprawl. This impact is of relatively recent vintage, however. Pike County's settlement had been in progress for several years before Atlanta even came into existence as a junction of two railroads in a wilderness. In fact, Mitchell notes that this northern area of Pike (principally the first and second land districts) was commonly referred to as the "wilderness" in the earlier years of its settlement. She further observes that prior to 1840 all the northern part of Pike was exceedingly primitive and undeveloped.

Rather, Pike's earliest development followed, to a great extent, the Alabama Road traversing the County's eastern and southern sectors. The town of Barnesville came into being in the first decade of Pike's existence, obviously influenced appreciably by its close proximity to the Alabama Road. Barnesville had its beginning following the settlement of Gideon Barnes in 1826 and his establishment of a tavern and a stage station. He operated a stage line connecting Macon and Columbus. Also located on a major stage route between Washington and New Orleans, Barnesville quickly became a fast-growing community in Pike County.

Before 1850, Barnesville, then in the eastern part of Pike County, was enjoying the economic and commercial stimulus of railroad transportation, certainly a boon to any community in a day when any other form of automated transportation was nonexistent. The Monroe Railroad and Banking Company, chartered by the State of Georgia in 1833, reached Barnesville with a rail line by 1841, and by 1846 the line had been completed over the whole length of 101 miles from Macon to Atlanta with Barnesville strategically located about midway between these two points. Organized as the Macon and Monroe Railroad, in 1847 it became the Macon and Western. This railroad rapidly became a mainline freight and passenger line which, upon consolidation with the Central of Georgia Railroad (initially Central Railroad & Banking Company) in 1873, extended from Atlanta to Savannah. It is today a part of the giant rail network of the Norfolk Southern Corporation.

More than forty years passed before any of the County's towns other than Barnesville were favored with railroad transportation. The impact on Barnesville over this interim was tremendous. What was previously a little frontier hamlet was by the 1880s transformed into the County's largest metropolis and its major manufacturing and commercial center.

Barnesville's superior industrial status in the County stemming from its more favored rail connection is not to be underestimated. It could boast twenty mainline passenger trains daily traveling east and west through the town and ten freight trains daily east and west. This rail transportation advantage catapulted Barnesville into the position of Pike's largest industrial center. Two buggy manufacturing firms, that of Summers and that of Smith, located in Barnesville, resulting in the town's becoming the largest buggy manufacturing center in the South. Barnesville has been described, at the height of the horse-and-buggy age, as a manufacturer of transportation as Detroit became for the automobile industry. Similarly, Barnesville had the first and only textile manufacturing operations in the County by the turn of the twentieth century, as well as several large general merchandise firms and dealers in farm machinery, livestock (livery stables, etc.). Also, Barnesville became a major educational center. Gordon Junior College, now a part of the University of Georgia system, was chartered in 1851.

Thus, it appears quite understandable that the removal of the substantial eastern flank of Pike County to form the new county of Lamar in 1920, which included the town of Barnesville, resulted in, no doubt, the most profound revamping of Pike's geography, topography and economic base to be experienced in the entire history of Pike County. This separation was the culmination of a fight for some fifty years for a new county by residents who felt themselves at an "uncomfortable distance" from both Zebulon and Forsyth, the county seats of Pike and Monroe, respectively. A portion of the new county was taken from Monroe.

Not until the 1880s were rail connections and service established to towns in Pike County other than Barnesville. In 1887, the Georgia, Midland & Gulf Railroad Company laid its tracks from Atlanta to Columbus connecting the towns of Concord and Molena. The same year (1887), the Atlanta and Fort Valley road laid tracks through the towns of

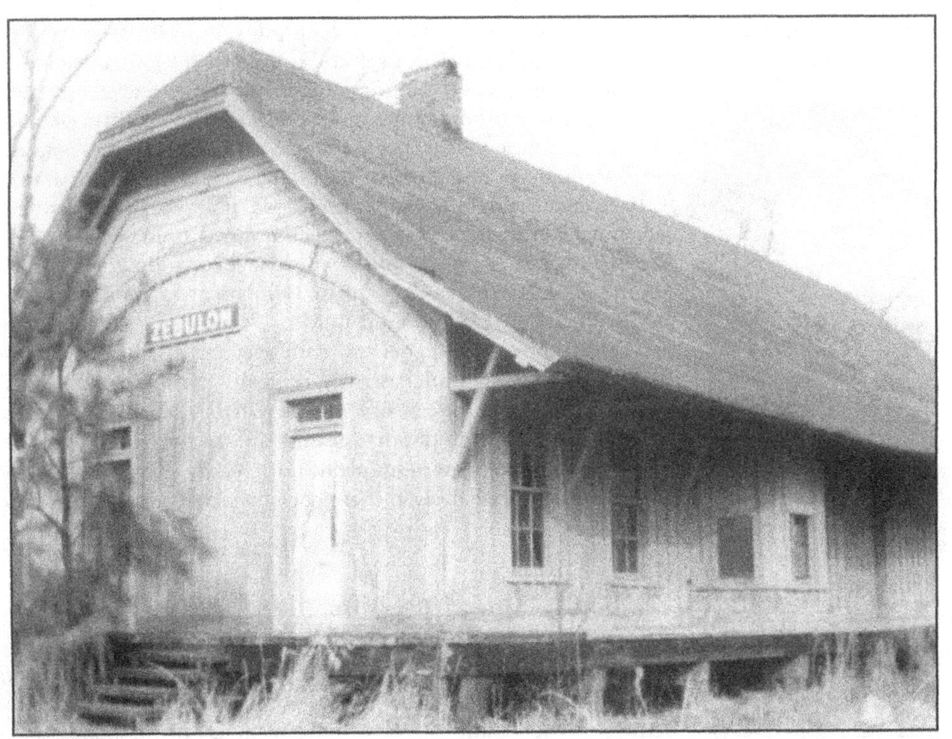

Old RR Station, Zebulon, GA, 1986. Courtesy of Lynwood and Anita Johnson (now owned by The Pike County Lions Club).

Zebulon and Meansville. These two lines converged near Griffin at Williamson and used common trackage into Atlanta. The Atlanta & Fort Valley Railroad was completed by 1888.

The impact of the advent of railroad transportation in the County, in addition to that already noted for Barnesville, within the setting of its time, was truly profound and should not be underestimated. The structure and character of the towns and communities reached by rail were markedly affected, not only in terms of their economic significance, but also in terms of their topography and demography. For example, Pike County affords at least two instances of towns/communities being rendered completely defunct and becoming extinct when the coming of a railroad diverted this locus of activity to another location. This phenomenon is seen in the case of Hard-Head situated a little west of Concord. This community became completely nonexistent when the railroad by-passed it in favor of the nearby Concord community. In fact, it would appear to be no coincidence that the Strickland firm, which became, perhaps, the County's largest mercantile operation serving the County's agrarian market of that day, established its operations in Concord in 1887—the same year that Concord became a point on the Georgia Midland & Gulf Railroad.

An even more striking example, perhaps, of this diversion phenomenon can be cited with regard to Meansville, in the southeastern section of the County. Until the coming of the Atlanta & Fort Valley rail line in 1887, the town of Meansville was located one mile east of its present location. All available recall and historical records indicate that Meansville at its original site was a flourishing little village, named for one of its key residents and landowners, John Means. It boasted stores, blacksmithing, sawmilling, and gristmilling operations and a church (the original location of Meansville Baptist Church). However, once the rail line was constructed a mile to the west, the economic and commercial activity naturally gravitated to that location, leaving only memories of the once-viable little center of activity.

However, by the third decade of the 1900s, the dominance of rail transportation was in steady decline. This decline, seen in the dominance of the railroads moving both passengers and freight, is marked not so much by the advent of gasoline-powered vehicles as it is by the development of serviceable road and highway systems. Certainly, the potential of the former could not be realized without installation of the latter. As unlikely as it may seem to our modern-day perspective, no paved roads existed within the present bounds of Pike County before 1931. In that year and in 1932 contracts were let for paving the entire span of U. S. Highway 19 from Pike's northern boundary with Spalding on the north to its southern boundary with Upson on the south. This brought a segment of the nation's Federal Highway System through Pike County.

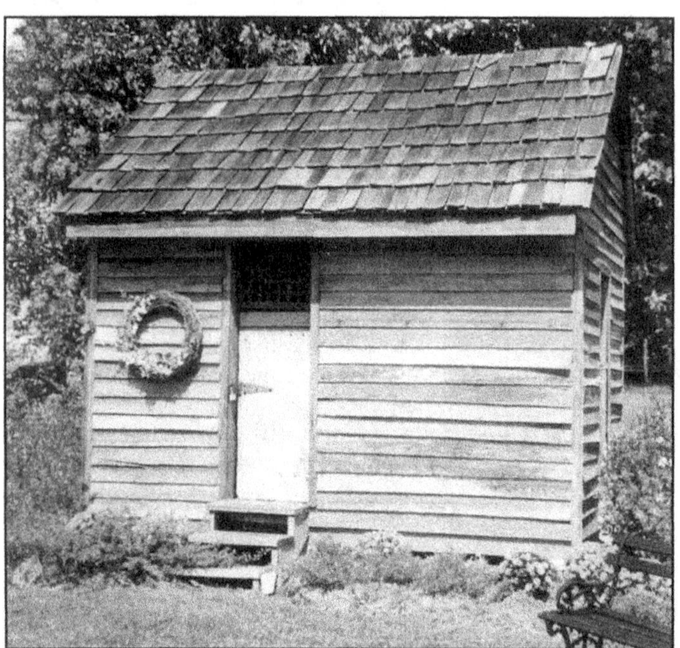

Old Molena Jail from the 1900's. Courtesy of Virginia Oglesby.

Several years elapsed between the construction of U. S. Highway 19, the County's first paved road, and the paving of its other significant thoroughfares. When in the 1940s federal matching funds were made available for the pavement of state highways, Highway No. 362, No. 18, and 109, all principally east-west routes through the County, were given State highway designation and paved surfaces. This achievement has been followed over the past twenty-five years or so with remarkable progress in the improvement and paving of secondary roads—often termed farm-to-market roads—in the County. This development has vastly affected population distribution and concentration with the easier access to markets and employment points from more distant locations in the County.

Some Pioneer Entrepreneurs

For approximately the first thirty years after Pike was formed, before the railroads became prevalent, all commercial freight—products being shipped to outside markets (mostly cotton) and goods shipped in—was transported by wagon teams t o and from Augusta and, later, Macon. A few enterprising individuals found themselves in a position to provide this essential service, thus exploiting a market which proved to be very profitable. Most prominent among these teamster operators were James Whatley and brothers, John and James Neal, the latter of whom continued with major transportation operations after John Neal moved away from the County. Both James Neal and James Whatley became virtually the largest land owners and the wealthiest men in the County. They were also large slaveholders, using trusted slaves to drive their teams in the movement of goods to and from the market points.

The profitability of their teamster enterprises enhanced the ability and the opportunity for citizens such as James Whatley and James Neal to use the lottery system by which Pike's lands were distributed to acquire vast landholdings in the County. The lottery system readily lent itself to acquisition of large land holdings and the proliferation of land transactions by those few early settlers who were in a position to buy up land lots drawn by others who did not wish to settle on them. A fortunate drawer need only pay a nominal fee ($19.00 in the 1821 lottery, for example) to claim the lot drawn. He was then free to homestead the lot, hold it, or resell it. As a result, a fortunate draw was merely a speculative move for many. They paid the small fee to claim the lot drawn, then were willing to sell it to another settler or to a land speculator, sometimes for little more than they had paid to claim the land.

Thus, those resident settlers with available resources to make these "fire-sale" land purchases could literally become land barons, and many did, as in the case of Neal and Whatley. In other instances, fortunate drawers did not homestead their land, nor did they sell it. They, for whatever reason, simply held it as if it were forgotten, with little or no property taxes in these newly settled counties where the land was located.

An Agrarian Economy in Transition

As was the case throughout most of the South, cotton early on became the chief commercial product of Pike County's farms. Early settlers in the County, as were those in much of the South, were seeking fresh, new lands on which to grow cotton. The cotton gin, invented in 1793, added impetus to this trend. At first, ginning operations were quite primitive, with farmers commonly having their own private gins powered by horses or mules in much the same way as were early cane mills. However, the improvement in technology and capacity of gins and the prevalence of steam power gave rise to the establishment of commercial ginning operations in nearly every small town and community in the County.

By the 1920s, substantial acreages in the County were diverted from cotton to peach production, thus introducing a measure of diversification in the County's single-crop agricultural economy. The County's soils and its climate proved quite favorable for the production of this fruit crop. Throughout the 1920s and the 1930s, peach orchards and peach packing sheds became quite prevalent over the County, with the shipment of fresh peaches by rail to markets outside Georgia and the South.

The growth of peach production in the County, more so than any other development, perhaps, prompted the establishment of canning plants by the early 1930s to process and can much of the County's peach crop for outside markets. Then, those enterprising individuals and firms operating canneries successfully expanded their canning operations to include other farm produce grown within the County, such as turnip greens, peas, and pimiento peppers. In fact, pimiento pepper production proved to be quite a lucrative cash crop for the County's farmers and became the first row crop to challenge and, perhaps, supersede cotton as Pike County farmers' principal cash crop. Introduced in the early 1930s, pimiento production remained dominant throughout the 1940s and began to wane in the 1950s. Its decline and demise saw a corresponding decline and eventual demise of cannery operations within the County, although they were sustained on into the 1960s and 1970s by processing farm products imported primarily from outside the County. The County's more substantial canning operations were conducted in Meansville, Zebulon and Concord.

By the 1970s, the profitability of more intensive agricultural production such as fruits and vegetables used in canning had markedly declined and many Pike County farmers were turning to less labor-intensive types of crops, such as cattle production, or were turning away from agriculture to industrial employment in nearby towns outside the County for their livelihoods. In fact, a phenomenon of note is the development of turkey production of substantial proportions over a period of some three decades beginning in the 1940s. This further contributed to the weakening of the dominance of cotton culture in the County's agricultural economy.

The Religious Climate in Historical Perspective

Pike's first settlers tended to reflect the rather homogeneous cultural and social patterns of their predominantly Scots-Irish heritage. They were, for the most part, products of the surge of religious revivalism that prevailed around the turn of the nineteenth century, profoundly affecting the lifestyles and mores of the frontier society from which these settlers had come. Characteristically, they took their religion seriously. Thus, it should be no surprise to find that churches were organized immediately upon their arrival in the new county.

Quite interesting is the fact that the Inferior Court minutes for 1824 show that the justices noted the need to establish "Meeting Houses" in the town of Zebulon, the county seat, and decreed that a lot be given and set aside exclusively for the "Methodist Society" and another one for the "Baptist Society." A factor which lent considerable impetus to this religious emphasis was the early Methodist system of an itinerating clergy, characterized by preachers who constantly traveled assigned circuits to organize and nurture congregations. Historians have noted that to the frontier first came the settler with ax and rifle, followed by the fabled Methodist circuit rider. To this add the fervent revivalism prevailing among frontier Baptists of this era and we have the prescription for a high level of religious consciousness among Pike's early society.

Fincher United Methodist Church, near Meansville, was established in 1822 and Zebulon Baptist Church was established about 1823 shortly after the County was created (December, 1822) and are reputed to be the first churches to be formed in the County. The Rev. Andrew Hamil, an itinerant Methodist preacher, was largely credited with establishing Fincher United Methodist Church and serving as its first pastor. The Rev. John Milner, a Baptist preacher and pioneer settler in eastern Pike County, was instrumental in forming some of the County's earliest Baptist congregations such as Zebulon Baptist, Mt. Olive in western Pike, and Sardis in eastern Pike, which later became the Barnesville Baptist Church.

Despite the keener religious sensitivity that frontier revivalism had fostered in these pioneer settlers, a pronounced commonality of form and expression was evident in their religious faith. Even though worshiping congregations sprang up rapidly as Pike's wilderness gave way to settled communities, after fifty years from the County's founding all of these congregations were of either Methodist or Baptist persuasion with the exception of Friendship Presbyterian Church near Williamson.

This homogeneity in religious character began to be appreciably mitigated by the last quarter of the nineteenth century with the emergence of several congregations organized by the Congregational Church and the Christian Church. More diversity in the County's religious faiths occurred around the turn of the twentieth century with the formation of the Mountain Gap Church, the County's first Pentecostal congregation, in 1898 with adherents recruited mostly from the nearby Methodist and Baptist churches. The formation of Rehobeth Church of the Nazarene followed in 1912; and over the years thereafter congregations of diverse faiths continued to emerge on the County's religious scene. Appendix A presents this development in greater detail.

A colorful facet of Pike's religious history for nearly one hundred years which deserves special note in this treatment was the Bluff Springs Methodist Camp Meeting located on the eastern side of the County. Beginning early in the County's history at a location on the Fincher United Methodist Church grounds, because of inadequate water supply the camp meeting was moved in 1853 to a location approximately equidistant—about two miles—from the towns of Meansville and Zebulon. Here, the camp meeting continued its annual meeting until the early 1940s with the exception of a short time following the Civil War when services were suspended, then resumed in 1878.

Always held in August each year when a farm population enjoyed more leisure time, this event attracted thousands to the camp grounds to not only hear powerful oratory in animated preaching, but also to indulge themselves in a few days of escape from the drudgery of farm life to enjoy a time of relaxed social interaction with family members and friends. Entire extended families moved, often bringing their livestock as well as other provisions, into the crude wood-framed "tents" which surrounded the "great arbor" in the center of the grounds.

The arbor was an open-sided pavilion-type structure large enough to seat a thousand or more worshipers with a speaker's platform and bare ground covered with wheat straw or sawdust—hence a true "sawdust trail."

In a day when transportation means were limited and alternative attractions were few, people flocked to the camp ground in such teeming throngs that on peak-attendance days, such as Sundays, the overflow in attendance from the great arbor was handled by improvising additional preaching stands with wagon bodies and stumps throughout the camp grounds so that several sermons were in progress simultaneously. As might be expected, the Camp Meeting became a favorite haunt, not only for those looking for a "good time," even for mischief, perhaps, for some, but also for aspiring politicians seeking opportunity for maximum exposure to a would-be constituency. In summary, Bluff Springs Camp Meeting, over its nearly a century of duration, became a Pike County institution in its own right. Perhaps, the Camp Meeting's impact is best felt in the sentiment expressed by a Mrs. Bonita Arnold who remembered attending Bluff Springs in her antebellum childhood: "Camp meetings afforded one of the greatest thrills of our childhood for camp meetings were not only spiritual feasts, but social as well."

The Mountain Gap Camp Meeting located about three miles southeast of Meansville boasts a similar rich tradition. While not as early in its origin as Bluff Springs Methodist Camp Meeting, the Mountain Gap Camp Meeting, which remains active today, has already achieved longer continuity than did Bluff Springs. Founded in 1900, Mountain Gap Camp Meeting, Pentecostal in belief and character, has continued viable for 104 years—that is, up to the present time. Never as large in scope and outreach as was Bluff Springs Camp Meeting, Mountain Gap Camp Meeting has, nevertheless, preserved and perpetuated the practice of an annual summer meeting with services under an open-air arbor, or tabernacle, even though on-the-grounds camping accommodations are no longer maintained. In fact, the Camp Meeting has experienced a resurgence in its viability, attracting larger numbers than at any time in recent years.

Educational Efforts in Historical Perspective

As in any frontier society, the early settlers in Pike were challenged by a dearth of educational opportunities. There were no schools and few who could teach them. The burden and responsibility for giving children any level of literacy were strictly a private undertaking at the parents' expense—a far cry from today's egalitarian approach to educating the children of the citizenry Thus, the first efforts by parents to give their youth some level of literacy was, in keeping with the custom of that day, through the medium of the so-called "private academy."

The academies were, in effect, the one-roomed schoolhouses that dotted the rural and wilderness landscape of the times, usually staffed by a single teacher who was hired by the parents of the students he taught.

In some cases, affluent landholders were able to engage live-in tutors just for their children alone. But, in most cases, the residents of a particular neighborhood or community would share the cost or labor input required to construct a small-usually a single room-structure to serve as a schoolhouse for children located in its proximity. Typically, a teacher was engaged to serve the school for a set charge per student, payable by the parents.

In these academies, students across the age spectrum, from beginners to the most advanced, were placed under the tutelage of a single teacher, whose instructional time and effort were divided among all the different levels, typically within the confines of a single room. As might be expected, the County's first academies appeared in the towns, the earliest on record being Zebulon Academy, established in 1825 Others appeared in communities over the County at the same sites as churches, which tended to be focal points in neighborhoods and communities, with academies using the church property and sometimes its facilities. Fincher School may be the earliest of these, located at the site of Fincher Methodist Church soon after this church was established in 1822.

Unfortunately, even though the names and approximate locations of many of these academies are known, extant county records offer little as to the dates they were established, the duration of their operation, and the teachers involved. Considerably more information is available regarding the dates of their closing or consolidation into the public schools, which appeared later. The list of the County's schools given in Appendix B includes as many of these academies as recent research has revealed and as much about the date they originated as is known, which, in many cases, is negligible. They do, however, represent the thrust of educational effort in Pike County from the time of its founding in 1822 until nearly the turn of the twentieth century.

A benchmark in the history of education in Pike County, perhaps, was the expression of the people of the County in favor of a public school system, as reported by a notice in the *Pike County Journal* in 1873. Even though such a system was several more years in coming, this was obviously a significant gesture, reflecting the education awareness of Pike's citizenry. Records make clear that Pike County's transition to a publicly supported school system evolved gradually in stages and not in a single stroke. By 1890, a County School Commissioner, later termed superintendent, had been named to coordinate and guide the educational efforts of the County's private academies. By 1897, a County Board of Education was already in place to exercise some oversight over the County's schools.

A major step toward a quality education system was taken in 1902 when teachers were examined by the office of the School Commissioner and graded according to their capability as a teacher. State participation in the County's school funding began in 1904 with the State Department of Education's Common School Fund.

Another benchmark in the development of a public school system in Pike County was the levying of the first county-wide school tax in 1921. With the County school system fully under supervision of a State School Superintendent in the 1920s, quality control measures were implemented, such as regulating the number of teachers in relation to the number of grades taught in the school

The process of consolidation of Pike County's schools began as early as 1947 when Concord's and Molena's separate high schools were consolidated as Concord-Molena High School, using the Molena High School facility. Before consolidation, only Zebulon, Molena, and Concord schools had grades one through eleven. All others in the County had grades one through seven only. Further consolidation occurred when in 1956 all the County's black schools were consolidated at the Concord school facility. By 1969, however, the County's schools, all grades, had been totally integrated.

The consolidation process continued with construction of new facilities on a 125-acre site at Zebulon so that by the 1987-1988 school year all schools and all grades were consolidated at this single site. Further construction and expansion have continued at this site to the present to bring to fruition the County's current modern consolidated school complex.

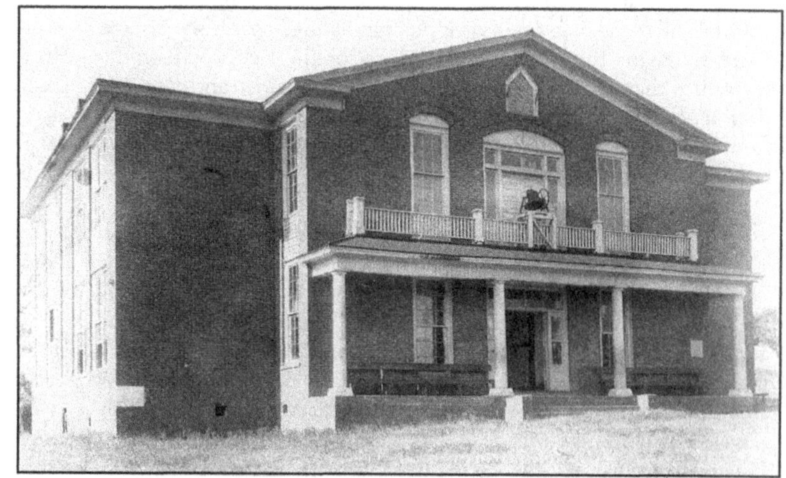

Williamson School, early 1920s, now demolished. Courtesy of Rachel McClelland.

Churches of Pike County in Order of their Date of Establishment

1822 Fincher United Methodist Church. Began under a brush arbor. "Believed to be the oldest church in Pike County." (Rev. Richard W. Rogers in his *History of Pike County, 1822-1922.*)
1823 Zebulon Methodist Church
1823 Zebulon First Baptist Church
1823 Williamson United Methodist Church, originally Red Oak Methodist Church, founded as a log church.
1827 Mt. Olive Baptist Church, located on Hwy 109 near Molena. Revs. John and Pitt Milner constituted the presbytery.
1828 Century Nelson United Methodist Church, located in Old Alabama Road.
1828 Friendship Baptist Church, located in Second District.
ca. 1830s Flat Rock Methodist Church, located one mile south of Hollonville on Concord Road. Later moved to center of Hollonville.
1835 Friendship Presbyterian Church, located in Concord. Until 1869 was located about four miles west of present site.
1837 Shoal Creek Baptist Church, near Hollonville.
1838 Concord Baptist Church, first organized as Hebron Baptist Church. Changed to Concord Baptist Church in 1942 when moved into Concord.
1840 Ebenezer United Methodist Church, located five miles east of Zebulon on Hwy 18.
1850 Concord United Methodist Church (originally known as Salem Methodist Church).
1851 Meansville Congregational Church. Established as New Hope Congregational Methodist Church. United with the Congregational Christian Church in 1888.
1856 Free Liberty United Methodist Church, located at Williamson.
1863 Nazareth Baptist Church, first organized as Weaver Baptist Church.
1865 Beulah Baptist Church, located at Lifsey Springs.
Before 1865 Mt. Hope Baptist Church
1866 Roberts Chapel United Methodist Church
1869 Providence Baptist Church. Moved to Williamson and became Williamson Baptist Church in 1892.
1869 Flat Rock Primitive Baptist Church, located on U. S. Highway 19.
1869 Philadelphia Methodist Church, located at Meansville
ca. 1871 Fairfield C. M. E. Church, located at Hollonville.
1872 Fuller Chapel United Methodist Church, located at Zebulon
1874 Hollonville Baptist Church
ca. 1876 Mt. Calvary Baptist Church, located off Eppinger Rd., near Concord.
ca. 1877 Mt. Gilead Baptist Church, located U. S. Highway 19, Second District.
ca. 1879 Antioch Baptist Church, U. S. Highway 19, Second District.
1879 Bethany Christian Church near Williamson
1882 Hollonville United Methodist Church. Established by removal of Flat Rock Methodist Church from one mile south of Hollonville on Concord Road into center of Hollonville. Flat Rock was established ca. 1830.
1882 New Hope Baptist Church, located in Second District.
1885 Meansville Baptist Church
ca. 1886 Chapel Hill Baptist Church, located near Williamson
1888 Molena Baptist Church
1892 Molena Methodist Church
1893 Liberty Chapel Congregational Church, located one mile from Lifsey Springs.
1894 Neal Baptist Church, located between Concord and Molena.
1898 Mountain Gap Pentecostal Holiness Church, located on Pine Valley Road three miles south of Meansville.
1902 Concord Christian Church, located in Concord.
1907 New Hebron Baptist Church, located about three miles west of Concord.
1911 Williamson Christian Church (1989 History of Pike County says 1917)
1912 Rehobeth Church of the Nazarene, located near Lifsey Springs.
1940s Pine Mountain Church of the Nazarene, located on U. S. Highway 19 about five miles south of Zebulon.
1966 Vega Community Church, located on Vega Road.
1970s Pike County Assembly of God, located on U. S. Highway 19, three miles south of Zebulon.
1979 Church of Joy, located at Rover, near Williamson.
1980 Prayer Mountain Ministries, located on U. S. Hwy 19, about five miles south of Zebulon.
1988 Emmanuel Baptist, located on U. S. Highway 19, three miles south of Zebulon.
2003 Christ's Chapel Assembly of God, located at Zebulon.

Mt. Olive Baptist (black, located on Highway 109 near Molena. No date available, but some years after 1827.

Mt. Nebo Baptist Church, located near Meansville. No date available.

New Pleasant Hill C. M. E. Church, located at Concord. No further date available.

NOTE: The above list is based upon the most complete information available at the time of this writing. It does not preclude the possibility of other churches for which there is no known record

APPENDIX B

LIST OF PRIVATE ACADEMIES AND SCHOOLS IN PIKE COUNTY

Beeks School — Near Hollonville. Existed in late 1800s.
Beauchamp School — Located in Second District.
Beulah Church School — Located at Lifsey Springs. Established about 1900.
Concord School — Existed before 1900. Became Concord High

	School in 1900.
Cook School	Located near Lifsey Springs. Existed before 1900. Consolidated with Lifsey Springs School in 1943.
Dunbar School	Located near Williamson. Consolidated with Williamson in 1936.
Fincher School	Located at site of Fincher Methodist Church. Established soon after the establishment of Fincher Methodist Church in 1822. Combined with Meansville School in 1922.
Flat Rock School	Located in Second District. Dates to soon after Pike County was created in 1822.
Friendship School	Located in New Hope Community. Consolidated with New Hope School.
Hall's Academy	Located near Taylor Springs on Vega Road. Existed will before 1900.
Hollonville School	Grew out of Shoal Creek School located at Shoal Creek Primitive Baptist Church, the latter existing as early as 1880s.
John Means Institute	Located in Meansville. Dates from 1900 or before.
Johnson Academy	Established in 1896 in New Hebron Community. Later consolidated with Concord School.
Jolly School	Located near Concord. Probably founded before 1900. Known to be existing in early 1900s.
Lifsey School	Located at Lifsey Springs. Consolidated with Cook School in 1843.
Midway School	Located between Zebulon and Williamson. Replaced Pine Forest School in 1897.
Molena School	Located at Molena. Formed in 1926 by consolidation of Union, Lawrence, and Neal Schools.
Mount Gilead School	Located in Second District.
Neal School	Located between Concord and Molena. Consolidated as Molena School in 1926.
New Hope School	Located near New Hope Baptist Church. Existed before 1900. New building constructed in 1903.
Old Meansville School	Located between Meansville and Old Meansville. Existed in late 1800s.
Pedenville School	Located at community of Pedenville. Built about 1840. Replaced with new school building in late 1870s.
Roberts School	Located at Roberts Chapel Methodist Church. Built in 1915.
Shoal Creek School	Located at Shoal Creek Primitive Baptist Church. Existed as early as the 1800s.
Union School	Located between Lifsey Springs and Molena. Consolidated as Molena School in 1926.
Lawrence School	Located near Molena. Consolidated as Molena School in 1926.
Pine Forest School	Located between Zebulon and Williamson. Existed in 1880s. Replaced by Midway School in 1897.
Vega School	In Vega community about three miles south of Meansville. Dates to 1900 or before.
Warm Springs Academy	Located at Lifsey Springs. Built about 1890 or before on land donated by John Lifsey.
Weaver School	Located at Nazareth Baptist Church. Existed before 1890.
Williamson School	Existed before 1915, when new building was constructed. Continued until consolidation with Concord School in 1966.
Zebulon Academy	Established 1825 by legislative act.
Zebulon High School	In 1889, known as Excelsior Academy; in 1890, became Jeff Davis Institute; in 1903, became Griffin District Institute of the Methodist Episcopal Church; in 1912, deeded back to become Zebulon High School.
Zebulon School for Boys	In existence as early as the 1840s.
Zebulon School for Girls	In existence as early as the 1840s.

Black schools known to have existed, but for which no information is available as to location or date of existence.

Fairfield	Barrett Union	Antioch
Stroudsville	Brown Chapel	St. Elmo
Eady Creek	Broadway	Andrews Chapel
Baker Creek	Mt. Calvary	Piedmont
Free Liberty	Pine Grove	Bethlehem
Jolly	Holly Grove	Mt. Olive
Midway		

NOTE: The above list is reflective of available records and may not necessarily be exhaustive regarding schools over the history of Pike County.

LIST OF SOURCES

Adams, James W. *A Study of the Effect of Government Aid and Other Factors on the Economic Development of Three Selected Areas in Georgia.* Atlanta, GA: Georgia State University, 1971

Adams, James W. "A Tale of Two Brothers." Paper presented to Upson Historical Society, October 17, 2003. Thomaston-Upson County Archives, Thomaston, GA.

Bechtel, Douglas, and Susan R. Boatwright, Editors. *The Georgia County Guide.* The University of Georgia, Fifteenth Edition 1996.

Bogue, Donald J., and Calvin J. Beale. *Economic Areas of the United States.* Glencoe, Ill.: The Free Press, 1961.

Gilman, Glen. *Human Relations in the Industrial Southeast.* Chapel Hill, NC: University of North Carolina Press, 1956.

Historical Committee. *Sesquicentennial 1822-1972, Pike County, Georgia.*

History of Pike County. Published by Retired Teachers of Pike County and *The Pike County Journal and Reporter.* Dallas, TX: Curtis Media Corporation, 1989.

Lambdin, Mrs. Augusta, and Mrs. Edward A. Fish, Editors. *History of Lamar County, 1825-1932.* Barnesville, GA: The Barnesville News-Gazette, 1932.

Mitchell, Lizzie R. *History of Pike County, Georgia, 1822-1922.* Spartanburg, SC: The Reprint Company, Publishers, 1980.

Nottingham, Carolyn Walker, and Evelyn Hannah. *History of Upson County, Georgia.* .Vidalia, GA: Georgia Genealogical Reprints, 1969.

U. S. Census of Pike County, GA, Microcopy 432, Roll No. 80.

White, Rev. George. *Historical Collections of Georgia.* New York: Pudney and Russell, 1855.

Pictorial History

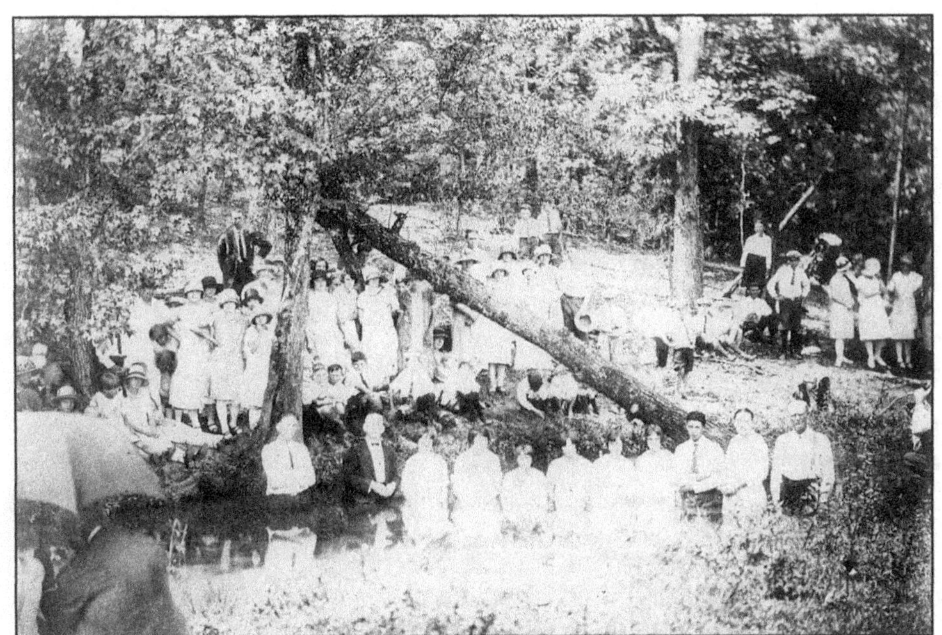

New Hope Baptist Church baptizing. Courtesy of Susan Brown Parham.

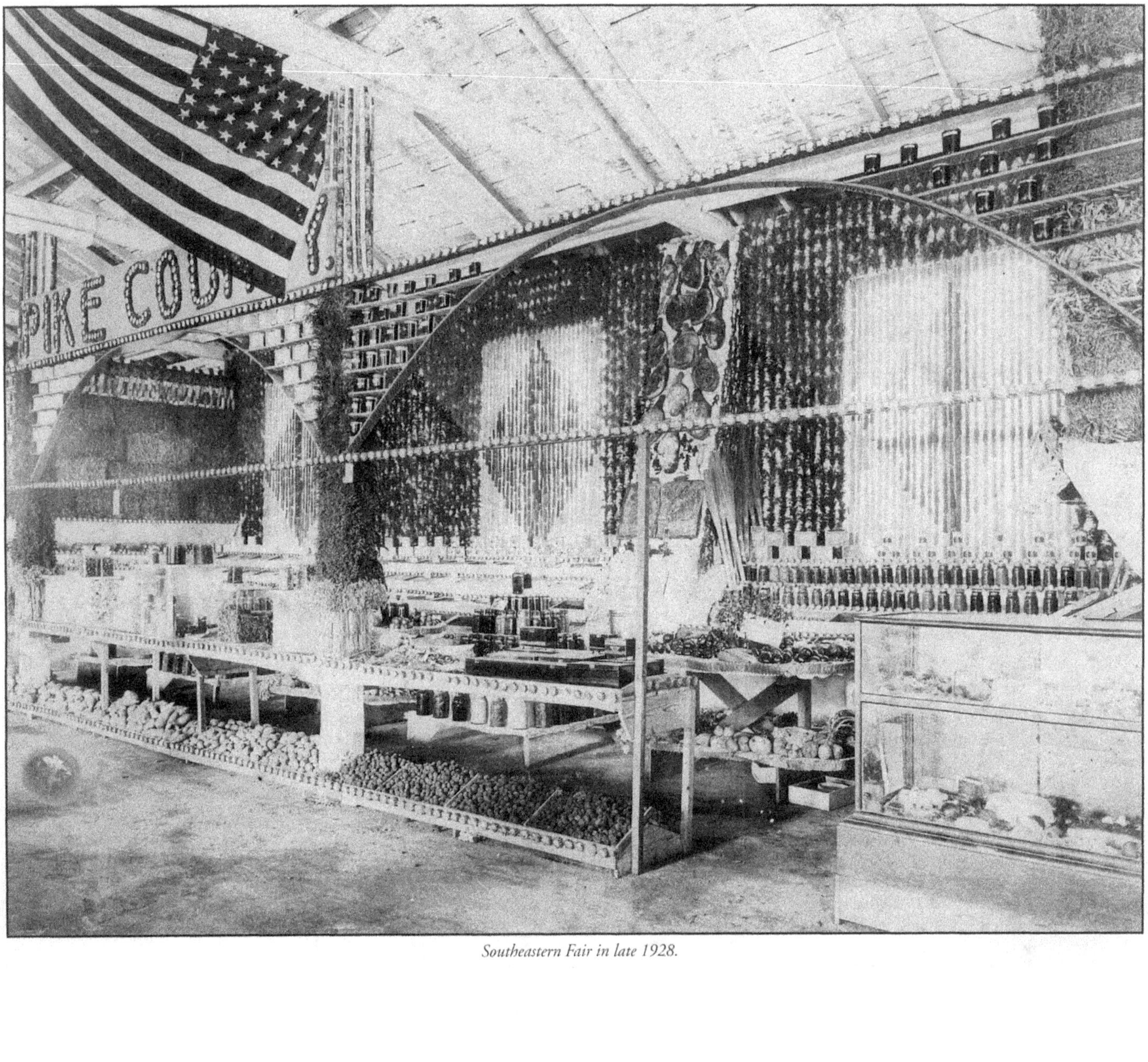

Southeastern Fair in late 1928.

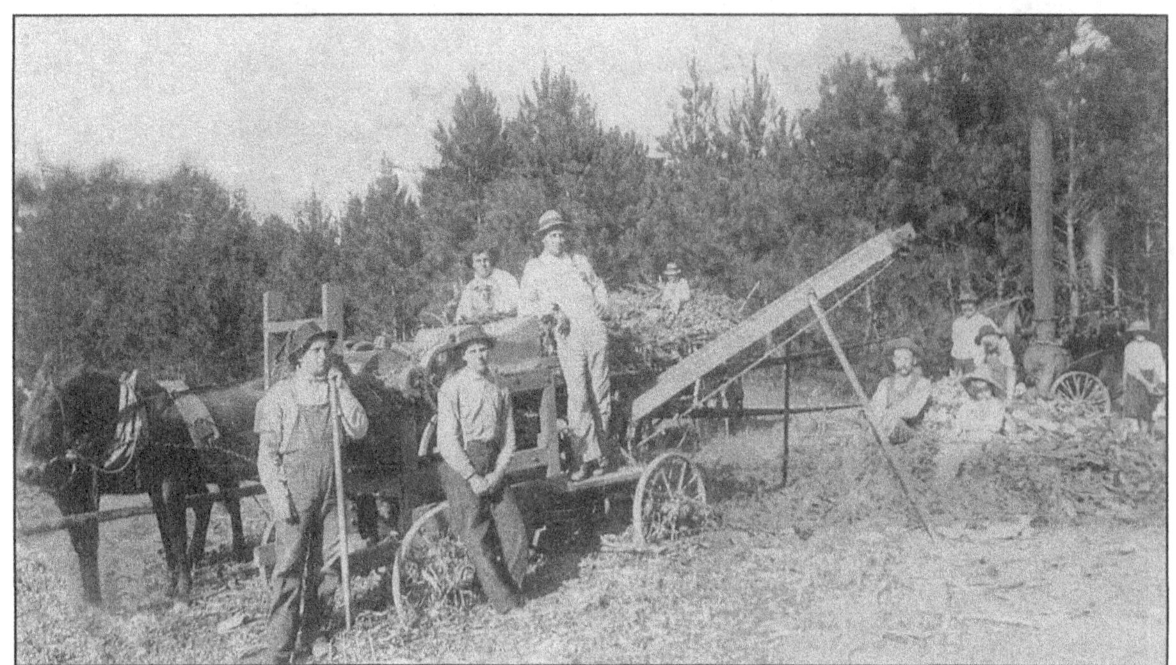

Corn shredder. David Kendrick Sr., Wilson Morrow, Thomas C. Morrow and William Morrow. Courtesy of Walter Kendrick.

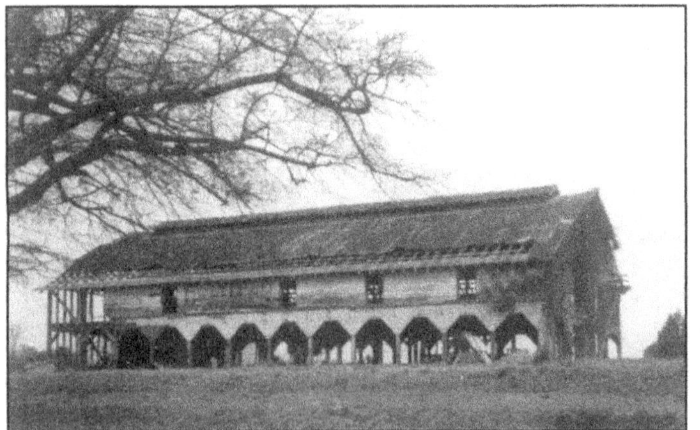

Peach Shed located in Molena, Georgia, now demolished. Courtesy of Stephanie Bradley.

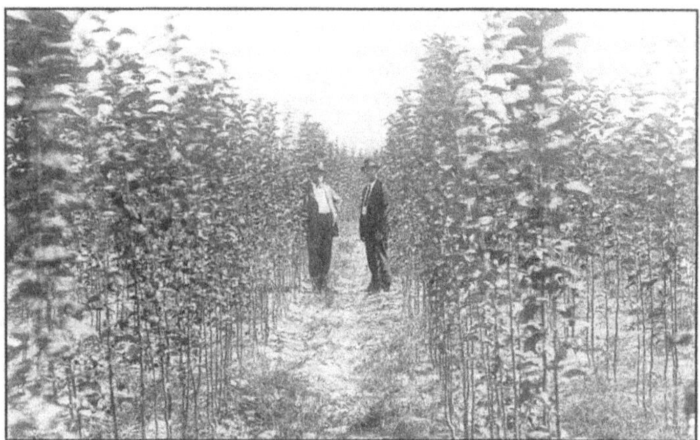

Charlie Smith and F.L. Adams. Courtesy of Rachel McClelland.

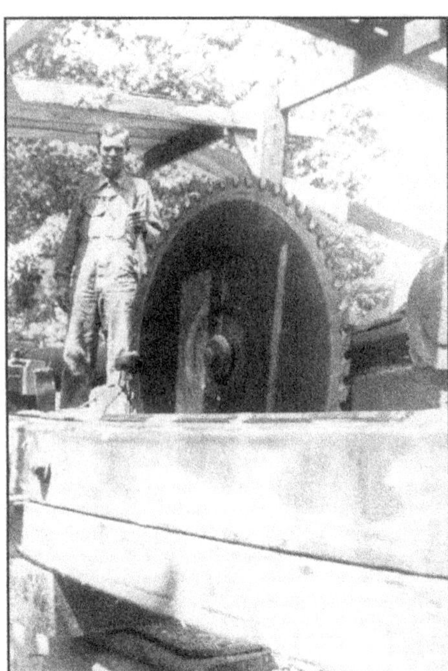

Fred Douglas McDaniel, 1950's. Courtesy of Joann Fenley.

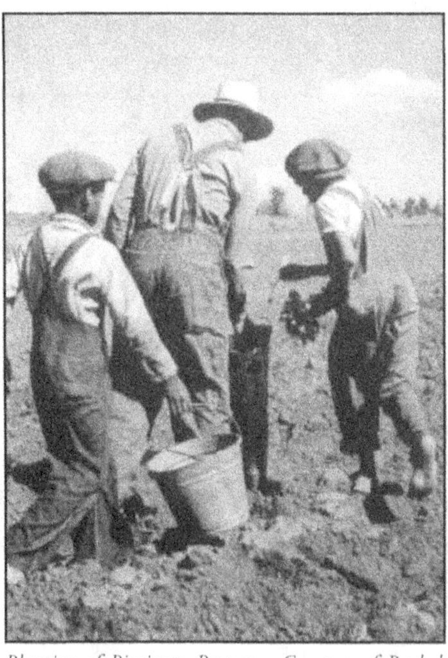

Planting of Pimiento Peppers. Courtesy of Rachel McClelland.

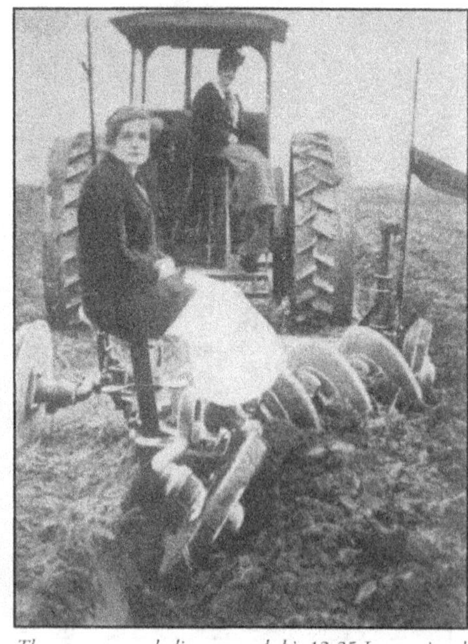

These two young ladies operated this 12-25 International tractor and plow on the 6th district farm A&M school at Barnesville. Courtesy of JBG.

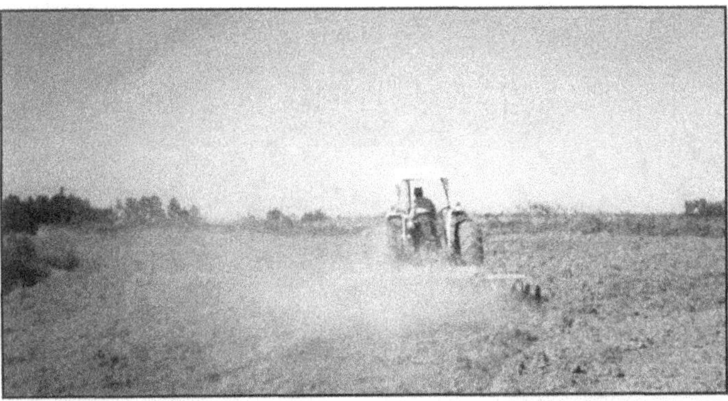

Wilbur Elliott on his tractor, doing what he loved. He was a dedicated farmer all his life. Courtesy of Jane Gaulding.

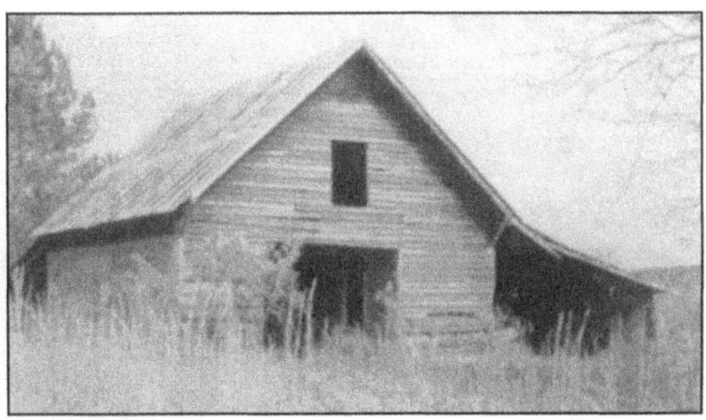

The barn at the Howard homeplace. Courtesy of Mrs. Clyde Gibson.

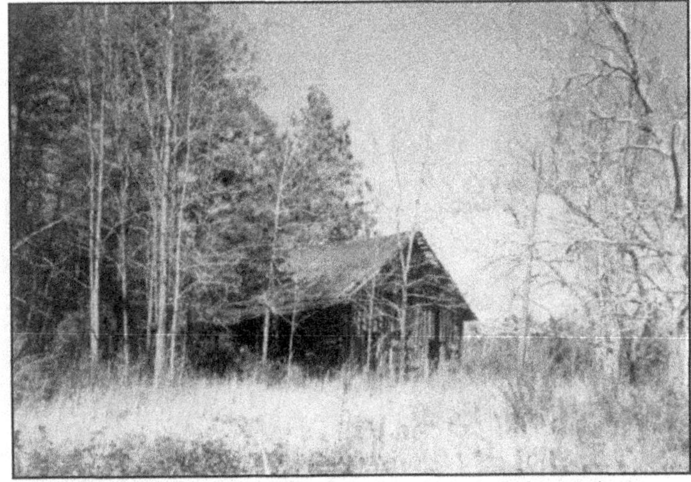

Old barn on Bishop homeplace in Jugtown. Courtesy of Sylvia Wright.

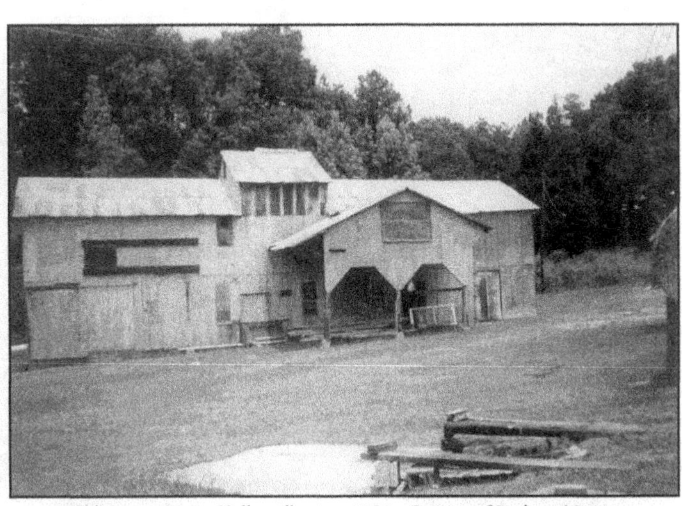

Old Cotton Gin in Hollonville, circa 1997. Courtesy of Barbara Martin.

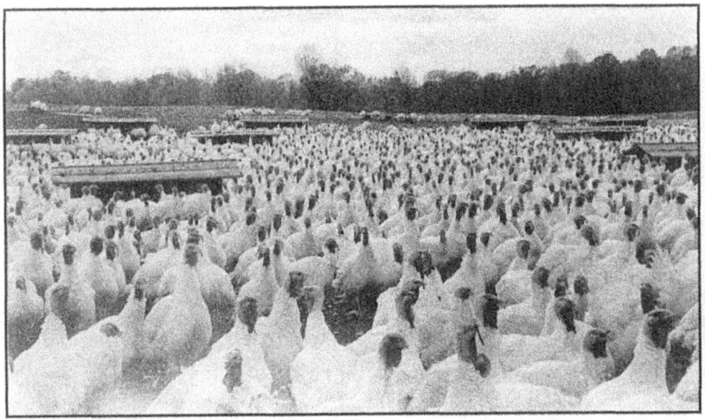

Turkeys in Molena, Georgia. Courtesy of Rachel McClelland.

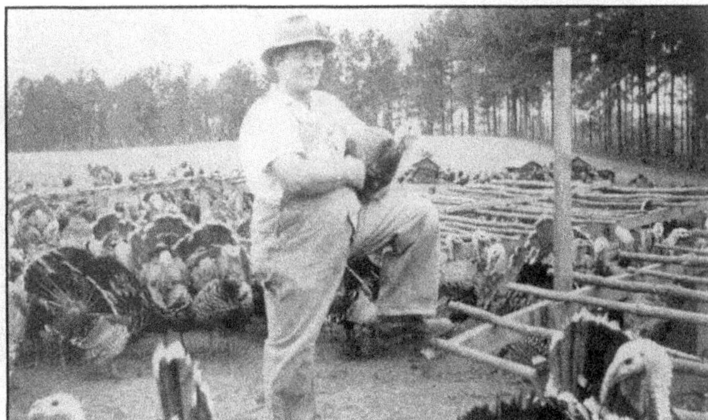

Lloyd Hamlett with turkeys he raised, circa 1956-57. Courtesy of Louise Hamlett.

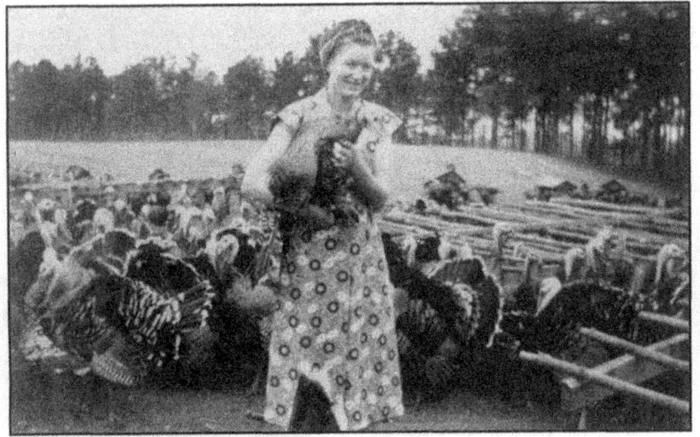

Louise Hamlett with turkeys, circa 1957. Courtesy of Louise Hamlett.

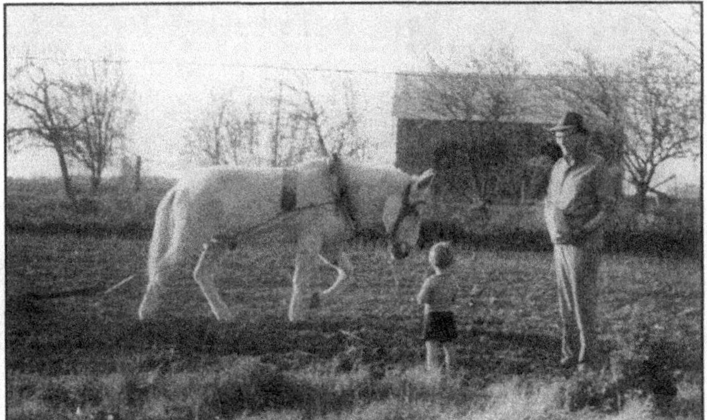

Emmett O. Caldwell and Grandson Jerry Caldwell planting a garden. Courtesy of Kenneth Caldwell.

Pilkenton Barker Mill on Old Zebulon Road, built in the late 1850's or early 1860's by Robert Pilkenton. Located on Elkins Creek in the Mount Olive Community east of the present town of Molena. It ceased operation in 1955 and was moved to the Vignos farm in 1978, then burned in 1999. Courtesy of Carol Barton.

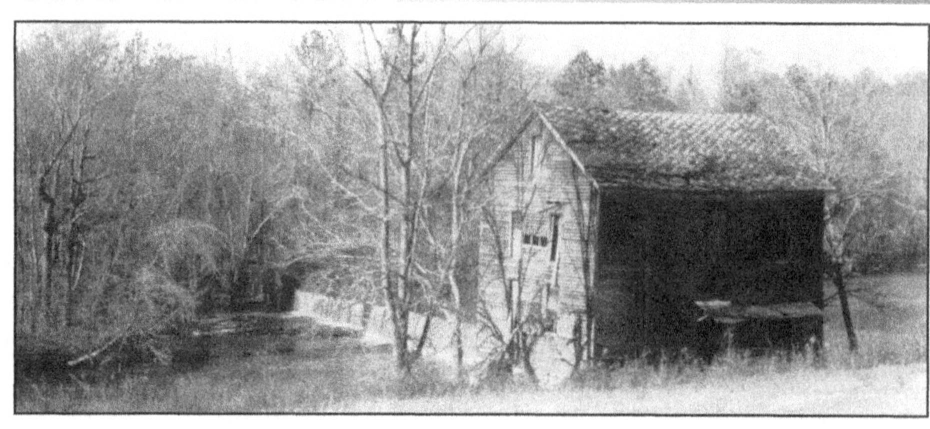

Pilkenton-Barker mill after it was moved to Vignos farm and restored. Courtesy of Carol Barton.

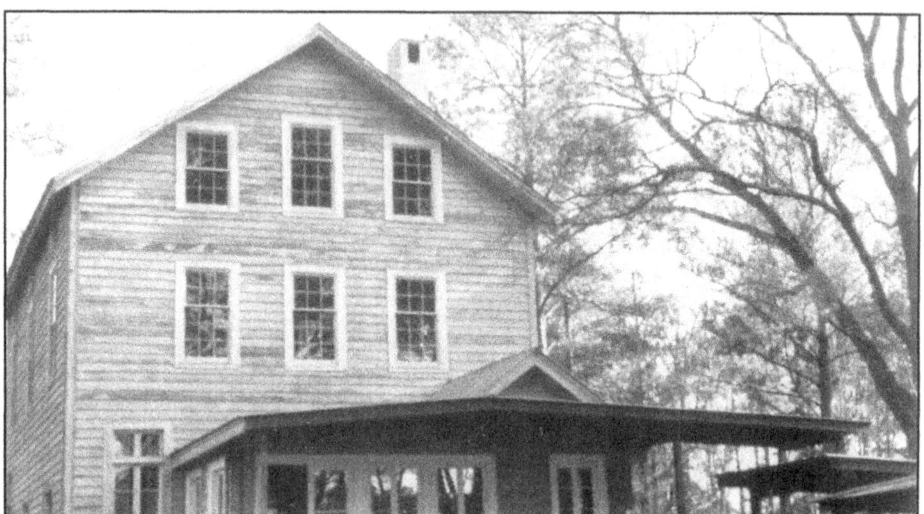

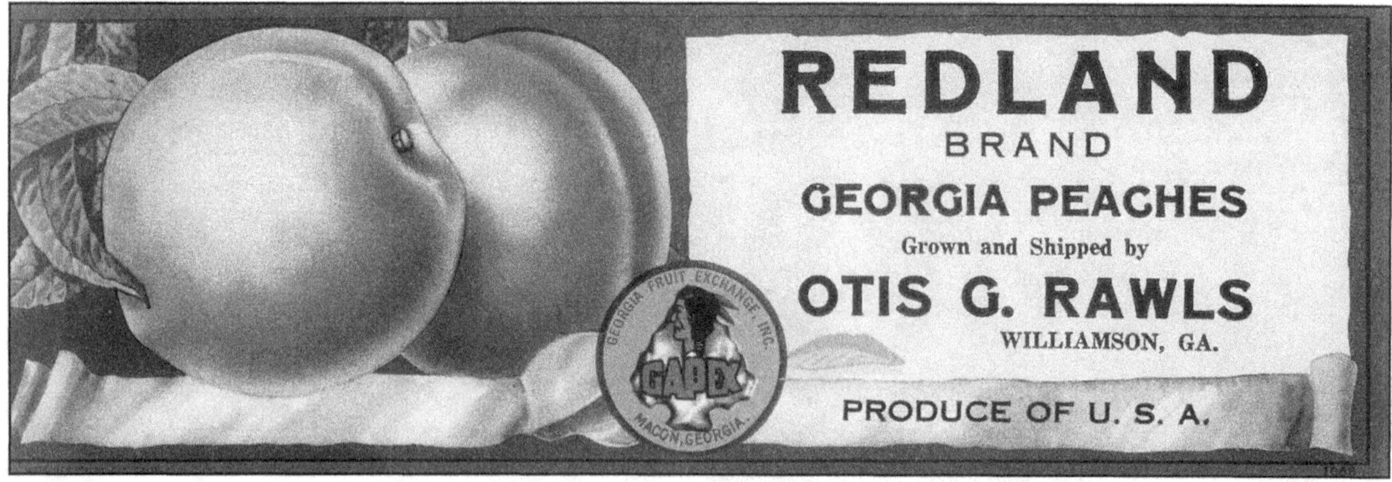

Advertisment for Redland Brand Georgia peaches. Courtesy of Bob Williamson.

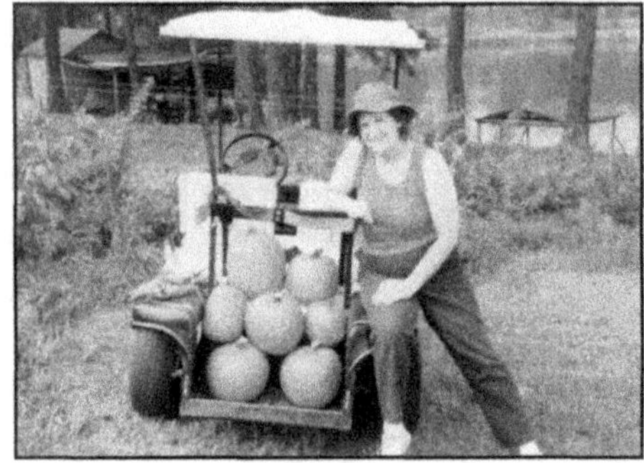

Sonya Morton and her homegrown pumpkins. Courtesy of Tom Morton.

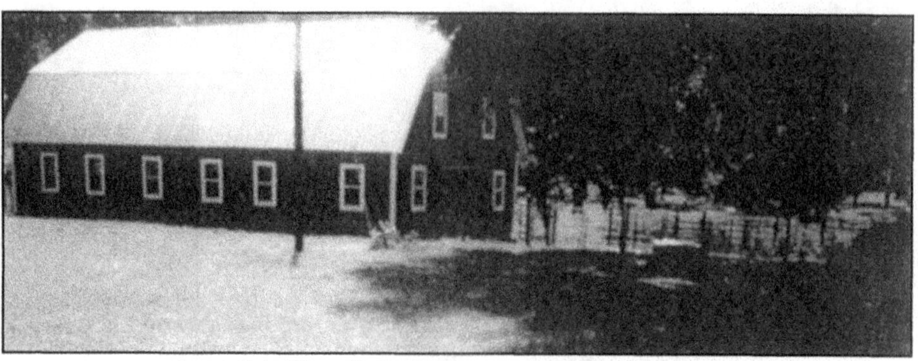

Barn built by Clinton H. Capel, after restoration. Courtesy of Elna Capel.

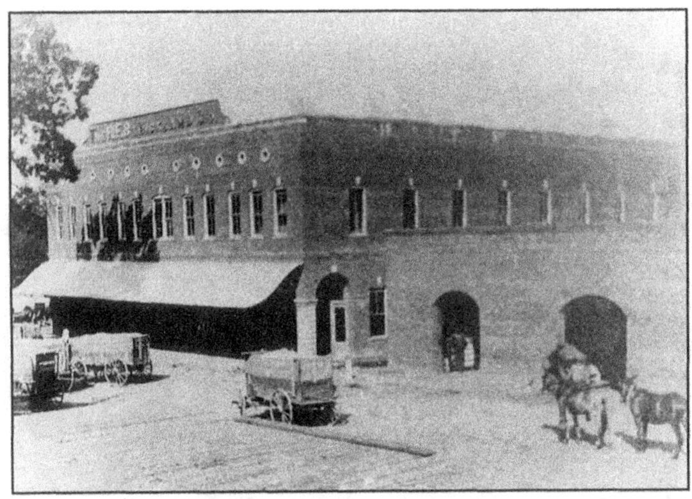

R.F. Strickland Store, Concord.

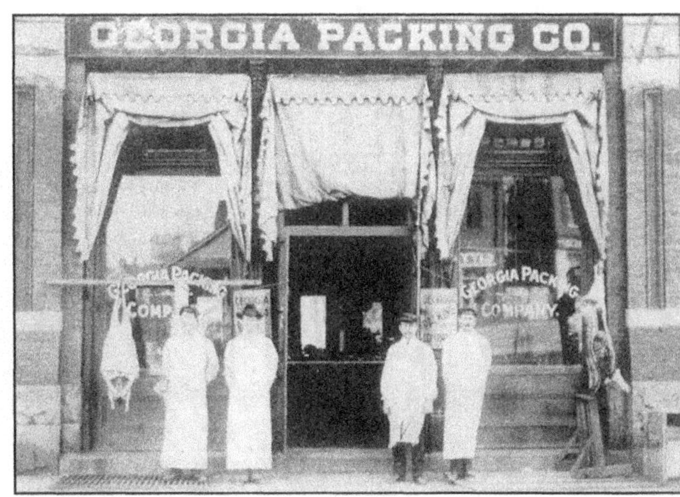

Georgia Packing Company located in Macon, run by Pike Countians. Courtesy of Jane Gaulding.

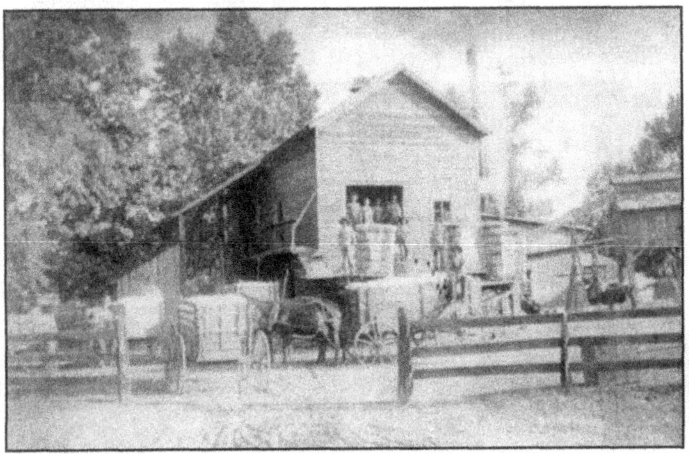

Cotton Gin of Elkins Creek near Molena. Courtesy of Elna Capel.

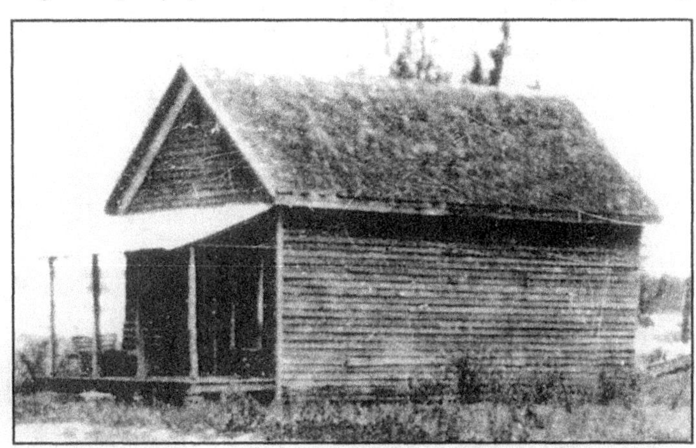

County store operated by Clinton H. Capel from the mid 20's through the late 40's. Lightning destroyed it in the mid 50's. Courtesy of Elna Capel.

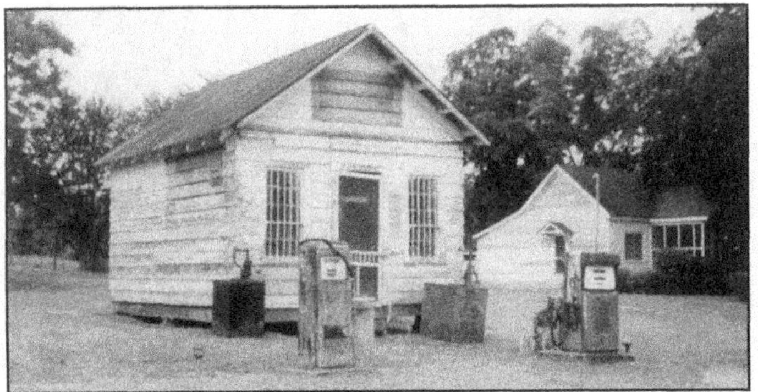

Jones Grocery Store, as it looks today. It once was a very busy business and gathering place in Pike County, located on Hwy. 109 East of Molena, GA. Robert Cecil Jones built the store in the 1930's and he ran it until his death in 1961. Courtesy of Jane Gaulding.

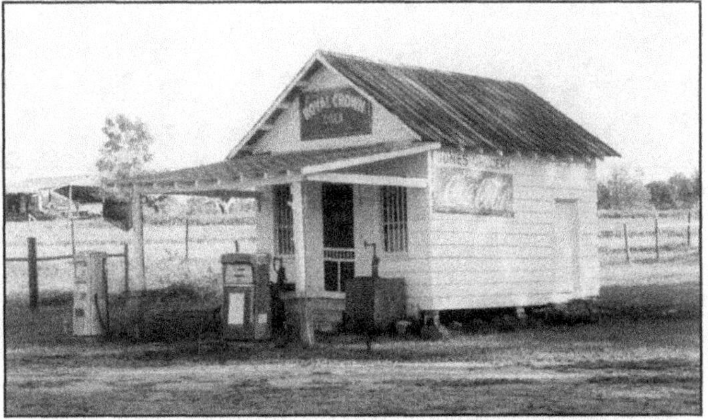

R.C. Jones Grocery, Hwy. 109 Molena. Courtesy of Robert F. Jones.

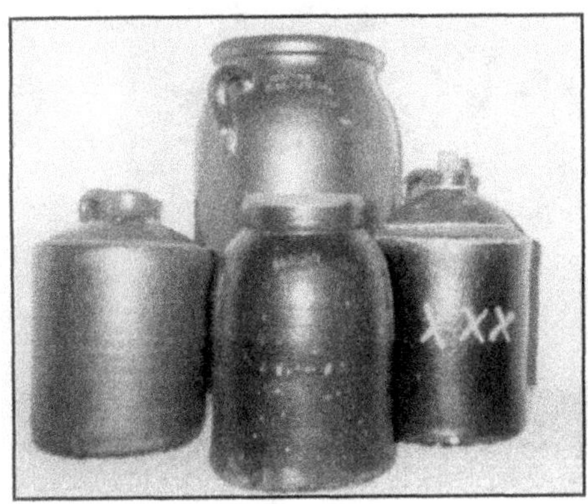

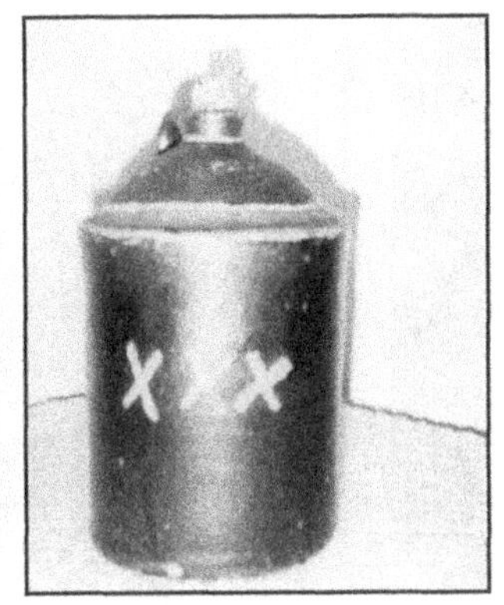

Left: The jug with initials H.B. and W.D. Bishop was turned by W.D. Bishop and fired by his grandson, Hugh J. Bishop. It is the only known piece with both W.D. Bishop and H.B. on it. The churn was made by J.D. Bishop, W.D.'s brother and Jasper's son. The small crock was made by Jasper (J.A.) Bishop, before the Civil War. Courtesy of Bonnie Gardner.

Right: This moonshine jug was made by Curtis (C.G.) Bishop. The story is told that when C.G. made a jug for moonshine, he would bury the filled jug under flowers that his wife, Amzie Etheridge Bishop like to see blooming in the Spring. When the flowers bloomed, Curtis knew where to find his jug. Courtesy of Bonnie Gardner.

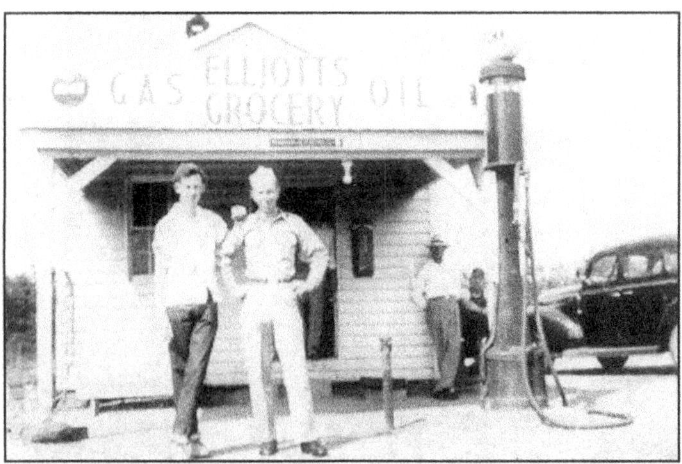

Harvey Bush and Wilbur Elliott standing in front of Elliott's Grocery Store on Hwy. 18E in Zebulon. The store was located in the Weaver Community and was the gathering place. Every night different families would come and the men would sit around the store and the women would sit around the house and the children would play in the yard. This was before TV, when neighbors stuck together. Courtesy of Jane Gaulding.

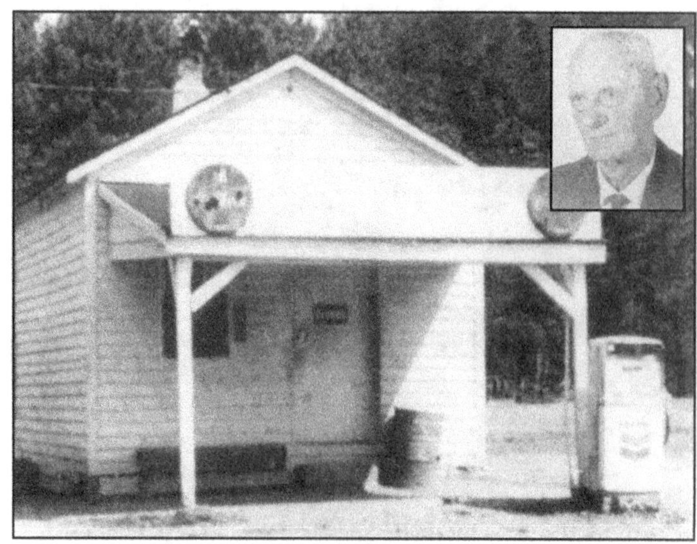

Above: Elliott's Store, a landmark in Pike County. Inset: W.R. "Bill" Elliott. Courtesy of Rachel Shaw.

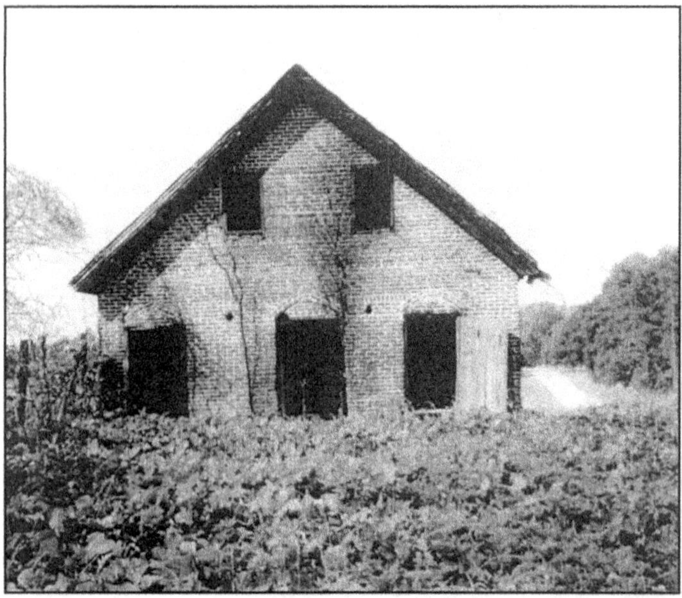

This brick building was once used as a liquor warehouse for a government liquor still. It was built shortly after the Civil War. Courtesy of Elna Capel.

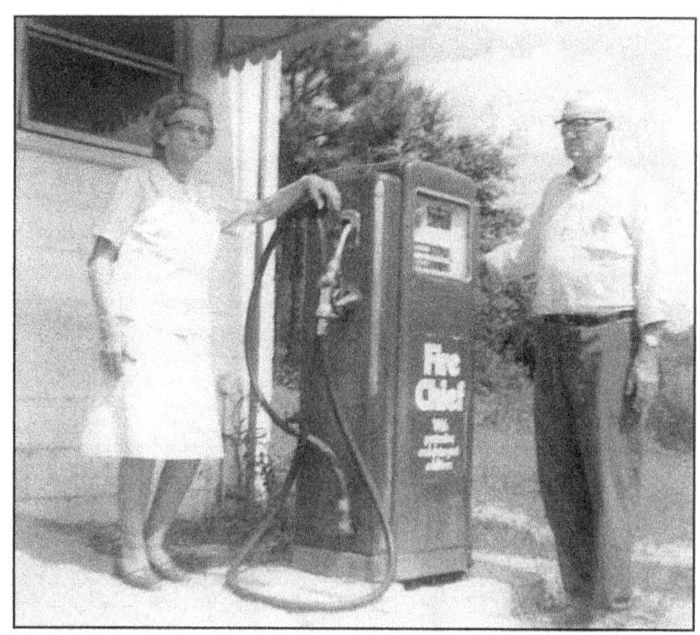

Grady and Essie Jones at their country grocery store in 1972. Courtesy of Rosalee King.

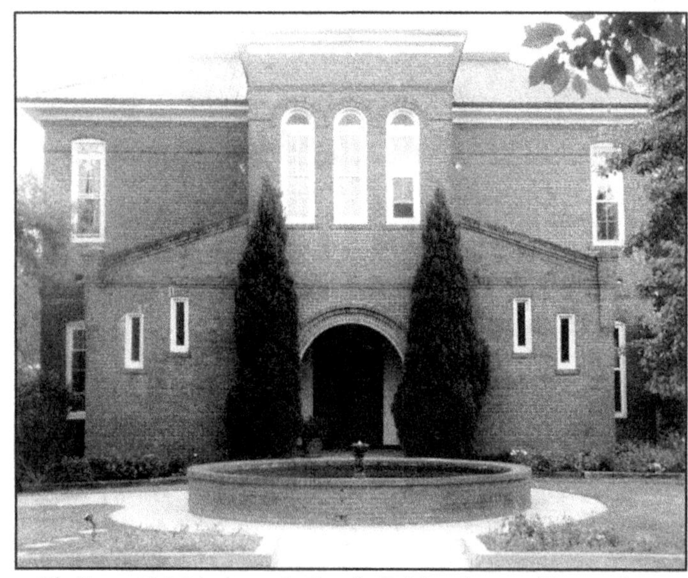

Pike County High School, now the Chandler Building. Courtesy of Branwyn Reeves.

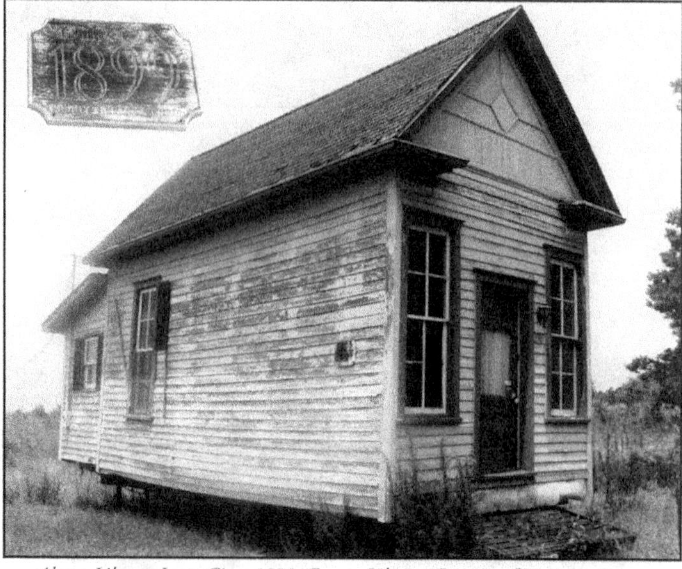

Above: Library. Inset: Circa 1899, County Library. Courtesy of Branwyn Reeves.

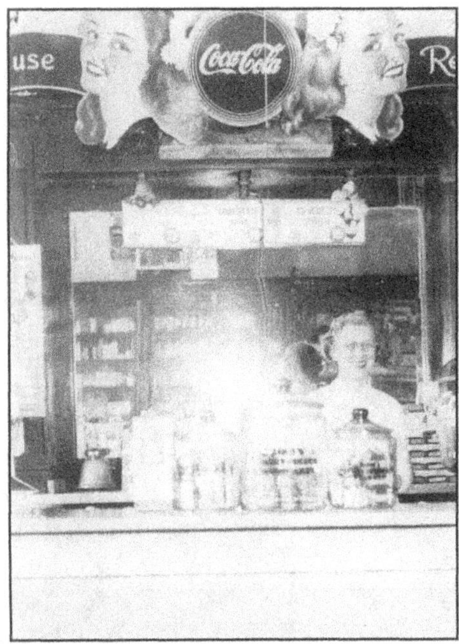

Soda Fountain at City Pharmacy in the early 1950's. Courtesy of W.S. Rodgers.

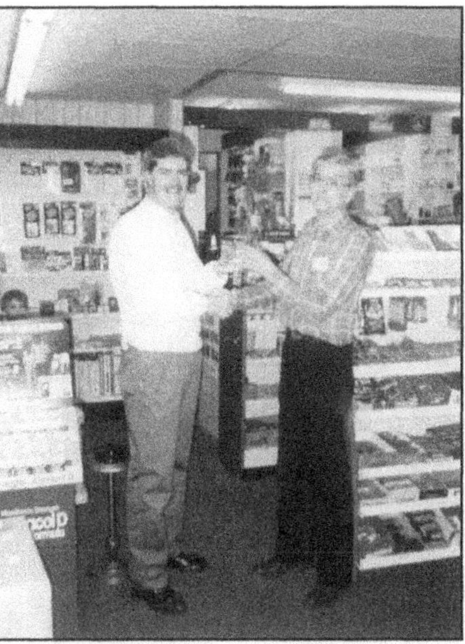

W.S. Rodgers turning over ownership of City Pharmacy to Ken Caskins on December 31, 1988. Courtesy of W.S. Rodgers.

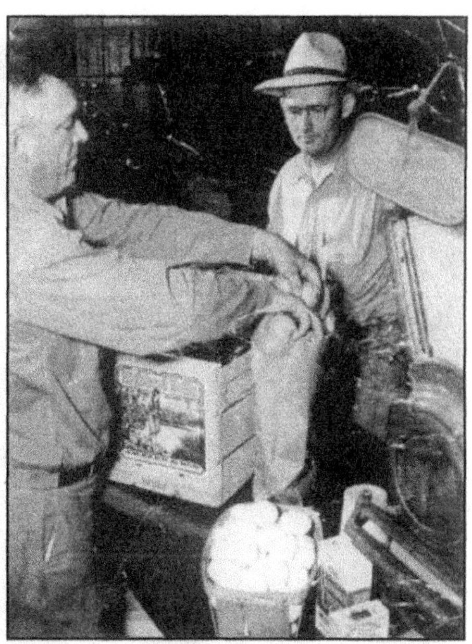

Holloway Norris barters eggs for oranges with Julius McGee at Pine Mountain Service Station. Courtesy of Rachel McClelland.

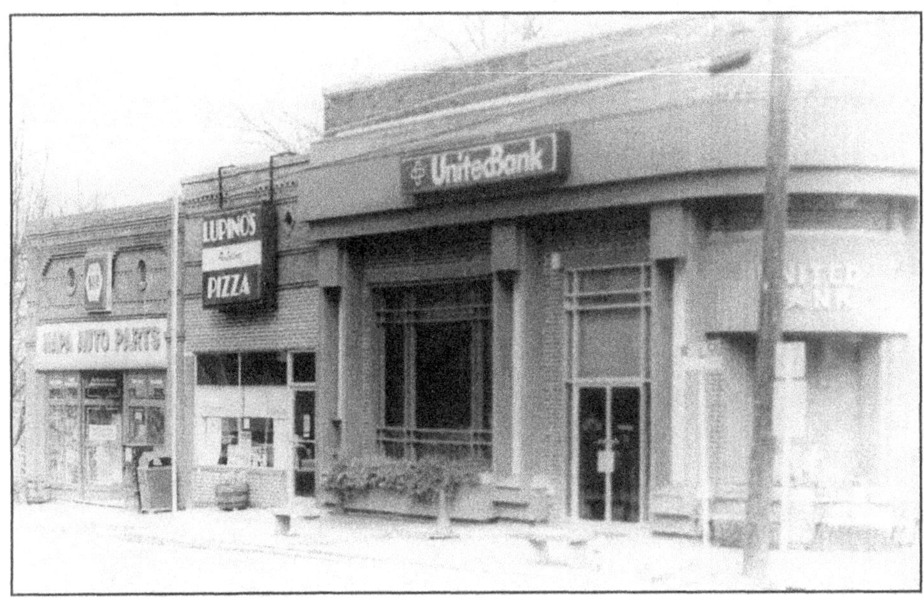

View of a street in Zebulon. Courtesy of Rosalee King.

Prices Reduced

On All Voiles, Crepes,

Pongee, Etc.

Good Line of Men's and Boys' Dress Shirts.

Full Supply of Hosiery at Bargain Prices.

Also Enamel Ware, Crockery

Groceries and Hardware.

Bring us your chickens and eggs

W. E. STOREY

Lifsey Springs

Zebulon, Ga., Friday, Aug. 6, 1926.

The country store which stood for many years.

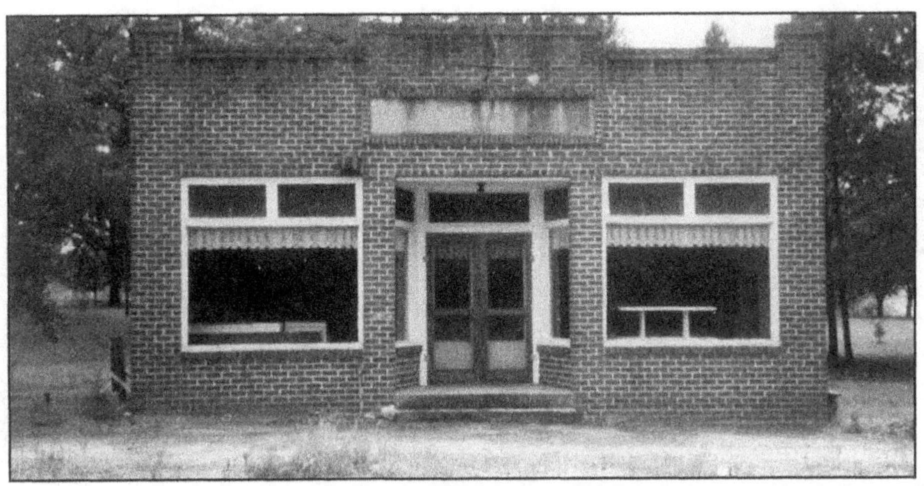

Bankston Grocery Store, Lifsey Springs, owned by Ed and Ethel Bankston, built in 1942. It is now a church. Courtesy of Hazel Osbolt and Melissa Carraway.

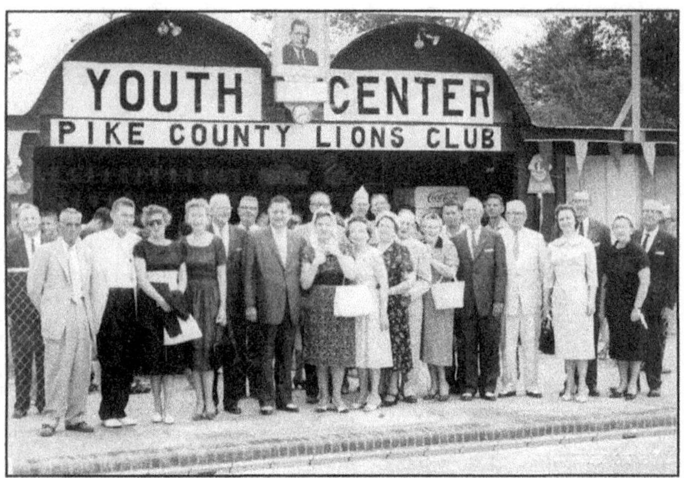

Grand opening of the Lions Club Youth Center in Pike County. Mr. George Bates, whom the center was dedicated to stands on left, front row. Courtesy of Hazel Osbolt and Melissa Carraway.

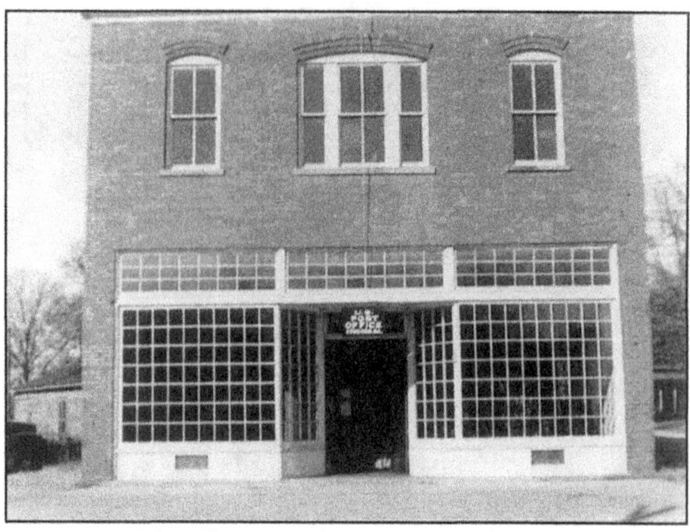

US Post Office in Concord Georgia. Courtesy of Joy Walker.

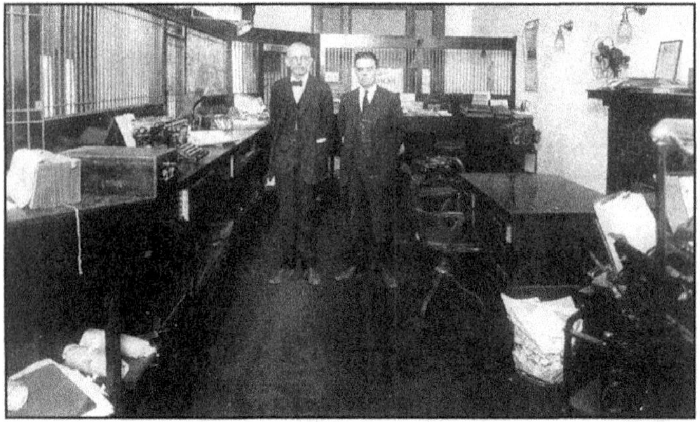

Mr. C.R. Gwyn, Sr. and Mr. John H. Baker in the Bank at Zebulon, GA. Courtesy of Betty Copeland.

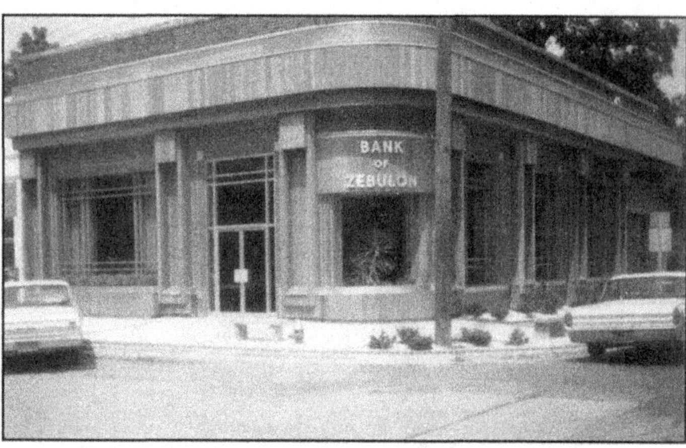

The bank of Zebulon is proud of their newly renovated building, 1966.

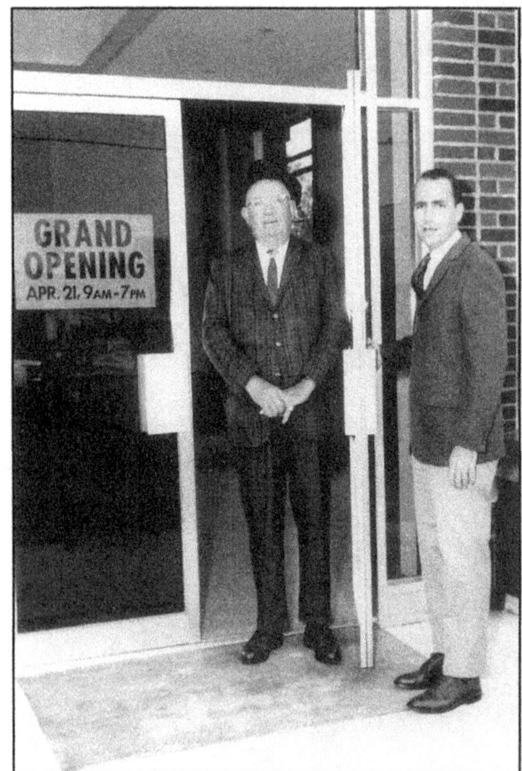

Mr. Joel Edwards and Mr. Bill Edwards at the grand opening of the Bank of Zebulon following their renovation, April 1966.

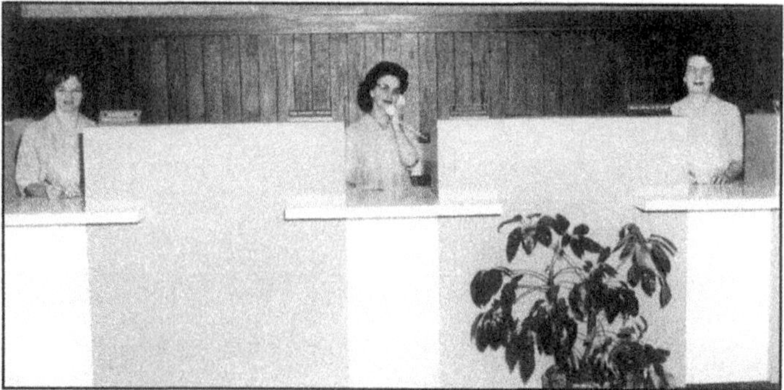

Sue Allen, Margaret Rawlins and Carolyn Gilbert. 1966.

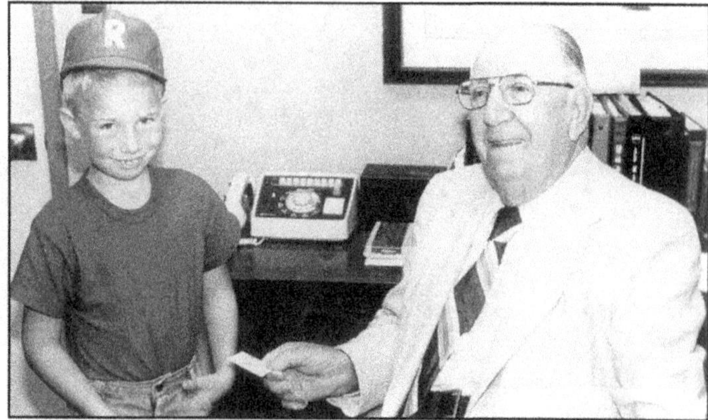

Mr. Joel Edwards serving a young community member, Chris Coleman, May 1981.

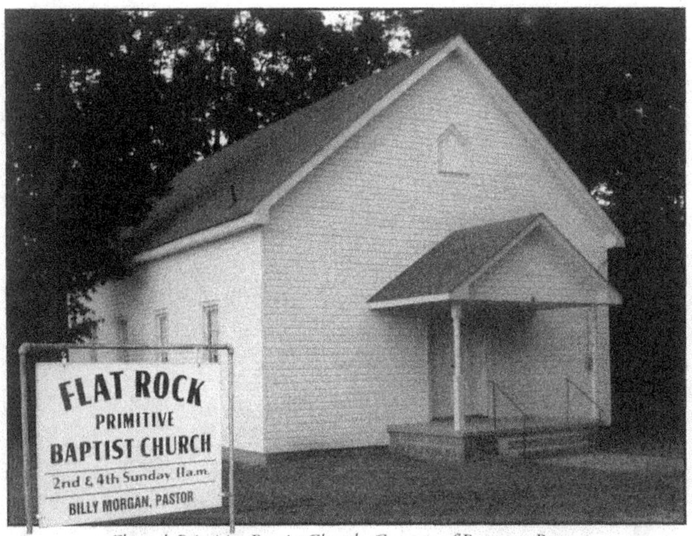

Flatrock Primitive Baptist Church. Courtesy of Branwyn Reeves.

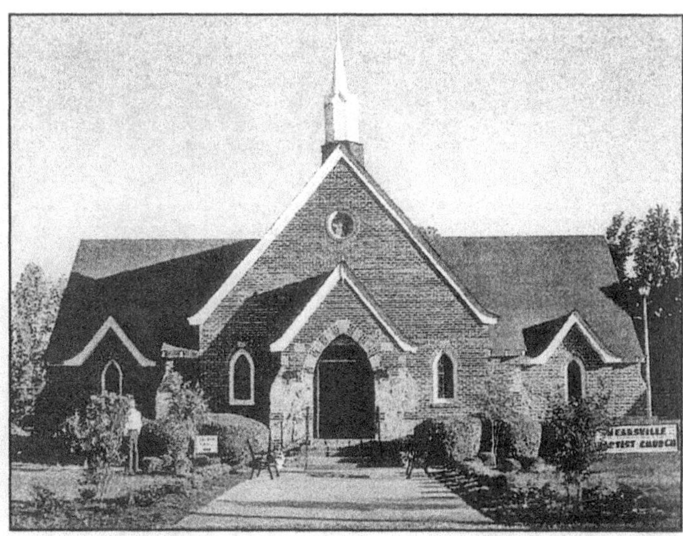

Meansville Baptist Church, founded in 1885. Courtesy of Bonnie Gardner.

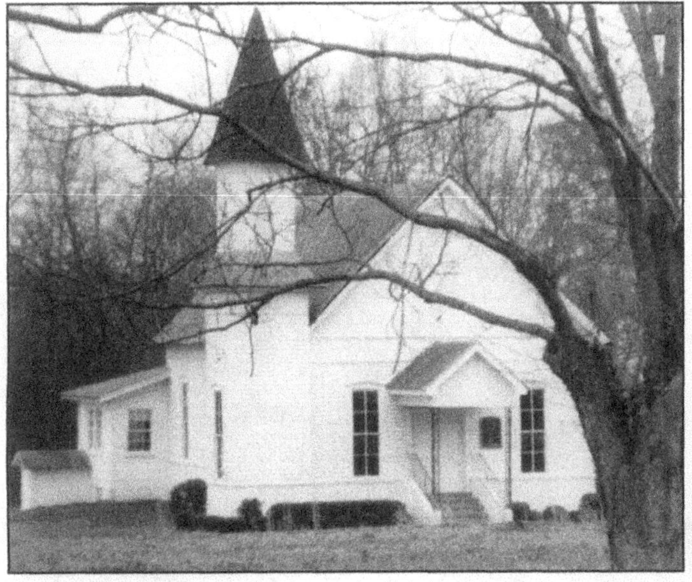

Exterior of Molena Methodist Church, now the Christian Outreach Center. Courtesy of Stephanie Bradley.

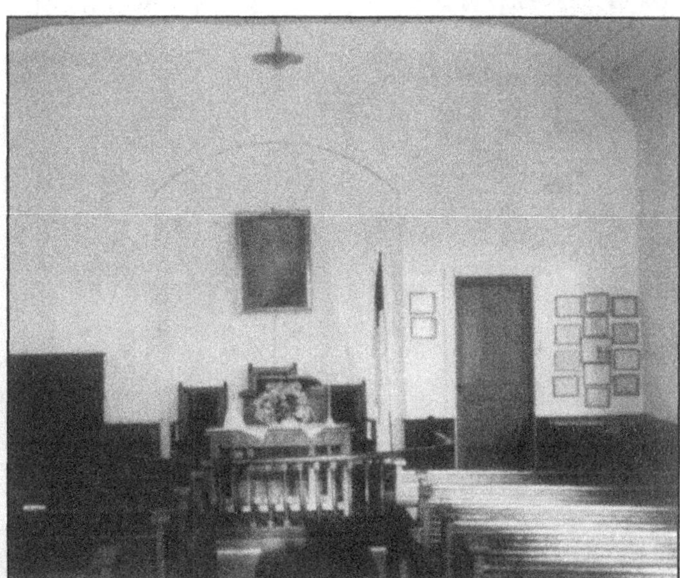

Inside Molena Methodist Church. Courtesy of Stephanie Bradley.

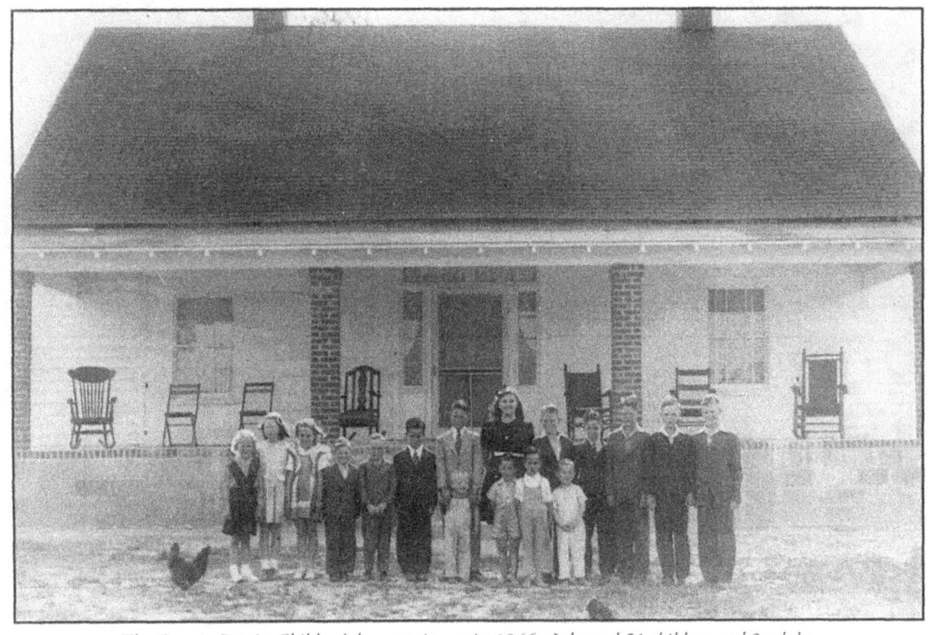

The Georgia Baptist Children's home as it was in 1946. It housed 51 children and 2 adults.

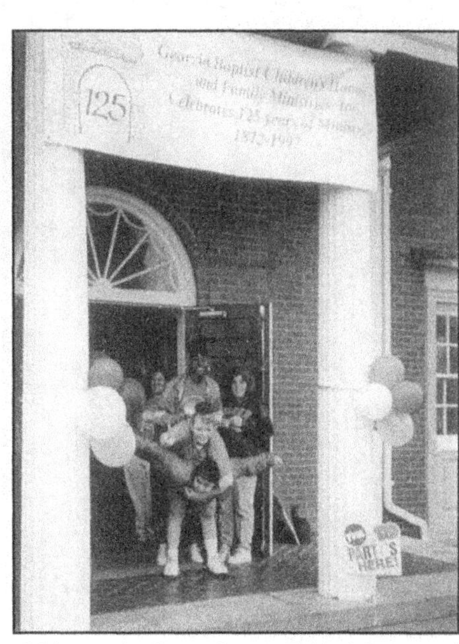

Celebrating the Georgia Baptist Children's home 125th anniversary in 1997.

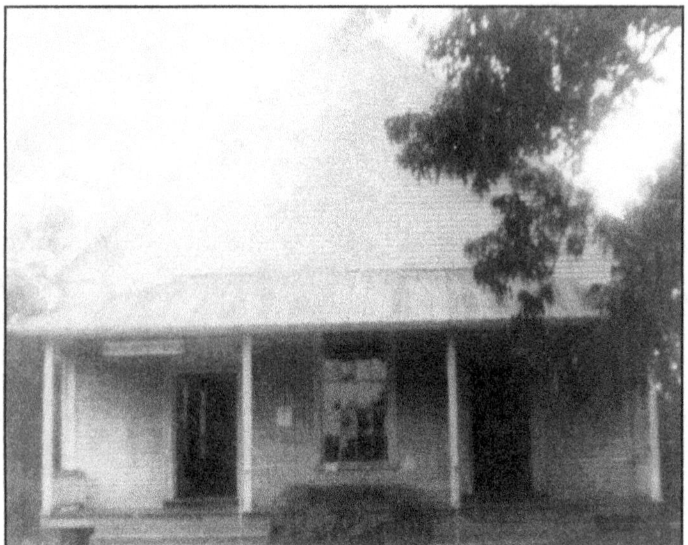
Old Mt. Olive Baptist Church. Courtesy of Geneva Sanders and Anna Belle McDaniel.

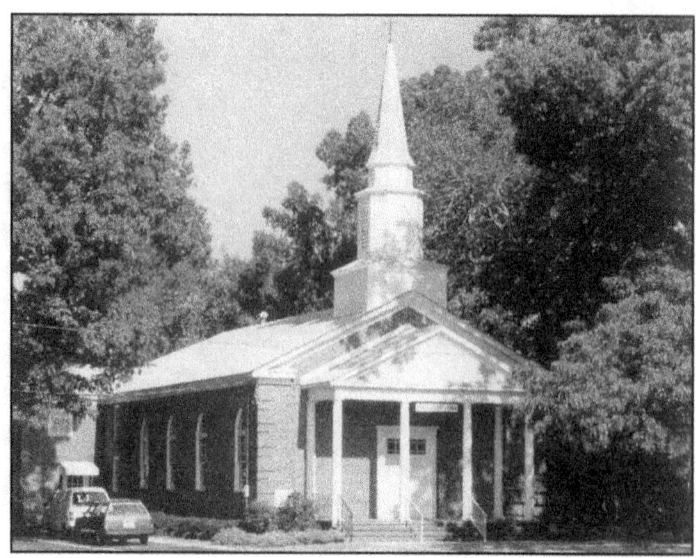
New Mt. Olive Baptist Church. Courtesy of Geneva Sanders.

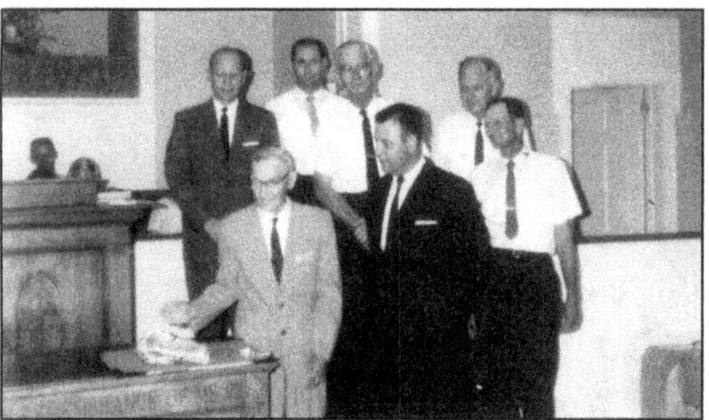
Burning of note at Mt. Olive. J.T. Pilkenton, Rev. Bob Williams, Jack Pilkenton, Tom Pilkenton, Render Lawrence, Bill and Walter Pilkenton. Courtesy of Geneva Sanders.

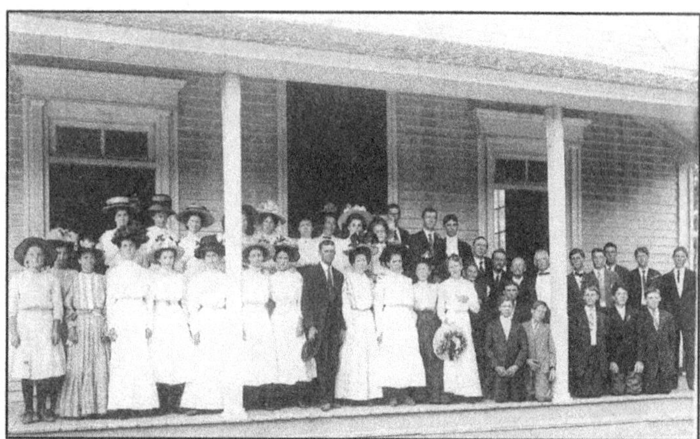
Mt. Olive Church, Sept. 5, 1909.

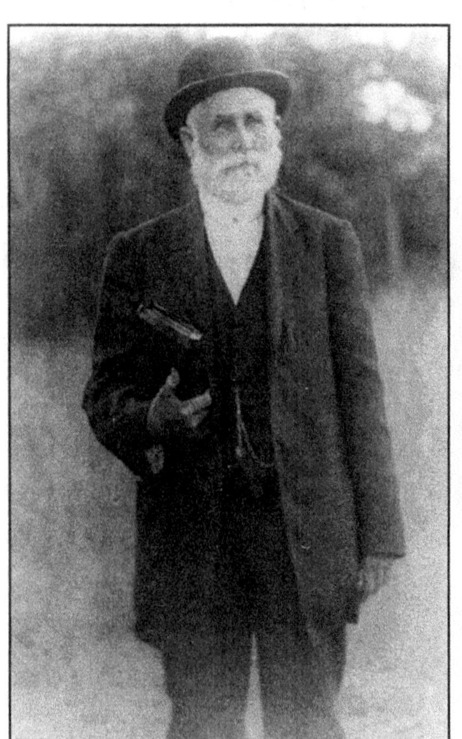
Rev. William H. Graham, the first pastor of Liberty Chapel Church in 1892. Courtesy of Wayne Foster.

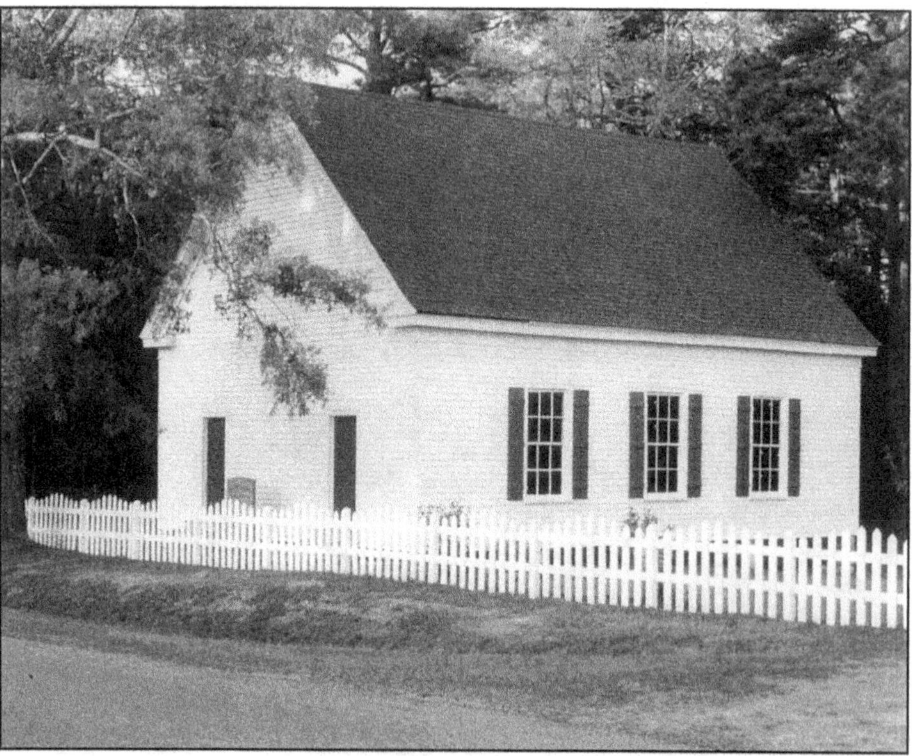
Liberty Chapel, founded January 7, 1892. Courtesy of Wayne Foster.

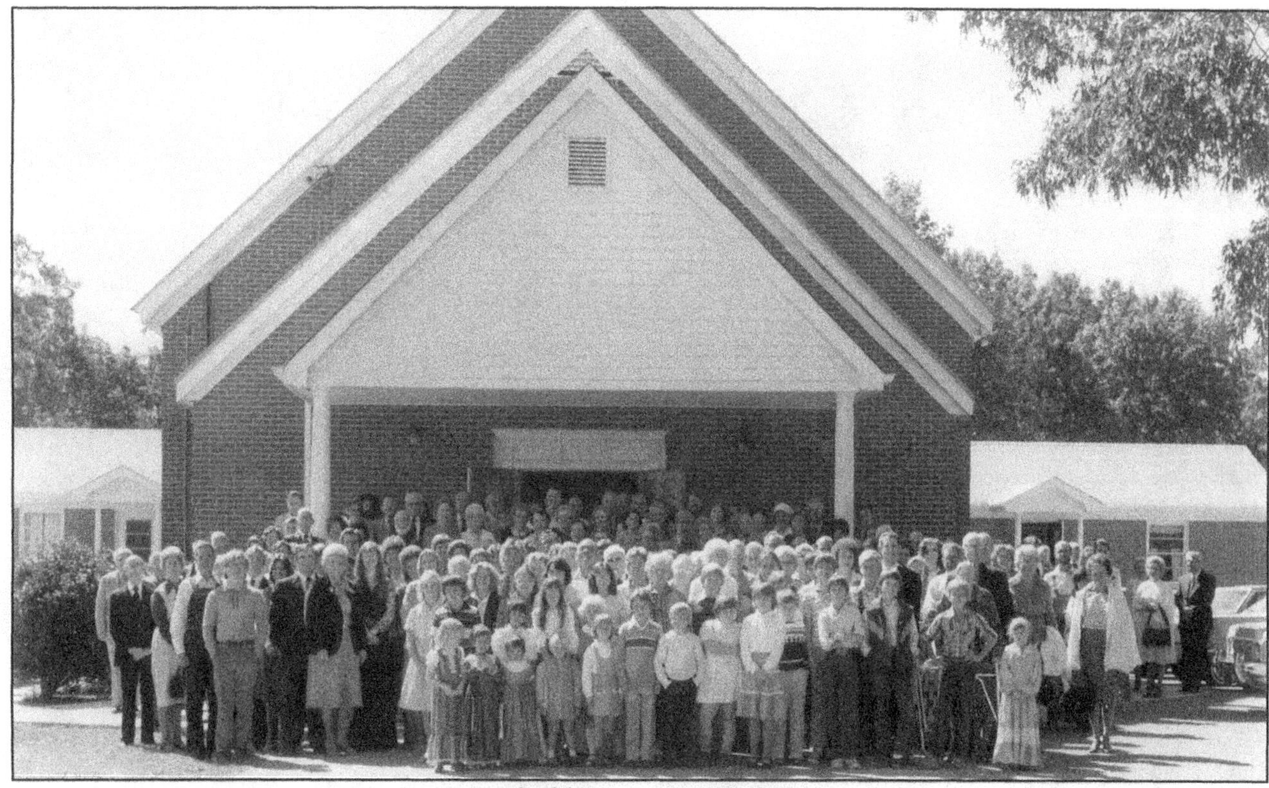

New Hope Baptist Church homecoming. Courtesy of Susan Brown Parham.

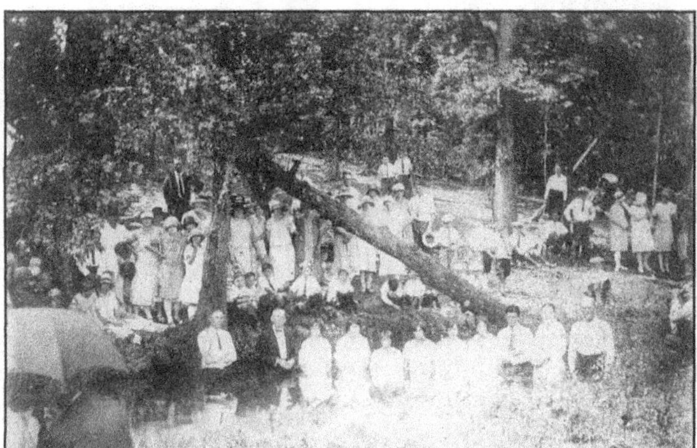

New Hope Baptist Church members. Courtesy of Patsy Vaughn.

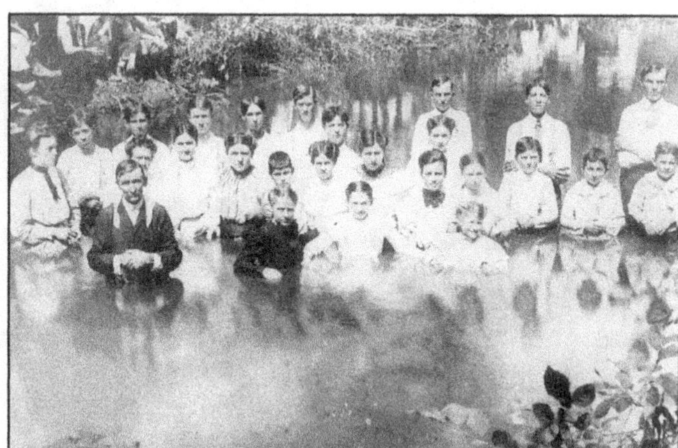

New Hope Baptist Church members being baptized. Courtesy of Patsy Vaughn.

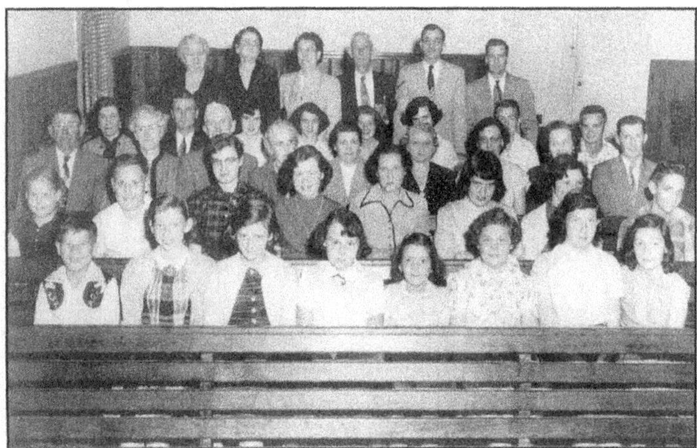

Group picture taken at New Hope Baptist Church, circa 1957. Courtesy of Rachel Shaw.

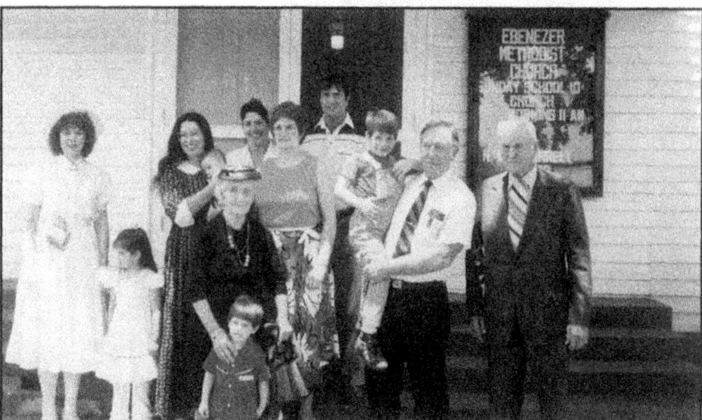

Old Fashion Day, June 24, 1990 at the Ebenezer United Methodist Church. Some of the Elliott family descendants: Lula Elliott (standing in front with great-grandson, Chris Elliott). Others, L-R: Rachel (Hammock) Shaw, Laura Chambley, Denise (Elliott) Chambley holding her nephew-Dustin Elliott, Valerie, Helen, Keith Elliott, Wilbur holding grandson, Darrell Elliott, Jesse England "Bully" Elliott. Courtesy of Jane Gaulding.

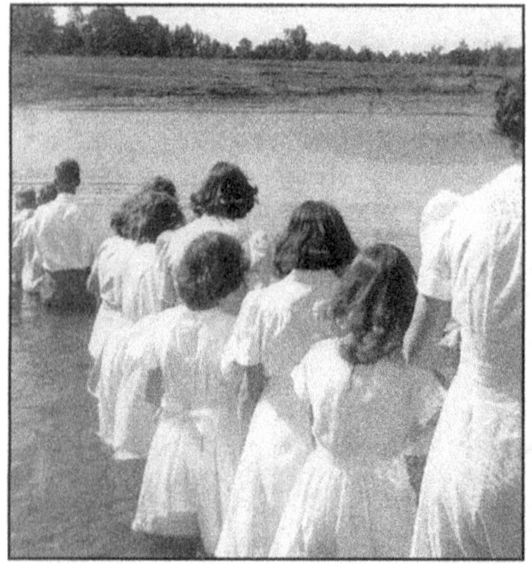

Beulah Baptist Church baptism service at Ode Cook's Lake on Cook Rd. Courtesy of Rosalee King.

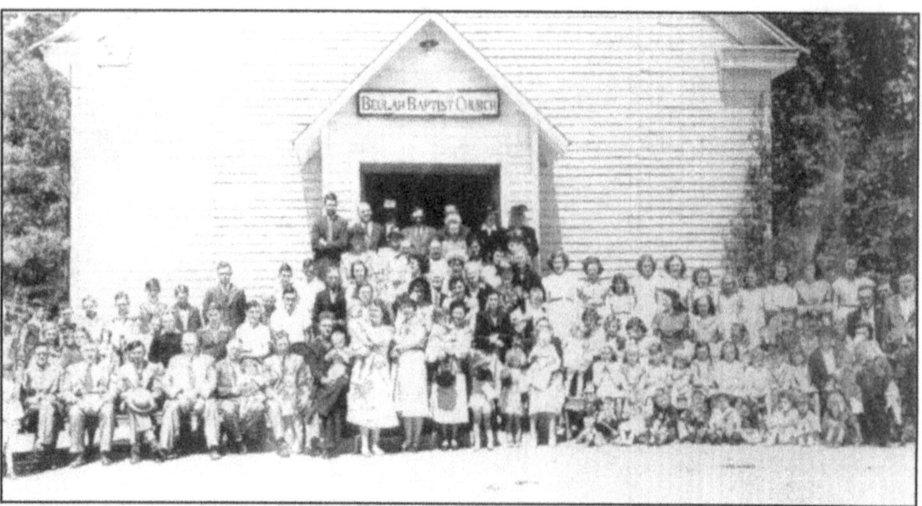

Beulah Baptist Church, 1949. Courtesy of Virginia Brooks.

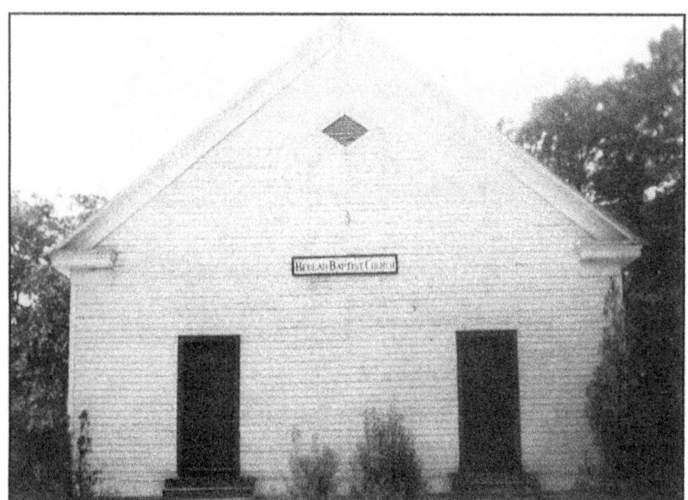

Beulah Baptist Missionary Church, circa 1920-40. Courtesy of Virginia Brooks.

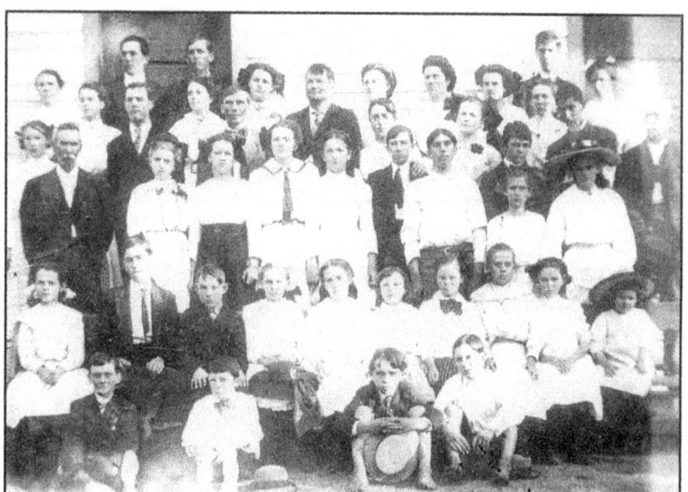

Mt. Gilead Baptist Sunday School. Courtesy of Sam Bunn.

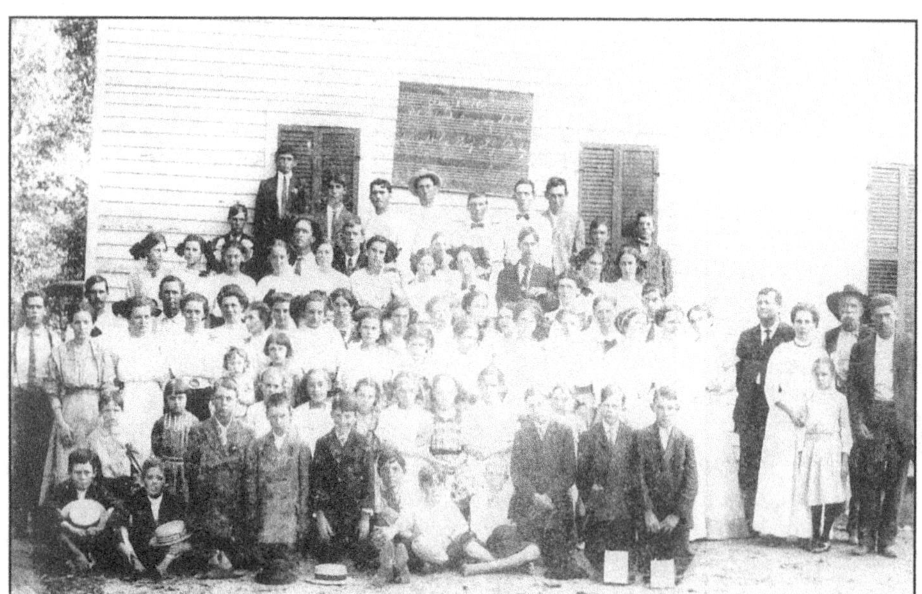

Mt. Gilead Baptist Church, 1911. Courtesy of Sam Bunn.

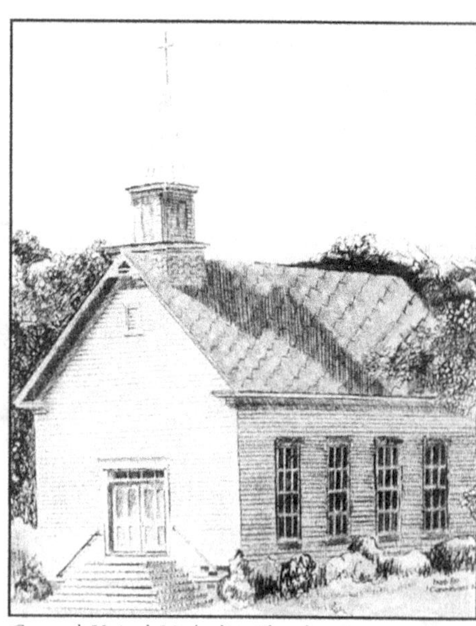

Concord United Methodist Church. Courtesy of Fred Oxford.

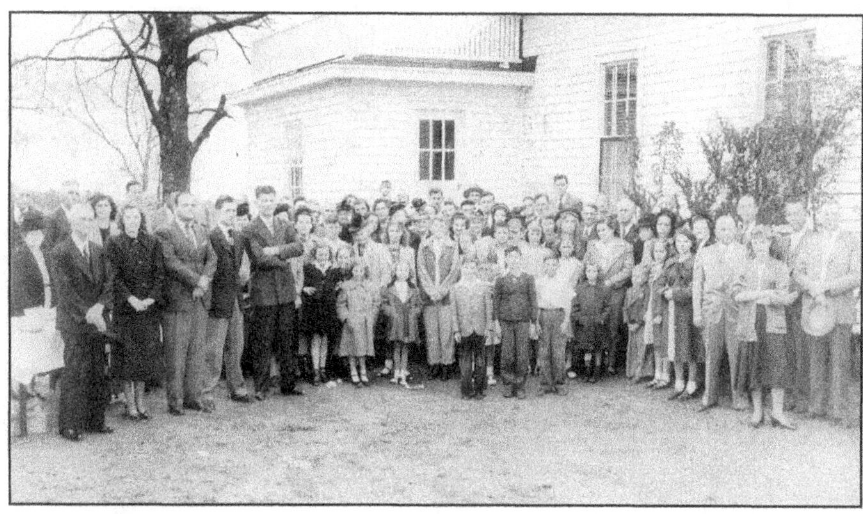

Nazareth Baptist Church, Milner Road in Zebulon, GA. Homecoming day, circa 1947 or 1948. Courtesy of Jane Gaulding.

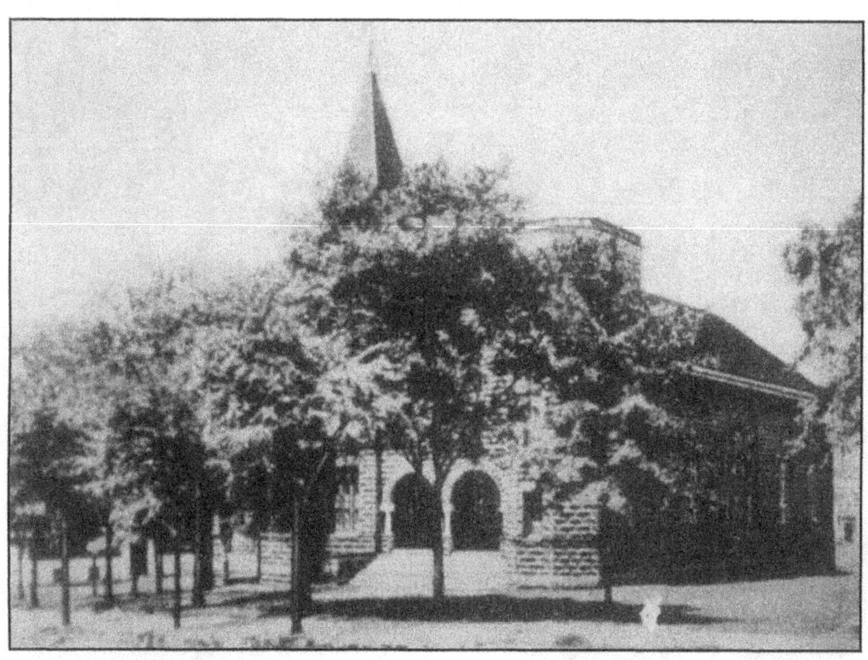

First Methodist Church in Barnesville. Courtesy of JBG.

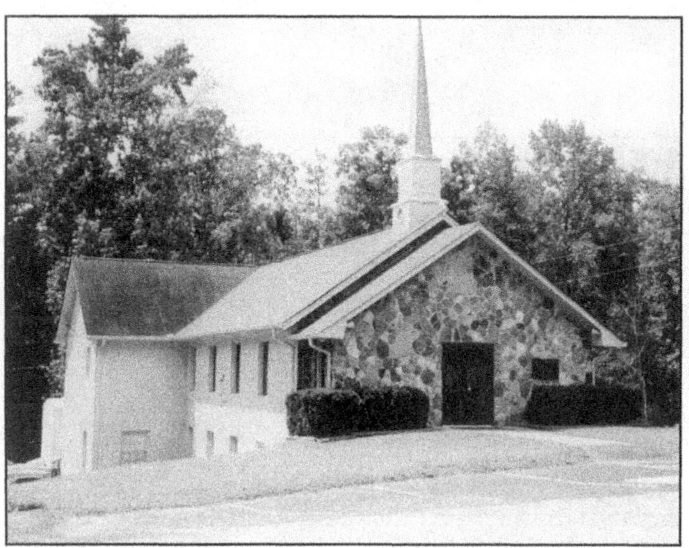

Mountain Gap Church, established in 1898. Courtesy of James Adams.

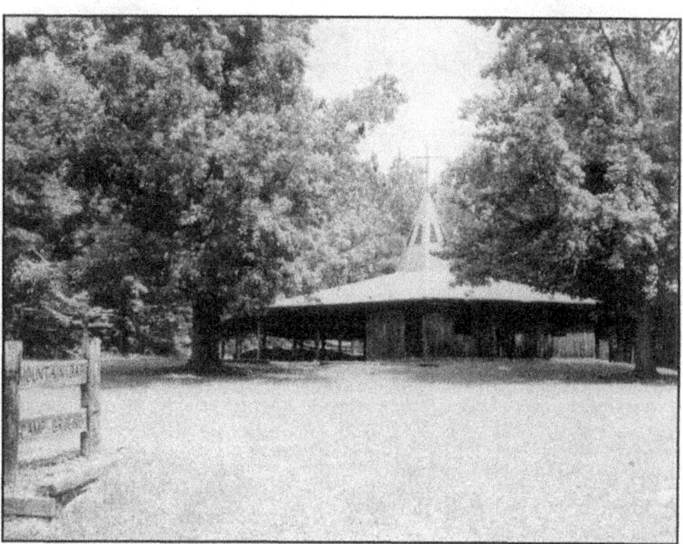

Mountain Gap Camp, meeting tabernacle, built in 1977. Courtesy of James Adams.

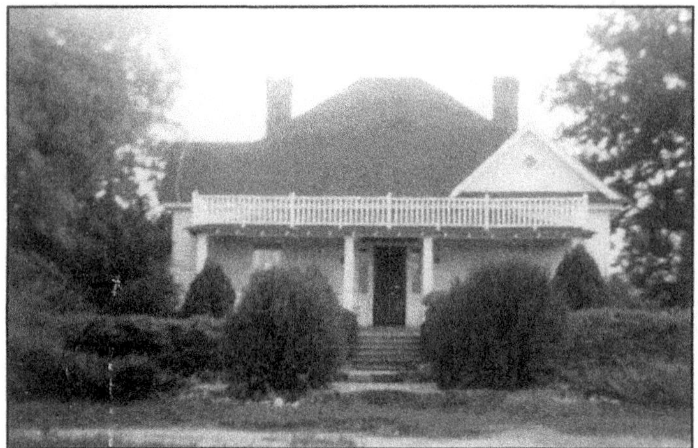

The Howard homeplace at Lifsey Springs. Courtesy of Mrs. Clyde Gibson.

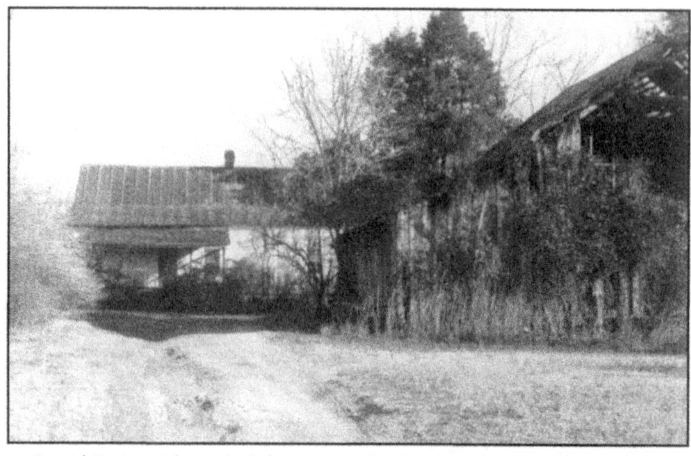

Daniel Eppinger's home, built between 1824 and 1830. Courtesy of Carol Barton.

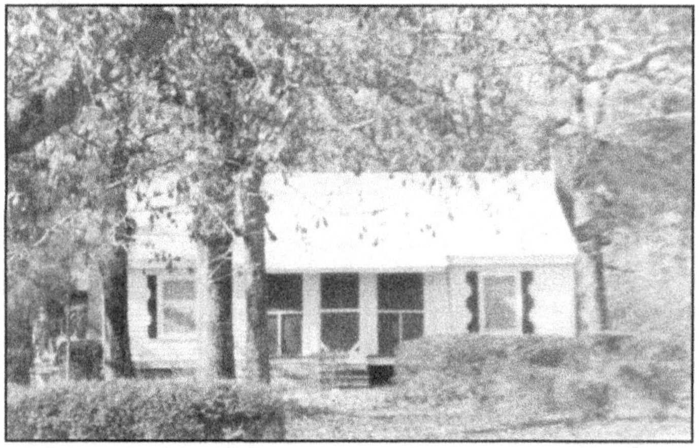

The Brown's Pike Co. homeplace on New Hope Road. Courtesy of Susan Brown Parham.

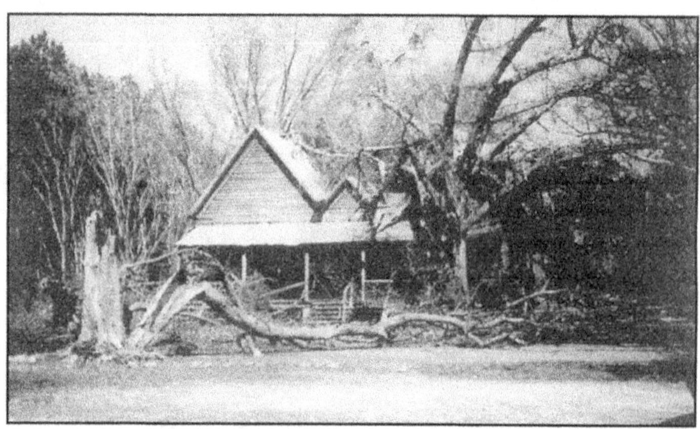

Robert Chapman's house showing the damage it received from a tornado in the 1960's. Courtesy of Robert Chapman.

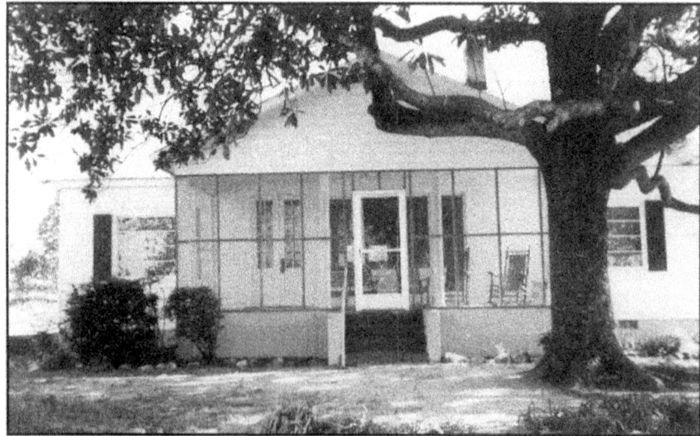

R.C. and Jewel Pilkenton Jones home on Hwy. 109, Molena, GA. Courtesy of Robert F. Jones.

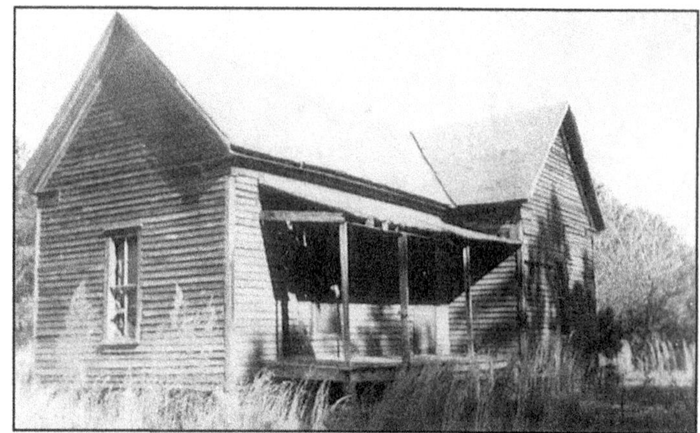

Old tenant house where Rosalee and J.M. Buck King started their life off together in 1934, now demolished. Courtesy of Rosalee King.

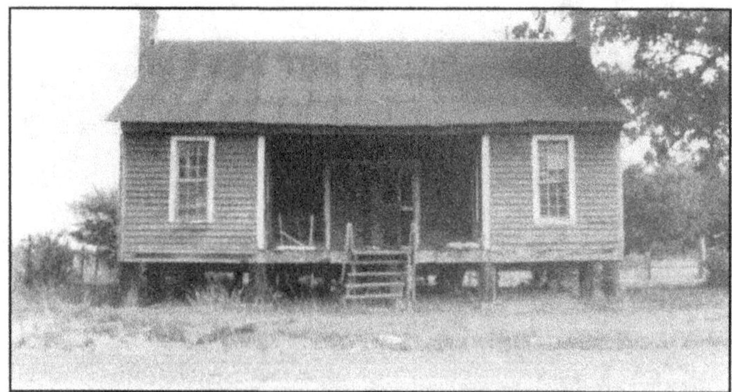

Martin Luther Bennett home in Molena, GA. Courtesy of Robert F. Jones.

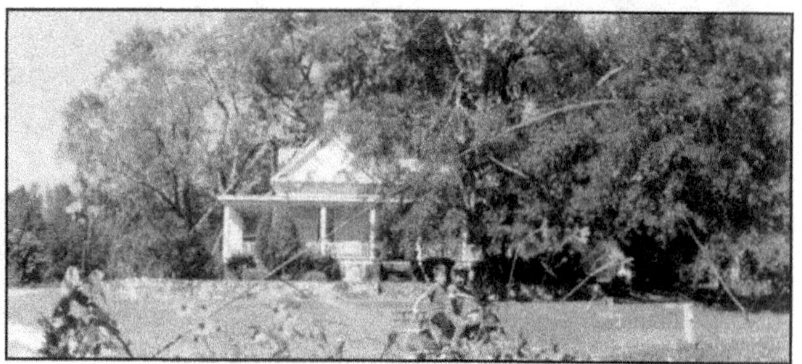

Homeplace of Ed and Ethel Bankston of Lifsey Springs. The Bankston's owned Bankston Lumber Co. on the square in Zebulon in the building which is now attorney Virgil Brown's, office. They also owned Bankston's grocery in Lifsey Springs which Mrs. Bankston ran. Courtesy of Hazel Osbolt and Melissa Carraway.

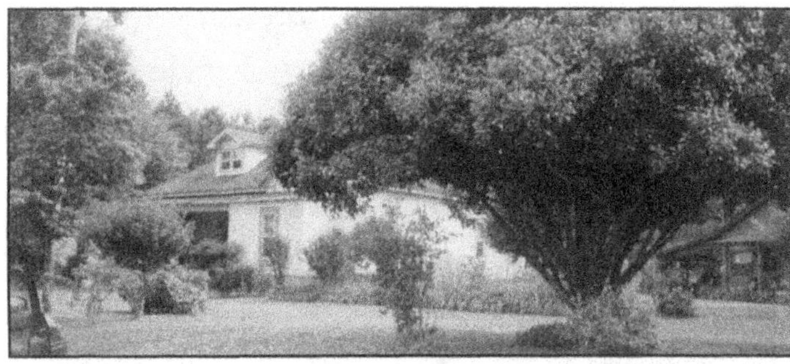

The third and final home of Bob and Dora (Bush) Elliott. It was across the road from where Dora was born and raised. Her parents, Rev. and Mrs. Jones Bush, owned a large amount of land in this area. Not sure if this house was already built when they moved there in 1913-1914. Her mother died in 1903 and her father died in 1913. She inherited the homeplace. Bob and Doris along with their 10 children lived in this house. Bob died in 1951 and Dora died in 1963. After her death all her property was auctioned off and eventually split up. It was very upsetting to some of the Bush descendents that this land was out of the family. This house was bought by the Helms family and it remains in that family today. Courtesy of Jane Gaulding.

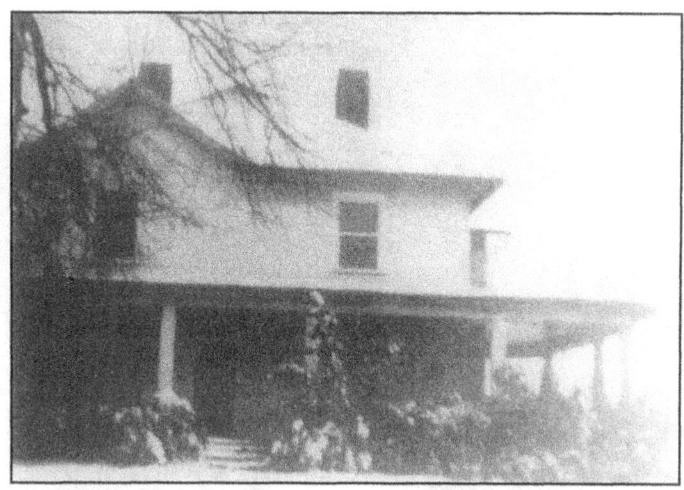

Home of G.M. Rawls, Williamson, GA, taken March of 1923. Courtesy of Helen Kendrick and Betty Copeland.

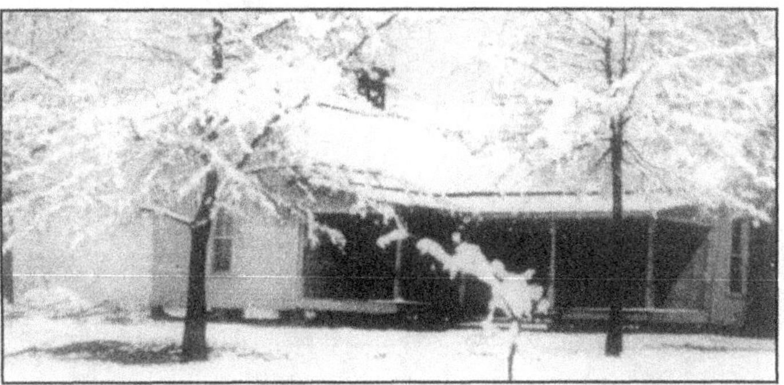

Home of Otis G. Rawls, Williamson, GA. Taken March, 1923 — built about 1895. Courtesy of Betty Copeland.

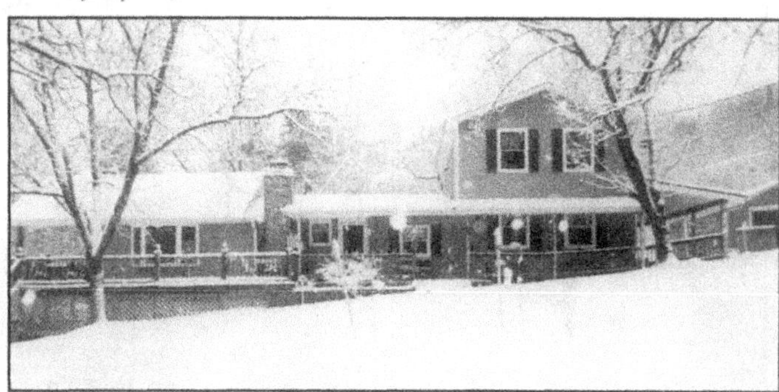

A winter wonderland in January 2002 on Sunshine Mountain Farm, the Bishop-Byrd-Gardner homeplace. Courtesy of Bonnie Gardner.

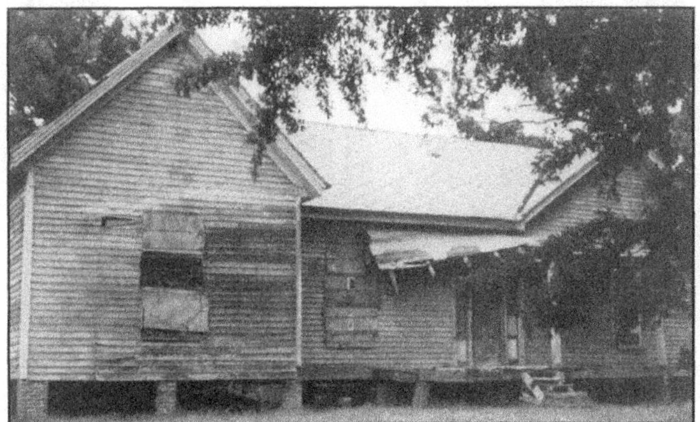

Former home of Robert and Bathsheba Riggins Pilkenton, Molena, GA, circa 1970's. Courtesy of Robert F. Jones.

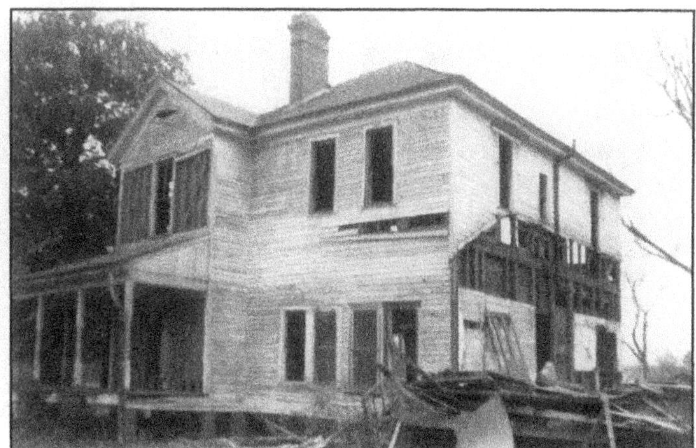

Gilbert House, moved in March of 1991. Courtesy of Stephanie Bradley.

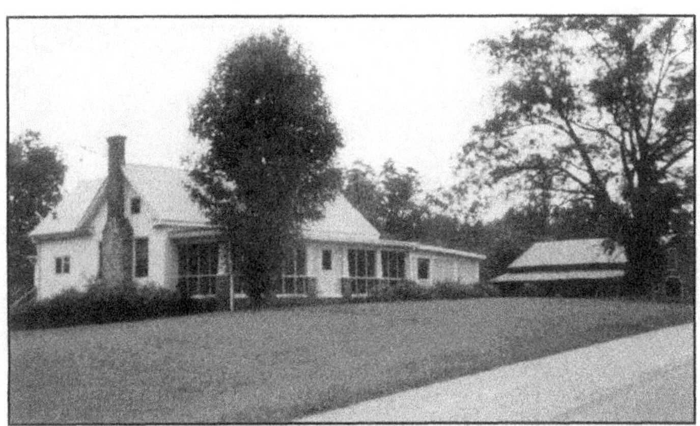

Maxie and Sarah Jordan's homeplace on Old Zebulon Road. Courtesy of Jane Gaulding.

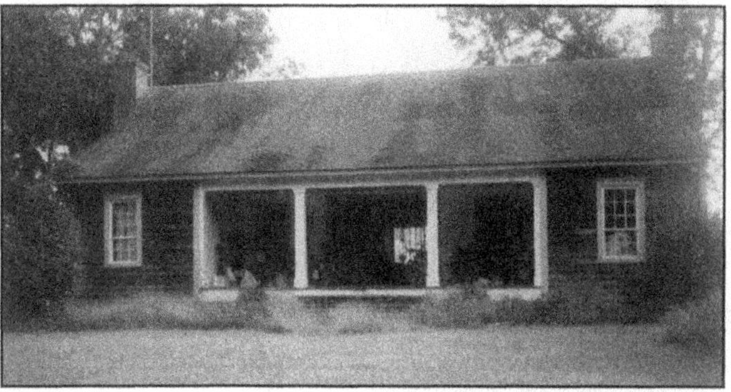

The Cauthen House, originally was in Pike Co. but was later moved to Lamar Co. It has been said that the house has a secret room that was used to help the slaves escape to the Underground Railroad. Courtesy of Rebecca Cauthen.

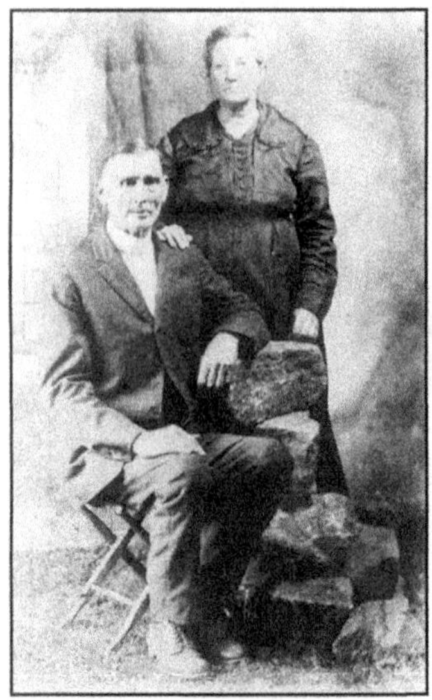

Mr. and Mrs. J.W. Self, 1925. Courtesy of Louise Hamlett.

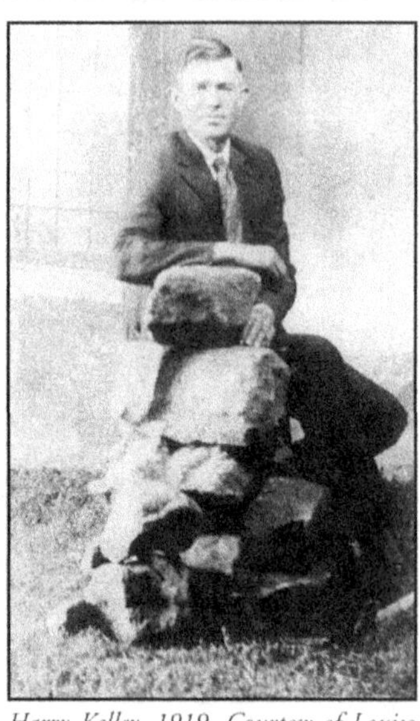

Harry Kelley, 1919. Courtesy of Louise Hamlett.

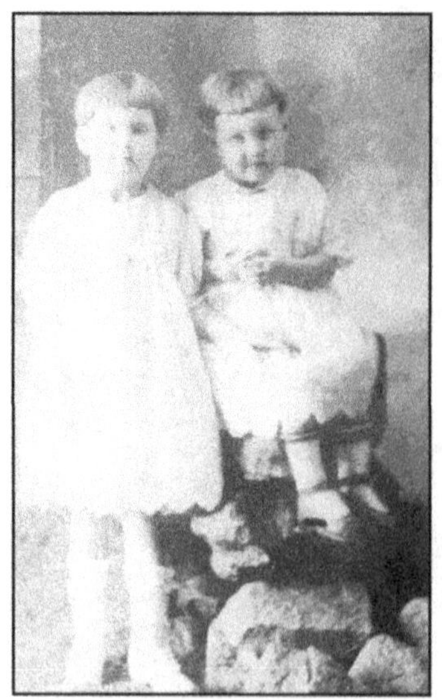

Louise and Dorothy Kelly, 1919. Courtesy of Louise Hamlett.

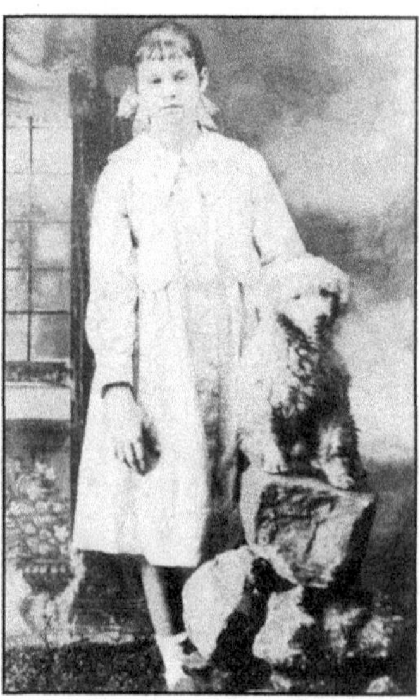

Doris Self, 1925. Courtesy of Louise Hamlett.

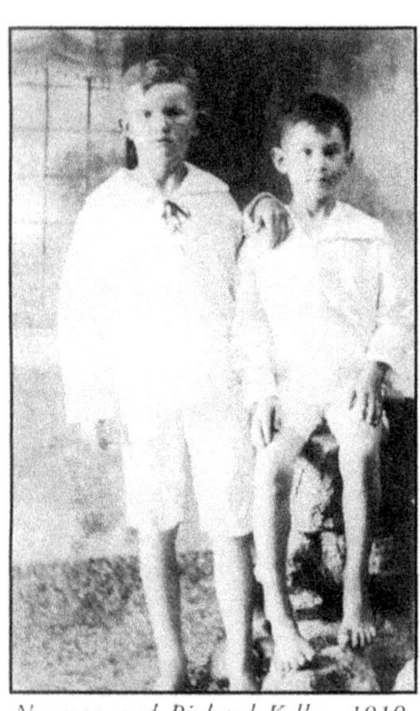

Norman and Richard Kelley, 1919. Courtesy of Louise Hamlett.

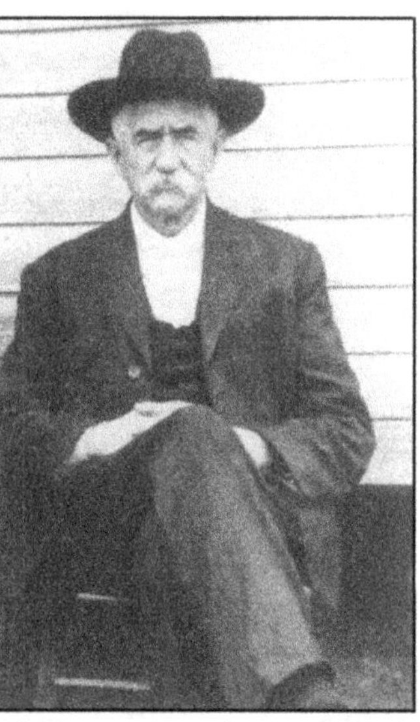

John Benjamin Harris (1857-1946), made circa 1920. Courtesy of Lanny Cauthen.

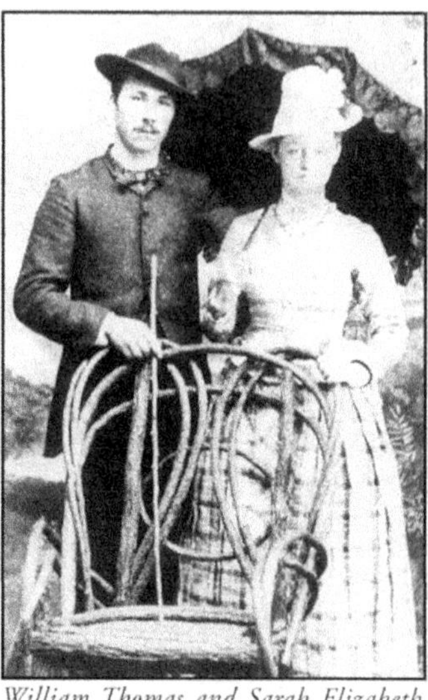

William Thomas and Sarah Elizabeth (Pounds) Cauthen, Sept. 4, 1887. Courtesy of Lanny Cauthen.

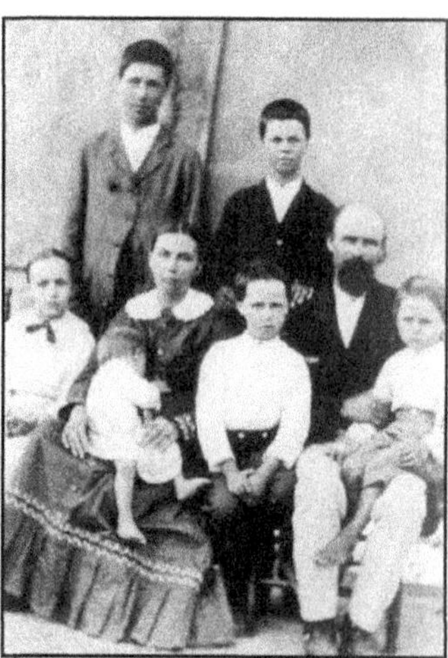

William Harvey Cauthen and Family: William Thomas, Edward Alexander, Mary Lula, Sarah, Elijah Franklin, John Robert, William Harvey and Charles Washington. Courtesy of Lanny Cauthen.

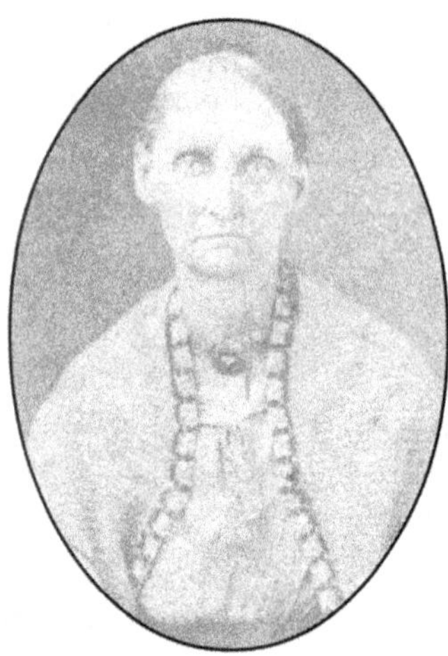

Susan Pyron Harris (1809-1885), made circa 1880. Courtesy of Lanny Cauthen.

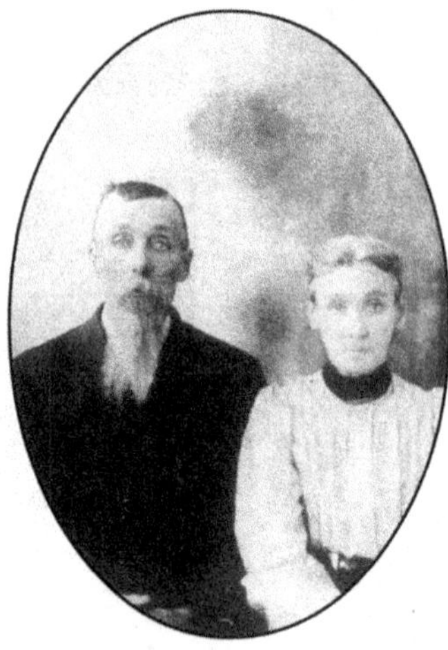

Henry Clay and Susan Randall (Harden) Harris, 1900. Courtesy of Lanny Cauthen.

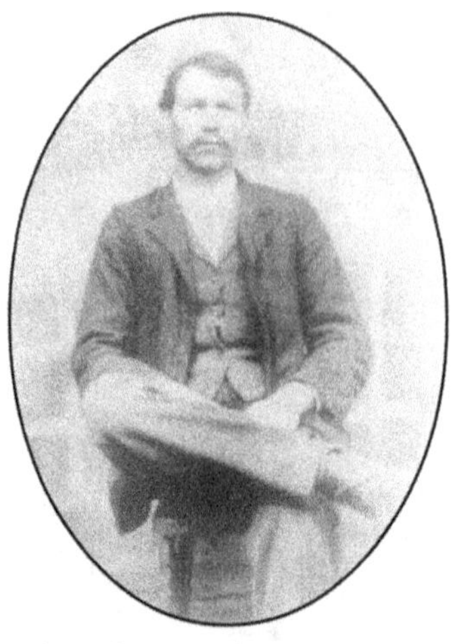

John Robert Cauthen (1876-1965). Courtesy of Lanny Cauthen.

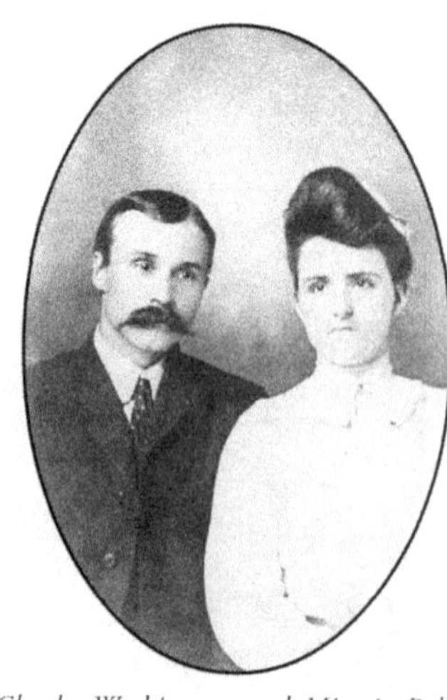

Charles Washington and Minnie Bell (Kendrick) Cauthen, about 1903. Courtesy of Lanny Cauthen.

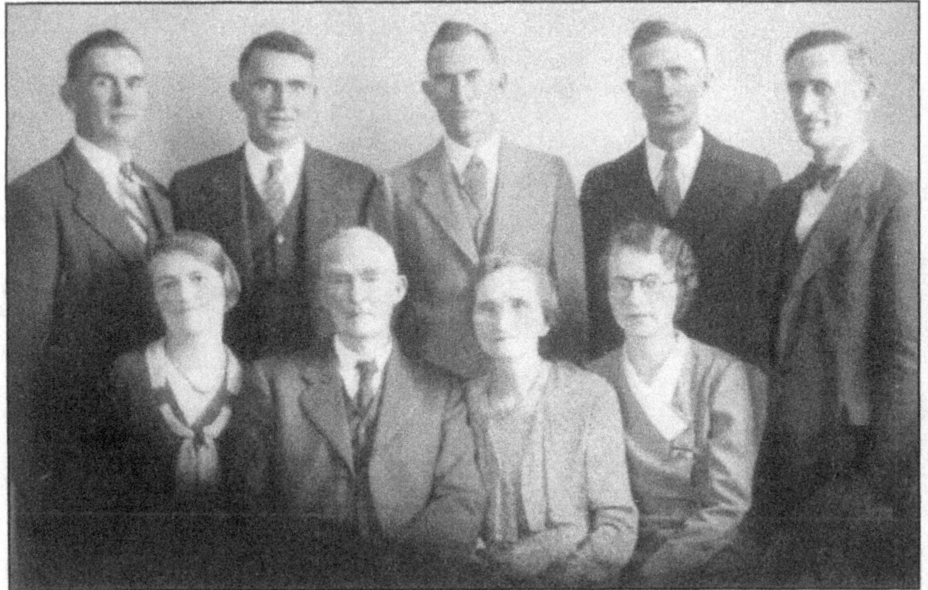

William Edward Caldwell family, 1933. Front row: Jewel Caldwell McKinley, William Edward Caldwell, Sarah Jane Grubbs Caldwell and Olene Caldwell Bogle. Back row: Jim, Henry, Emmett, Worthy and Roy. Courtesy of Kenneth Caldwell.

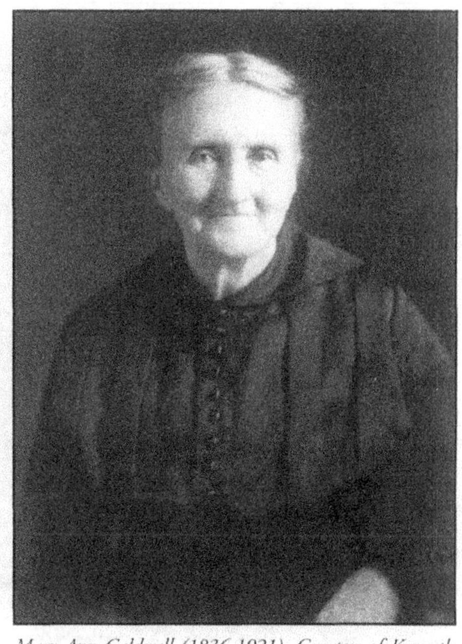

Mary Ann Caldwell (1836-1921). Courtesy of Kenneth Caldwell.

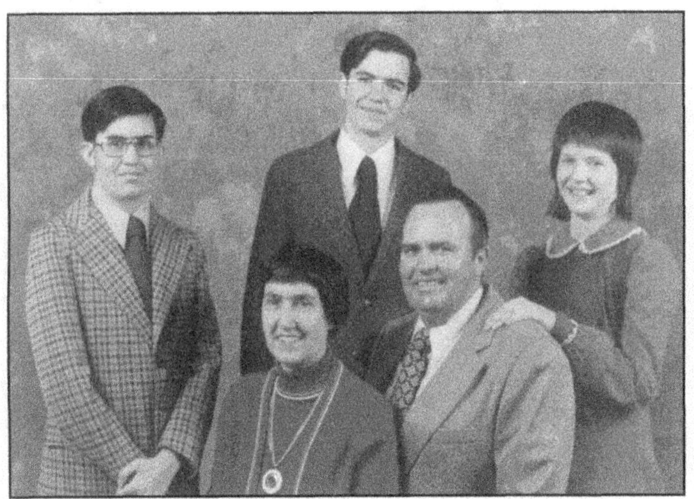

Kenneth, Ruth, William, Emmett and Penny Caldwell, circa 1970's. Courtesy of Kenneth Caldwell.

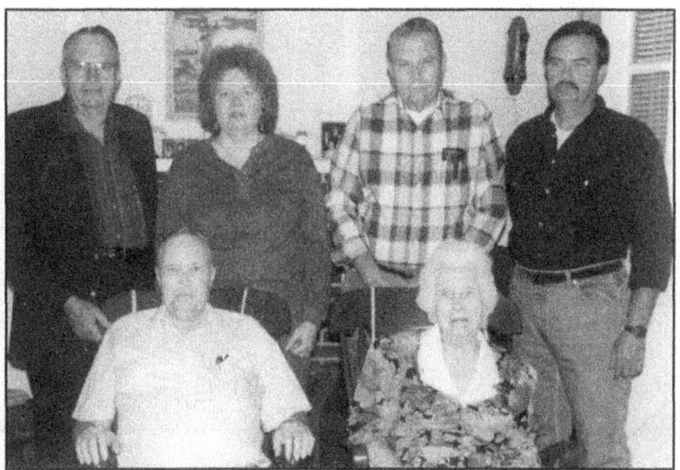

Family of Emmett O. Caldwell Sr. Front row: Ronald W. Caldwell and Lucile Hawkins Caldwell. Back row: Owen Caldwell, Ann Caldwell Wheeless, Charles W. Caldwell and Wendel G. Caldwell. Courtesy of Kenneth Caldwell.

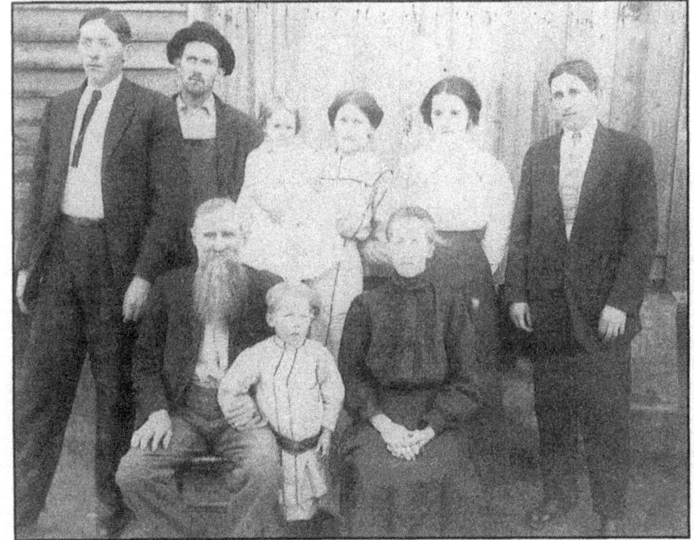

Front row: Thomas Franklin Kendrick, Thomas Clark and Lucy Lynch Kendrick. Back row: Milton B. Kendrick, John (Bud) Kendrick, Evie Kendrick Clark, Maude Clark, Pearl Kendrick and Walter Kendrick Sr. Courtesy of Walter Kendrick.

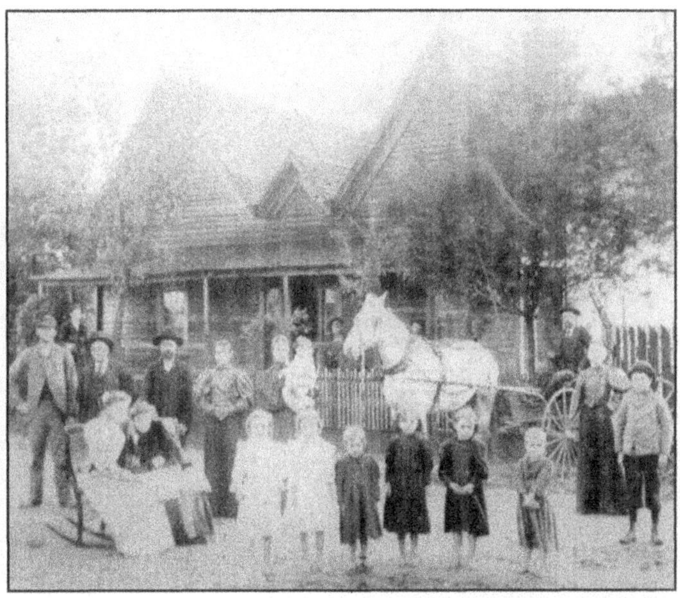

J.C. Chapman homeplace, circa late 1800's. It is still standing. Courtesy of Robert Chapman.

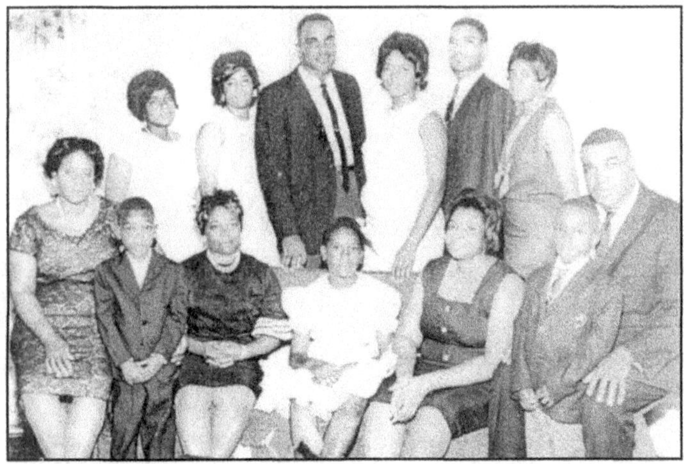

The Lee family: Mattie Francis Lee, Martha Lee Burden, Ellen Lee Randolph, James Lee, Evelyn Lee, Henry Hall, Mattie Lee Hall, Scottie Lee, Mary Harmon, Albberta Lee Willis, Eva Heard, David Lee Jr., and Dave Lee, 1965. Courtesy of Martha Burden.

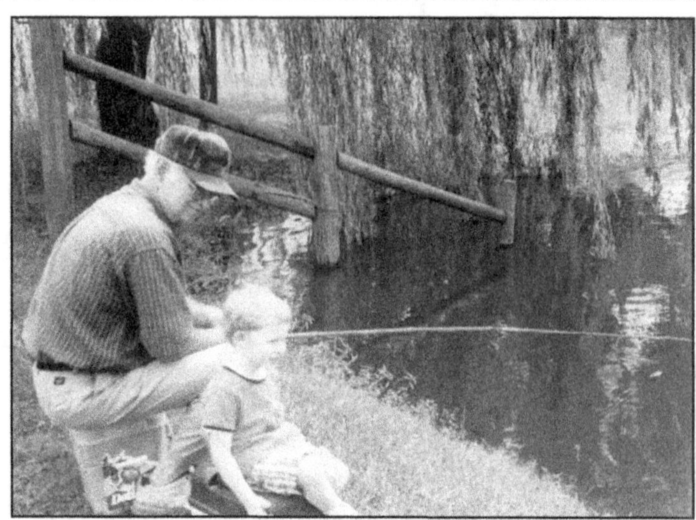

James William Lawrence and Zack Lawrence. Courtesy of Billy Lawrence.

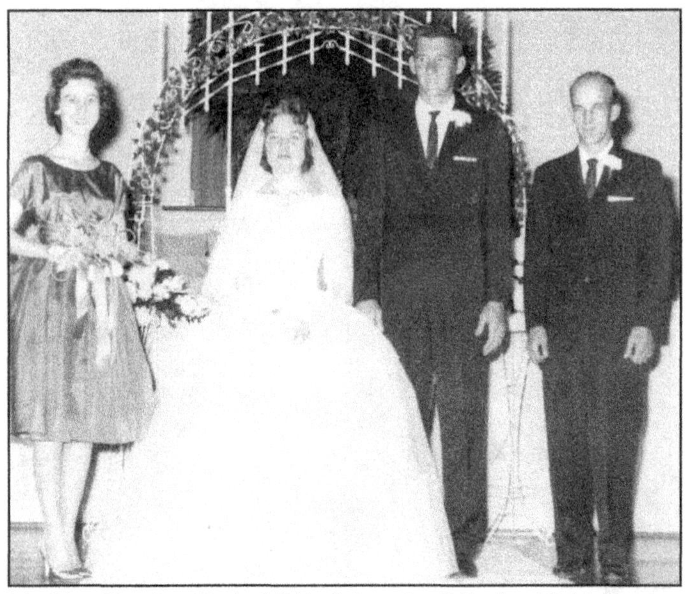

Jake Selsor, Mary Jean Moreland Caldwell, James Lee Caldwell and Ralph Paramore, 1961. Courtesy of James Caldwell.

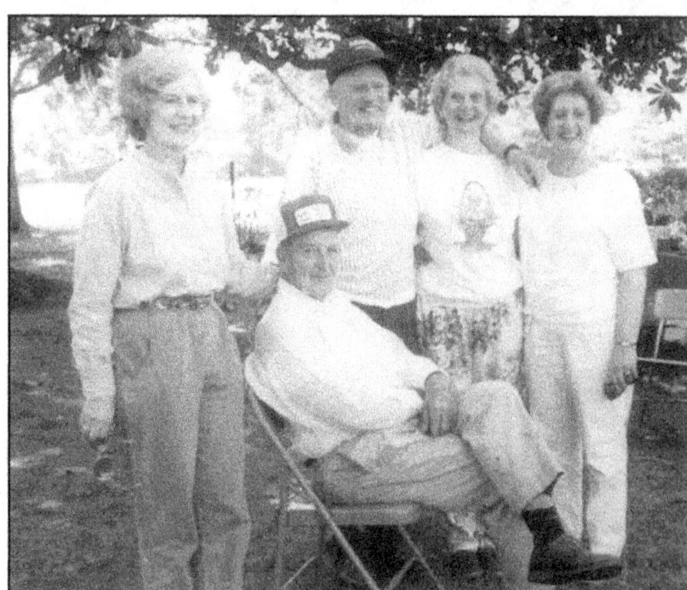

Martha Jones Austin, Henry Jones, Fred Jones, Virginia Jones Tucker and Jefflyn Jones Williams at the Jones homeplace on Hwy. 109, Molena, GA. Courtesy of Robert F. Jones.

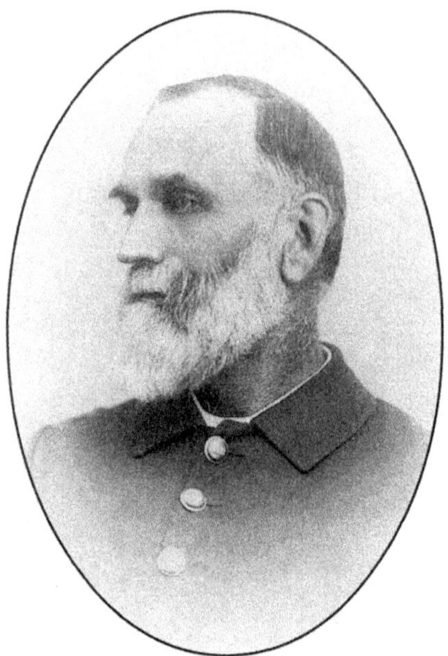

Azmon Benson Shackelford (1833-1912), wounded at Chickamauga, Sept. 17, 1862. Courtesy of Cora Shackelford.

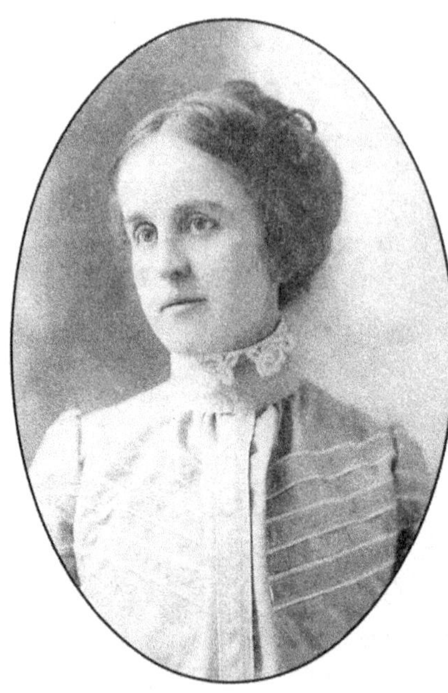

Frances (Fannie) Ann Shackelford. Courtesy of Cora Shackelford, circa 1891.

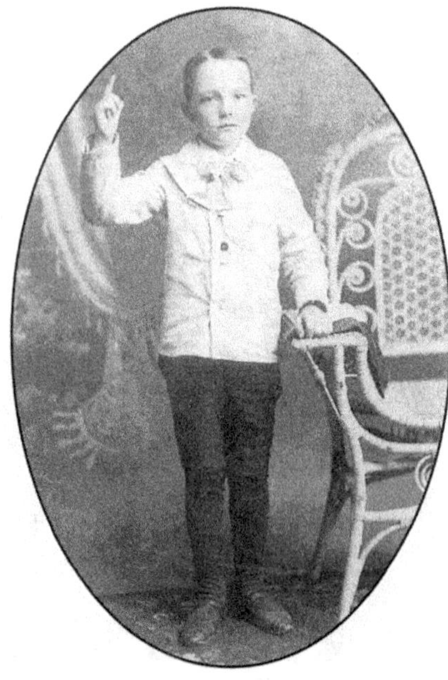

Junius M. Shackelford (1880-1973). Courtesy of Cora Shackelford.

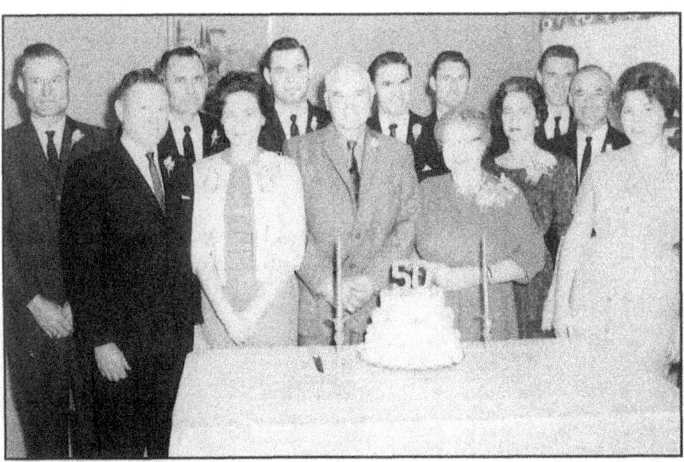

50th wedding anniversary of John Stephen Shackelford Sr. and Ethel B. Pitts. Back row: Alton Drewery, John Stephen Jr., Charles Ray, Byron Lewis, William Ray and Riley Allen. Williard Murray, Lois Inell, John Stephen Sr., Ethel B. Pitts, Alice Marie, Howell Benson and Mary Lucille. Courtesy of Cora Shackelford.

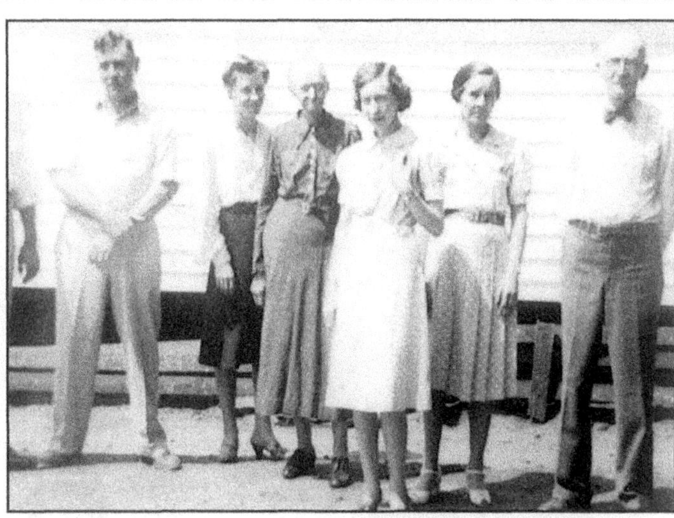

Mary Shackelford Martin, Lula Ross Shackelford, Maude Shackelford Sappington and Opal Shackelford Carter, man on left unknown. Courtesy of Ophelia Shackelford.

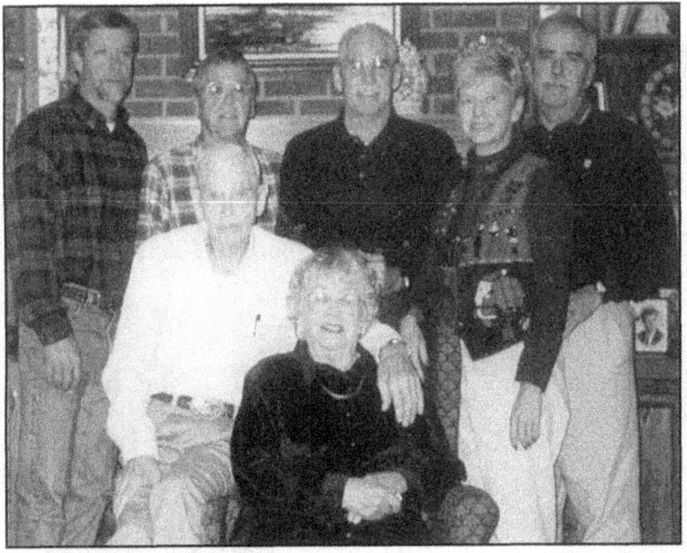

Alton, Wendell, Norman, Alice, Mitchell Jr., C.M. and Hattie Turner. Courtesy of the Clark Mitchell Turner Sr. Family.

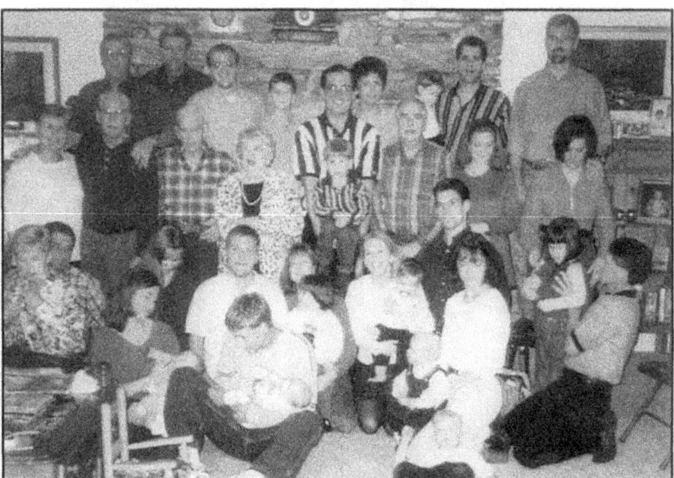

Wendell, Alton, Nikki, Powell, Buck, Etta, Mitchell, Clark, Norm, Yvonne, Norman, C.M., Hattie, Sean, Mitchell Jr., Janice, Lori Anne, Alice, Rick, Heather, Renee, Katie, Shannon, Turner, Bert, Leigh, Natalie, Cole, Trent, Camryn, Alex, Brittany, Matt and Curtis. Not pictured: Shane, Shannon, Abi, Holly Turner, Carter Mullinax, Reagan and Ty Turner. Courtesy of the Clark Mitchell Turner Sr. Family.

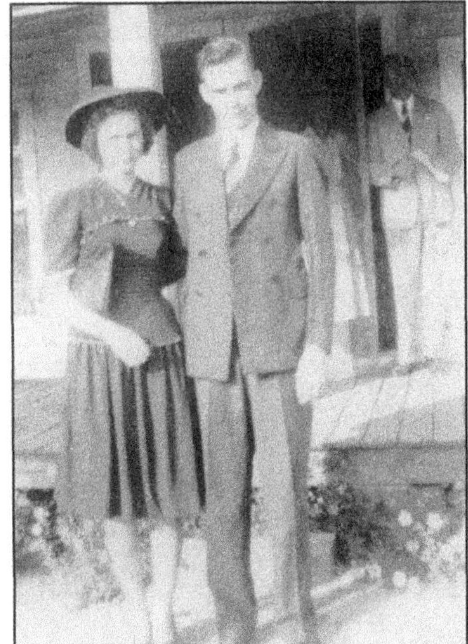

Alton and Virginia Brooks. Courtesy of Virginia Brooks.

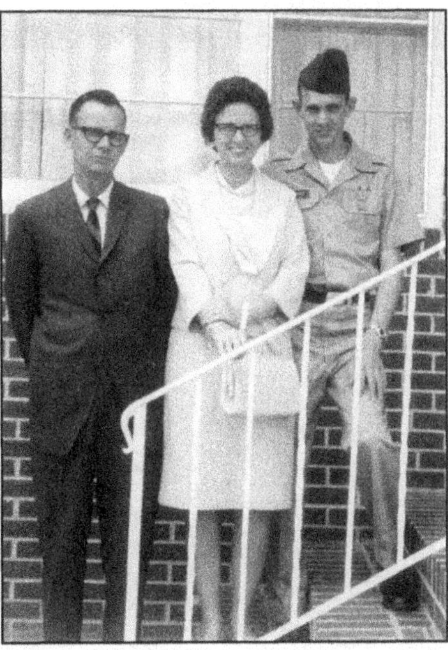

Alton, Virginia and Dennis, 1968. Courtesy of Virginia Brooks.

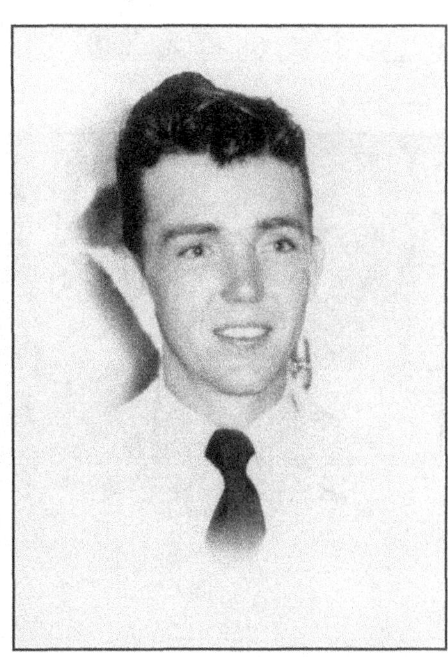

Pvt. Harvey Williard Vaughn. Courtesy of Patsy Vaughn.

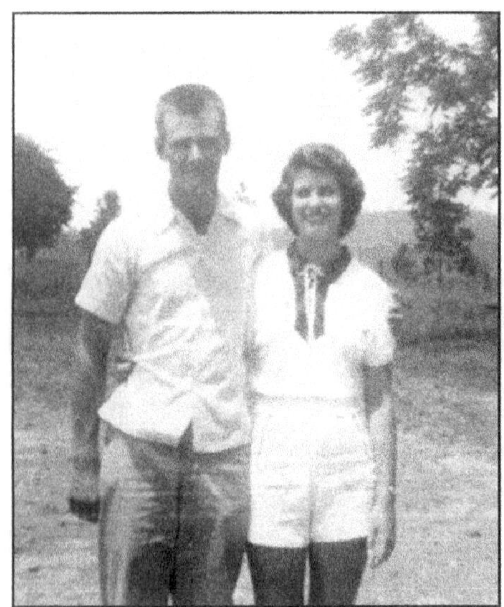

Twins, Donald and Dorothy Bishop, 1953. Courtesy of Sylvia Wright.

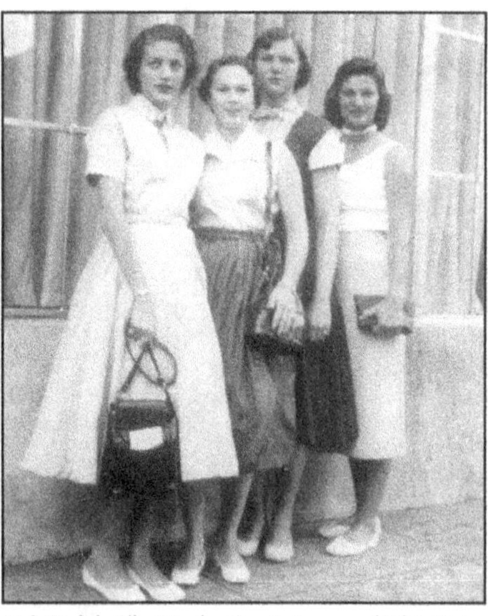

Dale English, Ellen Manley, Connie Rogers and Sylvia Bishop during their senior trip in 1955. Courtesy of Sylvia Wright.

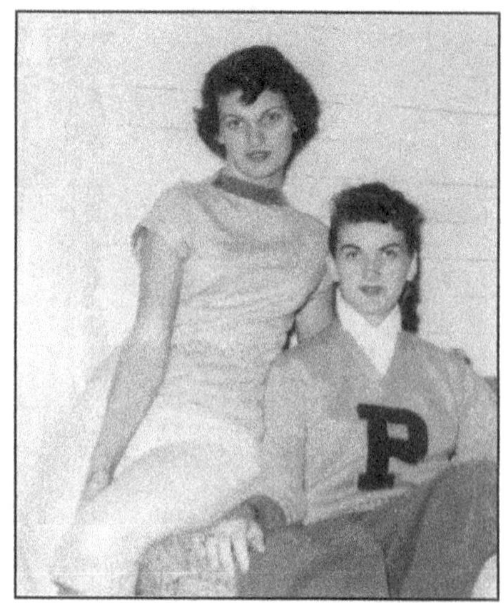

Sylvia and Jan Bishop, Pike County cheerleader, 1957-58. Courtesy of Sylvia Wright.

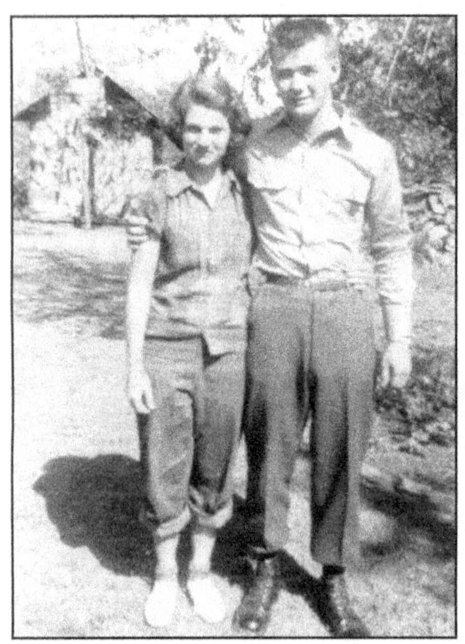

Sylvia and Donald Bishop in the early 1950's. Courtesy of Sylvia Wright.

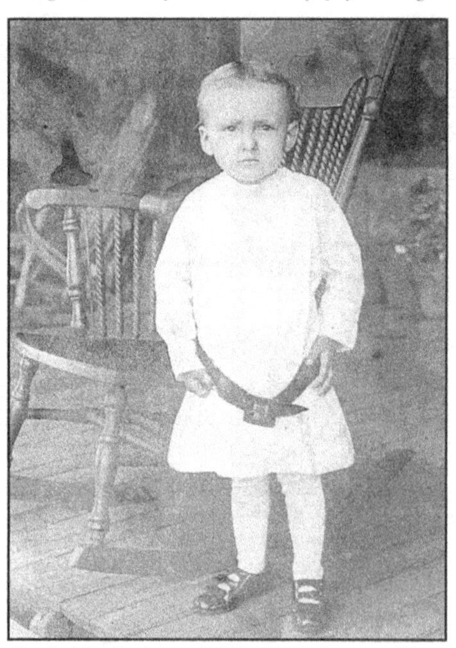

Hartford Lee Bankston. (1912-1915). Courtesy of Grace Ward.

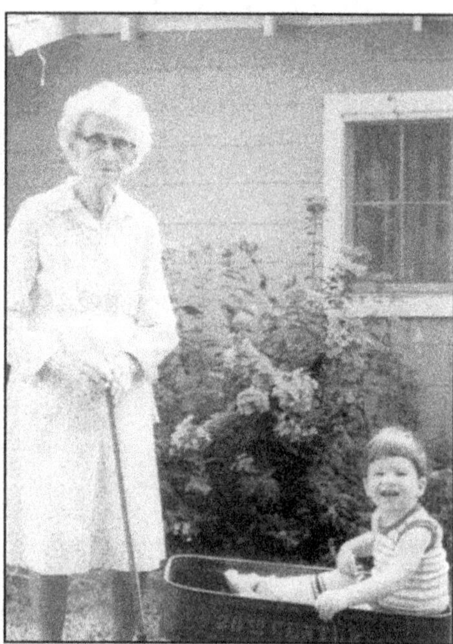

Essie Bankston, 90, and Lee Ward. Courtesy of Grace Ward.

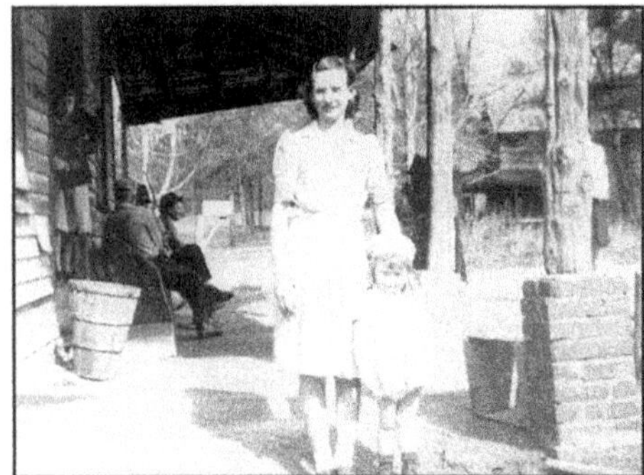

The background of this photo shows the Odd Fellows Hall at Lifsey springs. Courtesy of Grace Ward.

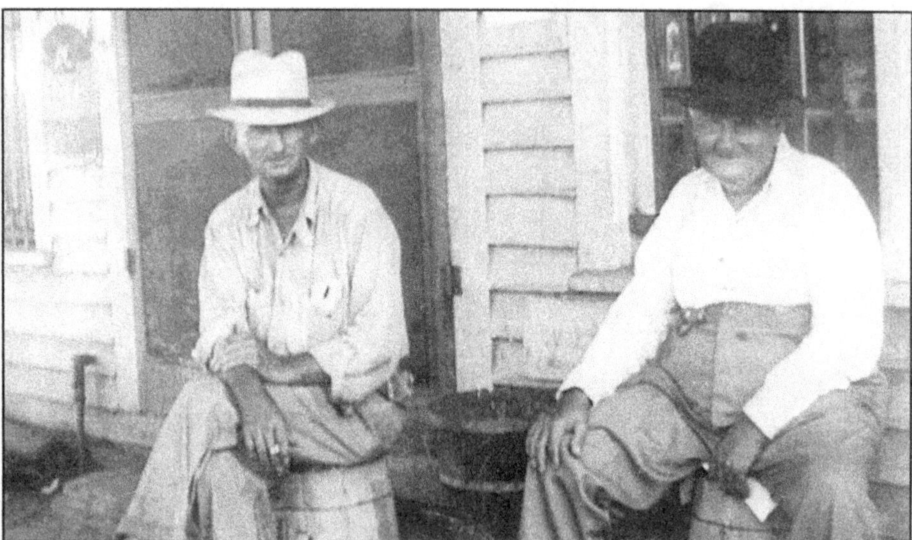

Ed Bankston and Chester Chapman, circa 1930's. Courtesy of Grace Ward.

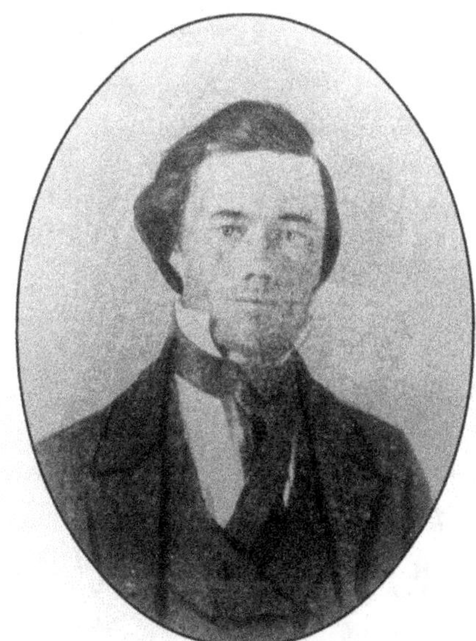

Rev. Jones Bush (1827-1913), he was a Congregational Methodist Preacher and lived near Weaver, Pike County. Courtesy of William Ridley.

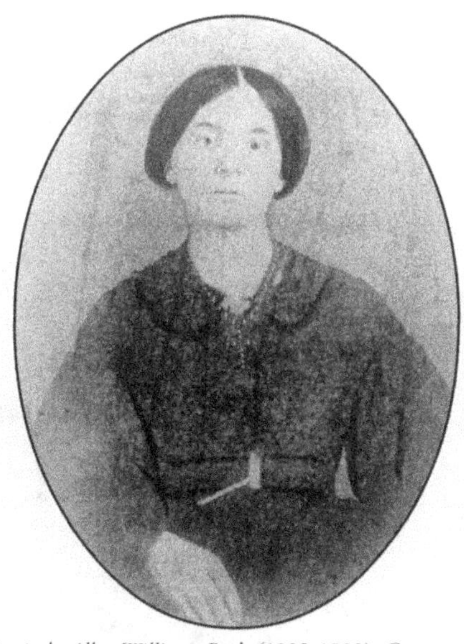

Lucinda Allen Williams Bush (1833-1903). Courtesy of William Ridley.

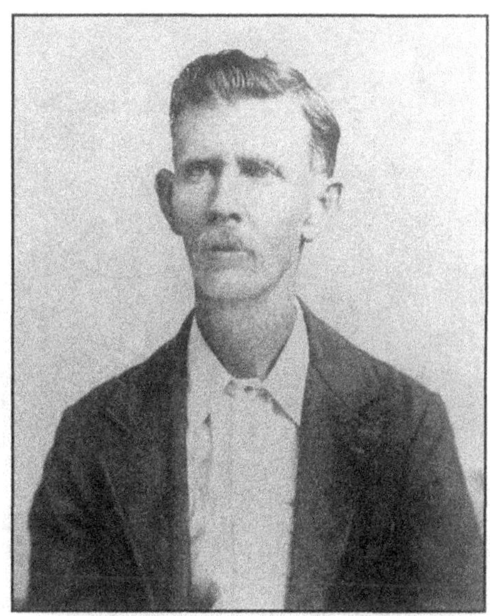

George W. Ridley (1833-1904), he was a farmer, Civil War veteran, preacher, general store owner and postmaster at Weaver. Courtesy of William Ridley.

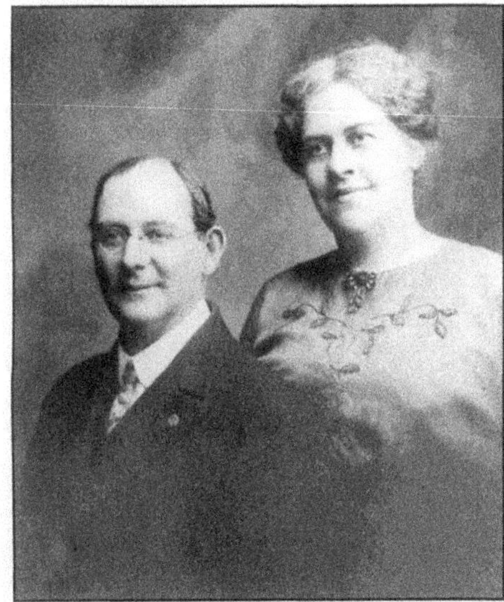

George Benjamin Ridley (1868-1934) and Buena Vista Brook Ridley (1876-1951). Courtesy of William Ridley.

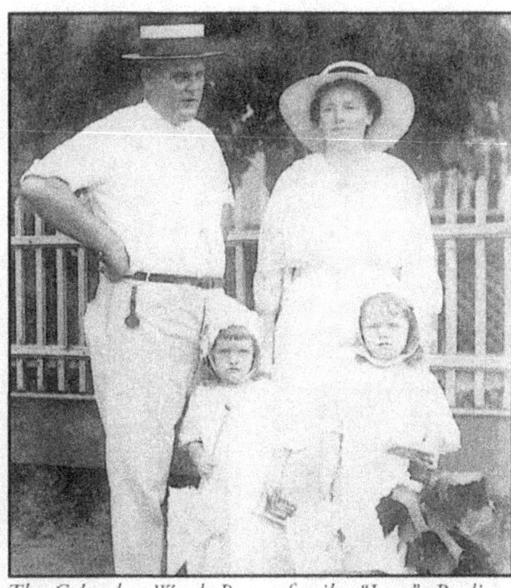

The Columbus Worth Pettett family: "Lum", Pauline, Ophelia and Louise. Columbus Worth was Republican Party chairman, teacher, Devout Baptist and Mason. Courtesy of William Ridley.

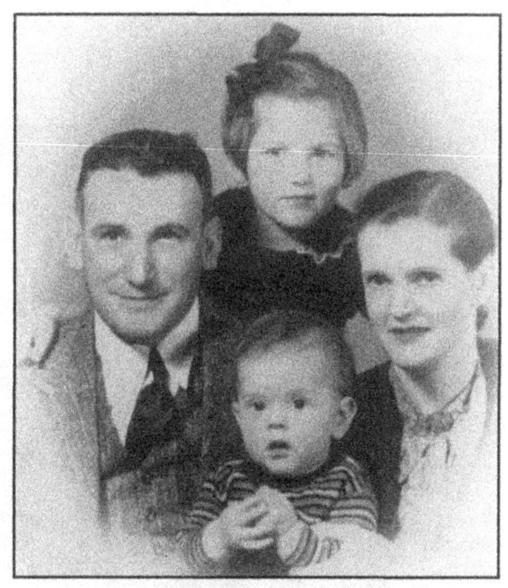

The William Edward Ridley, Sr. family of Williamson in 1941: Ed, Pauline, Louise and Billy. Courtesy of William Ridley.

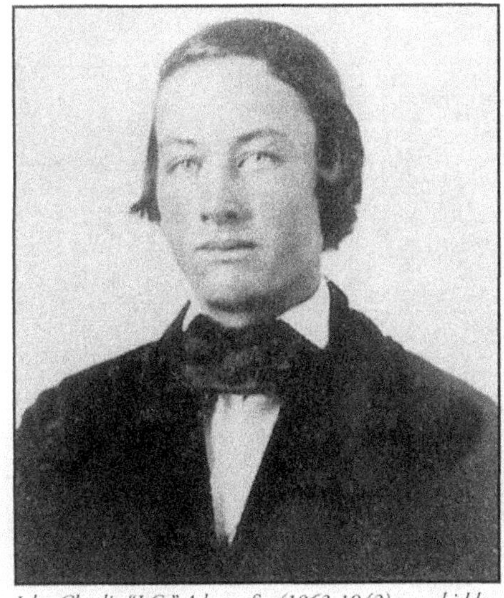

John Charlie "J.C." Adams, Sr. (1863-1943), was hidden in a fireplace when Sherman came through. Courtesy of William Ridley.

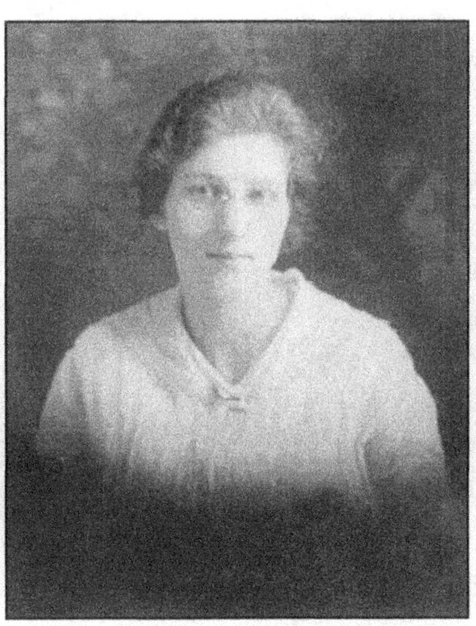

Essie Shivers Callahan. Courtesy of Ophelia Shackelford.

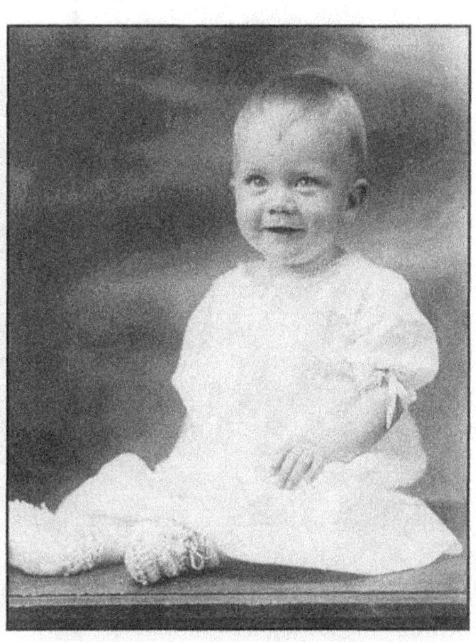

Marvel Artis Elliott. Courtesy of Jane Gaulding.

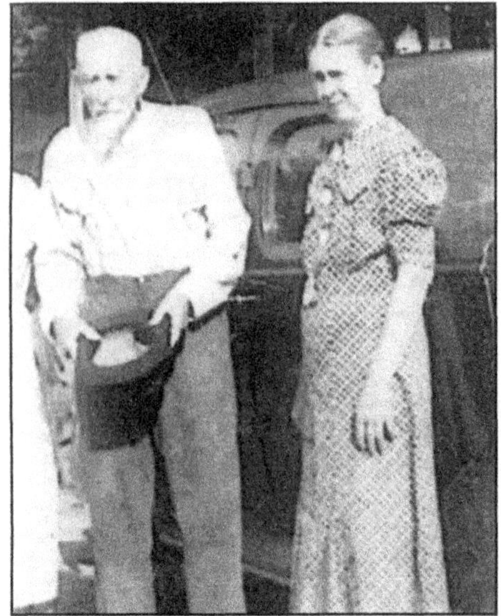

Thomas M. Cauthen born 1851 in Pike Co., GA and daughter Della Cauthen Jones, born 1876 in Pike Co. Della married Arlin E. Jones, also born in Pike Co. in 1871. Thomas was the son of William Cauthen and grandson of Thomas H. and Rebecca Williamson Jones. Thomas M. was married to Arminda J. "Minty" Weathers in 1873 in Pike Co. Courtesy of Trevia Hood.

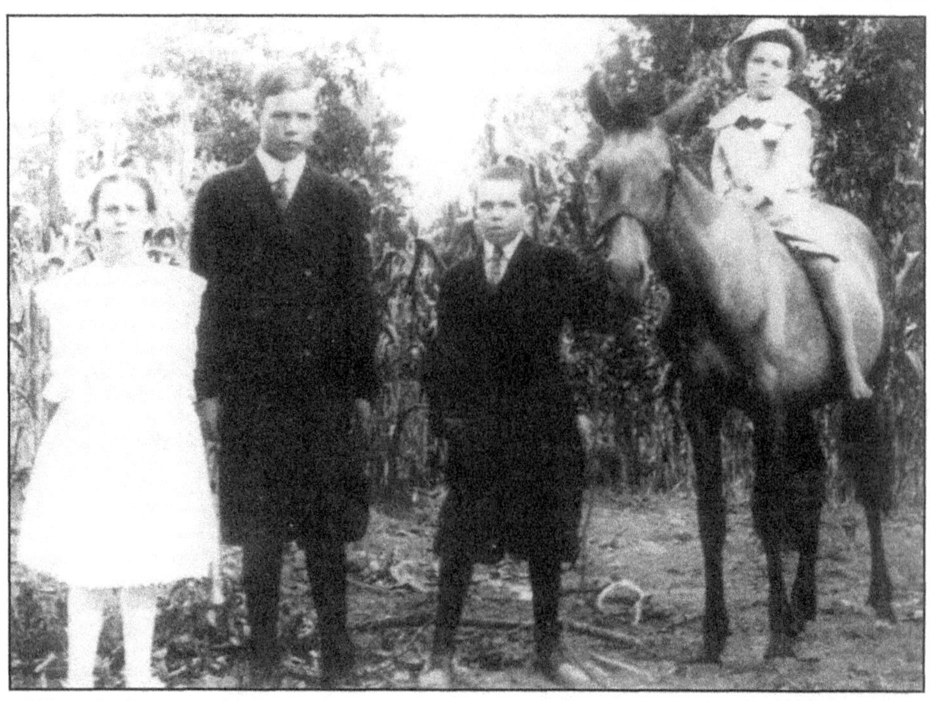

Children of Arlin Jones and Della Cauthen Jones: Ethel Jones Godsey, Walter Raymon Jones, Ed Jones and Ora Jones. Courtesy of Trevia Hood.

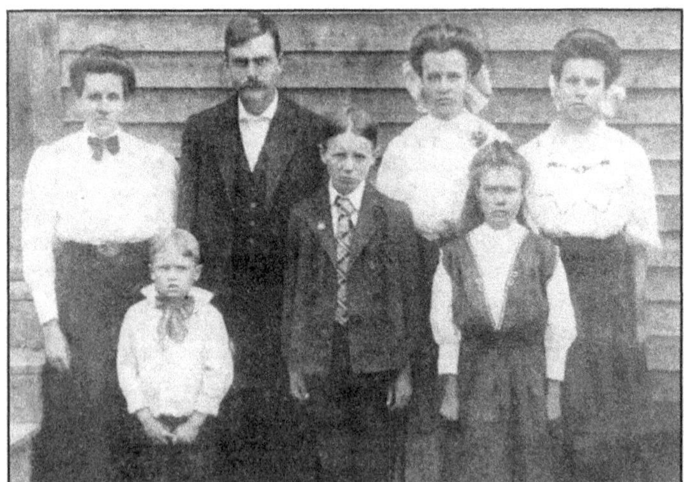

1913 family photo. Back row: Sarah Gibson, Sidney Isiah Gibson, Ester Gibson Kersey and Ethel Gibson Bankston. Front row: Hezikihah Gibson, Grady Gibson and Eunice Gibson Dunn. Courtesy of Hazel Osbolt and Melissa Carraway.

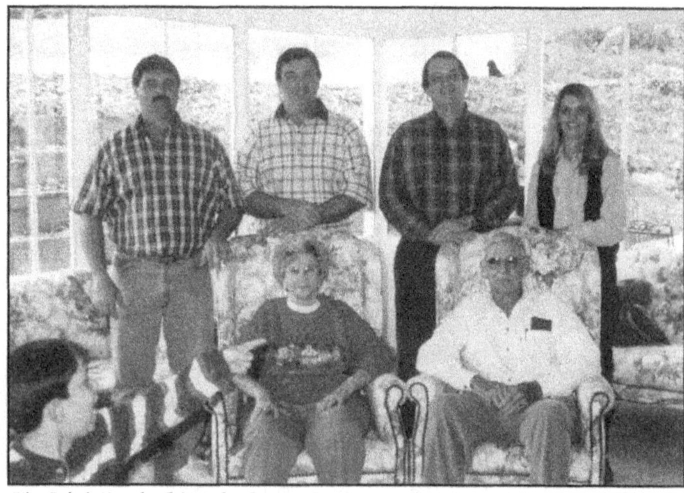

The Osbolt Family of the Lifsey Springs Community. Standing: Johnny, Terry, Charles and Melissa. Seated Hazel Bankston Osbolt and John A. Osbolt. Courtesy of Hazel Osbolt and Melissa Carraway.

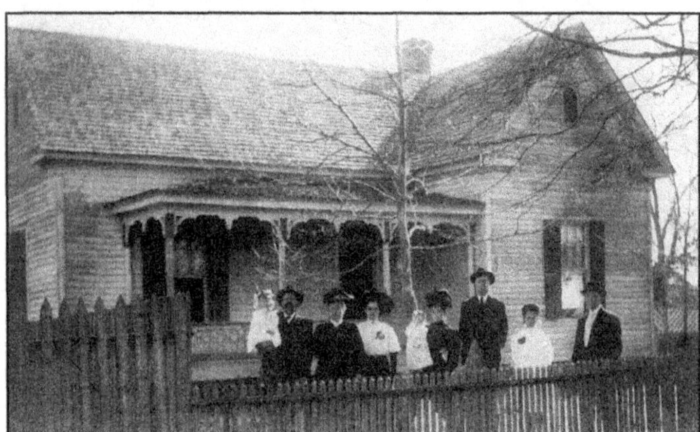

Kendrick homeplace at 2750 Zebulon Rd. Mr. and Mrs. William Alexander Kendrick, Geraldine Cauthen, Minnie Kendrick Cauthen, Cora Kendrick Gresham, Thelma Gresham, John Lemuel Gresham, Eva Kendrick Peek and Robert Kendrick. The home is now owned by Mr. Gene R. Sarsfield. The house was built in 1890 by Mr. Banks. The Kendricks came to Pike County in 1823. Courtesy of Helen Kendrick and Betty Copeland.

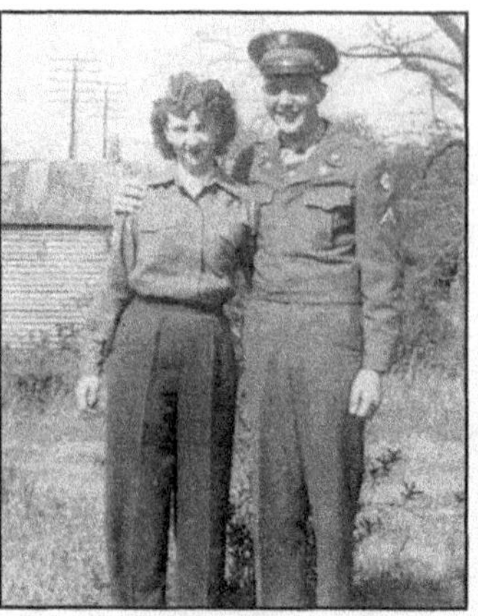

Williamson Jail House, Connell's Store and Pitts home in background, pictured are Montez and Walter (Buddy) Hardy, circa 1945 or 1950. Courtesy of Helen Kendrick and Betty Copeland.

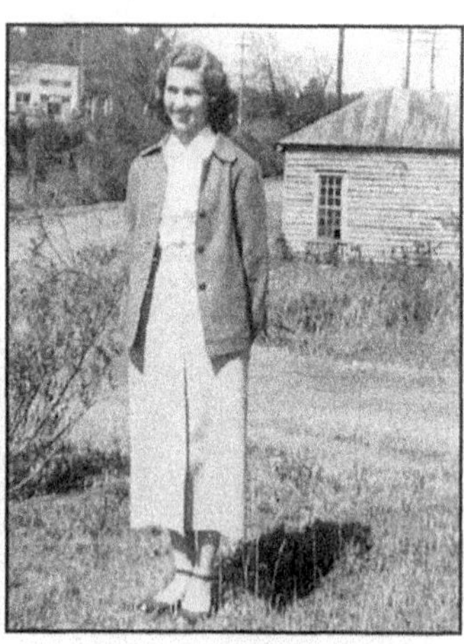

Peggy Taylor Hardy, 1945 or 1950. In the background is Connell's store and the Williamson jail house. Courtesy of Helen Kendrick and Betty Copeland.

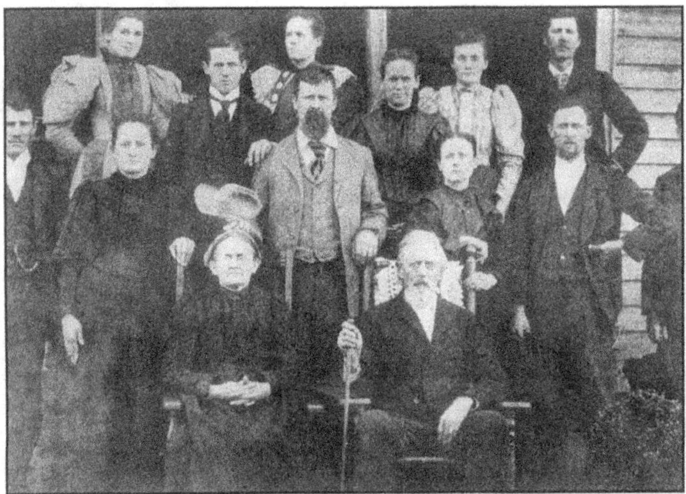

Front row: Anne Hawkins Bevil and James Burton Bevil. Second row: Oscar Bevil, Lizzie Bevil Ballard, Tom Bevil, Mary Frances Bevil Jones, Johnny Bevil and Frank Bevil. Third row: Pellie Bevil Weathers, Bloomer Bevil, Anna Bevil Harris, Carrie Bevil Ballard, Martha Bevil Reeves, Charlie Bevil and Billie Bevil (not pictured). Courtesy of Frances Aaron.

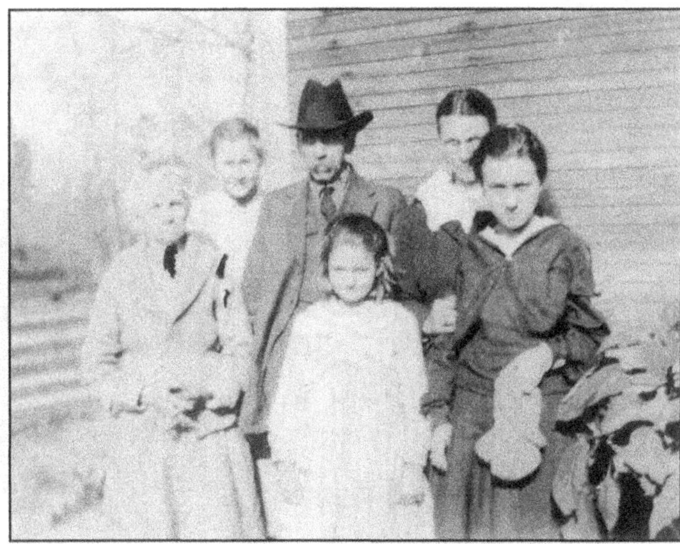

Martha Bell Jones Bunkley, Annie Jones, John Millard Filmore Jones, Nancy Jones Stewart, Odell Jones and Nellie Key, circa 1917. Courtesy of Frances Aaron.

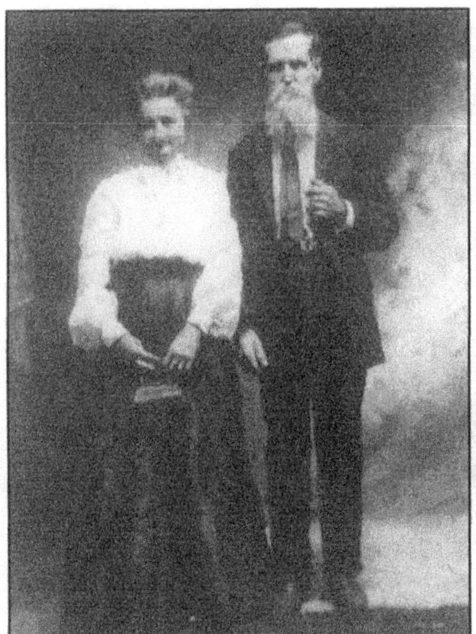

Robert Jackson Mangham and Eliza R. Elliot around 1889. Courtesy of Ray and Earline Mangham.

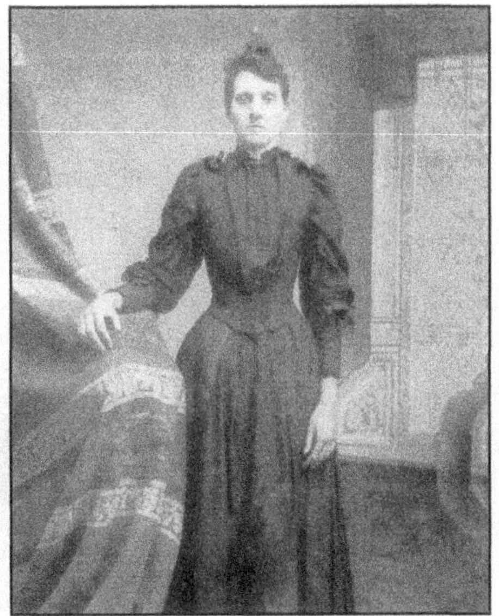

Abbigail (Abbie) Littlejohn, born February 25, 1869 and died December 11, 1923, she was buried in the Mangham Family Cemetary in Lifsey Springs. Courtesy of Ray and Earline Mangham.

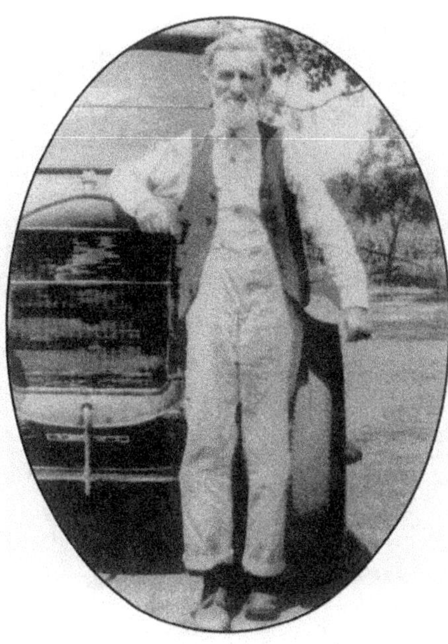

R.J. Mangham, circa 1921. Courtesy of Ray and Earline Mangham.

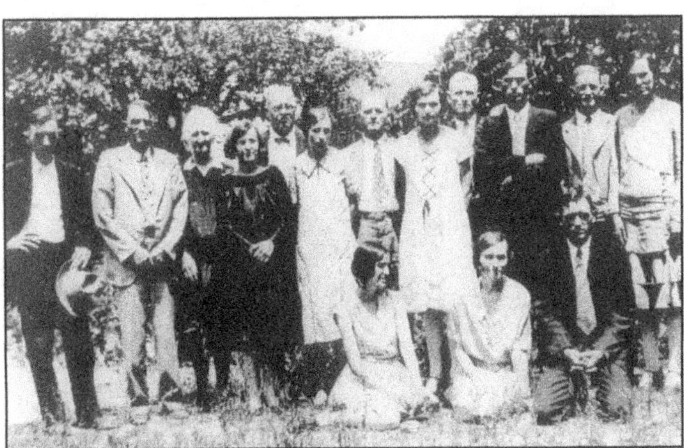

Some of the 23 children of R.J. Mangham, 1929. Courtesy of Ray and Earline Mangham.

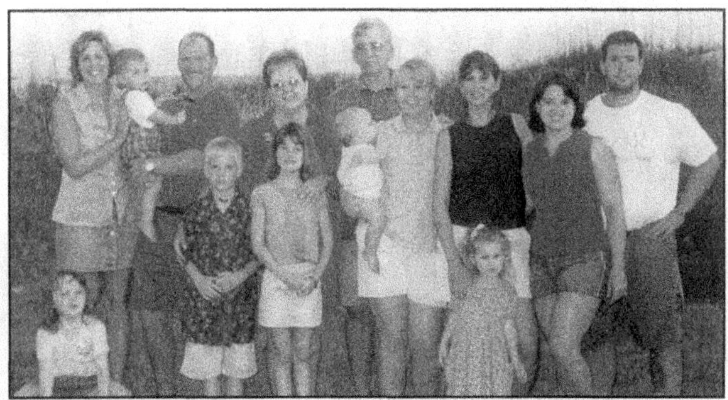

The Paul and Ruthie (Norris) Faulds family: Kaitlyn Faulds, Wanda Faulds, Richard Faulds, Evan Scott, Justin Faulds, Ruthie Faulds, Megan Popwell, Paul Faulds, Carey Faulds, Louis Silverstein, Debra Faulds Scott, Kirsten Scott, Amy Faulds Sandefur and Mark Sandefur. Not pictured Lee Scott. Courtesy of Ruthie Faulds.

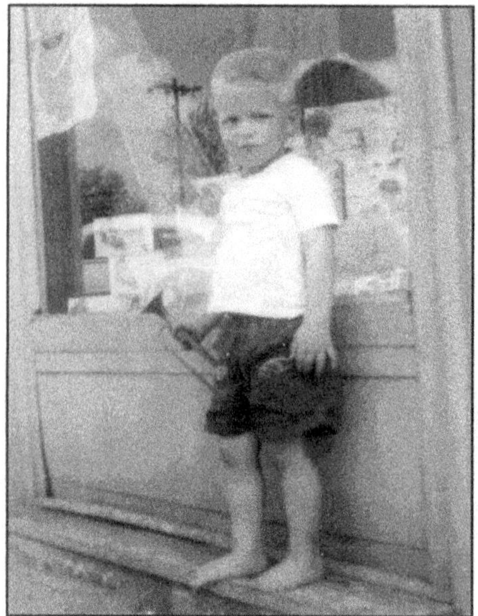

Farris Rodgers outside the original City Pharmacy, circa 1955 or 1956. Courtesy of W.S. Rodgers.

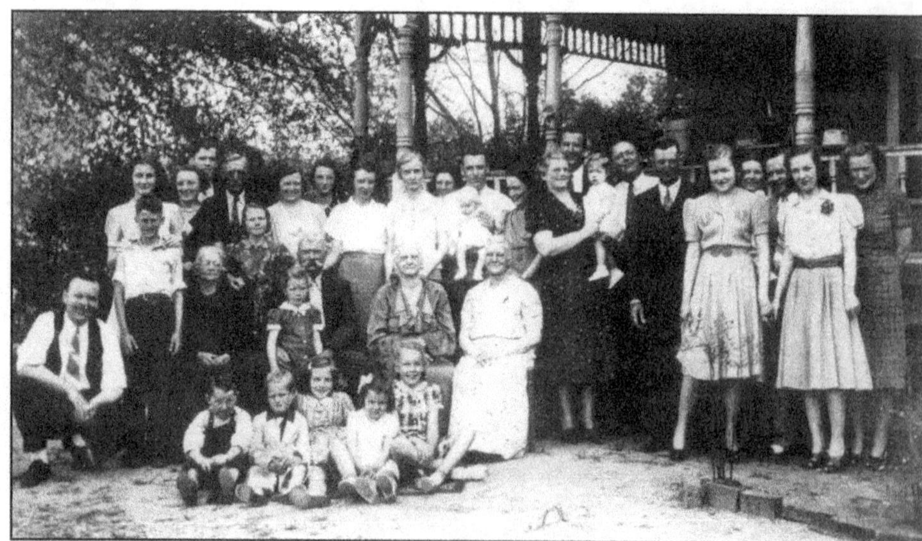

The Thomas Jefferson and Willie Anna Simerly Cochran family reunion taken at home in Concord circa 1938. Seated in chairs left to right are Mrs. Emma Crawford, Jeff and Willie Cochran and Mrs. Dora Strickland. The property is now owned by Pat and Jack Goodman. Pat's grandmother, Gladys C. Caldwell is pictured standing behind her mother, Willie. Courtesy of Ann Yearwood.

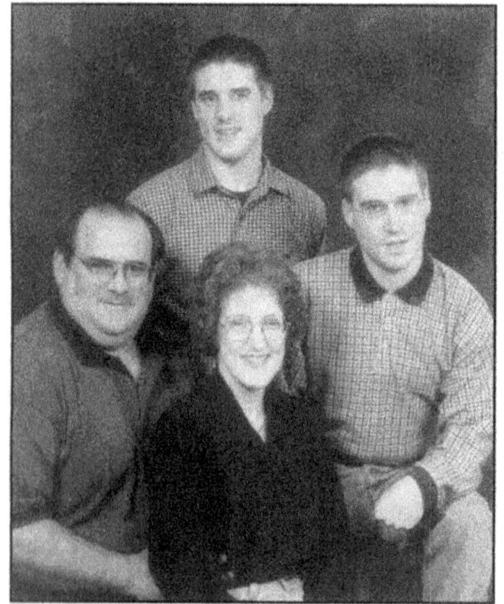

Ann, David, Nathan and Sam Wright. Courtesy of W.S. Rodgers.

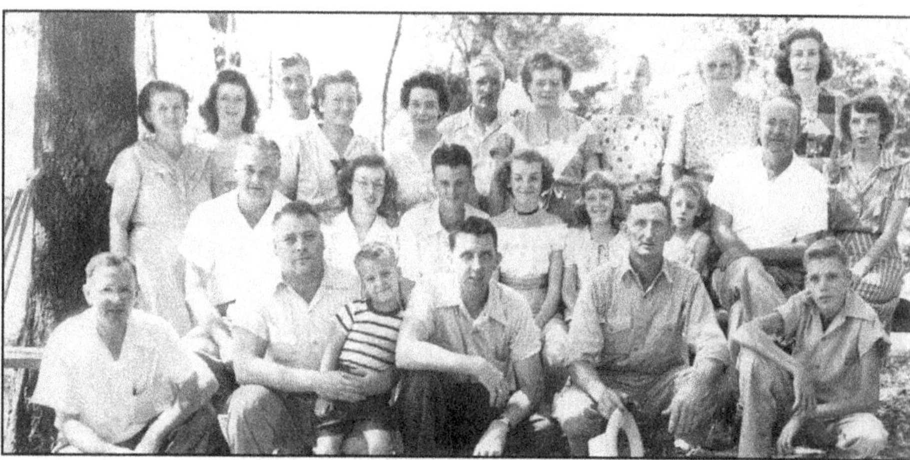

Descendants of the Thomas Jefferson Cochran family taken on the bank of Flint River at the 1949 family reunion. Pictured front row are: Ben Hill Morgan, Claude Cochran, Eddie Cochran, Guy Whiting, Johnny Caldwell and Jimmy Wesley. Second row: Frank Cochran, Jean Griffin, Cochran Caldwell, Ann Whatley-Whiting, Gloria Irvin, Janice Cochran, Roy Irvin and Billie C. Whiting. Third row: Dolly C. Morgan, Marcile Wesley-Crutchfield, Paul Crutchfield, Mae C. Griffin, Louise Cochran, Douglas Wesley, Grace C. Wesley, Gladys C. Caldwell, Nellie C. Irvin and Dorris Caldwell. The property is now owned by Cochran Caldwell. Courtesy of Ann Yearwood.

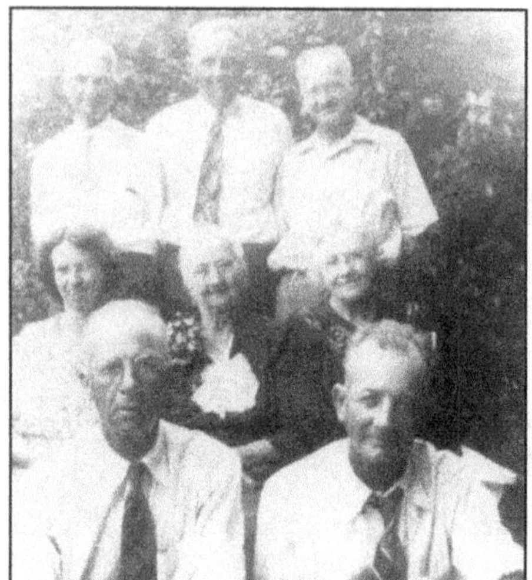

Front row: Clarence Beckham and George Beckham. Second row: Ruby Beckham, Grandma Beckham and Ida B. Cooper. Third row: Claude Beckham, Roger Beckham and Enoch Beckham. Courtesy of Geneva Sanders.

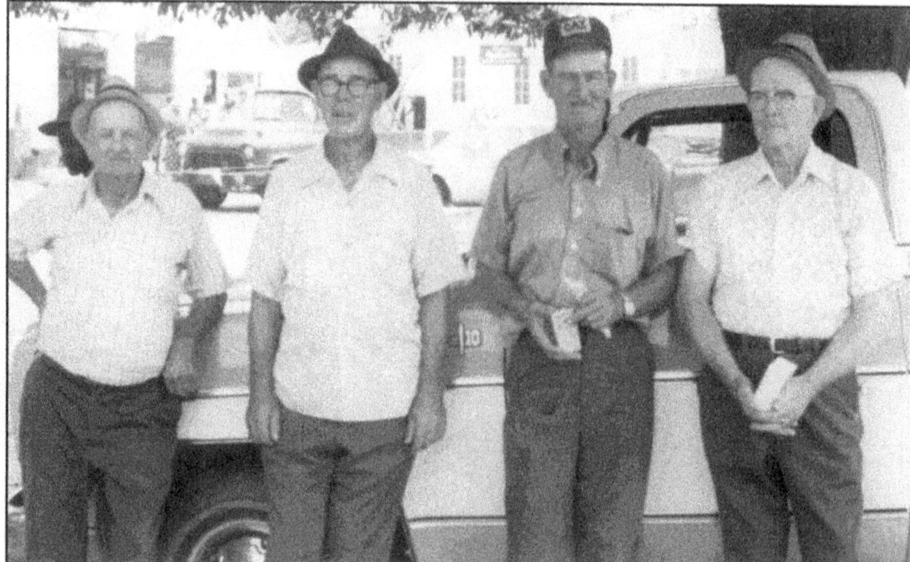

George Beckham, Jim Foster, Jack Lawrence and Lester McCrary. Courtesy of Geneva Sanders.

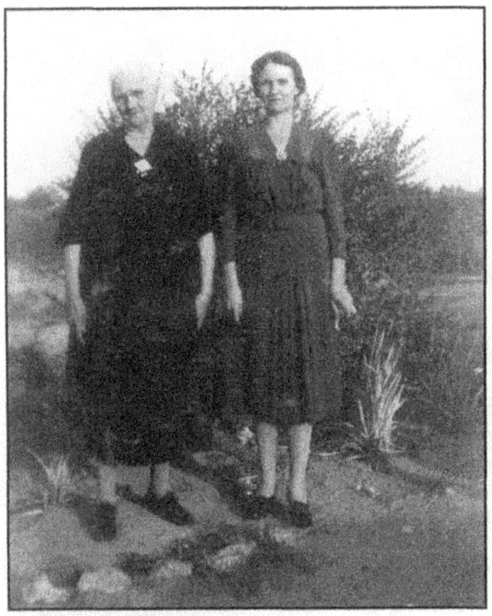

Ella and Ruby Beckham. Courtesy of Geneva Sanders.

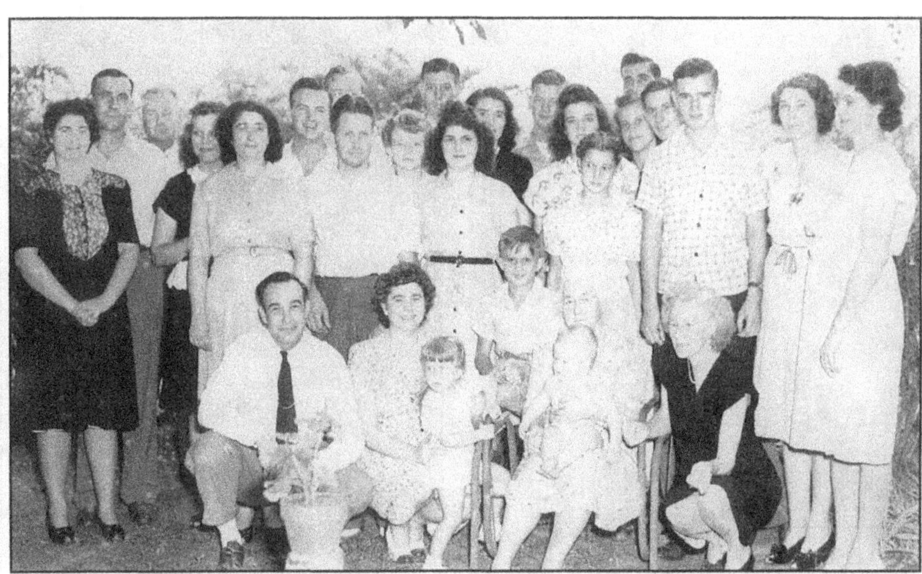

Children and grandchildren of Clifford and Minnie Hancock. Courtesy of Geneva Sanders.

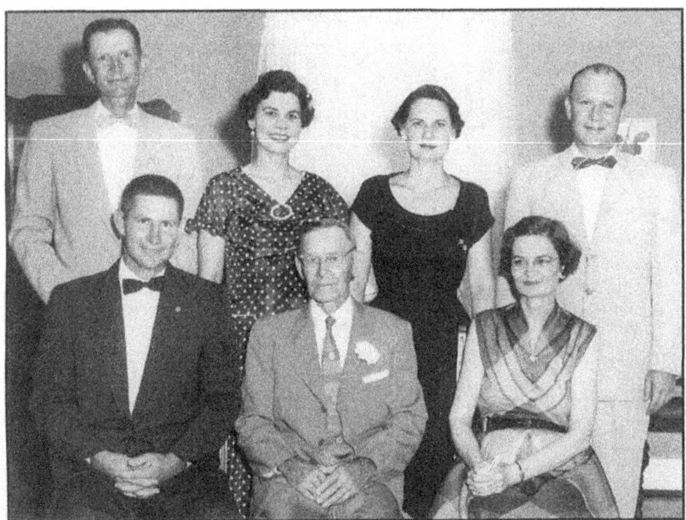

John Thomas Pilkenton family: Walter, John, Elizabeth, Jack, Nelle, Fay and Thomas. Courtesy of Geneva Sanders.

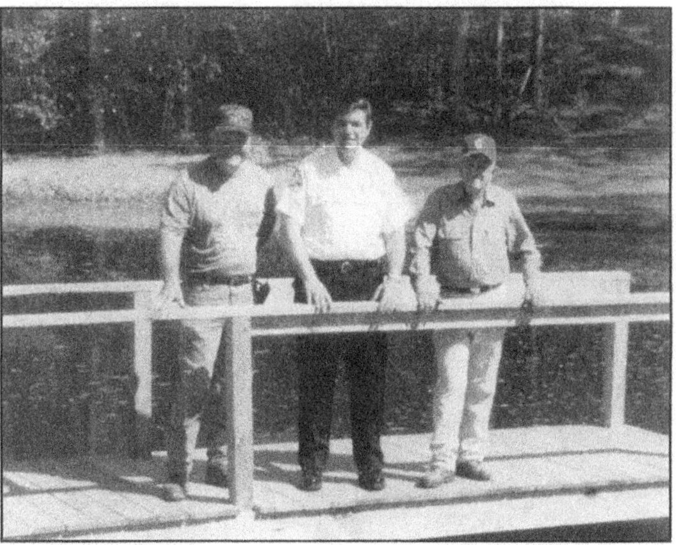

Eddie Brannon, Jimmy Thomas and David Kendrick. Courtesy of Rosalee King.

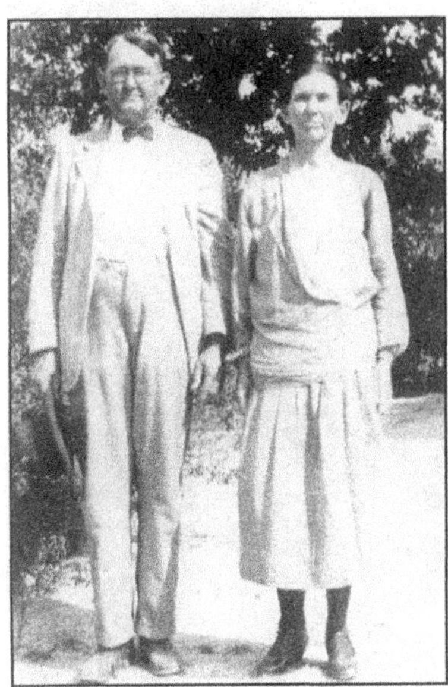

Jim King and Ella Mae King. Courtesy of Rosalee King.

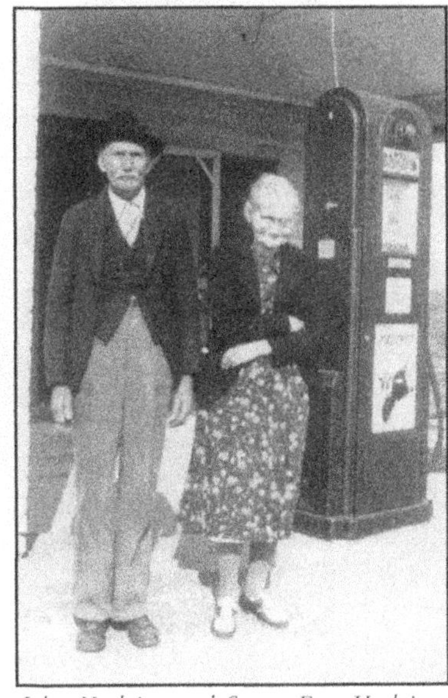

John Hudgins and Susan Etta Hudgins. Courtesy of Mrs. Clyde Gibson.

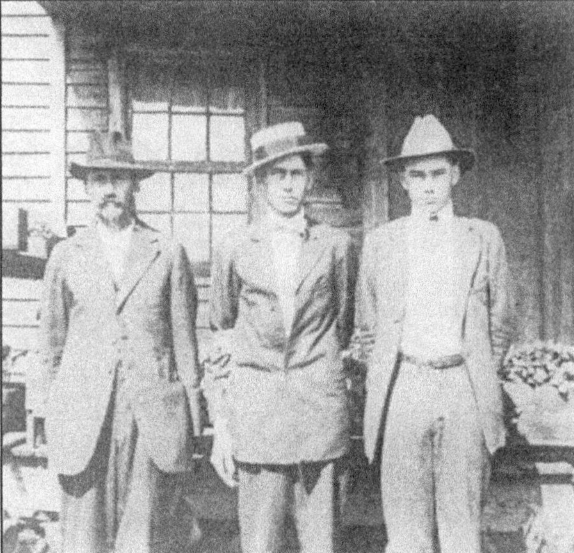

John Ambrose Hudgins, Ambrose Littleron Hudgins and Clyde Hudgins. Courtesy of Mrs. Clyde Gibson.

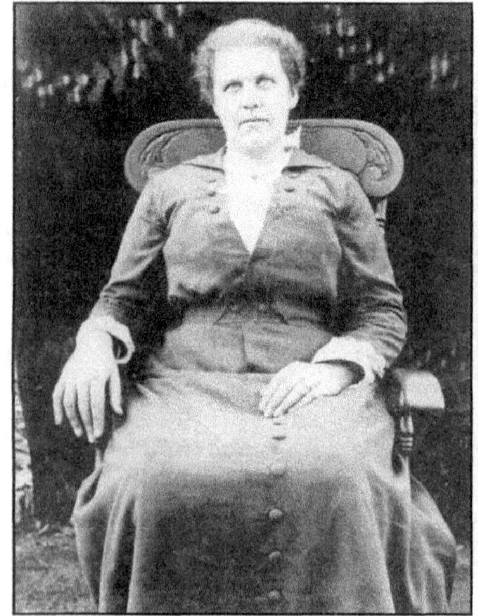

Ivie Howard. Courtesy of Mrs. Clyde Gibson.

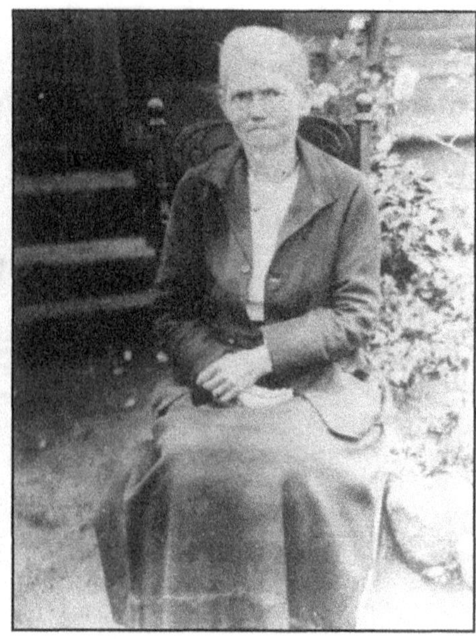

Susan Etta Hudgins. Courtesy of Mrs. Clyde Gibson.

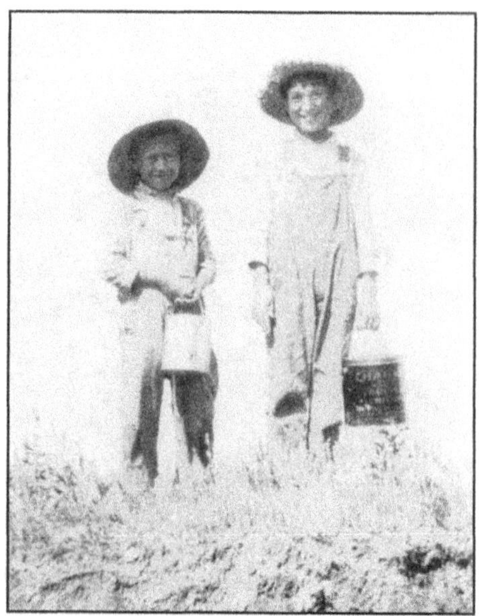

Horace Howard and Marvin Alexander, berry picking. Courtesy of Mrs. Clyde Gibson.

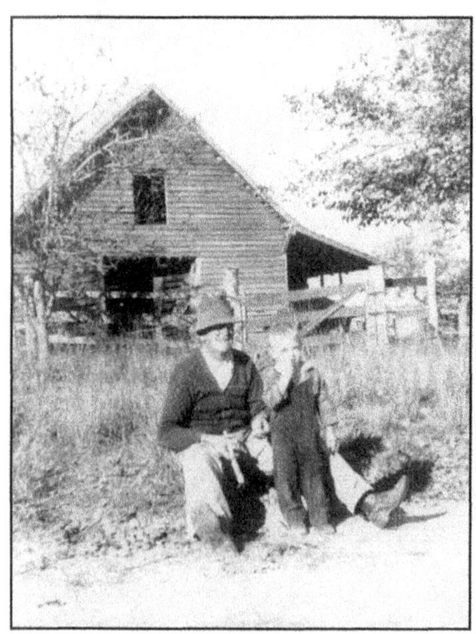

Will Howard and Terry Howard. Courtesy of Mrs. Clyde Gibson.

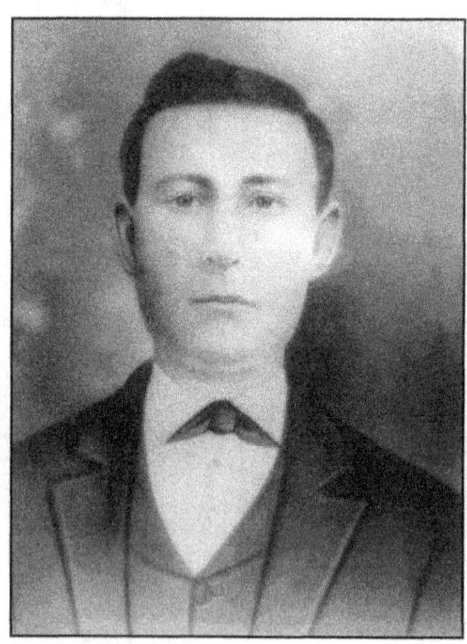

Lewis Stribling (1850-1930). Courtesy of Ralph Steele.

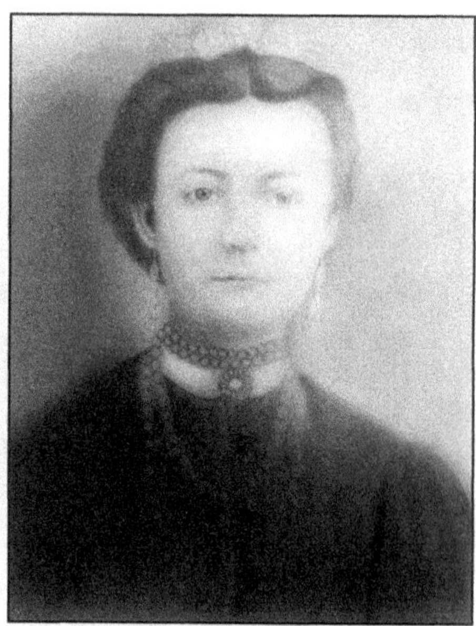

Sissie Riggins Stribling (1855-1929). Courtesy of Ralph Steele.

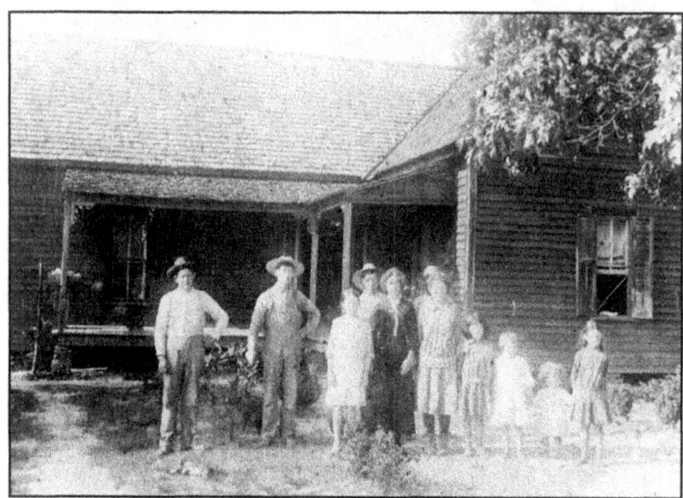

The homeplace of H.H. and Susan Reeves on Hwy. 109. Courtesy of Ralph Steele.

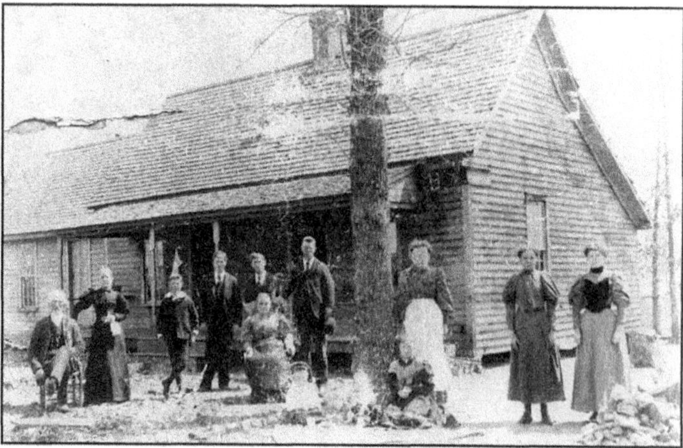

The home of Ruben and Emma Elliott on Hwy. 109 east of Molena, GA. Pictured: H.H. Reeves, Susan Reeves, George Andrew Reeves, Emma Reeves Elliott and Ruben Elliott, the others are unknown. Courtesy of Ralph Steele.

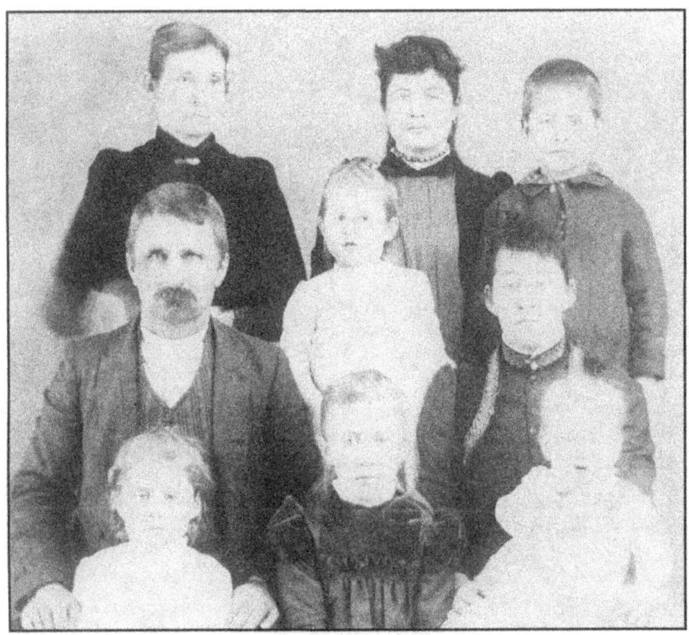

Back row: Nancy Barker Jordan, Rossie Pope Pilkenton and Fonza Lee Pilkenton. Center row: Robert Monroe Pilkenton, Nannie Alma Pilkenton and Mary Rebecca Jordan Pilkenton. Front row: Perla Mae Pilkenton, Julia Clyde Pilkenton and Henry Grady Pilkenton, circa 1891. Courtesy of Robert F. Jones.

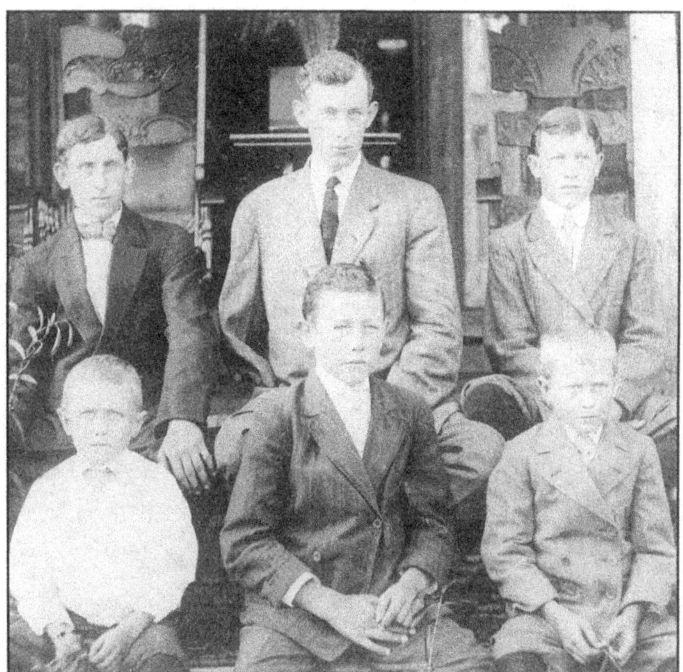

Back row: Robert Cecil Jones, William Luther Jones and Walter Beeks Jones. Front row: Jessie Willis Jones, Benjamin Hill Jones and Maxie Lewis Jones, circa 1910.

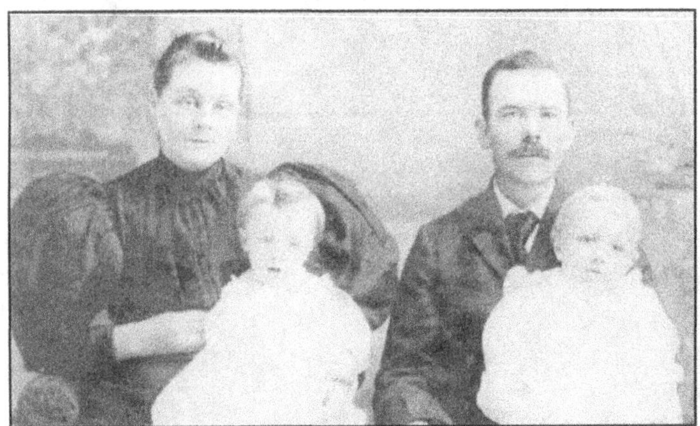

Thomas A., Elizabeth Collier, Oscar and Arthur Lifsey, circa 1895. Courtesy of James Adams.

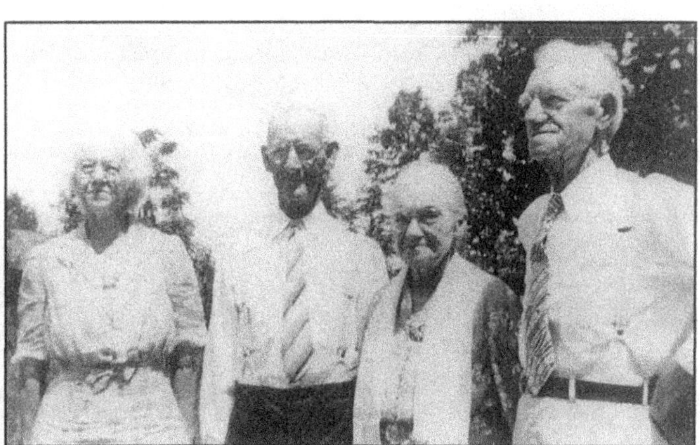

Eula Lifsey Howell, Edwin L. Lifsey, Rilla Lifsey Adams and Ben N. Lifsey, circa 1940's. Courtesy of James Adams.

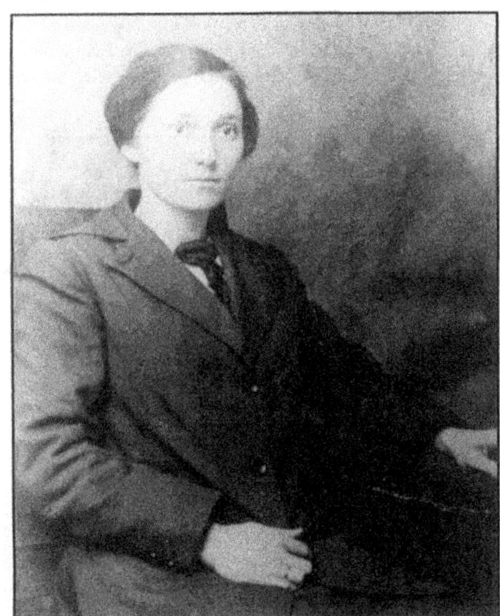

Bessie Mae Hudgins Howard. Courtesy of Mrs. Clyde Gibson.

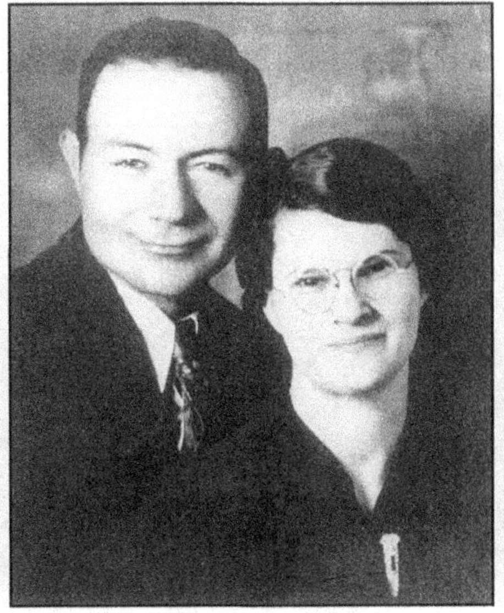

James Samuel and Bertha Brown Adams, circa 1940. Courtesy of James Adams.

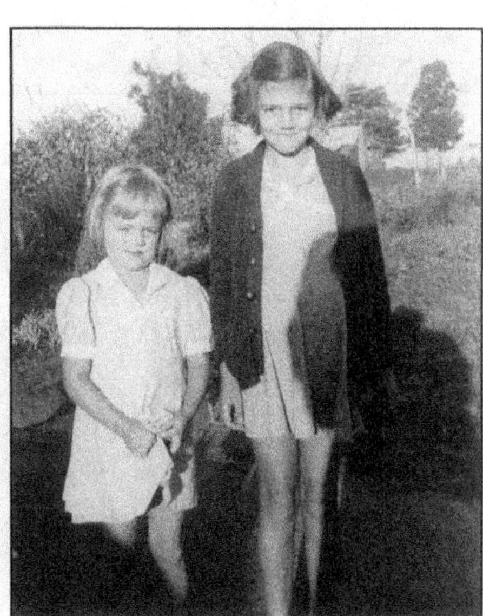

Cornelia Jane and Virginia Cynthia Smith. Courtesy of Virginia and Charles Oglesby.

Country home of E.H. Baker, Zebulon, GA Nov. 27, 1908. Florrie Baker, E.H. Baker, John H. Baker, Mary Baker and Mrs. E.H. Baker. Courtesy of Betty Copeland.

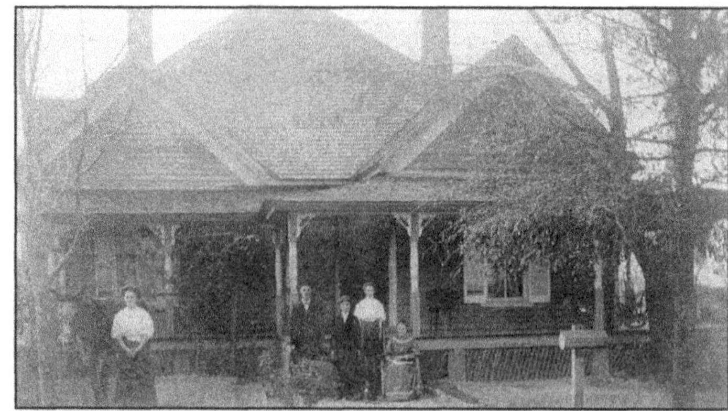

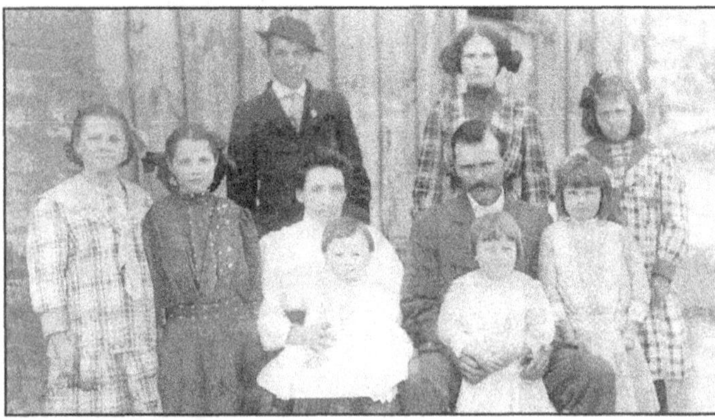

Thomas Marion Hawkins family, Front row (two smallest children): Clarence and Dora Hawkins Collins. Second row: Pearl Hawkins Caldwell, Lucile Hawkins Caldwell, Martha Ann Corley Hawkins, Florrie Lee Hawkins Burt, Herman Hawkins, Alma Hawkins Whatley, Eleanor Hawkins Jones, and youngest child J.T. not born. Courtesy of Kenneth Caldwell.

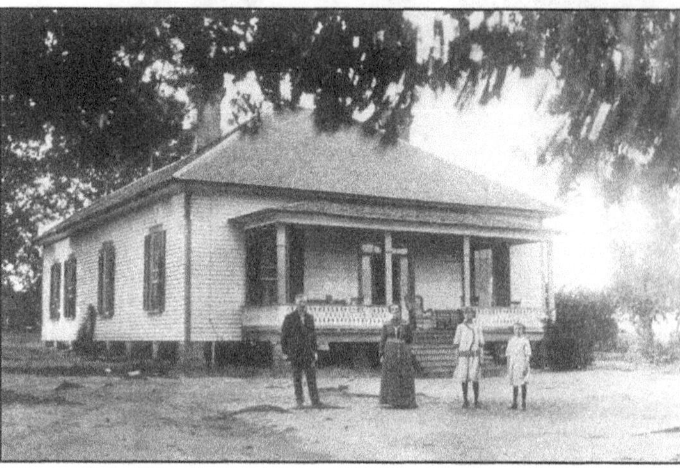

Left to right: William Edward Caldwell, Sarah Jane Grubbs Caldwell, Jewel Caldwell McKinley and Olene Caldwell Bogle. Courtesy of Kenneth Caldwell.

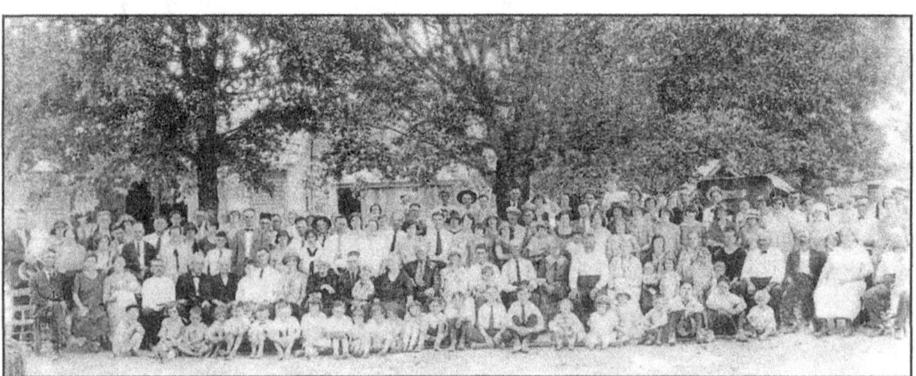

Bevil family reunion in Pike County, circa 1926. Courtesy of Frances Aaron.

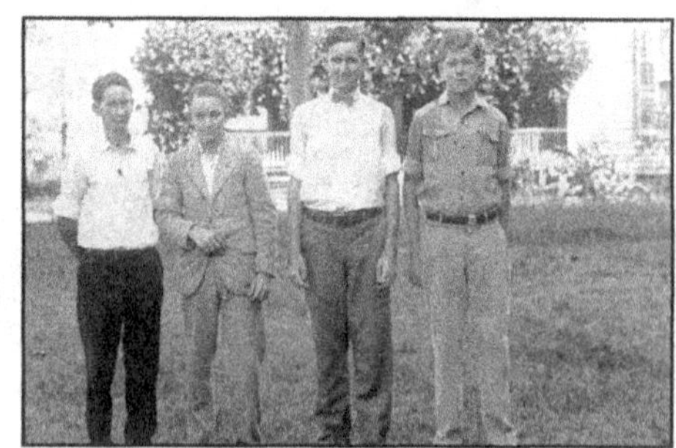

John H. Milner, Jr., Frank L. Adams, Jr., Hugh Morgan Milner and Harttez Barron, judges in chicken and cattle contest, Zebulon High School 1929-30. Courtesy of Rachel McClelland.

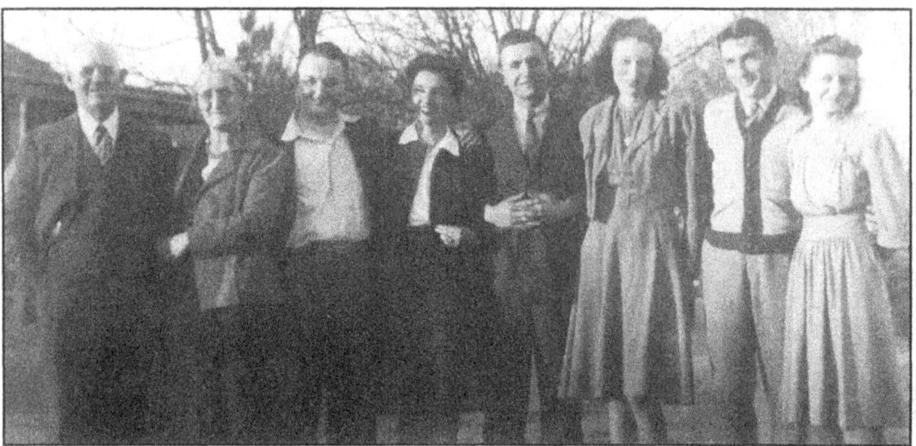

The Frank Lester Adams family: Frank L. Adams, Sr., Janie Pound Adams, Frank L. Adams, Jr., Esther Fernandez Adams, Charles Lee Adams, Hazel Perkins Adams, Linton Frankin Lee and Mary Lou Adams Lee. Courtesy of Andrea Noel.

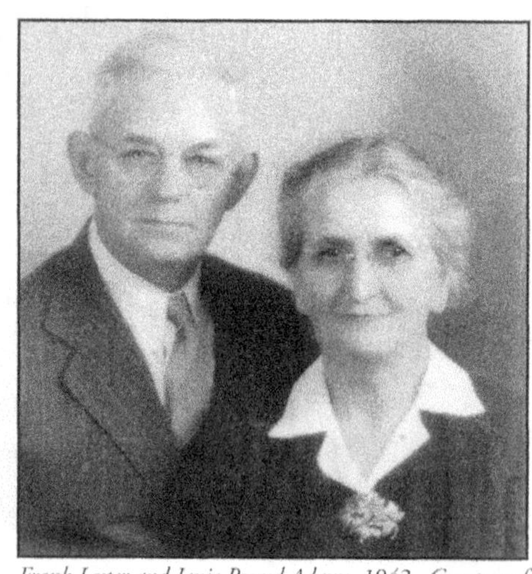

Frank Lester and Janie Pound Adams, 1942. Courtesy of Andrea Noel.

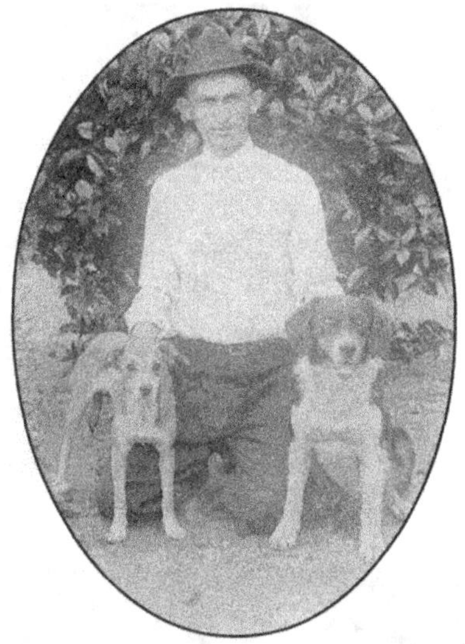

Ed Bankston, owner of Bankston Lumber Co. and Bankston Grocery Store. Courtesy of Hazel Osbolt and Melissa Carraway.

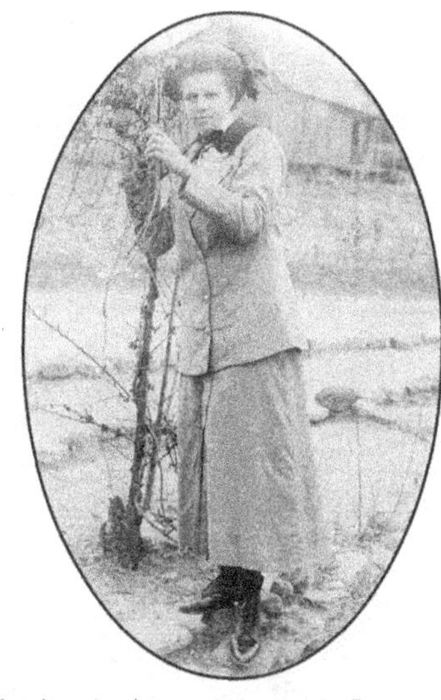

Ethel Gibson Bankston, 1913, age 17. Courtesy of Hazel Osbolt and Melissa Carraway.

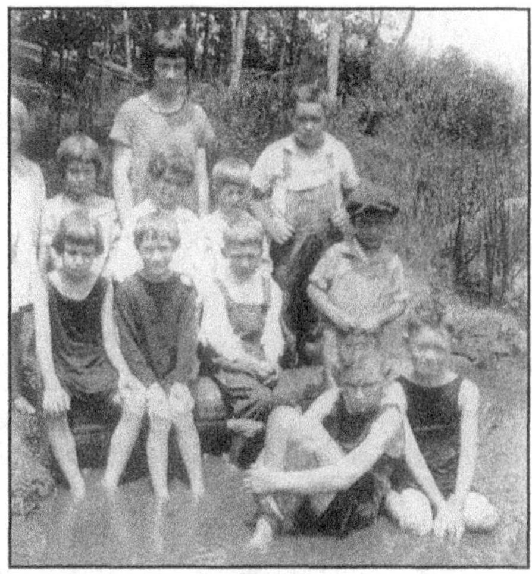

Robert F. Jones Sr. is seated in the center wearing overalls and his first cousin Rebecca Girard McCard is standing in rear and Evelyn Jones is on the far left, others are unknown, circa 1923. Courtesy of Robert F. Jones.

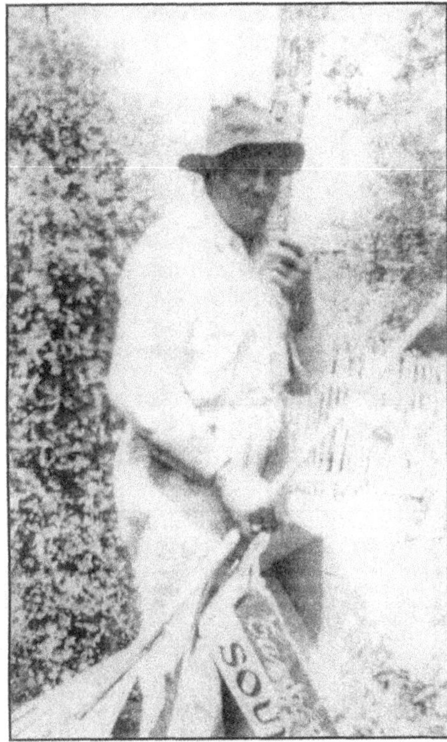

Ruth Driver. Courtesy of Fred Allen and Linda Dallas.

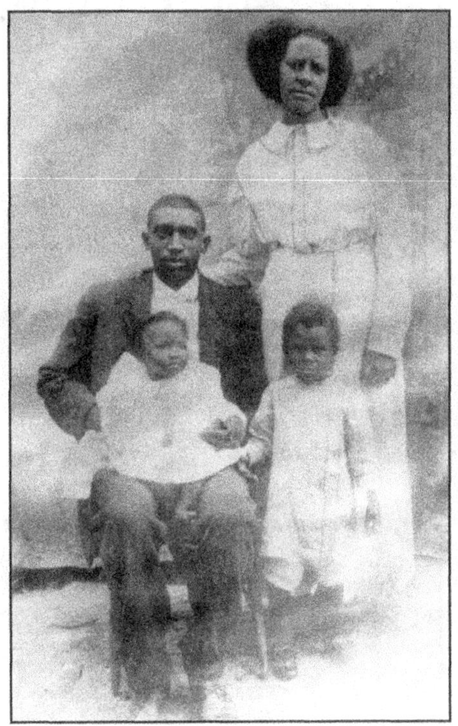

Oscar and Rosa Mae Reid with their children Olan Reid and Henry Reid. Courtesy of Fred Allen and Linda Dallas.

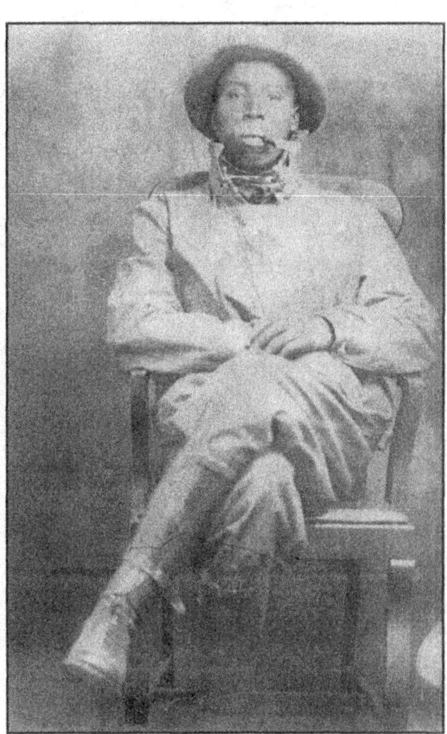

Cleveland "Law" Allen (1907-1963). Courtesy of Fred Allen and Linda Dallas.

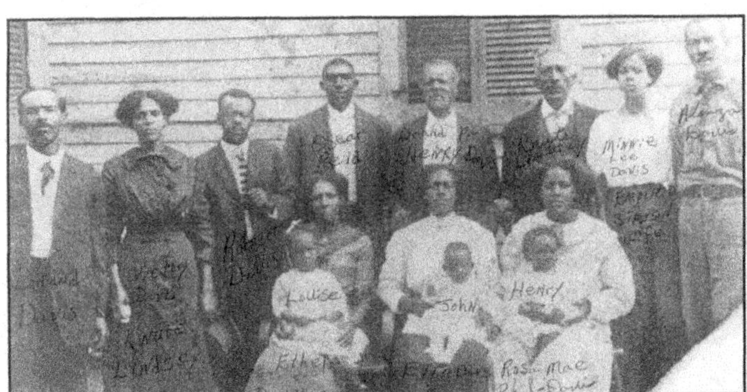

Henry Davis' family, in front of the Old Antioch Church, 1913. Henry Davis was the founder of the church. Standing: Doland Davis, Victory Davis, Robert Davis, Oscar Reid, Henry Davis, Knute Lindsey, Minnie Lee Davis, Alonza Davis. Seated: Ethel Davis holding Louise, Etta Davis holding John, Rosa Mae Reid-Davis holding Henry. Courtesy of Fred Allen and Linda Dallas.

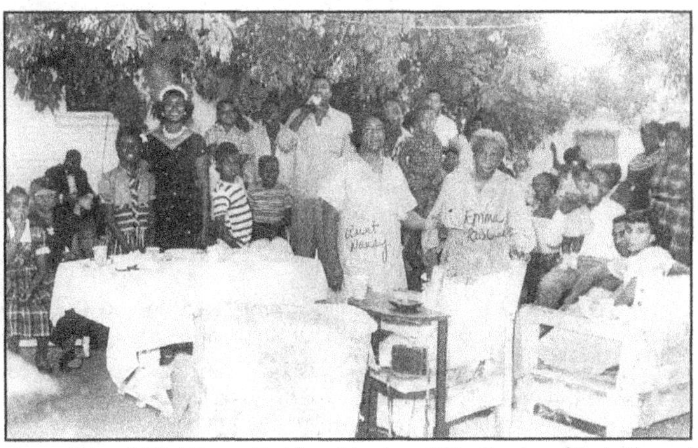

Emma Driver Reid's 108-year birthday celebration, 1960. Courtesy of Fred Allen and Linda Dallas.

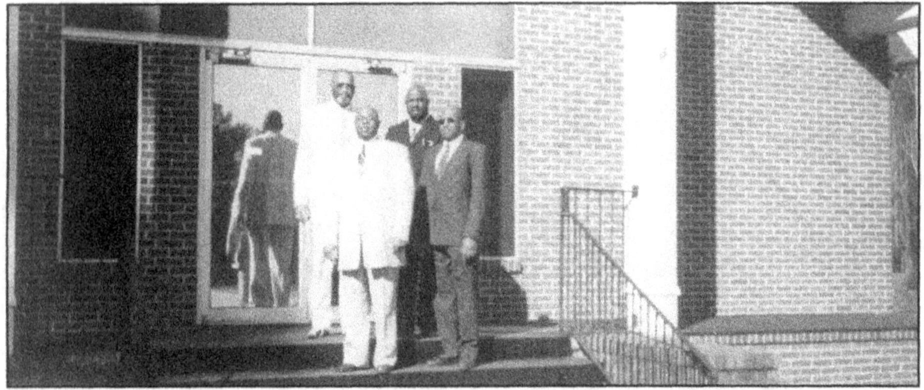

Members of Antioch Baptist Church, Back row: Fred Allen and Uland Nolley (Pastor). Front row: Kevin Watson and James Stillwell. Photo taken in 2004. Courtesy of Fred Allen and Linda Dallas.

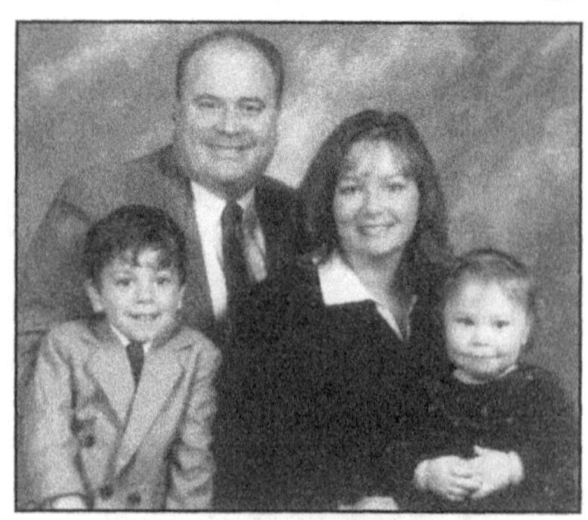

Robert, Elayne, Thomas Blake and Mary Elizabeth Morton. Courtesy of Robert L. Morton.

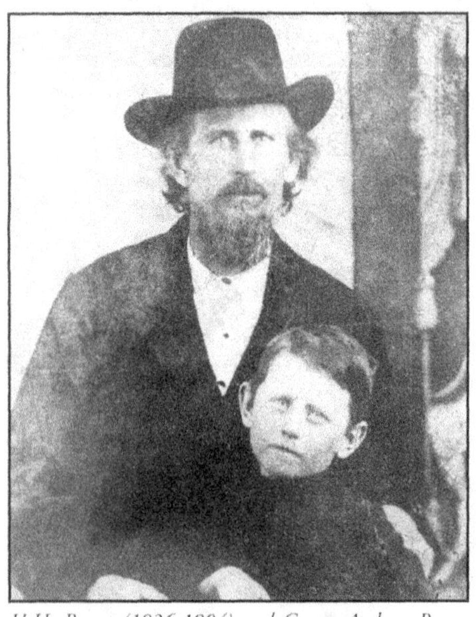

H.H. Reeves (1836-1904) and George Andrew Reeves (1874-1931). Courtesy of Ralph Steele.

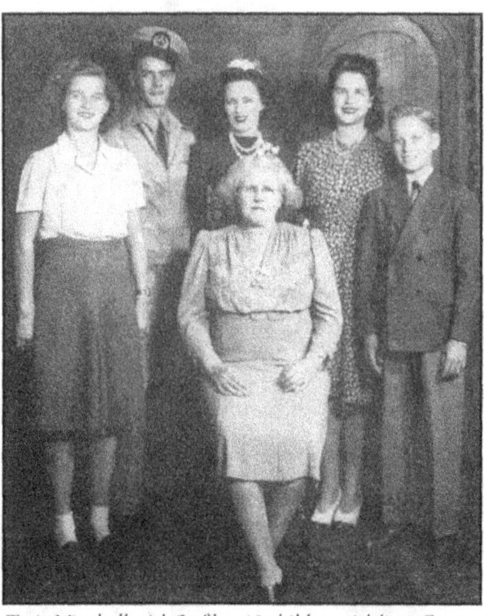

Tessie Marshall with 5 of her 10 children: Adeline, George, Cornelia, Tessie and Jesse Lee. Courtesy of Virginia and Charles Oglesby.

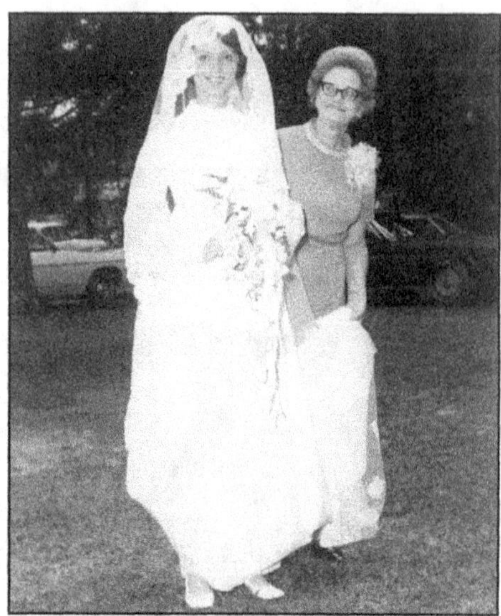

Sherry Johnson and Sara Marshall Smith outside of Friendship Presbyterian Church. Courtesy of Virginia and Charles Oglesby.

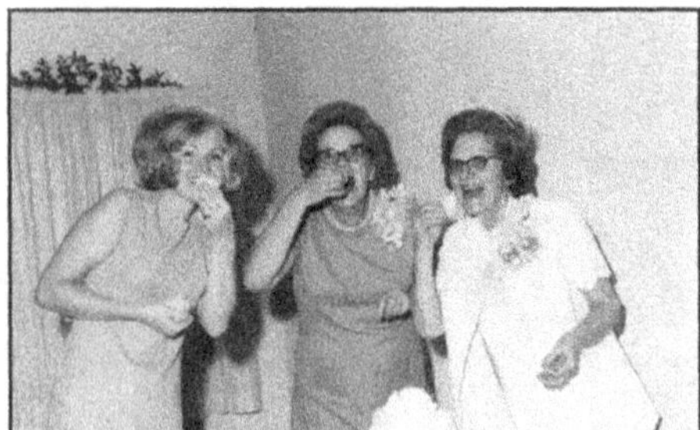

Ellen Johnson Lee, Sara Smith and Elizabeth Johnson. Courtesy of Virginia and Charles Oglesby.

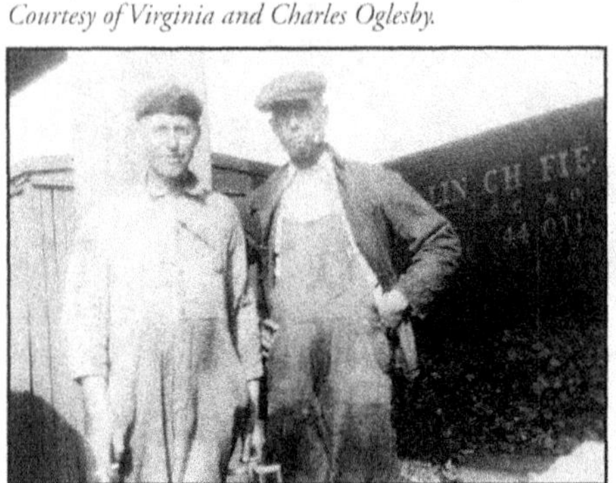

Jesse Lee Marshall and the other person is unknown. Courtesy of Virginia and Charles Oglesby.

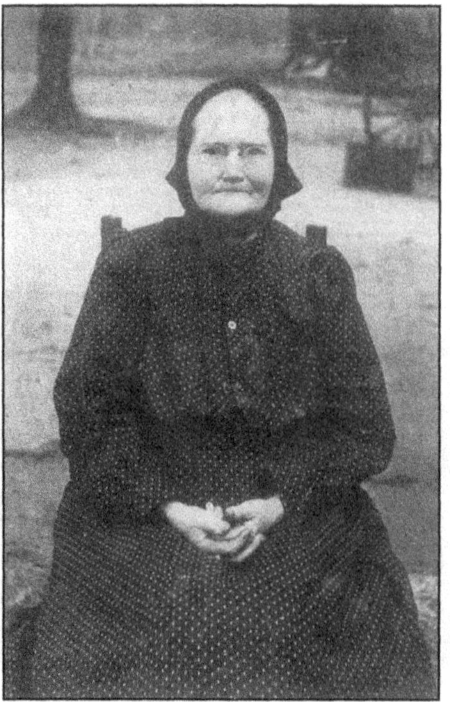

Margaret B. Kendrick. Courtesy of Kenneth Caldwell.

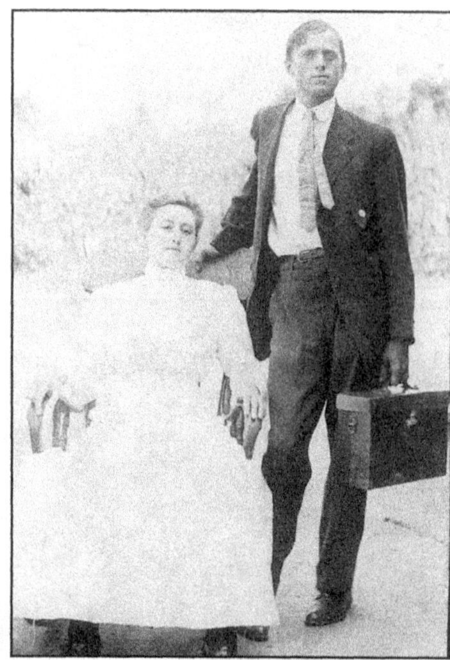

Bessie Watson Jones born 1893 in Upson County and Millard Grover Jones born 1890 in Pike County. Courtesy of Frances Aaron.

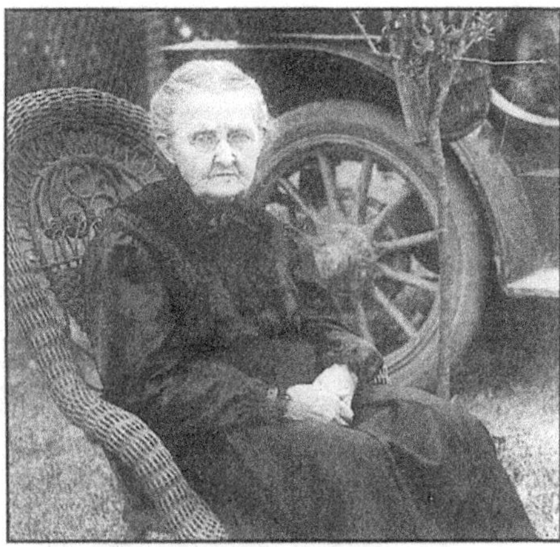
Ann Jane MacLean McElveen born Bulloch Co., Nov. 16, 1837-Nov. 23, 1923. Photo taken in front of home of Ida and Buster (A.A.) McElveen, Concord, GA about 1920. Ann Jane and her husband, William Elias McElveen (5th Cav. CSA) moved to Pike County, near Concord after the Civil War. Their children were James G., Sara, Willie A., John P., Allen Alvender, Mary Elizabeth, Minnie L. and Ada Gertrude. Courtesy of Barbara Snead Beasley.

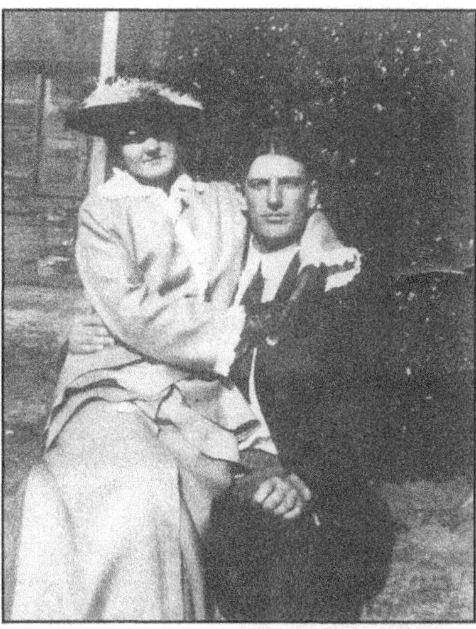
Amzie and Curtis Bishop on their wedding day, December 1915. Courtesy of Sylvia Wright.

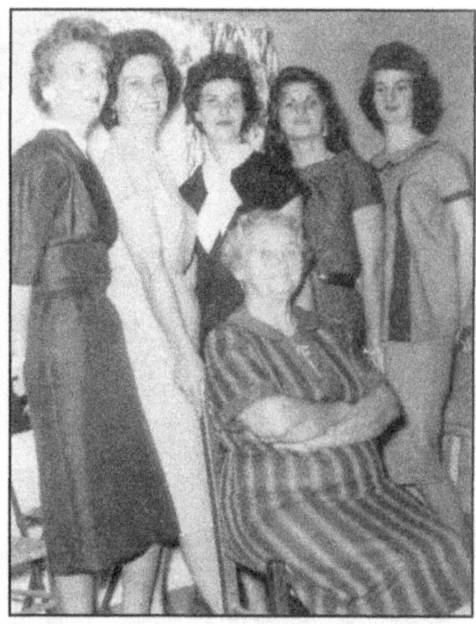
Amzie Bishop, Mary, Martha, Dorothy, Sylvia and Jan. Courtesy of Sylvia Wright.

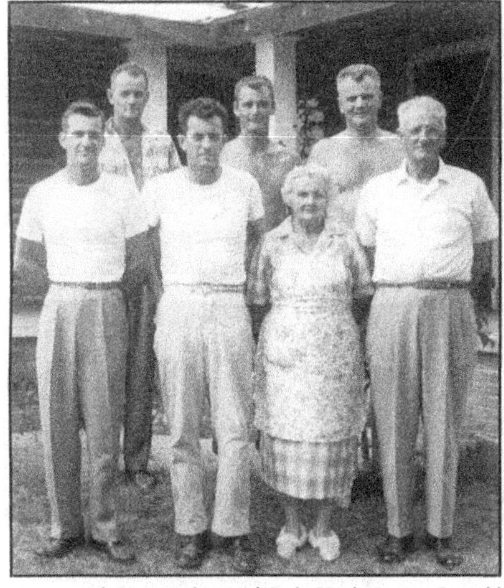
Amzie and Curtis Bishop with Jack, Hugh, Junior, Donald and Fred. Courtesy of Sylvia Wright.

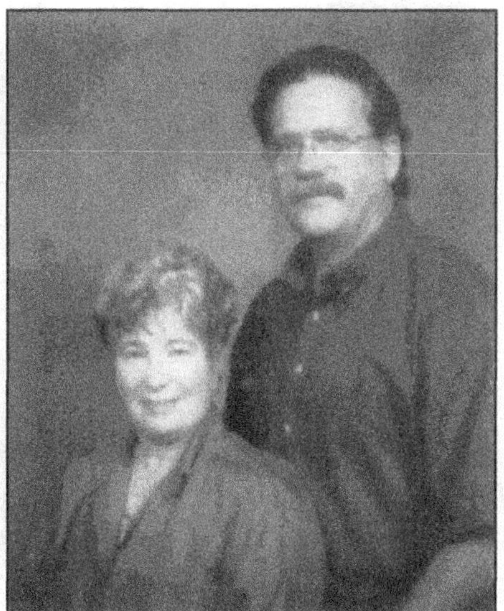
Ruth and Holloway Norris. Courtesy of Rachel McClelland.

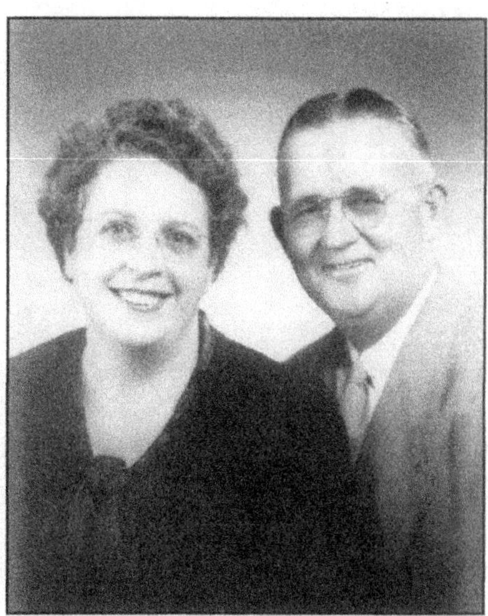
Bill and Judy Norris. Courtesy of Rachel McClelland.

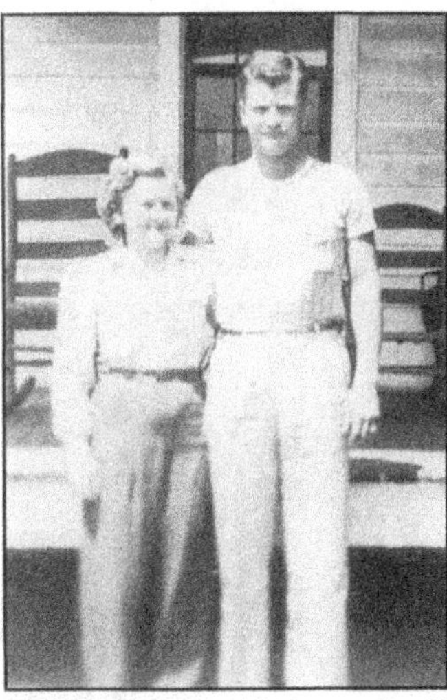
Willie Mae and Fred Bishop at the old homeplace, circa late 1930's. Courtesy of Sylvia B. Wright.

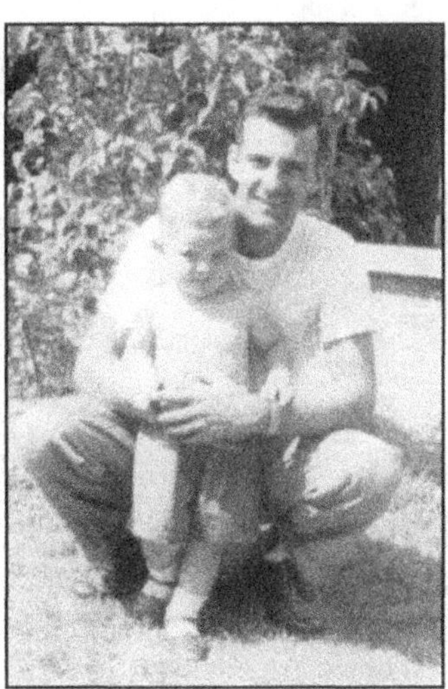
Jack Bishop at Old homeplace with his son Wayne. Courtesy of Sylvia and Bradford Wright.

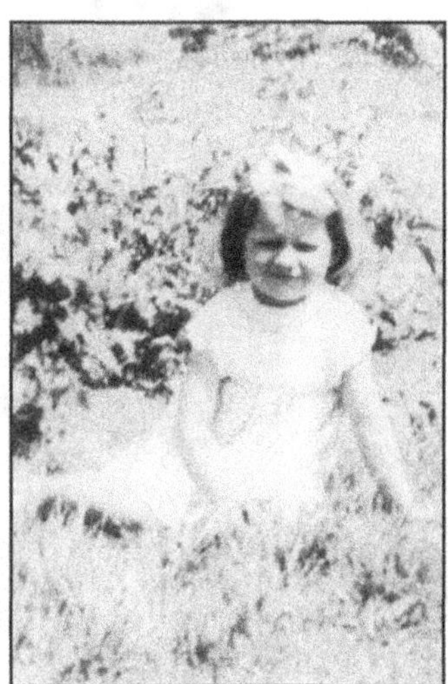
Sylvia Bishop at the old Bishop homeplace at the age of three. Courtesy of Sylvia B. Wright.

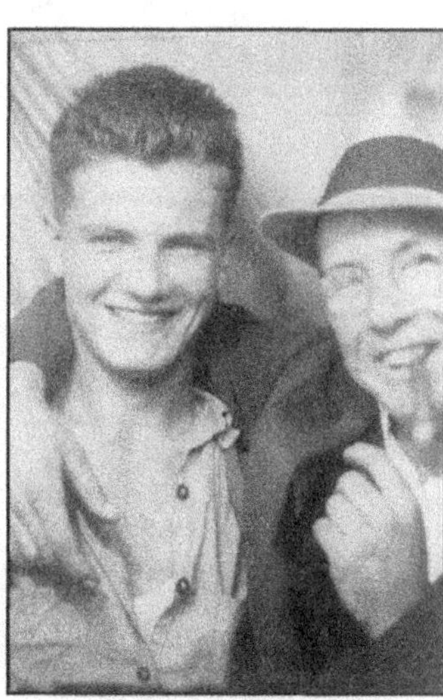
"Buddies" Fred Bishop and Horace Rogers, circa late 1930's.

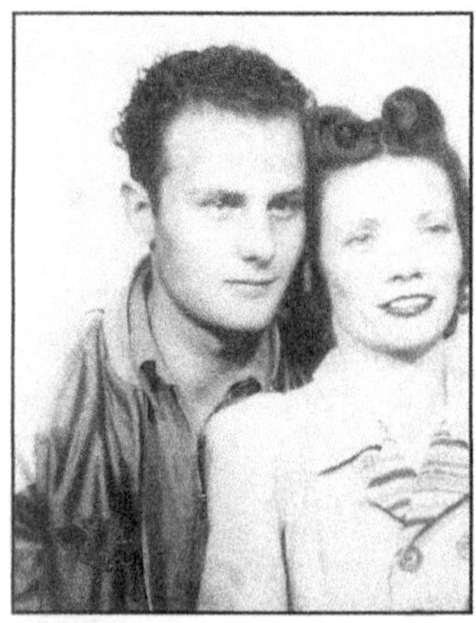

Hugh Joel Bishop Sr. and Pauline Brooks Bishop. Courtesy of Bonnie Gardner.

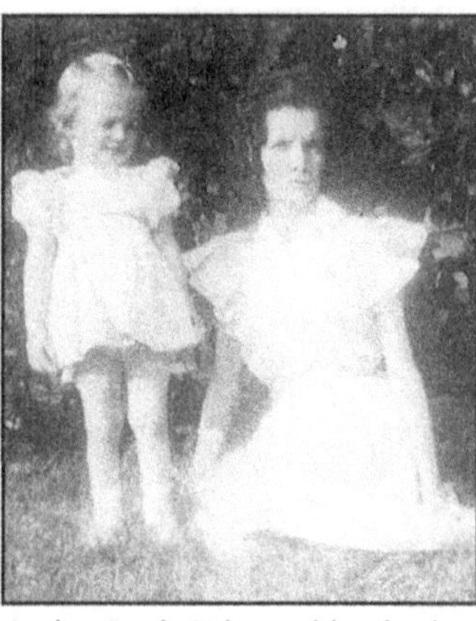

Pauline Brooks Bishop and her daughter Bonnie Pauline Bishop. Courtesy of Bonnie Gardner.

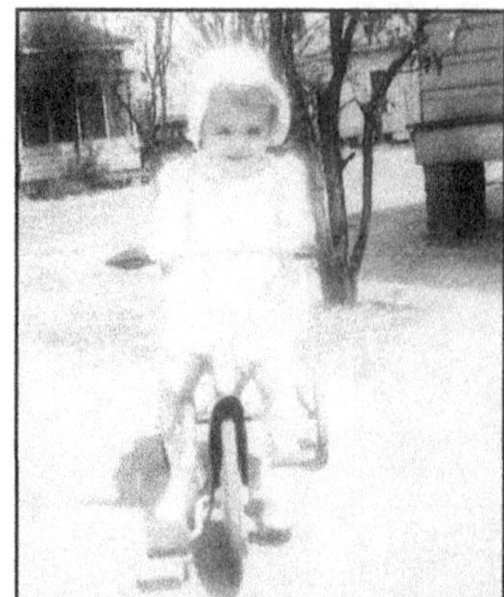

Bonnie Pauline Bishop in a 1944 picture riding her tricycle. Courtesy of Bonnie Gardner.

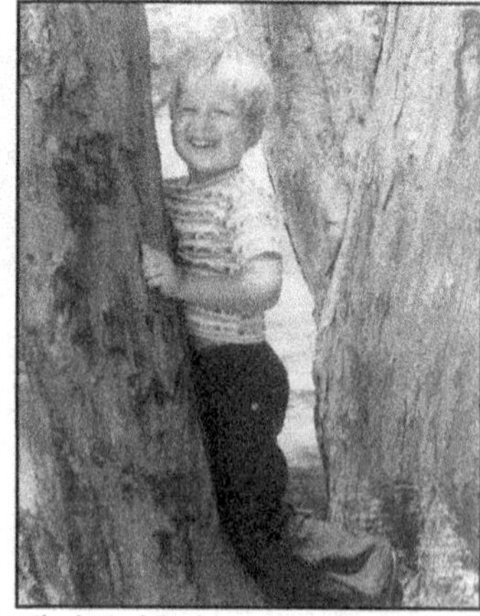

Chad Hugh Bishop tree climbing in 1979. Courtesy of Bonnie Gardner.

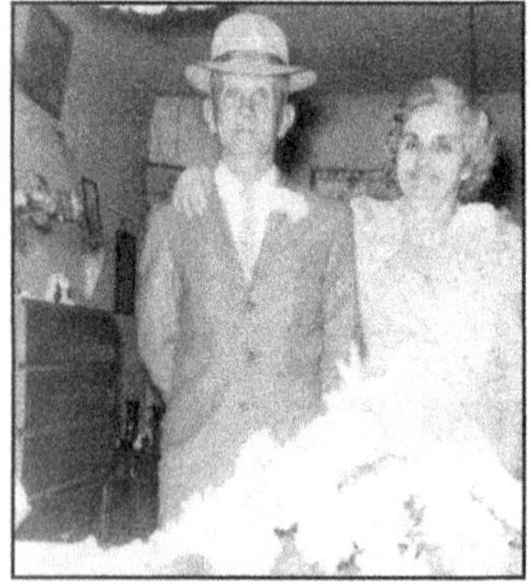

J.W. Brooks and Dora Rogers Broons celebrating their 50th wedding anniversary. Courtesy of Bonnie Gardner.

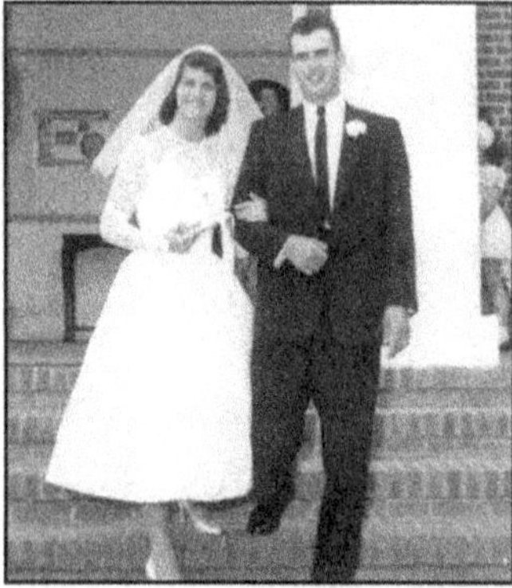

Sylvia Bishop and Bradford Wright on their wedding day in 1958. Courtesy of Sylvia B. Wright.

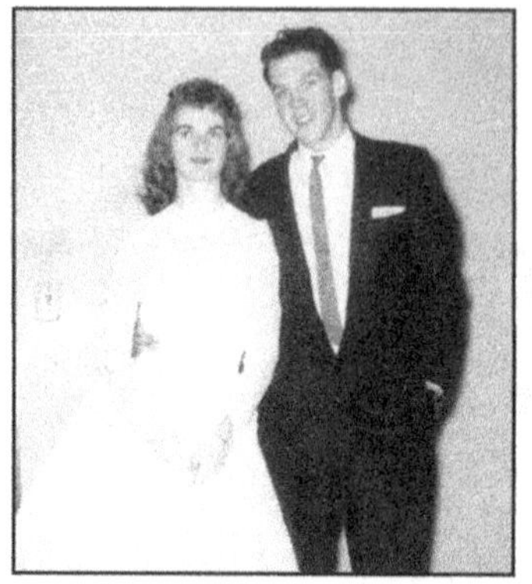

Jan Bishop and Billy Williams, wedding day, February 1960. Courtesy of Sylvia B. Wright.

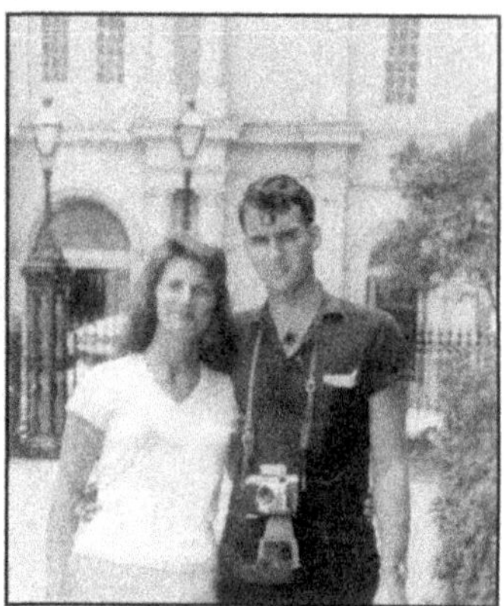

Sylvia Bishop Wright and Bradford Wright, 1959. Courtesy of Sylvia Wright.

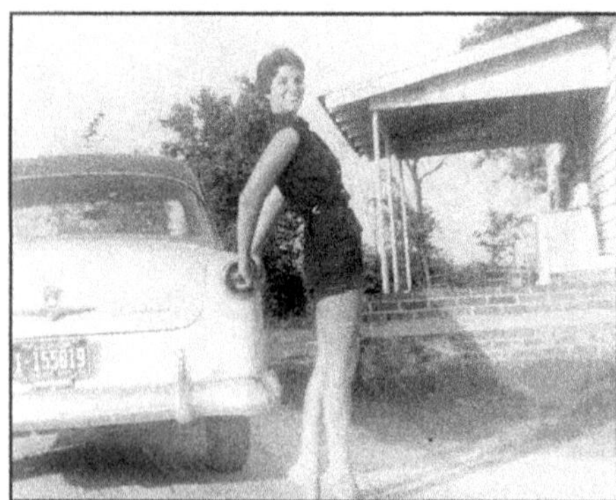

Dorothy Bishop at homeplace in 1958. Courtesy of Sylvia Wright.

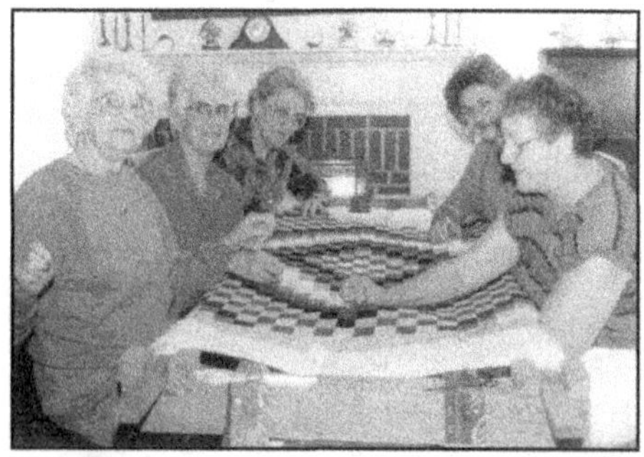

Sara Marshall Smith, Adeline Marshall Thorsen, Conelia Marshall Enyart, Virginia Smith Oglesby and Fran Enyart, working on Olympic Quilt, summer 1996. Courtesy of Virginia Oglesby.

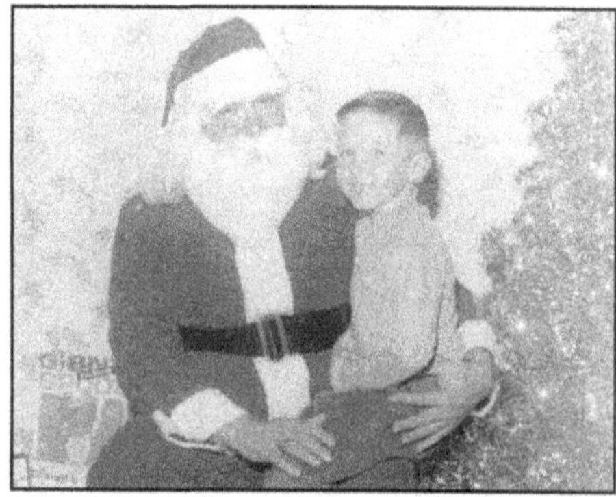

Kenneth Graham with Santa during Christmas of 1963. Courtesy of Dorothy Graham.

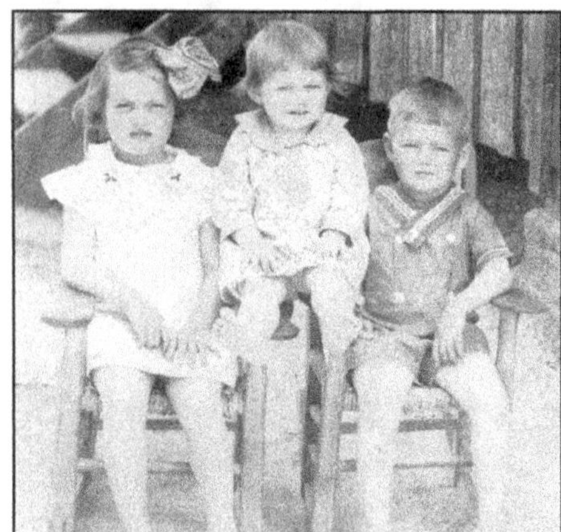

Dorothy, Sylvia and Donald Bishop, 1939. Courtesy of Sylvia Wright.

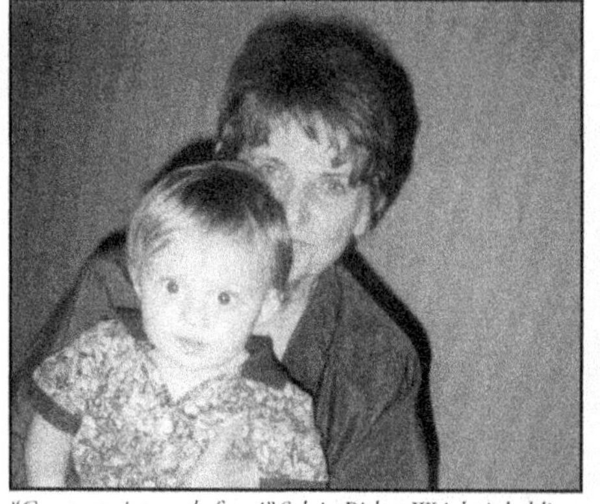

"Granmaw is proud of you!" Sylvia Bishop Wright is holding grandson, Jake. He had just had two bad shots at the doctor's office and he didn't even whimper! "My brave little man." Courtesy of Sylvia Wright.

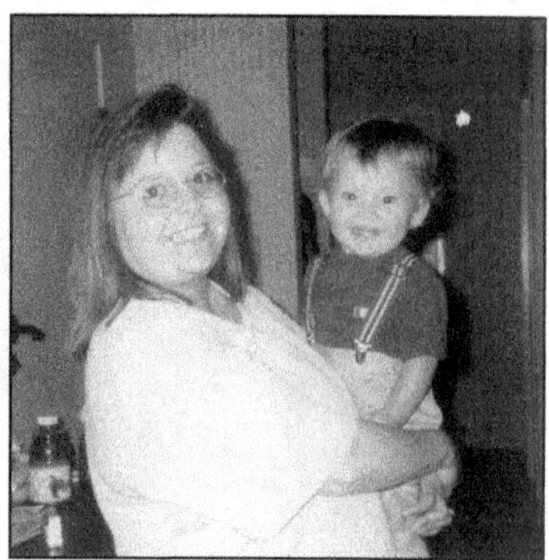

Cathy Wright with son, Jake. Courtesy of Sylvia Wright.

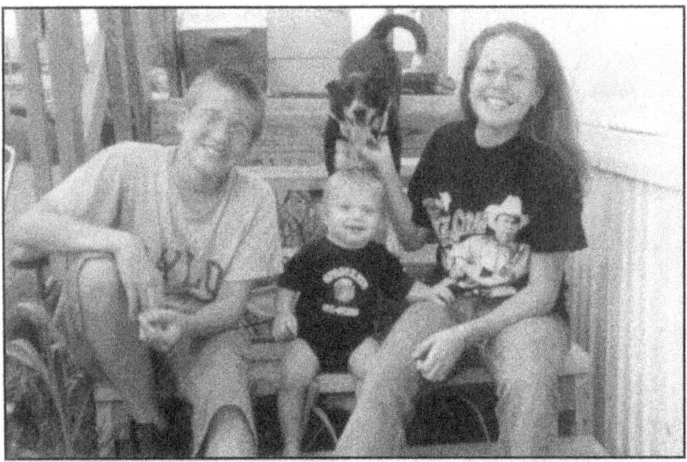

Marshall, Christine and Jake and their dog "Bo". Courtesy of Sylvia Wright.

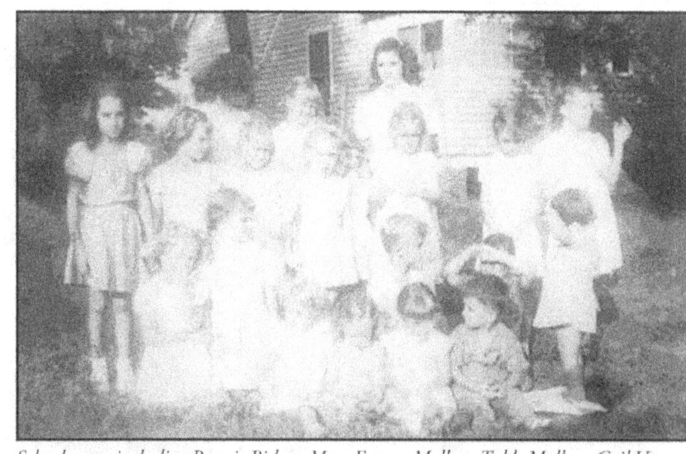

School mates including Bonnie Bishop, Mary Frances Mallory, Teddy Mallory, Gail Ussery and Jeanette Childs. Courtesy of Bonnie Gardner.

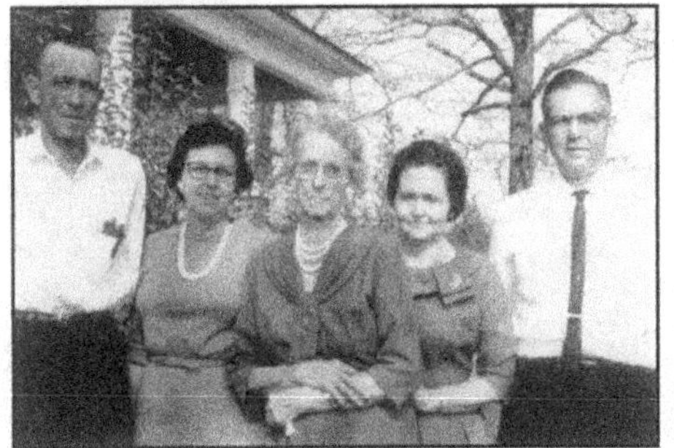

Jack Barker, Doris Barker Lawrence, Maggie Gregg Barker, Dimple Barker Smith and Williams Gregg Barker. Courtesy of Elsie Anderson.

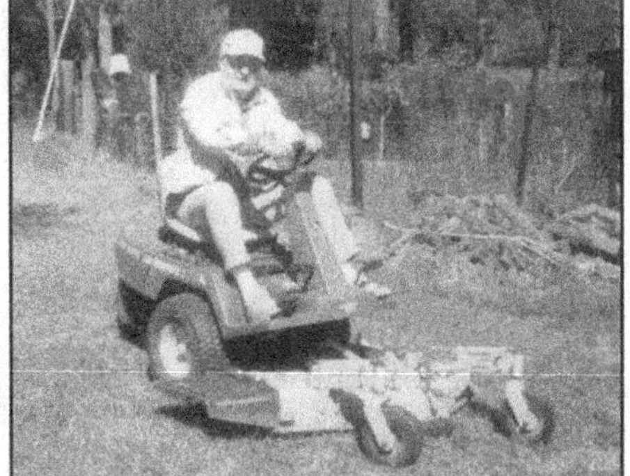

Tom Morton on his tractor. Courtesy of Tom Morton.

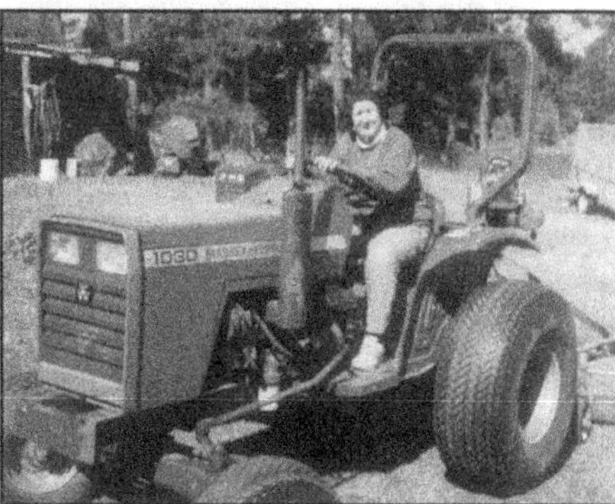

Sonya Morton on her tractor. Courtesy of Tom Morton.

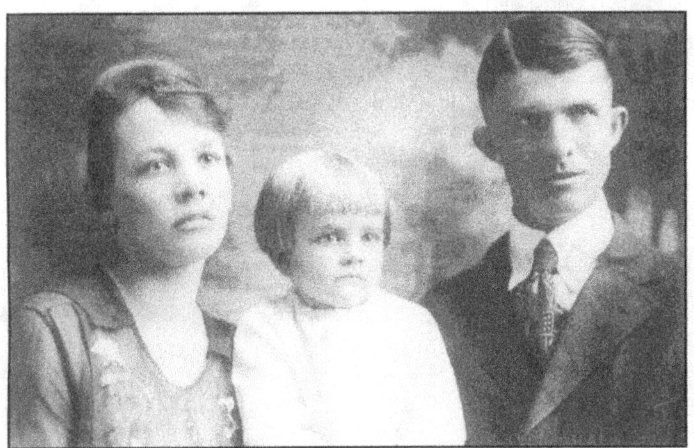

Pearl Stegar Williams, Wallace Gregg Williams and Helen (Williams) English, circa 1918 or 1919. Courtesy of D. English Smith.

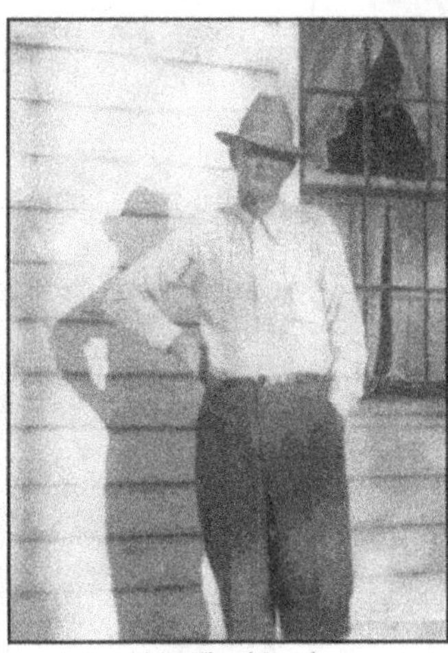

Mr. Claud Smith.

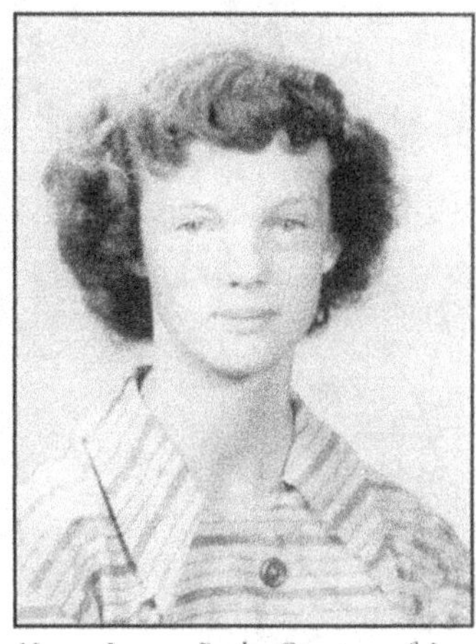

Nancy Joanne Bush. Courtesy of Jane Gaulding.

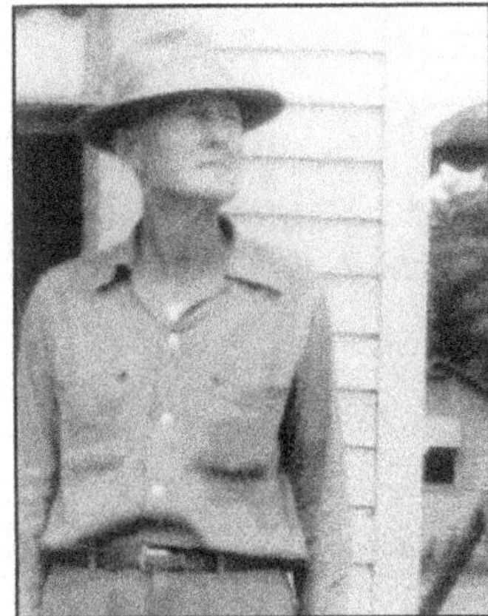

Thomas Jackson "Jack" Elliott. Courtesy of Jane Gaulding.

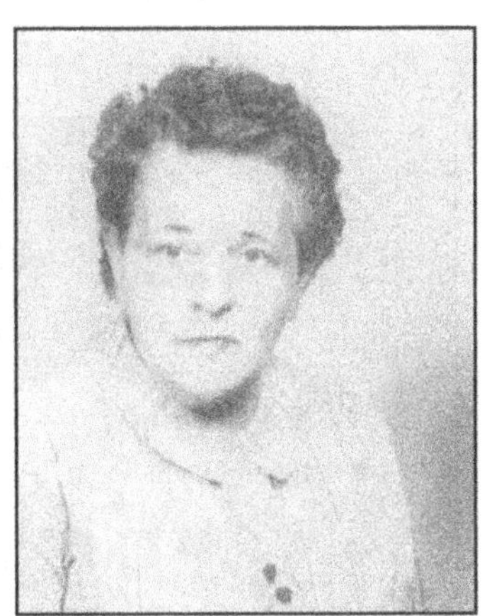

Elizabeth (Cloud) Elliott (1911-1979). Courtesy of Jane Gaulding.

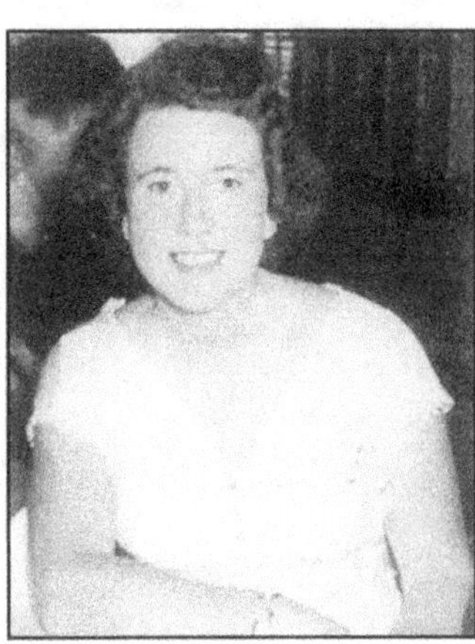

Sue Elliott (1937-1986). Courtesy of Jane Gaulding.

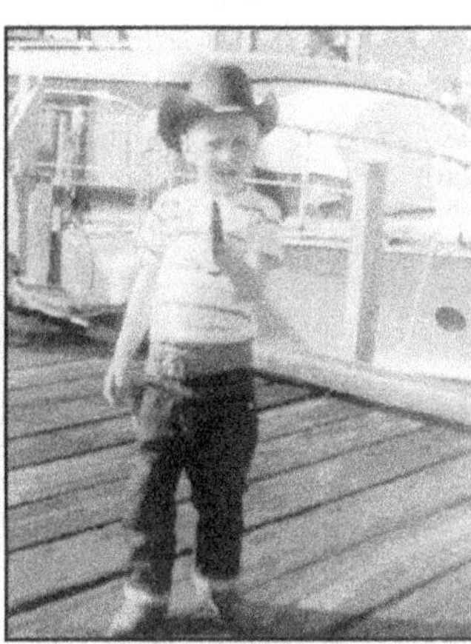

Stephen McCarty. Courtesy of Jane Gaulding.

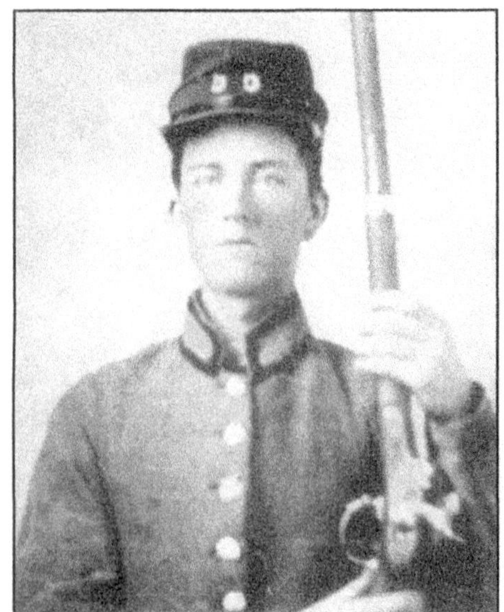

James Henry Barker, age 18 (1837-1908). Courtesy of Elsie Anderson.

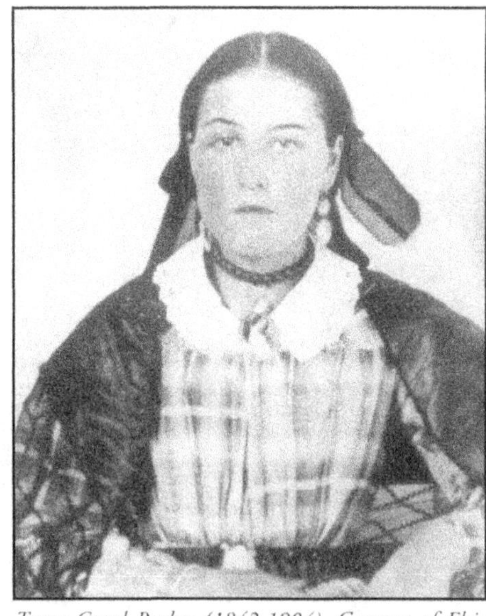

Teresa Capel Barker (1842-1904). Courtesy of Elsie Anderson.

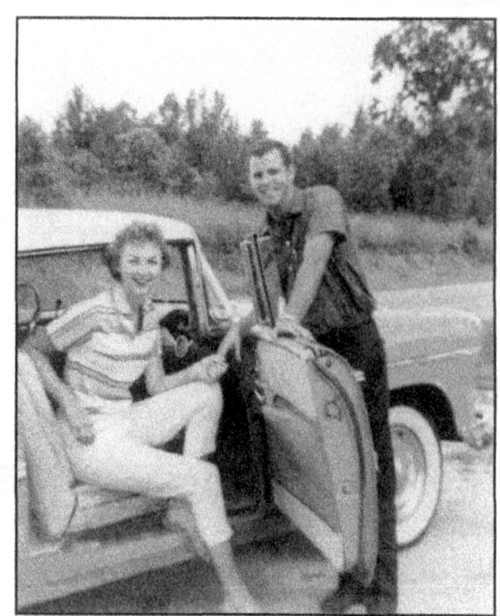

Elsie Lawrence and Melvin Anderson. Courtesy of Elsie Anderson.

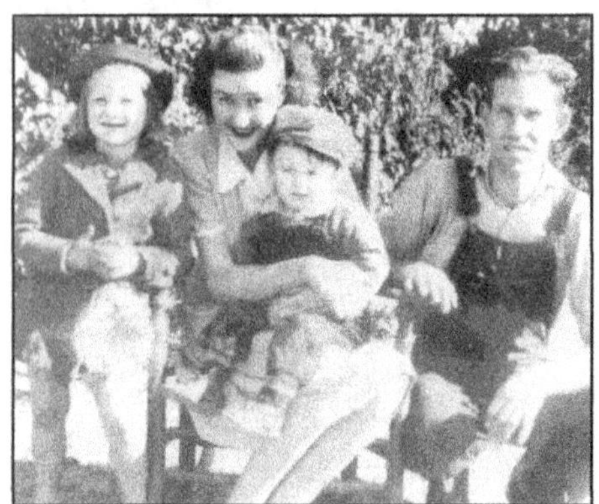

Annette Robbins, Estelle McDaniel Robbins, Harold Robbins and Ray Robbins, 1943. Courtesy of Joann Fenley.

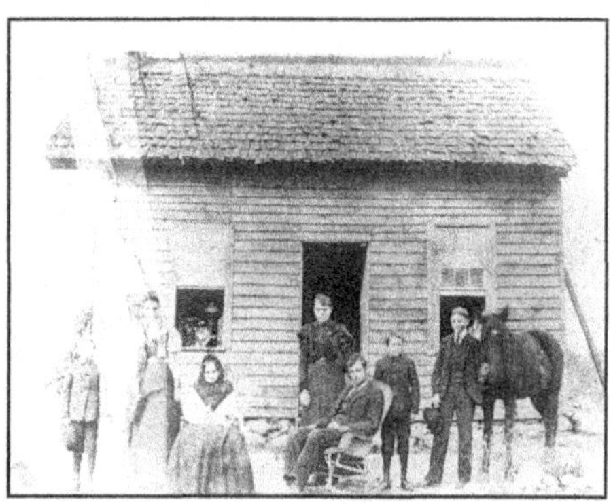

Smith homeplace about 1890: Otis Smith, Burkette Smith, Euel Smith, Bruce Smith, Archibald T. Smith and Ora Smith. Courtesy of Wayne Foster.

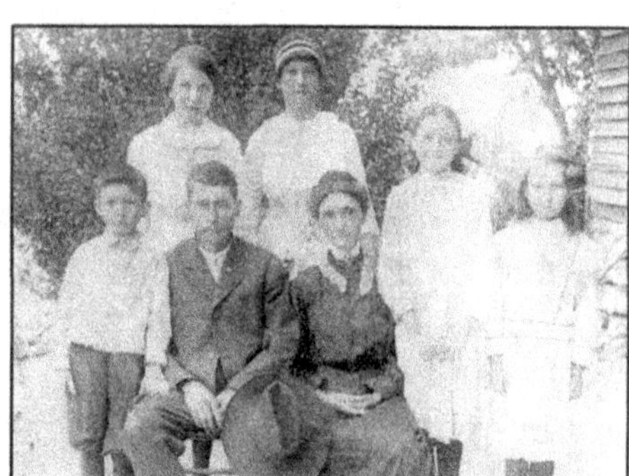

Quinton Oscar Turner, Martha Jane Ogletree Turner, William Elmer Turner, Fannie Mae Turner, Rosa Inese Turner, Lena Estelle Turner and Desa Lendra Turner. Courtesy of Joann Fenley.

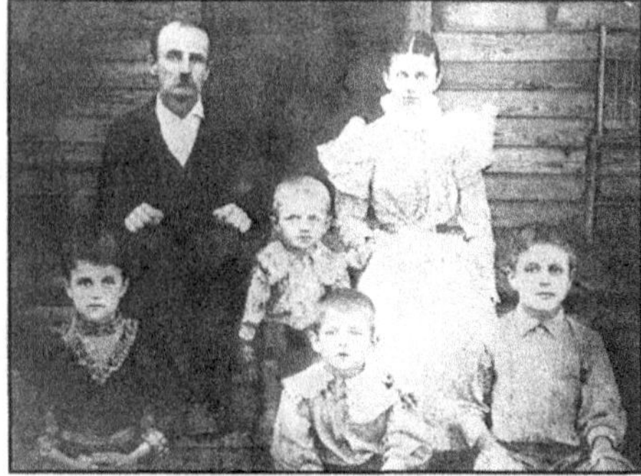

William Davis Bishop, Molly Melinda, Lonie, Curtis, Bosie (Ernest) and Bloomer, circa 1900. Courtesy of Sylvia Wright.

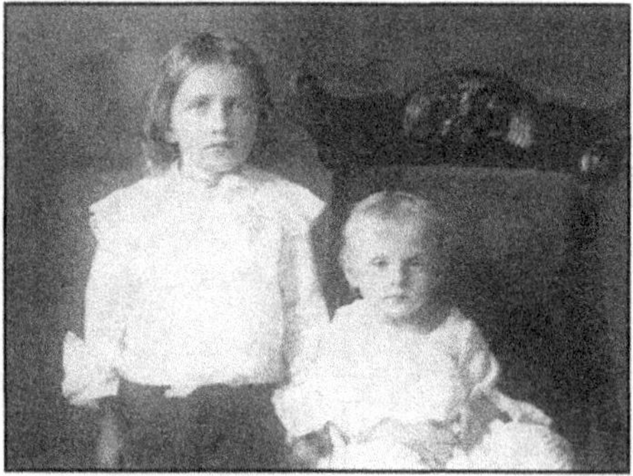

Rufus Loyal Dickens and Merial Edna Dickens. Courtesy of Anna Belle McDaniel.

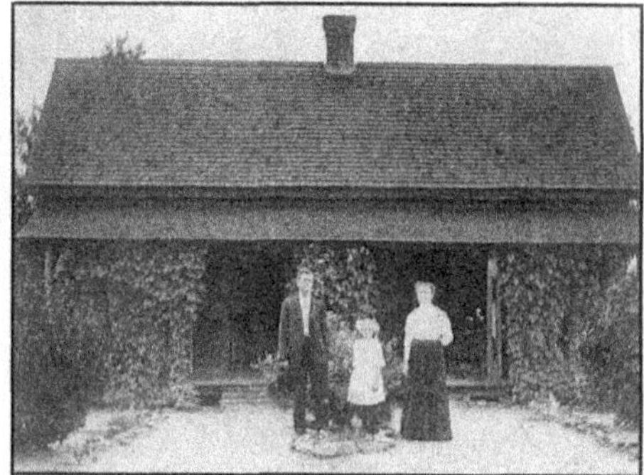

Jackson Thurston Dickens, Sara Thornton Dickens and Merial Edna Dickens. Courtesy of Anna Belle McDaniel.

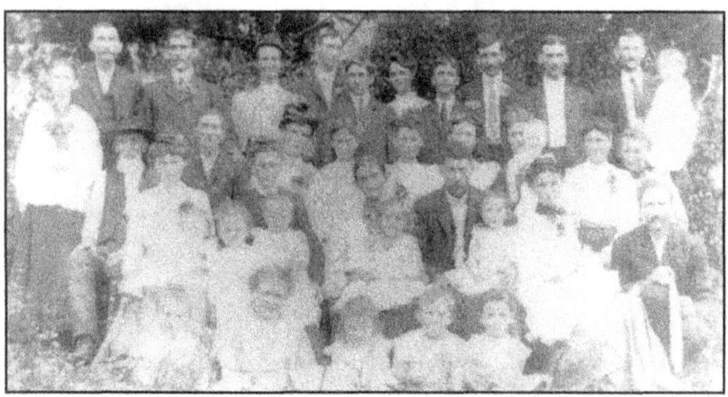

Ogletree family reunion, July 11, 1905. Courtesy of Joann Fenley.

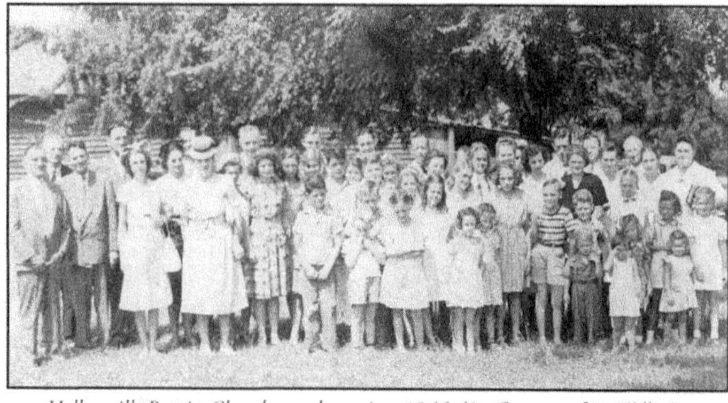

Hollonsville Baptist Church members, circa 1946-48. Courtesy of H. Willis Jr.

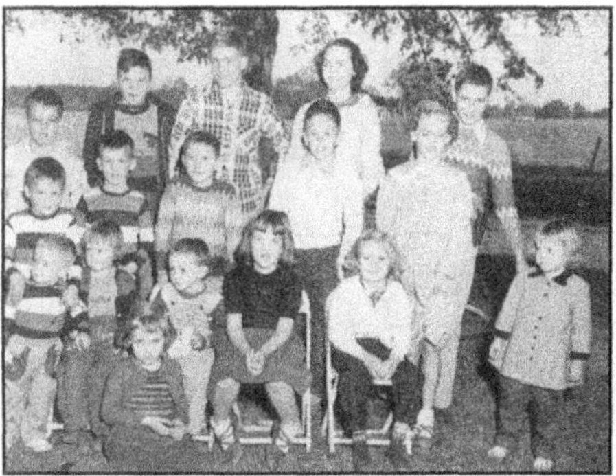
Back row: Jack Housch, Dick Milner, Milner Osborne, Carolyn Milner and John Milner III. Second row: Willis Bussey, Jimmy Bussey, George Milner, Morgan Milner II, Jane Osborne and Helen Housch. Front row: Sammy Bussey, Eugenia Milner, Beverly Milner, Tim Milner, Deanna Milner and Marcelle Milner. Pictured in side yard of home of Morgan and Nelle Milner's Turkey Farm, located on Hwy 19 just outside Zebulon. Grandchildren of John H. and Bessie Cannafax Milner. Date: about 1950. Courtesy of Eugenia Milner Henry.

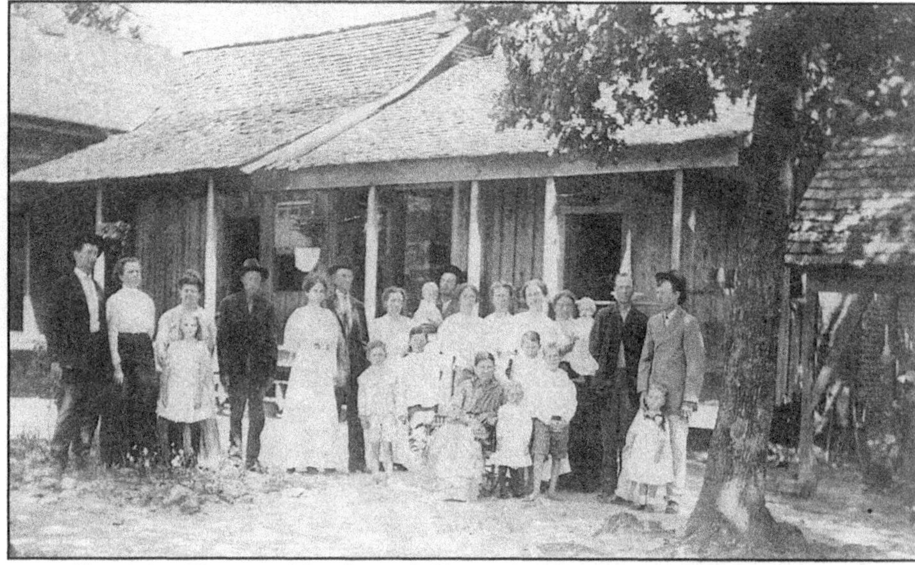
Henry Jackson Thornton and decendants at the Thornton homeplace. Courtesy of Anna Belle McDaniel.

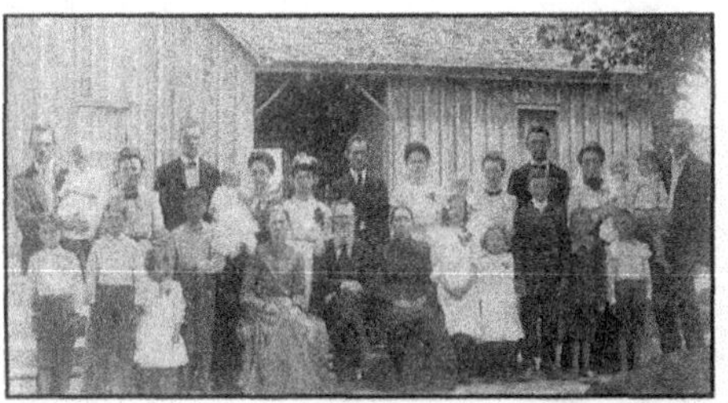
Thomas Caswell Brannon family home in Lifsey Springs, picture was made about 1906. Pictured: William Lafayette, Ola Moore, Ola Mae, Leon, Tandy, Lovett, Roz, V. Cook, Effie Mae Brannon Cook, Hoyt, Ivie, Fletcher, Lelia, Aunt Louisa Brannon, Thomas Caswell Brannon, Martha Elmyra Willingham Brannon, Eugenia Brannon Key, Robert Key, Eunice, Lois, Gladys, Clinton, Tom, Lula Ophelia Brannon Foster, Richard Foster, Raymond, Homer and Odessa. Courtesy of Wayne Foster.

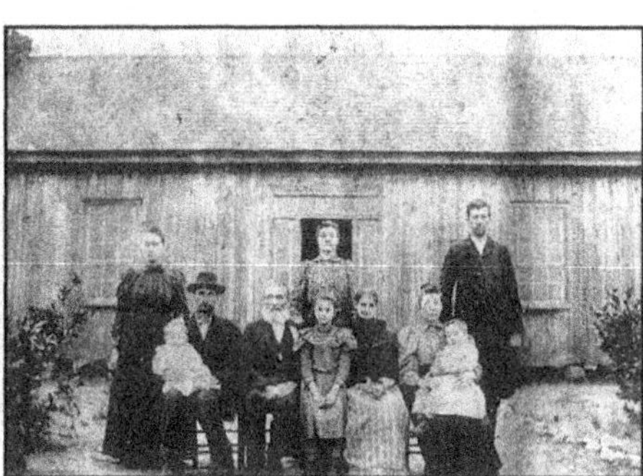
Foster home in the mid 1890's: Arizona Texas Brannon foster, Thomas Jefferson Foster, baby unknown, Burrell Jefferson Foster, Rebecca Adella Foster, Lemmer Estelle Foster, Easter Ameliar Hagans Foster, Julia Ann Foster Thompson, Lummie Thompson and Columbus David Thompson. Courtesy of Wayne Foster.

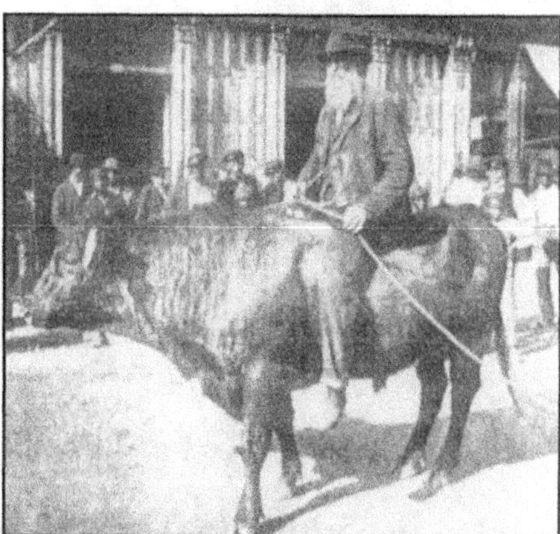
Mr. Milner on an oxen on Main St. in Zebulon. Courtesy of Tom Morton.

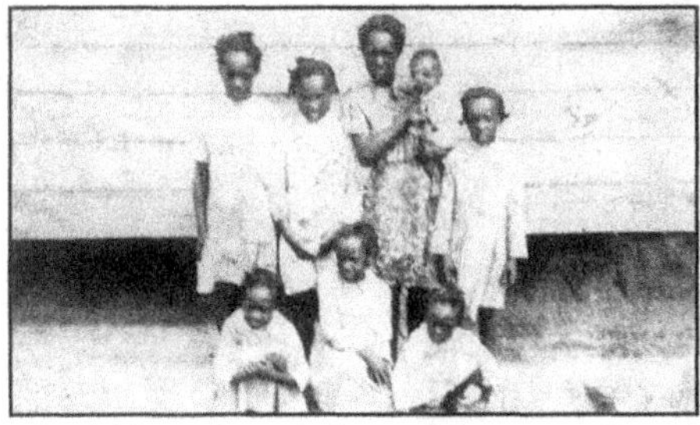
The children of Otis Bishop and Lee Myrtis (Harris) Caldwell. Left to right, kneeling: Eria Marie, Ozella and Geraldine. Standing: Minnie, Ida Mae, Lois (holding Otis Bishop), and Pearl Lena. Courtesy of Andrew Jones.

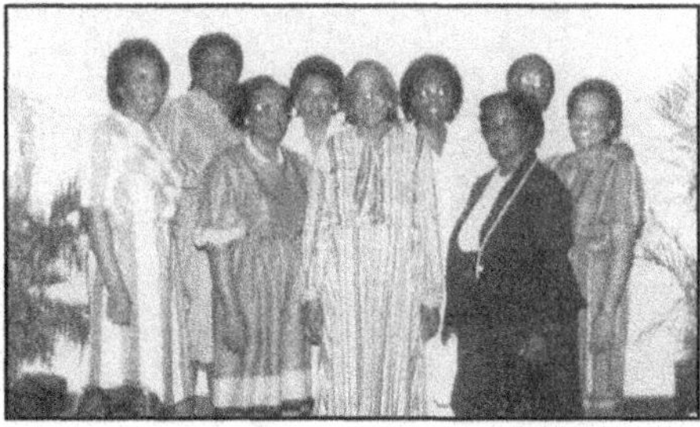
Caldwell children, as adults. Left to right, front row: Lois Caldwell, Lee Myrtis (Harris) Caldwell and Loet Moreland. Back row: Minnie, Eria Marie, Ozella, Geraldine, Otis Bishop and Pearl Lena. Courtesy of Andrew Jones.

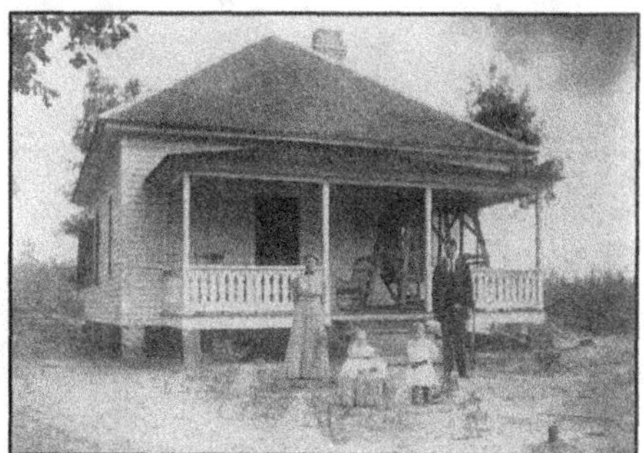
Charlie Osborne Cannafax and Cora Lee Wells. Courtesy of Joe Cannafax.

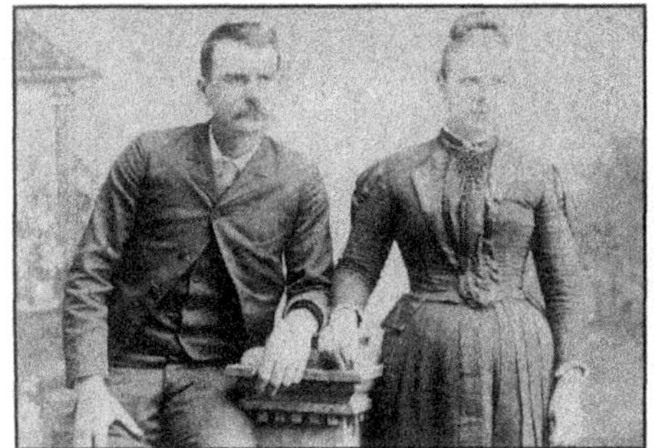
Henry Joe Cannafax and wife, Mattie Bush. Courtesy of Joe Cannafax.

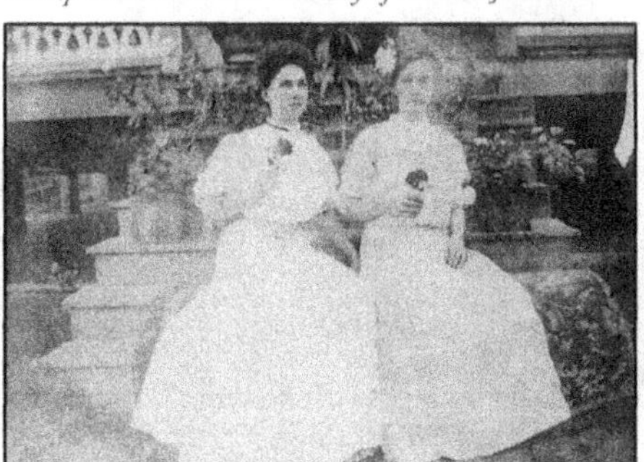
Two of the daughters of Parks Reno Coker and Nancy Althia Barrow. O'Dessa on right. Courtesy of Drew Payne.

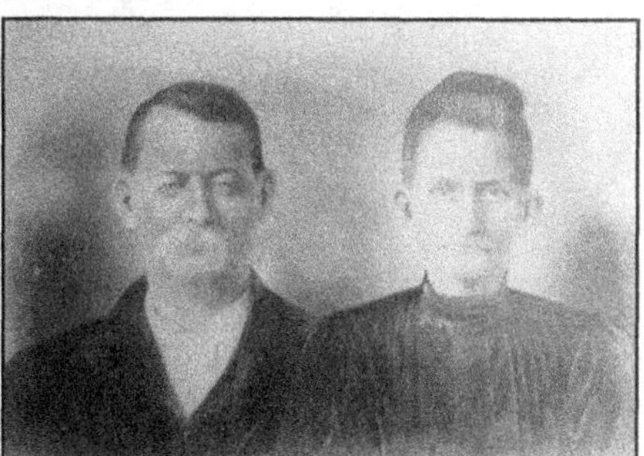
George Marshall and Amanda Calhoun Marshall, late 1800s. Courtesy of John Henderson.

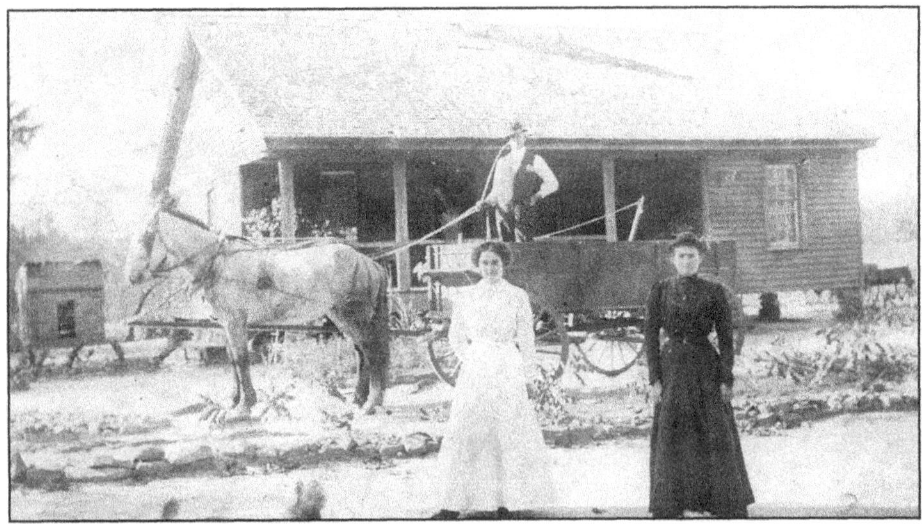

Four generations: J.C., Hilda, Cliff and Mellie "Grandma" Bankston. Picture taken on Bankston Circle-Marietta, GA, circa 1947. Courtesy of Hilda Bankston.

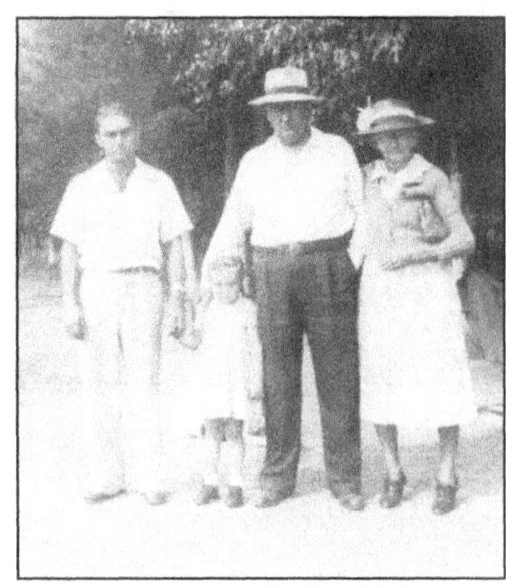

Vester Cannon in wagon with Effie and Lelia Cannon. Courtesy of Hilda Bankston.

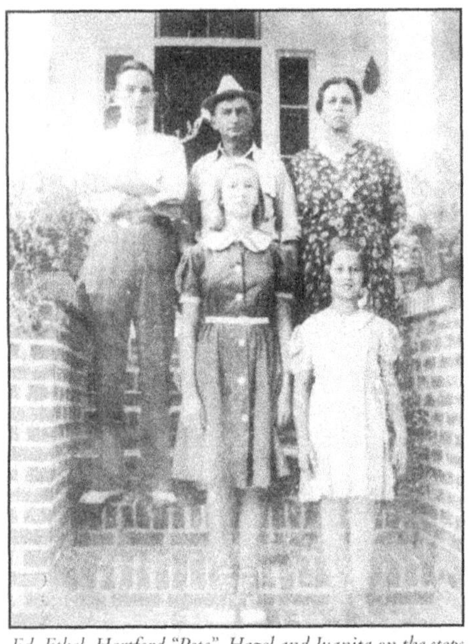

Ed, Ethel, Hartford "Pete", Hazel and Juanita on the steps of a house on Hwy 109W. Courtesy of Hilda Bankston.

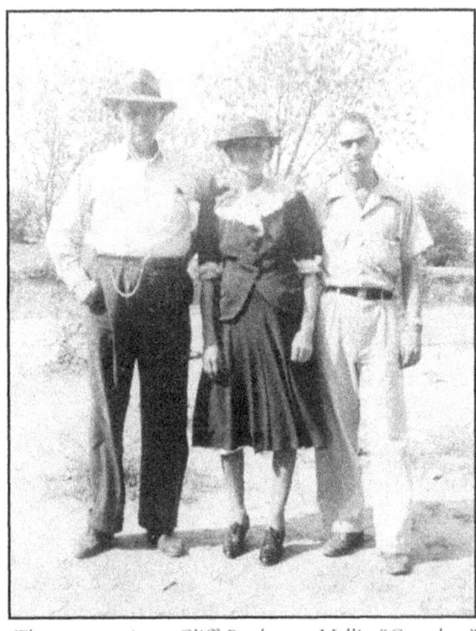

Three generations: Cliff Bankston, Mellie "Grandma" Bankston and J.C. Bankston, 1947. Courtesy of Hilda Bankston.

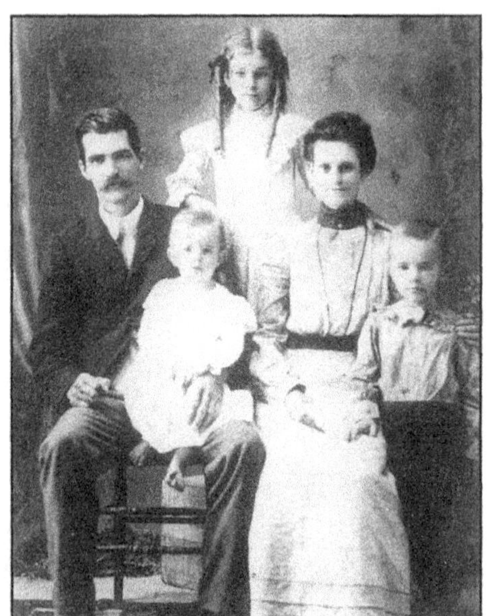

Walter and Ollie Mae Elliott Brown with three oldest children: Paul, Lorena and Quillian, circa 1903. Courtesy of James Adams.

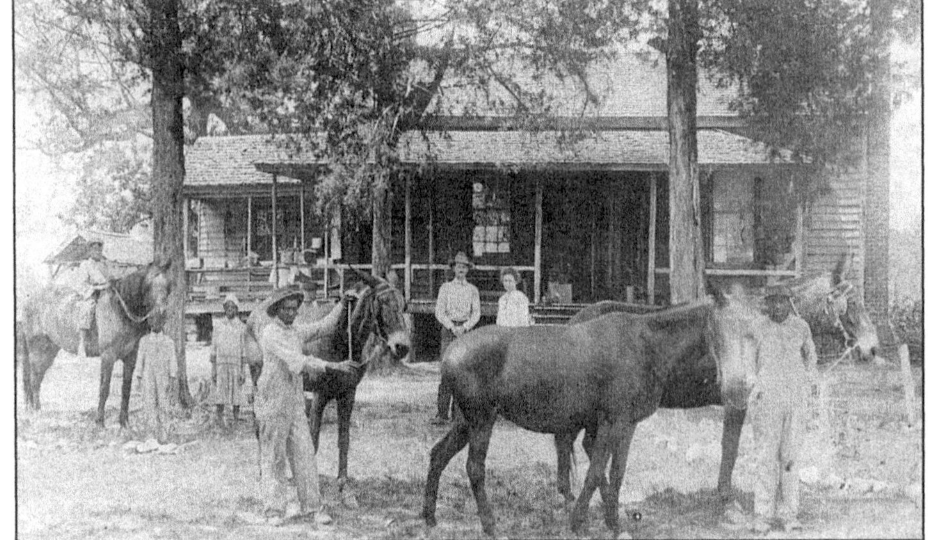

Farm scene with mules and laborers at the home of James W. and Opal Dunbar Elliott, circa 1920. Courtesy of James Adams.

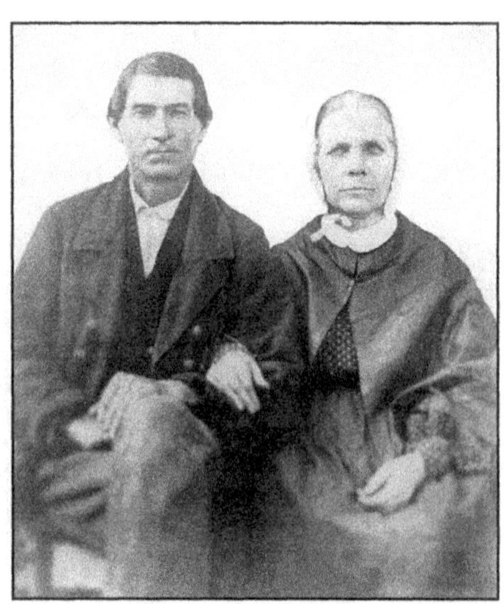

Nathan and Prudence Story Boyd. Pioneer couple and early settlers of the Meansville-Lifsey Springs community, circa 1860. Courtesy of James Adams.

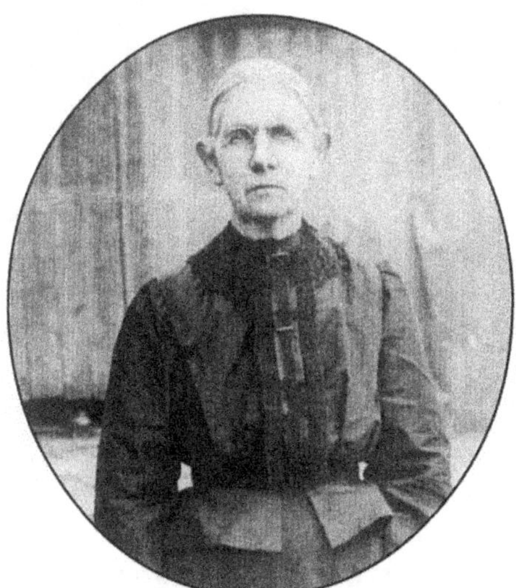

Lavonia Boyd Lifsey. Courtesy of James Adams.

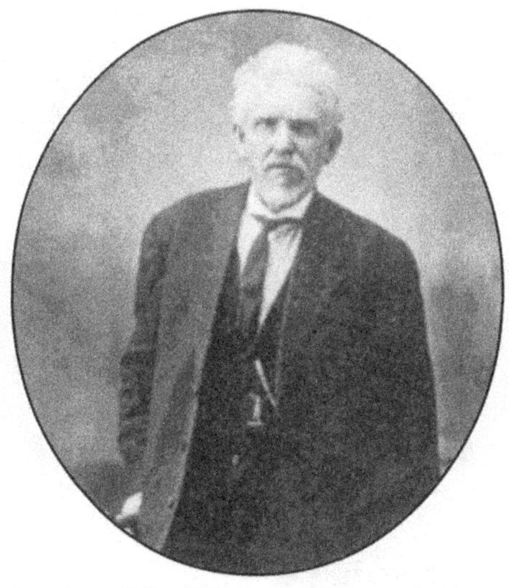

James Samuel "Tony" Lifsey, patriarch of a large family near Meansville. He served as Pike County tax collector for a number of years. Courtesy of James Adams.

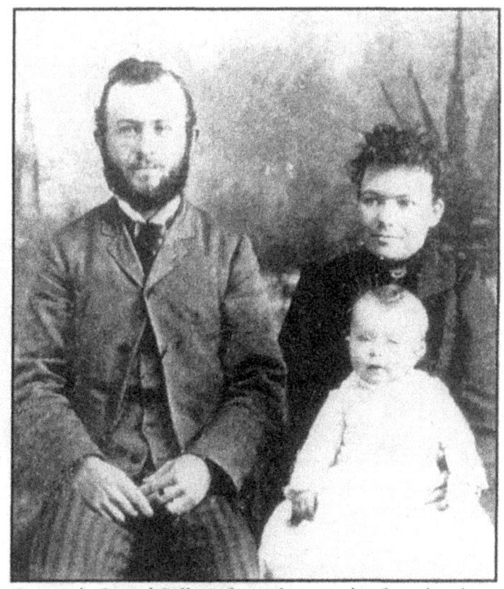

Jeremiah C. and Rilla Lifsey Adams and infant daughter, Estelle, circa 1895. Courtesy of James Adams.

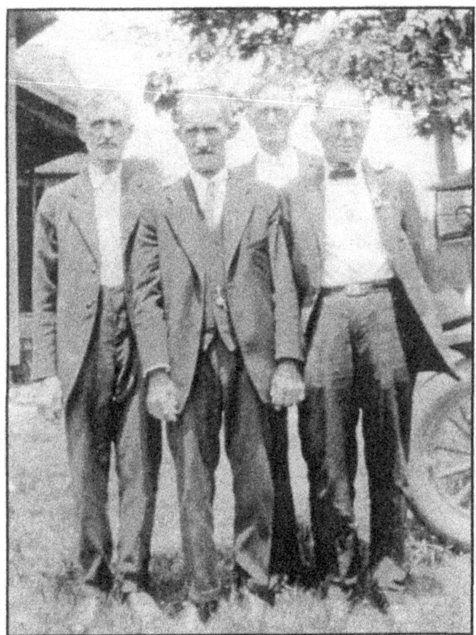

Richard B. Foster, Arthur Willingham, Gib Brannon and Lafayette Brannon, circa 1920's. Courtesy of Wayne Foster.

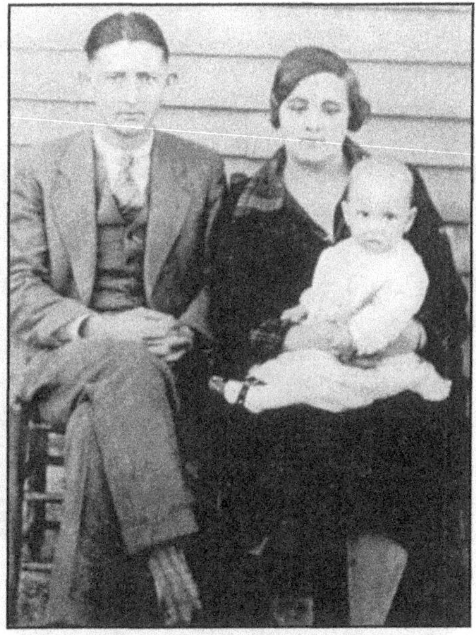

Willie Warren Campbell, Allie Maude Foster Campbell and Edward. Courtesy of Wayne Foster.

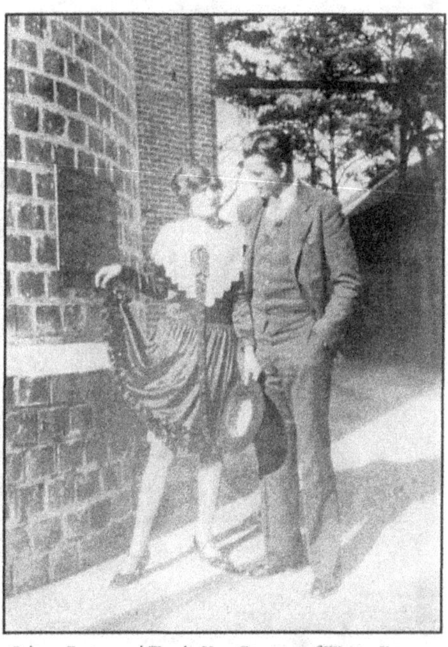

Odessa Foster and Tandy Key. Courtesy of Wayne Foster.

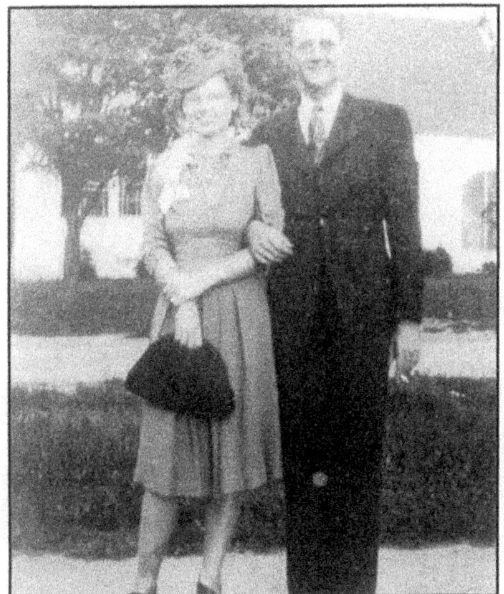

Frances Peugh and Walter Emmitt Foster. Courtesy of Wayne Foster.

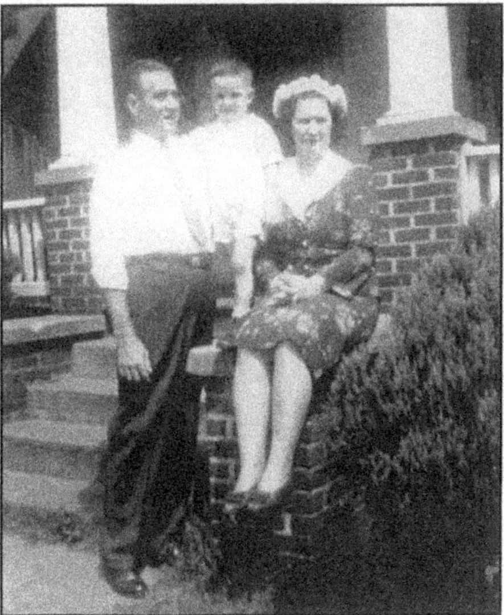

Amos and Alene Mullins Foster with Son Tommy. Courtesy of Wayne Foster.

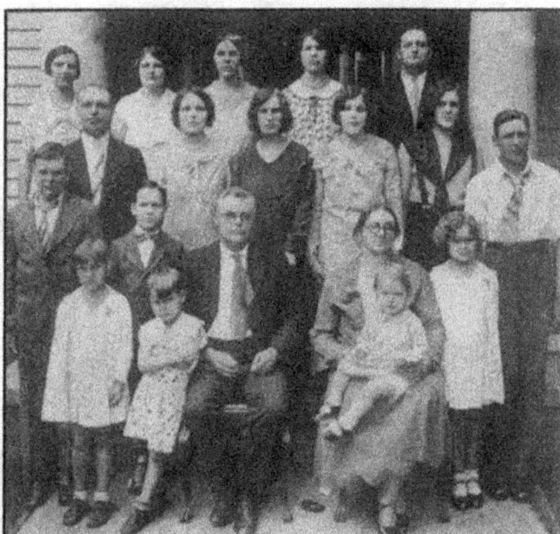

Edwin E. and Mary Etta Coggin Cook and their seventeen children. Courtesy of James Adams.

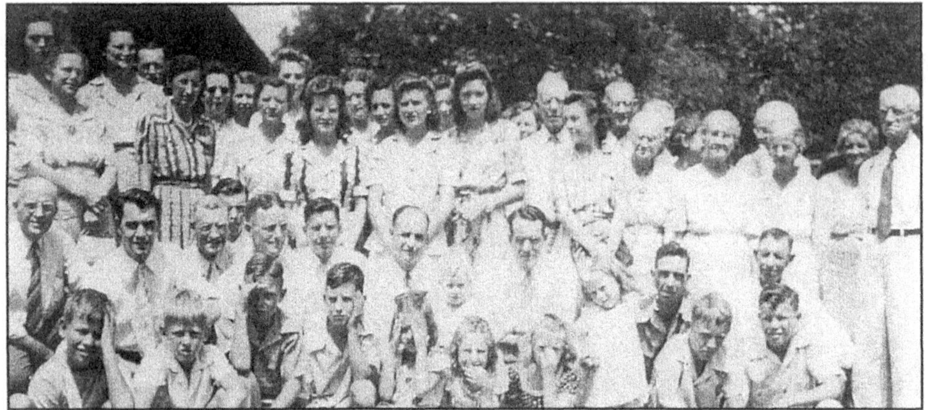

Family reunion of descendants of James S. and Lavonia Boyd Lifsey at the Bluff Springs Camp meeting grounds in 1942. Courtesy of James Adams.

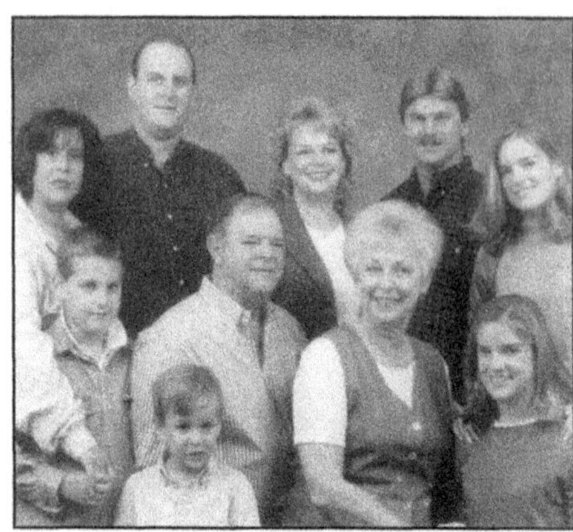

Melvin, Elsie, John, Jaime, Lawrence, Marshall, Jesse, Lisa, Joy and Jessica. Courtesy of Elsie Anderson.

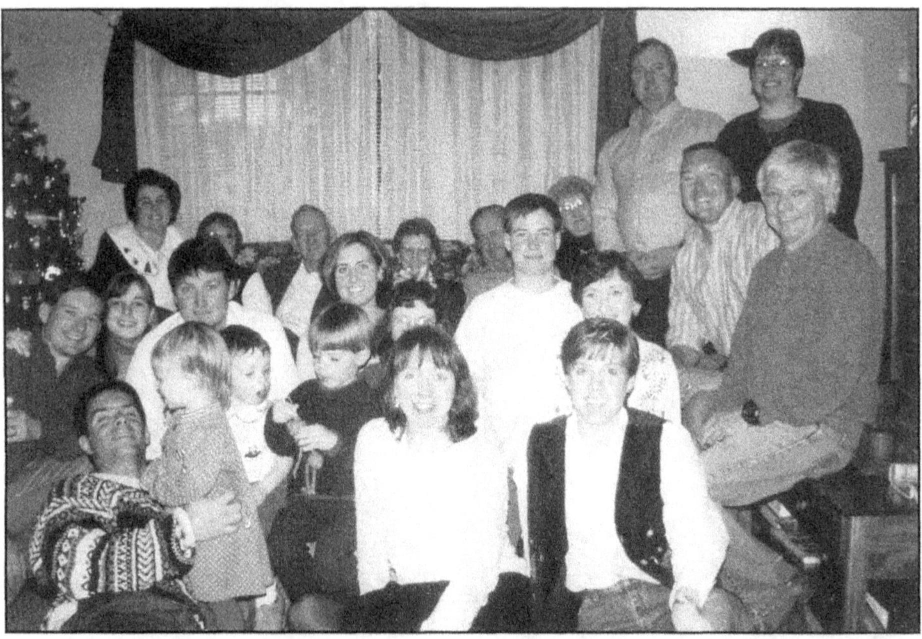

Christmas party of Rosalee King's family at the home of Eric and Wendy Haymans, 1997. Courtesy of Rosalee King.

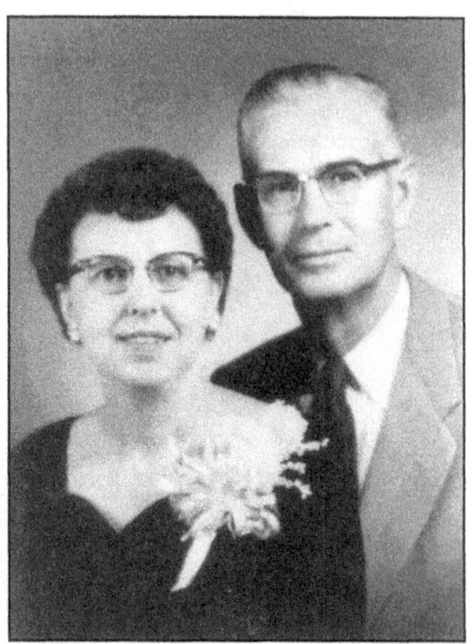

Doris Barker Lawrence and Robert Render Lawrence. Courtesy of Elsie Anderson.

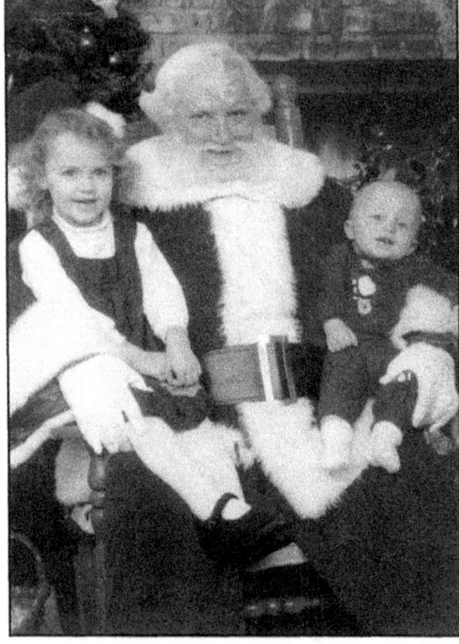

Megan Baker and Alex Evans, 2003. Courtesy of Rosalee King.

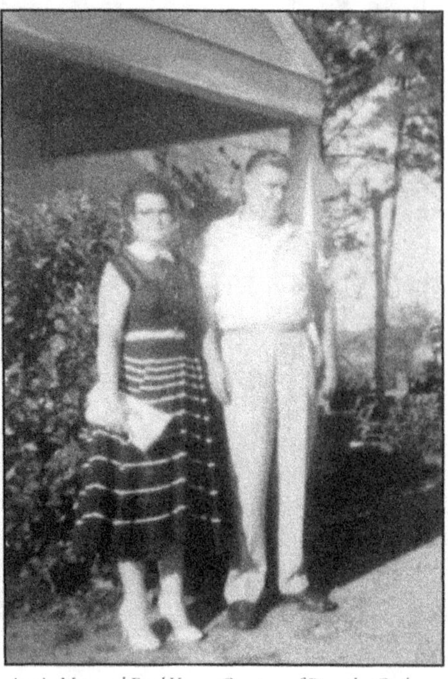

Annie Mae and Paul Yonce. Courtesy of Dorothy Graham.

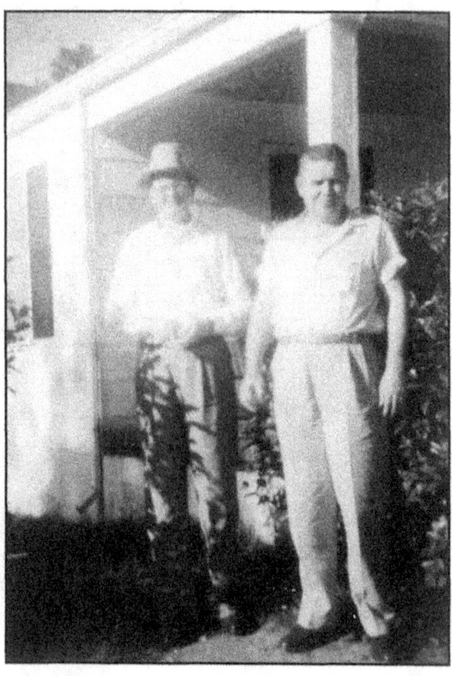

Claud Smith and Paul Yonce. Courtesy of Dorothy Graham.

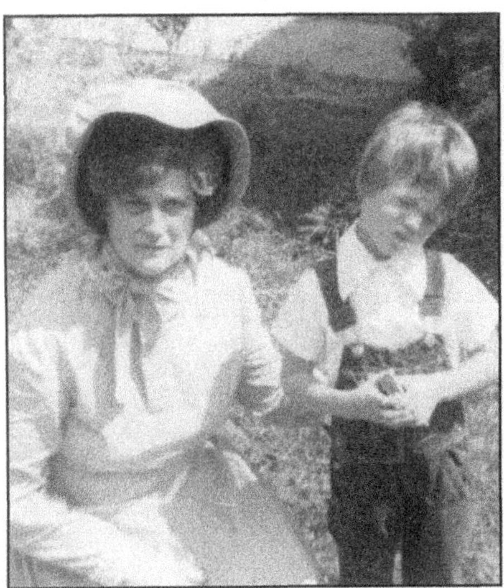

Will and Dorothy Graham, celebrating old fashion day at Mt. Gilead, June 1978. Courtesy of Dorothy Graham.

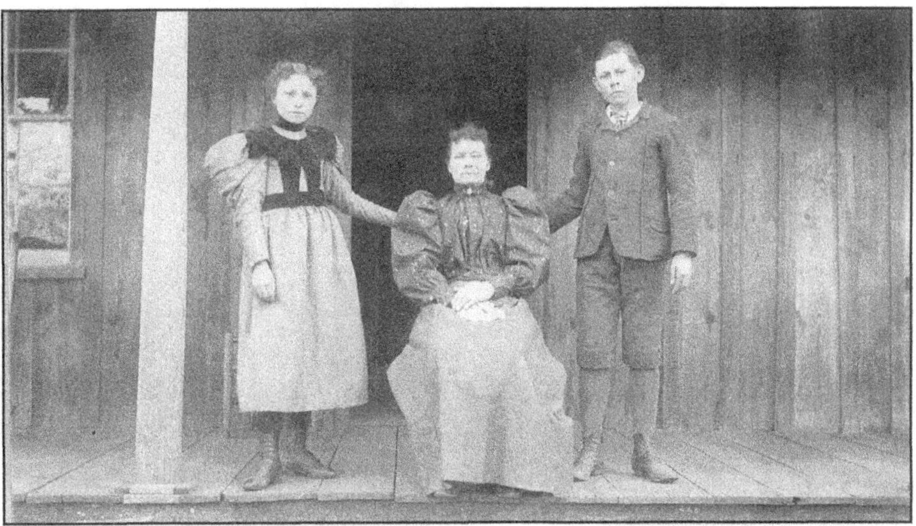

Ivie Bell Pilkenton Owen, Martha Sarah (Sallie) Hamlett Pilkenton and John Thomas Pilkenton, circa 1890's. Courtesy of Fay Pilkenton.

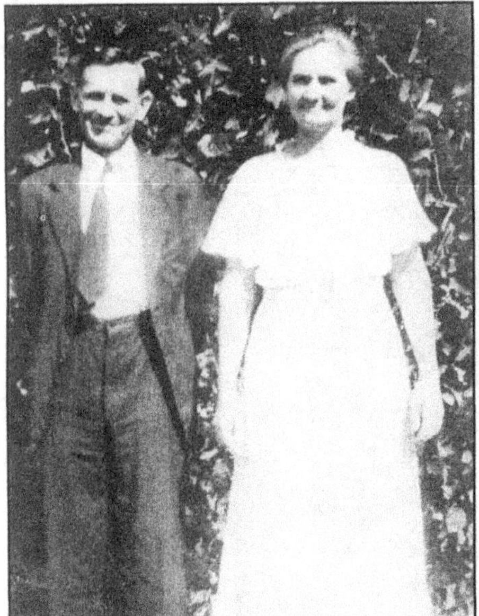

John Thomas and Clenda Pilkenton, circa 1935. Courtesy of Fay Pilkenton.

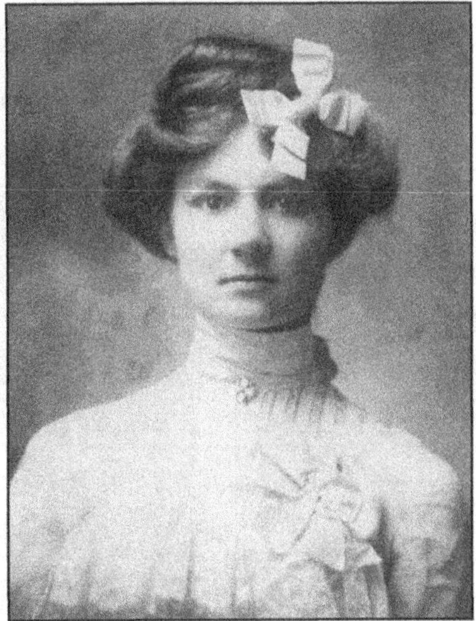

Clenda Lee Pilkenton, circa 1903. Courtesy of Fay Pilkenton.

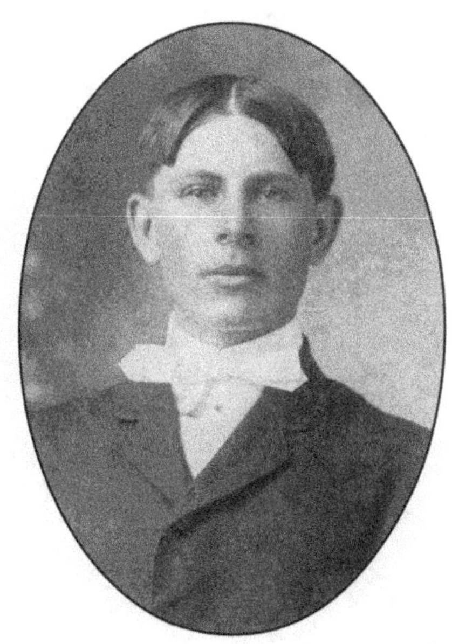

John Thomas Pilkenton, circa 1903. Courtesy of Fay Pilkenton.

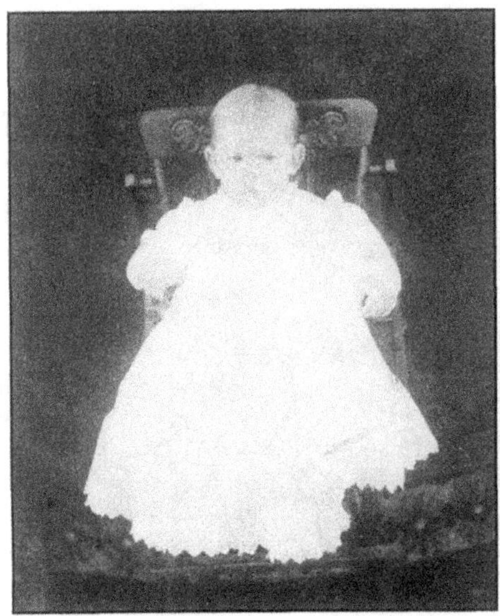

Sara Elizabeth Pilkenton, circa 1908. Courtesy of Fay Pilkenton.

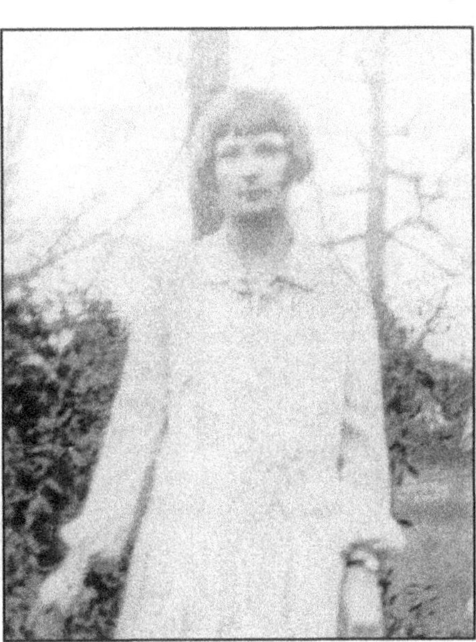

Charlie Reece Smith. Courtesy of Wayne Foster.

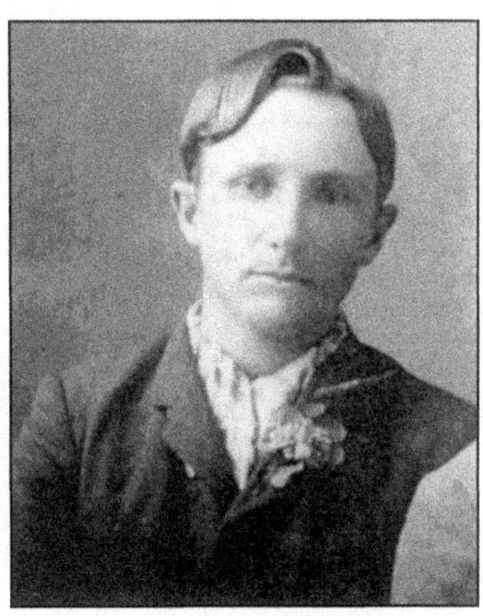

Arra Burkette Smith (1881-1937). Courtesy of Wayne Foster.

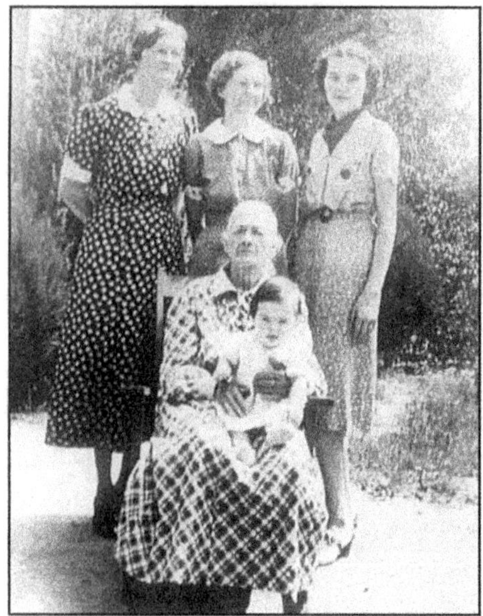

Five generations of the Crawford Family, Concord, GA: Annie Pope Banks Crawford, Lilla Inez Chappel Crawford, Martha Elizabeth Crawford Slade, Martha Emma Jane Cochran Crawrford and Barbara Angeline Slade. Picture was taken July of 1938 in the side yard of the home of Robert C. and Inez Crawford. Courtesy of Barbara Dayhuff.

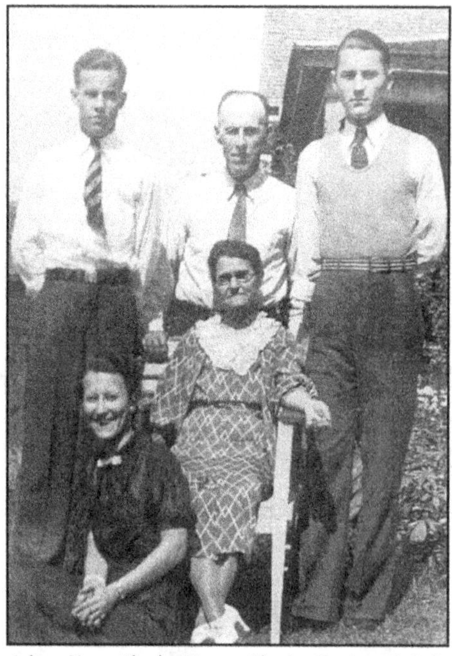

Julian Hoyt, Charles Simon, Charles Gordon, Ophelia Selina "Lena" Adams Slade and Edith Mertine Slade. Courtesy of Barbara Dayhuff.

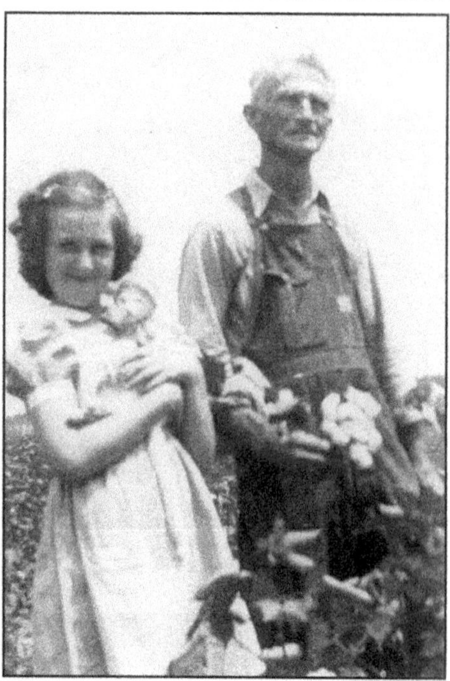

Archer Sylvester Weaver and Martha Johnson. Courtesy of Jeanette Adams.

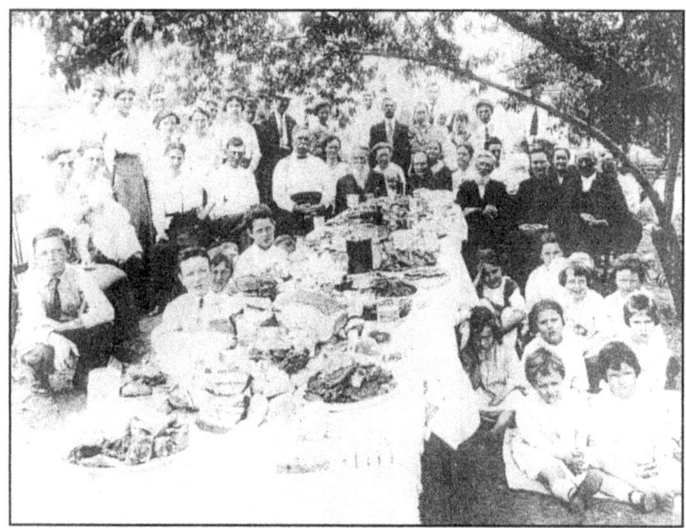

Pennington Reunion, Right side of table left to right: First row: Theresa Wing and Margaret Connell. Second row: Hattie Shell (Whatley), Arvazenia Wilson (Myers) and Eron Brooks (Whatley). Third row: Hattie Belle Wilson (Cash), Lucille Chappell (Nixon), Willie Belle Wing (Herbin) and Hattie Connell (Beaton. Fourth row: Mr. Jim Williams, Sara Elizabeth Pennington Chappell and James B. Chappell. Left side of table (little boys): Front to Back: Tom Connell, Emmett Chappell, Olin Chappell, J.C. Shell and Roy Chappell. Second row: Charlie Chappell, Sadie Pennington (Tingle), Gertrude Chappell (Anderson), Lillian, Annie Chappell (Milner), Ezelle Chappell (Brooks), Estelle Horton (Brooks), Mattie Lizzie Connell, Raymond E. Brooks, Jack Pennington, Nora Pennington, Blanche Pennington (Clark) and Leon Shell. At end of table: Seated: Bunk Pennington, Grandpa H.A. Pennington and Grandma Emily Ingram Sturdivant Pennington. Second row: Luna Pennington, Emma Pennington (Shell), Elizabeth Shell Smith, Dora Sturdivant, Georgia Pennington (huff), Viola Pennington (Connell), Belle Delk Morrison Wing Land and Mr. Wing. Third row: Henry Brooks, Roy Shell, Ida Chappell Bass (Huff), Agnes Huff, Oliver Chappell, Johnny Chappell, Belle Irvin Chappell, Hattie Willie, Lloyd Connell, Julia Chappell (Gardner), Hal Chappell and Alec Connell. Courtesy of Barbara Dayhuff.

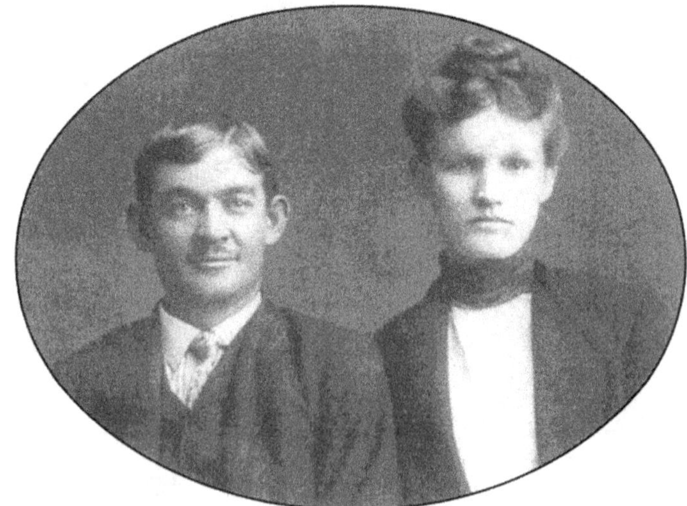

Eddie Montgomery and Martha Emma Jane Cochran Crawford. Courtesy of Barbara Dayhuff.

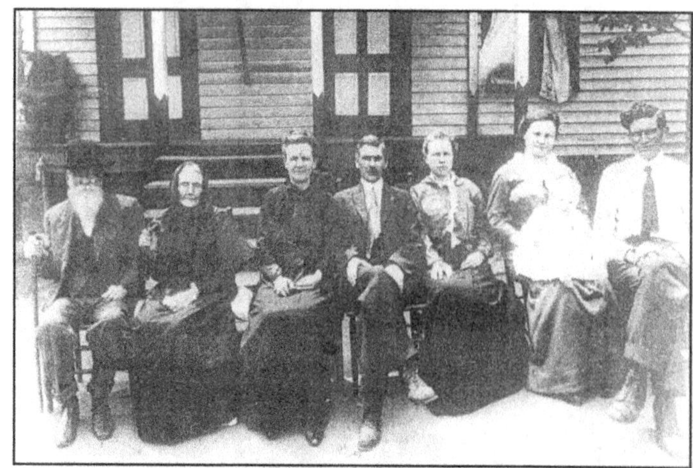

Henry Allen Pennington, Emily Ingram Pennington, Sara Elizabeth Pennington Chappell, John George Chappell, Belle Irving Chappell, Ida Chappell Huff, Agnes Hugg and Bass Huff, 1915. Courtesy of Barbara Dayhuff.

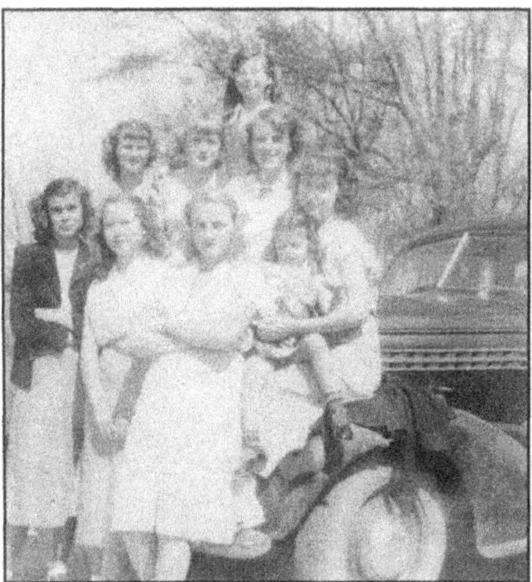

Faye Allen, Jackie Allen and Jeanette Allen, others unknown. Courtesy of Jeanette Adams.

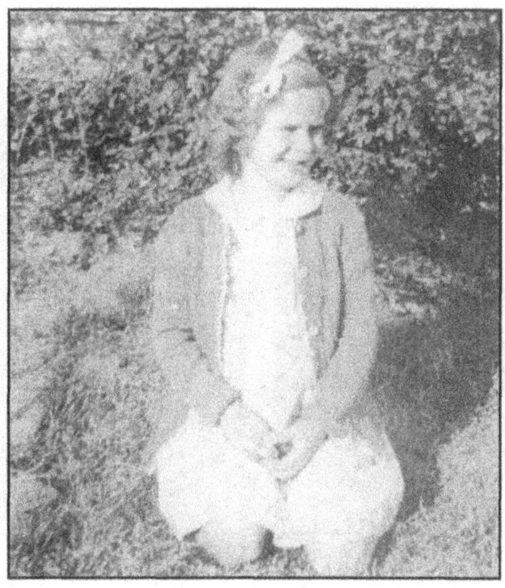

Jeanette Allen. Courtesy of Jeanette Adams.

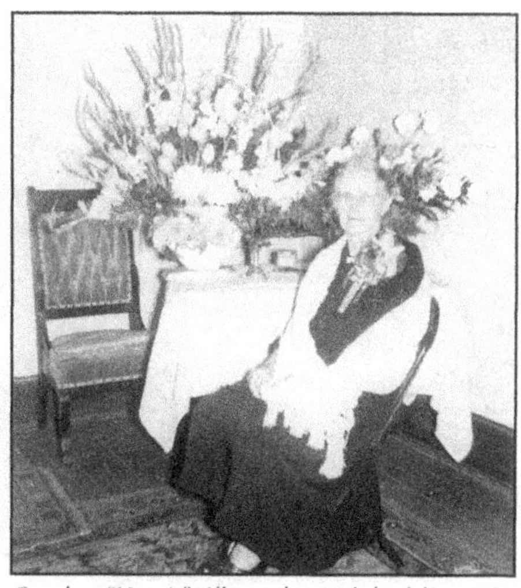

Grandma "Nannie" Allen at her 80th birthday, 1960. Courtesy of Jeanette Adams.

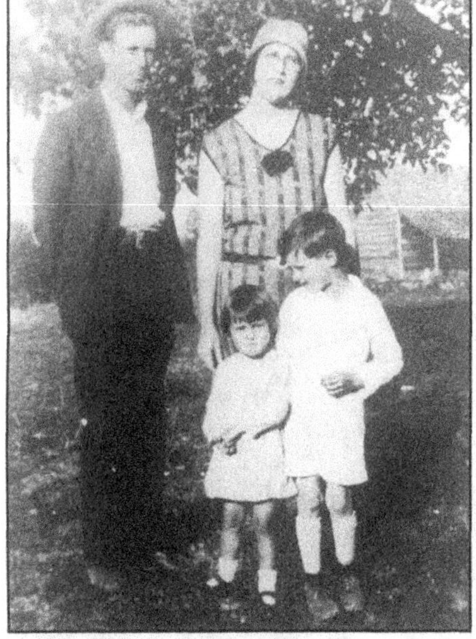

Charles (C.B.) Allen, Elizabeth Leone Weaver Allen, Elizabeth Rebecca Allen and Robert S. Allen, circa 1930. Courtesy of Robert Allen.

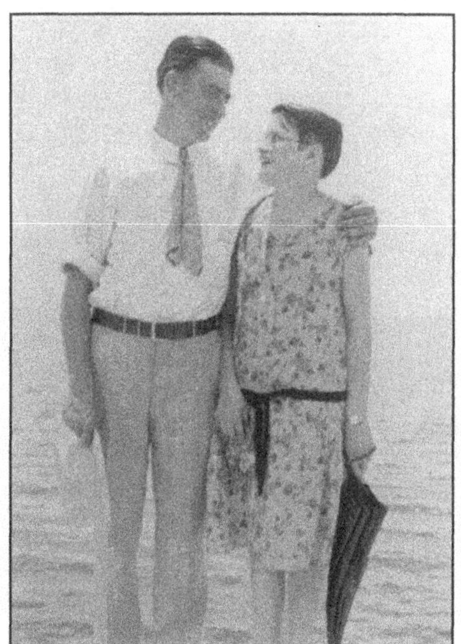

Rev. I.G. Johnson (1904-2001) and Mary E. Weaver Johnson (1909-1985). Courtesy of Robert Allen.

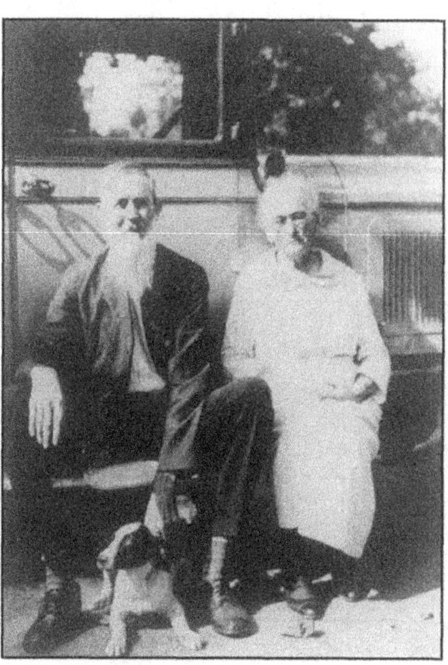

Rufus Alonza Buchanan (1853-1934) and Mary Ella Wood Buchanan (1859-1939). Courtesy of Robert Allen.

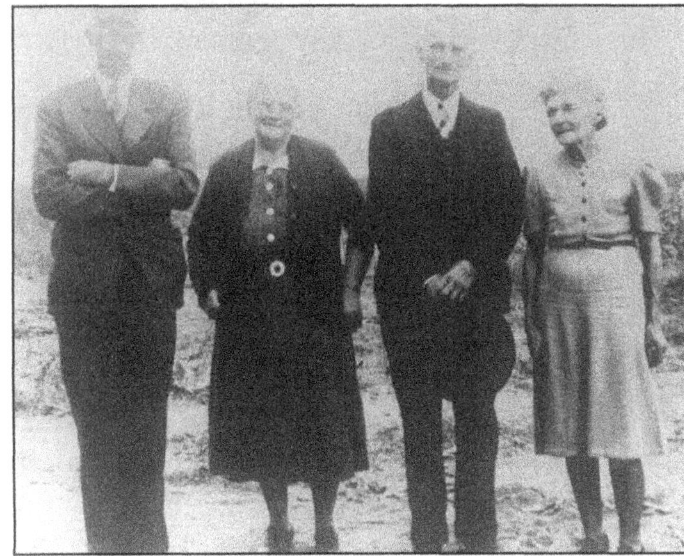

Eugene Franklin Weaver, Sophie Weaver Murphy, Archer S. Weaver and Della Weaver Ridley. Courtesy of Robert Allen.

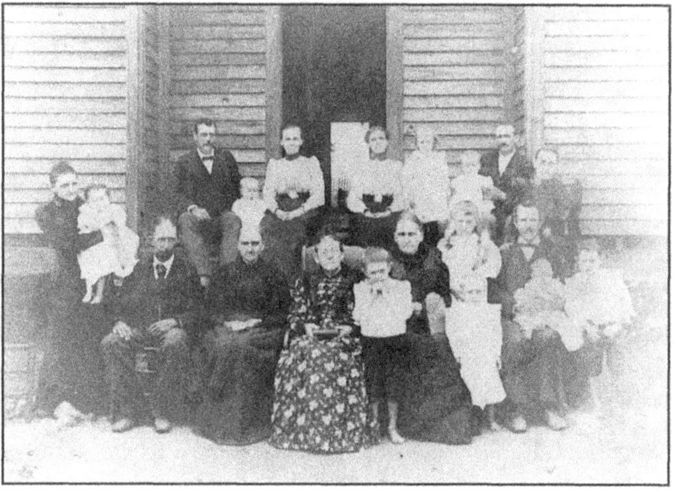

Front row: Mattie Maddox, Mary Cathy Maddox, Johnny Maddox, Martha Conner, Lesa Harp, Curtis W. Allen, Sallie Conner, Lena Allen, Thomas Marcellus Allen, Mary Elizabeth Allen, John Allen and Fitz Allen. Back row: George Allen, Collier Allen, Lilly Allen, Nannie Y. Allen, Lillian Allen, Clinton Allen, Robert L. Allen and Annie Victoria Allen. Courtesy of Robert Allen.

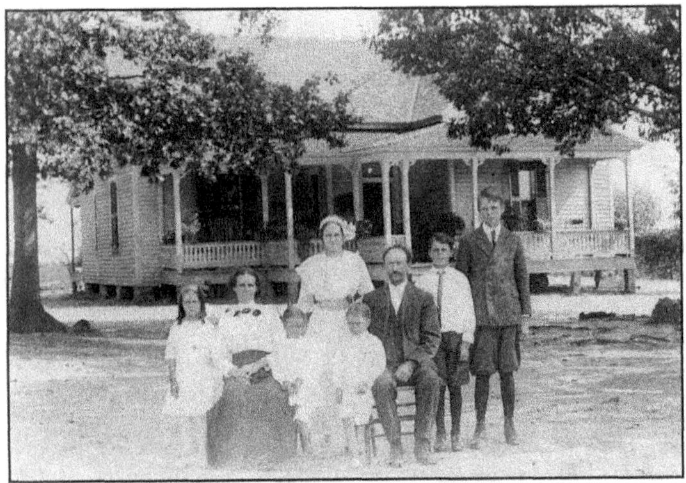

Mary Susie Allen, Nannie Yarbrough Allen, Lillian Lee Allen, Robert Lee Allen, Charles B. Allen, Jessie Clinton Allen, Thomas Lee Allen and William Douglas Allen, circa 1911. Courtesy of Robert Allen.

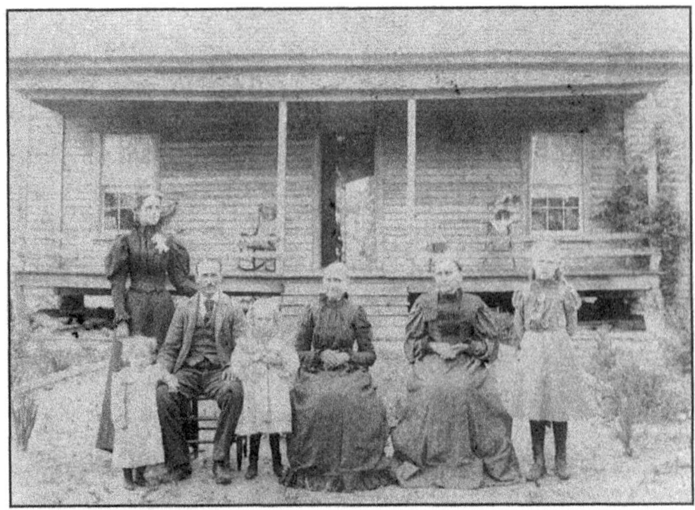

Nannie Yarbrough Allen, Robert Lee Allen, Martha Conner, Sallie Conner, Jessie Clinton Allen, Lillian Lee Allen and Lena Allen. Courtesy of Robert Allen.

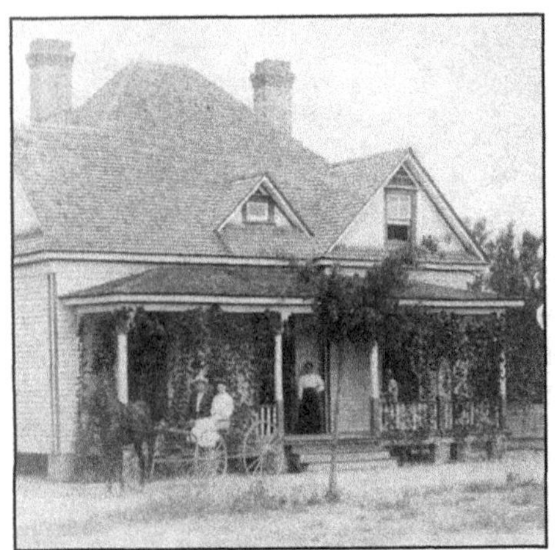

Ivie Bell Pilkenton and Cole Owen in buggy and Mrs. Sallie Pilkenton by front door. Ivie and Cole Owen owned and ran the Owen Hotel in Concord, GA, circa 1908. Courtesy of Fay Pilkenton.

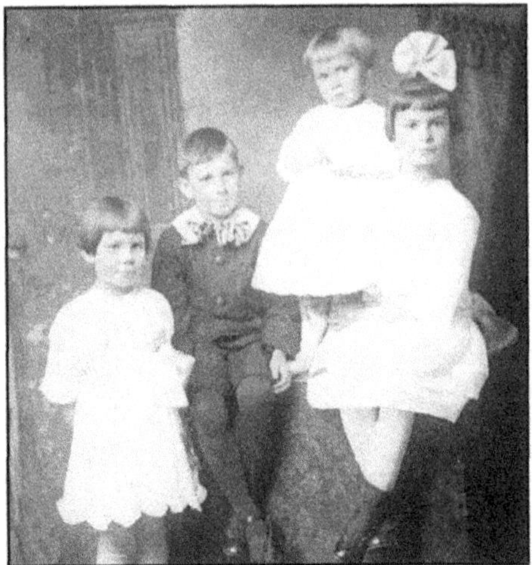

Nelle Pilkenton Presley, Thomas Pilkenton, Fay Pilkenton and Elizabeth Pilkenton, circa 1915. Courtesy of Fay Pilkenton.

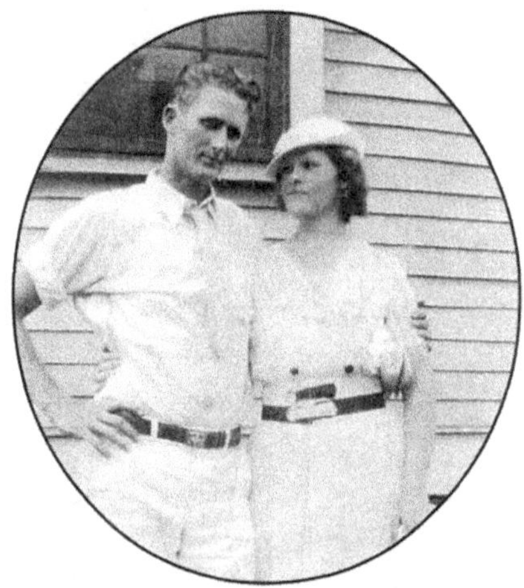

James Alton Foster and Ella Mae Cauthen. Married in Pike County June 16, 1934. James is the son of Richard and Lula Foster and Ella Mae is the daughter of W.D. and Ella H. Cauthen. Courtesy of Wayne Foster.

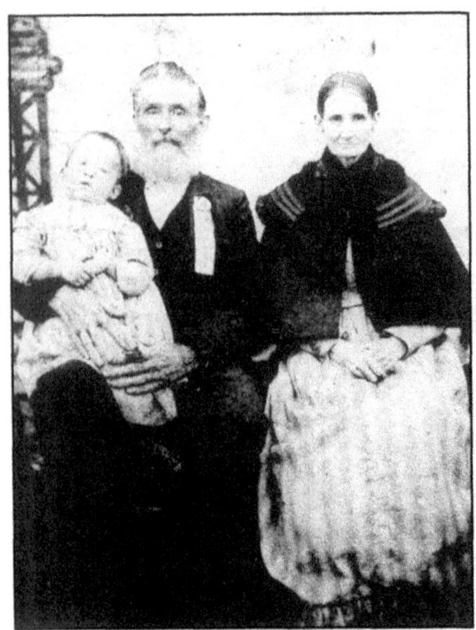

Burrell Jefferson Foster and Easter Ameliar Hagan Foster, 1896. Courtesy of Wayne Foster.

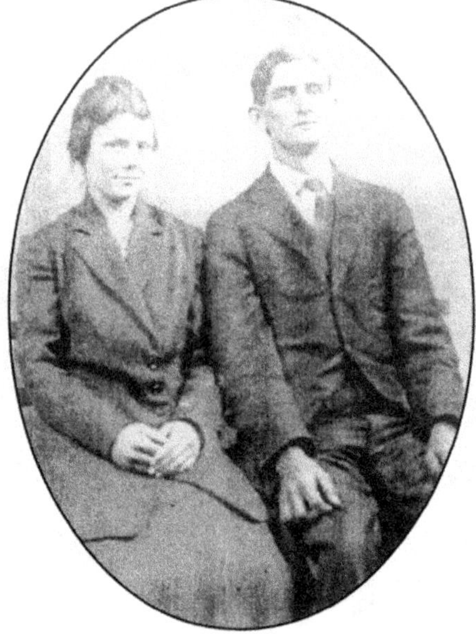

Maybelle Hamlett and Homer Foster. Courtesy of Wayne Foster.

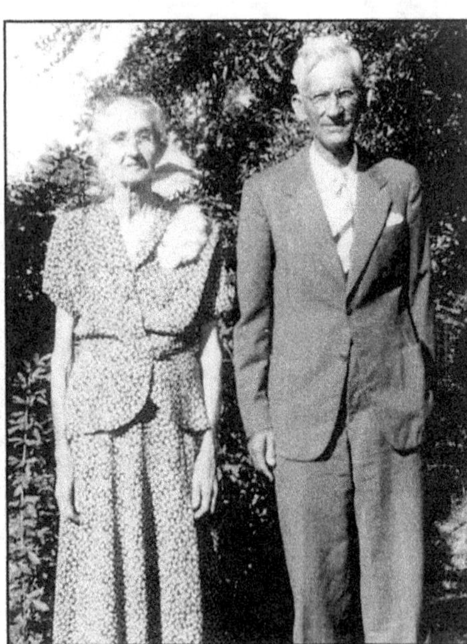

Fannie Ada Foster and Charles Floyd Langford. Courtesy of Wayne Foster.

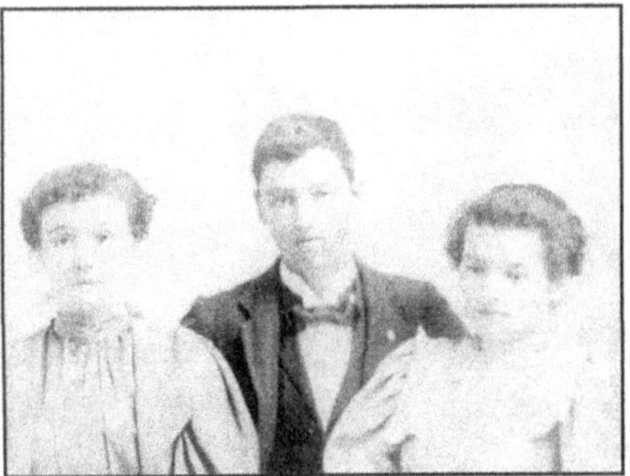

Rebecca Adella Foster, Charles F. Graham and Carrie Foster. Courtesy of Wayne Foster.

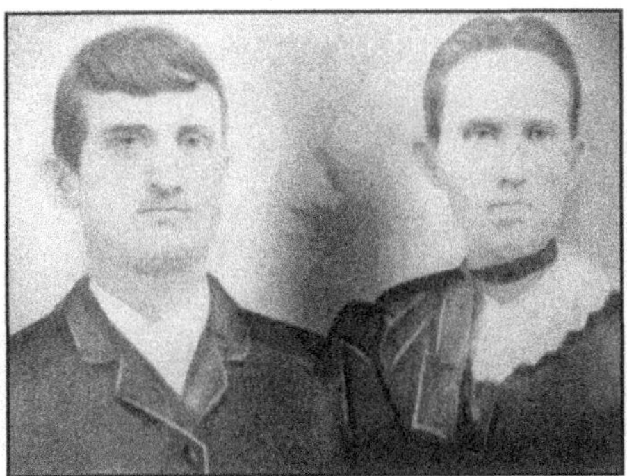

Thomas Jefferson Foster and Arizona Texas (Arrie) Brannon. Courtesy of Wayne Foster.

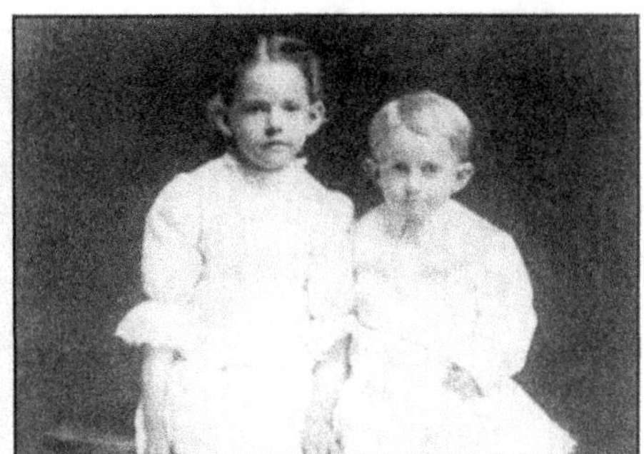

Birdie Mae and John Wilfred Cauthen, children of Jay and Emma Susan Cauthen, circa 1910. Courtesy of Wayne Foster.

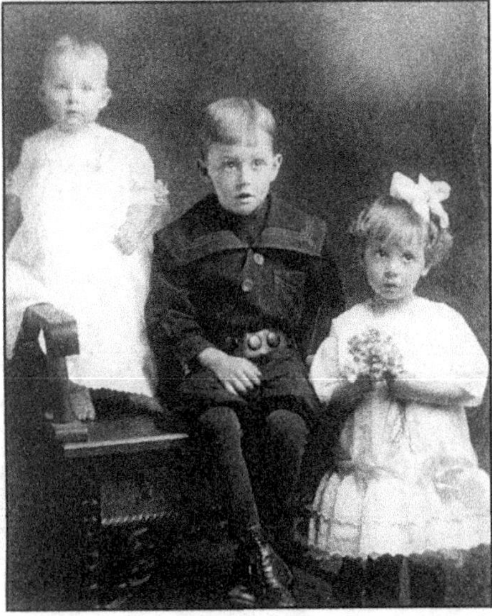

Ella Mae, Alvin and Emma Sue Cauthen, circa 1916. Courtesy of Wayne Foster.

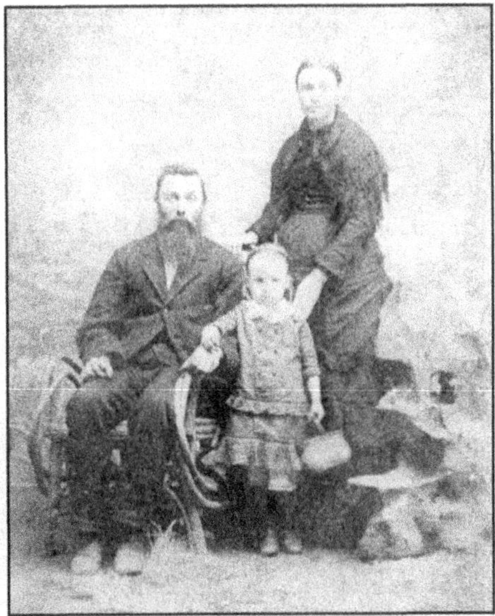

Henry Clay Harris and Susan R. Harris with daughter Ella Revachus Harris, about 1885. Courtesy of Wayne Foster.

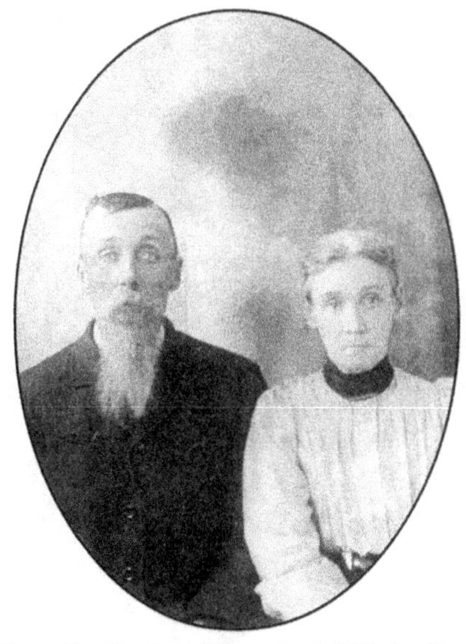

Henry Clay Harris and Susan Randall Harden Harris. Courtesy of Wayne Foster.

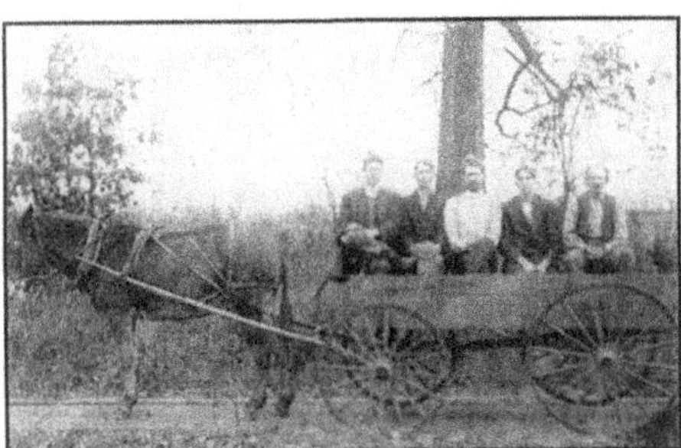

The Cauthen Family: Emma Sue, William Dennis Sr., Alvin, William Dennis Jr., Ella, Ruth and Ella Mae. Courtesy of Wayne Foster.

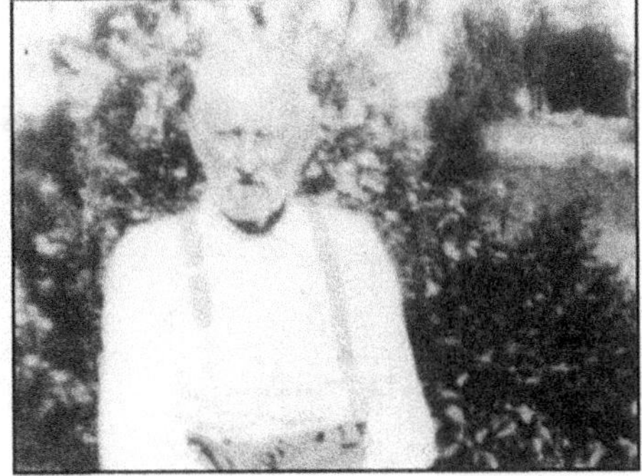

Wesley Franklin Brannon. Courtesy of Wayne Foster.

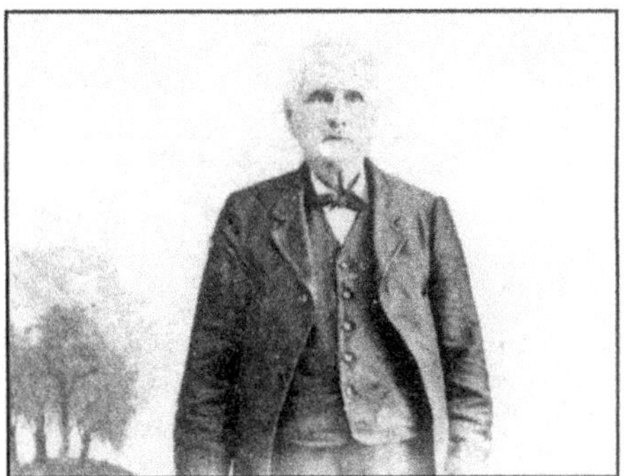

Rev. John Wesley Brannon. Courtesy of Wayne Foster.

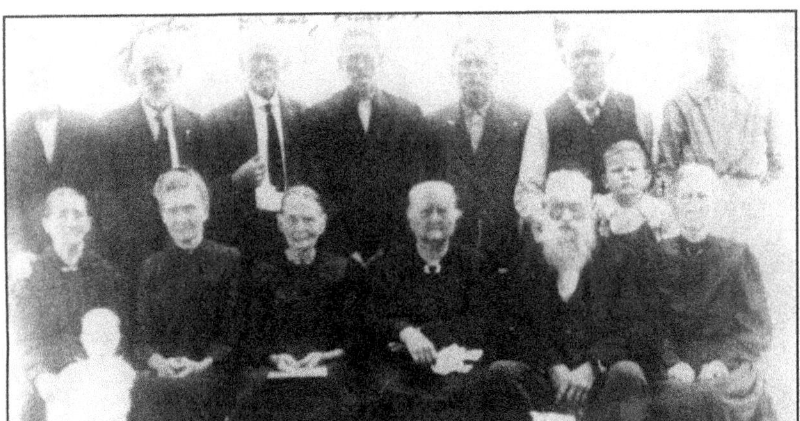

Children of John Wesley Brannon and Mary Aldine Gurffin: Back row: Thomas Caswell, John Wesley Jr., Wesley Franklin, Lambert H., Gilbert L., Robert Lee, Alice B. Stewart and Robert Edward Stewart. Front row: Martha Willingham Brannon, Martha, Edith Lifsey Brannon, Georgia Ann B. Jimmerson, Mary W. Holland, Alfred F. and Louisa Frances Brannon. Picture taken in 1915. Courtesy of Wayne Foster.

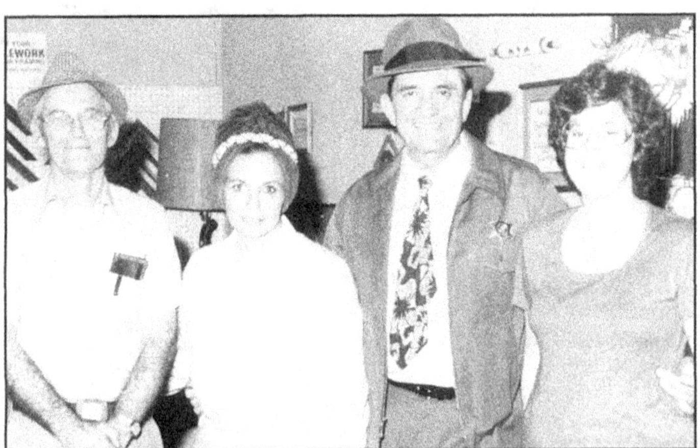

Emory Pasley, June Carter, Johnny Cash and Carol Pasley Spinks. Courtesy of Rachel McClelland.

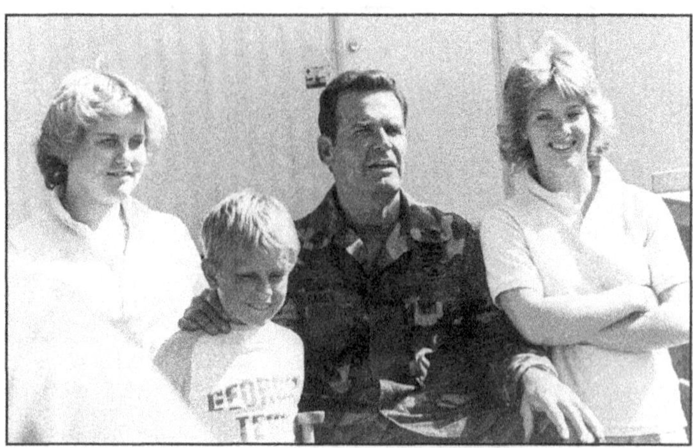

Meg Crane Underwood with James Garner and others unknown. Courtesy of Rachel McClelland.

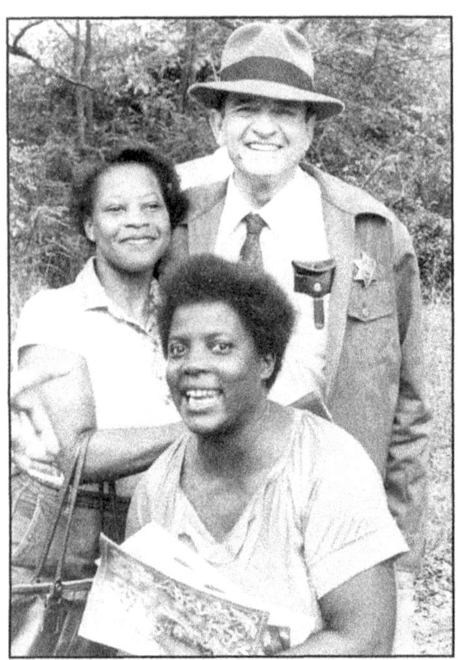

Joann Tucker with Johnny Cash. Courtesy of Rachel McClelland

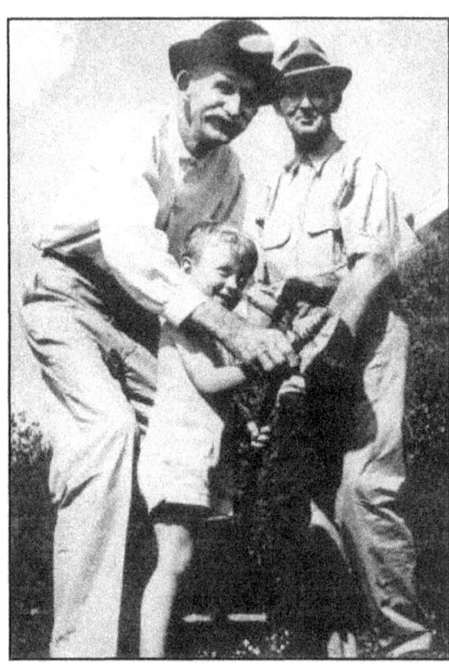

Will C. Norris, W. Holloway Norris and George C. Norris. Courtesy of Rachel McClelland.

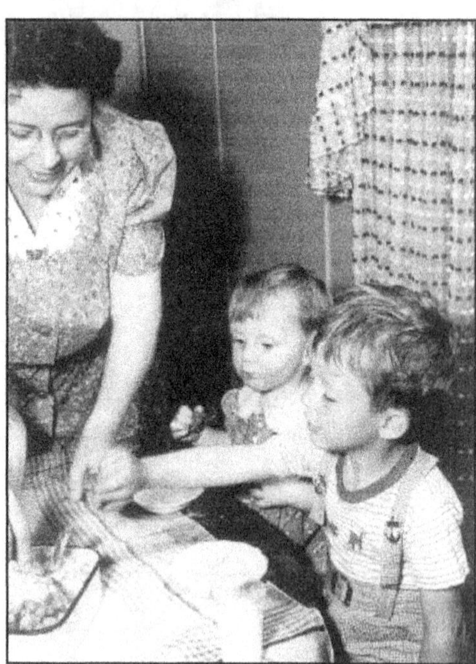

Mrs. Ruth Norris serves a meal to Rachel Norris McClelland and George Norris. Courtesy of Rachel McClelland.

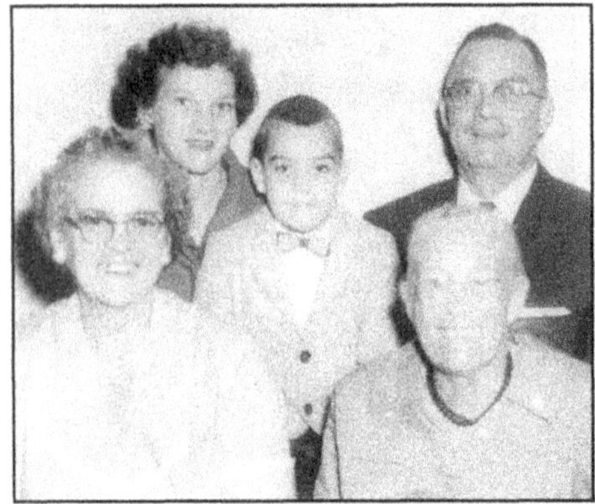

Five Generations: Anna Bevil Harris, Ethel Harris Mullins, Frank Mullins, Joann Mullins Trice and Blake Trice. Courtesy of Rachel Shaw.

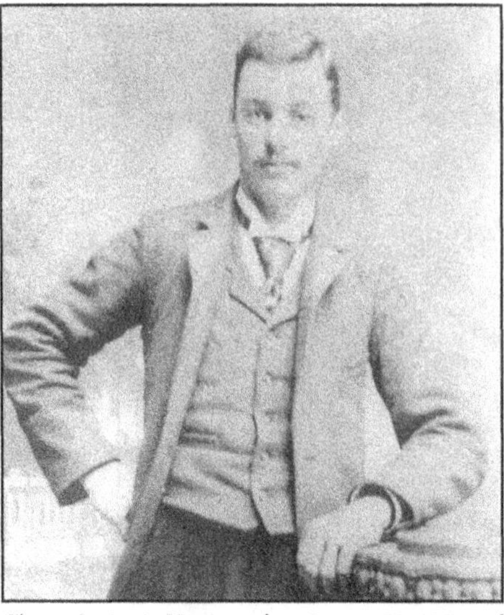

Thomas Benjamin Harris was born January 23, 1870 and died November 18, 1936. He was the son of Henry Clay and Susan Randall (Harden) Harris. Courtesy of Rachel Shaw.

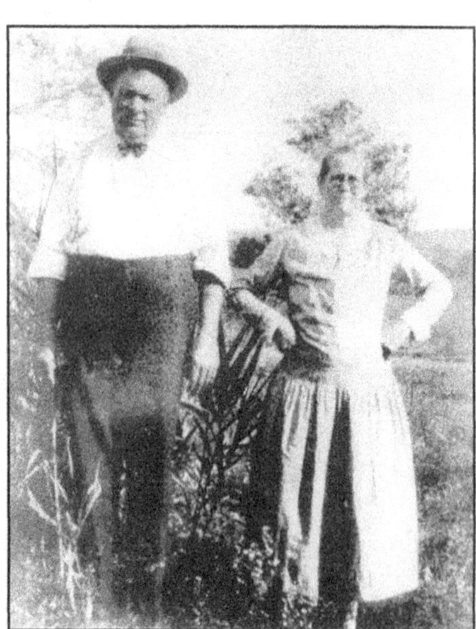

Thomas Benjamin Harris and Anna Bevil Harris. Courtesy of Rachel Shaw.

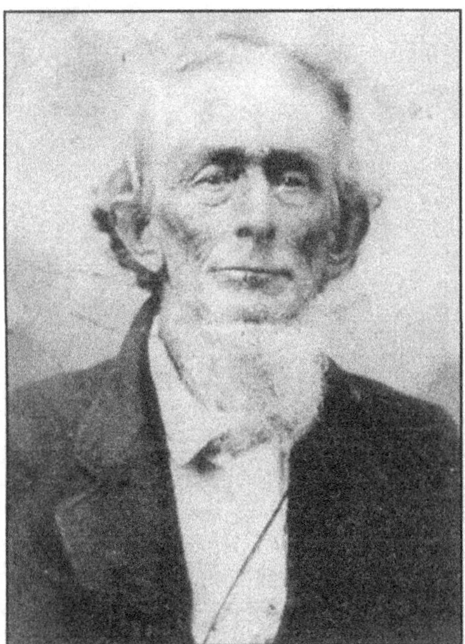

Levi Elliott. Courtesy of Jane Gaulding.

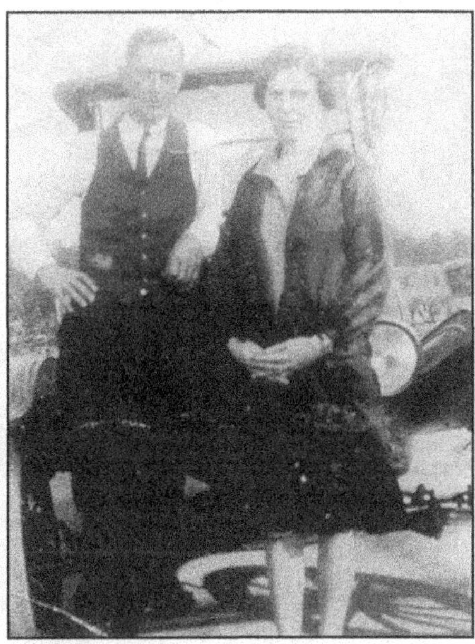

Bill and Lula Elliott standing in front of their Model T Ford in 1926 or 1927. Courtesy of Jane Gaulding.

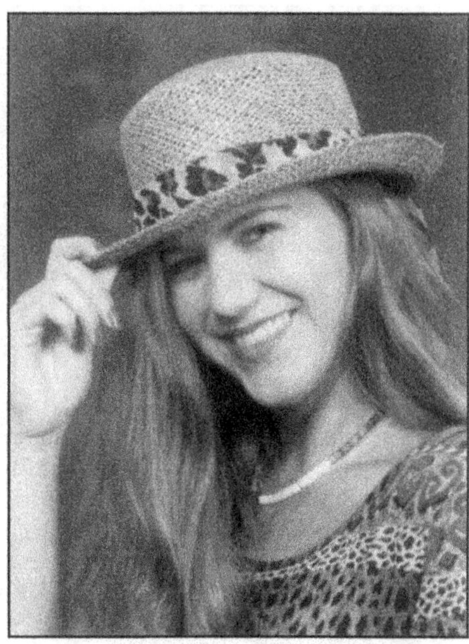

Amanda Hollar, Pike County Historical Society Secretary. Courtesy of Tom Morton.

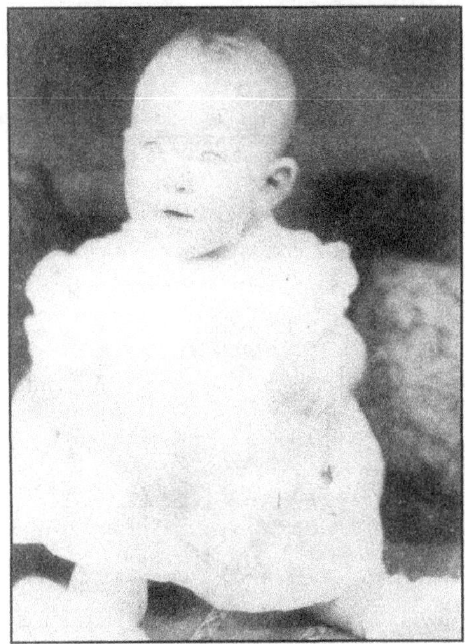

Sue Elliott (1937-1986). Courtesy of Jane Gaulding.

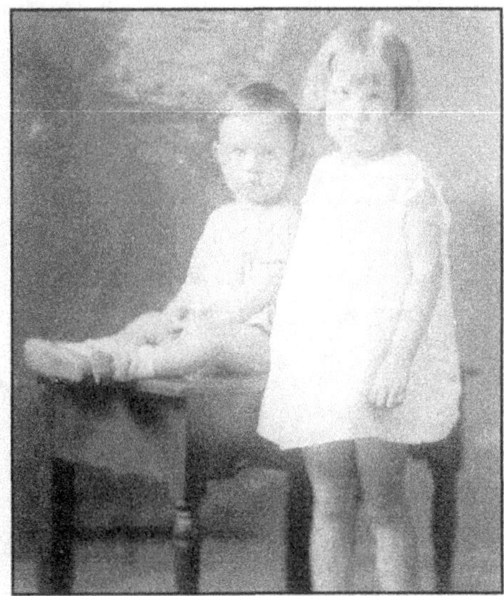

Standing: Jewell Willene Elliott, born Dec. 16, 1925, second child of William Robert "Bill" and Lula Elliott. Sitting: Wilbur Collins Elliott, born June 18, 1929, died Sept. 13, 1996, third child of Bill and Lula Elliott. Courtesy of Jane Gaulding.

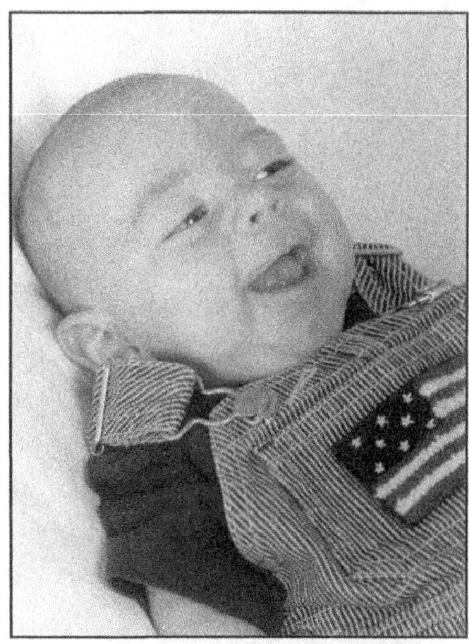

Thomas Blake Morton, one of Pike County's future citizens. Courtesy of Tom Morton.

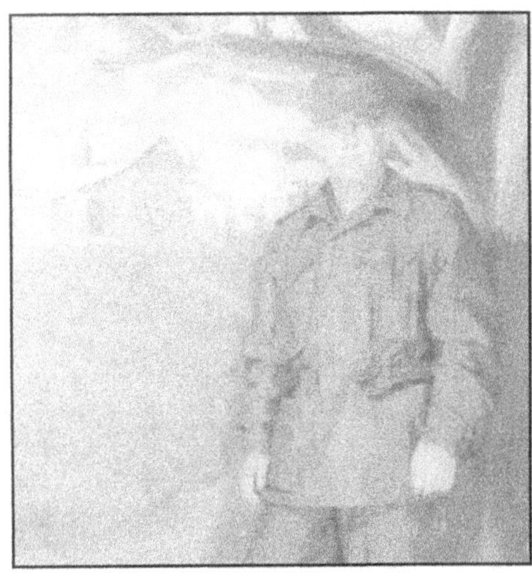

James Robert "Jimmy" Elliott (1935-1973). Courtesy of Jane Gaulding.

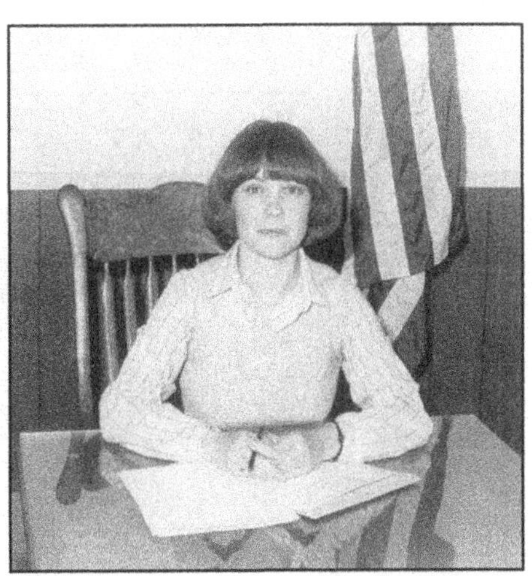

Joanna Gilmore Angle, first woman elected to Pike County Board Commissioners. Courtesy of Rachel McClelland.

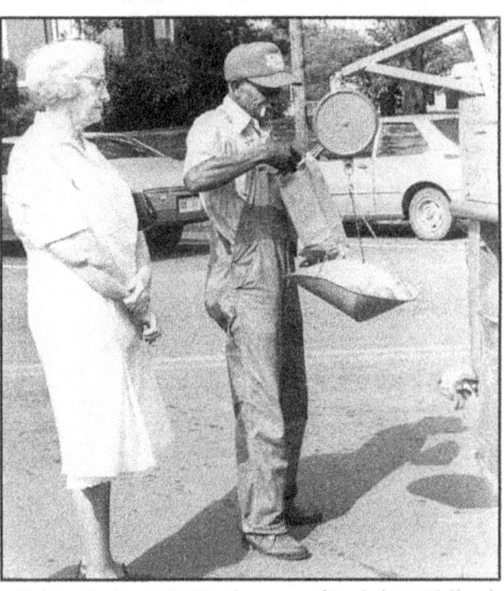

Calvin Hudson, 1970's. Courtesy of Rachel McClelland.

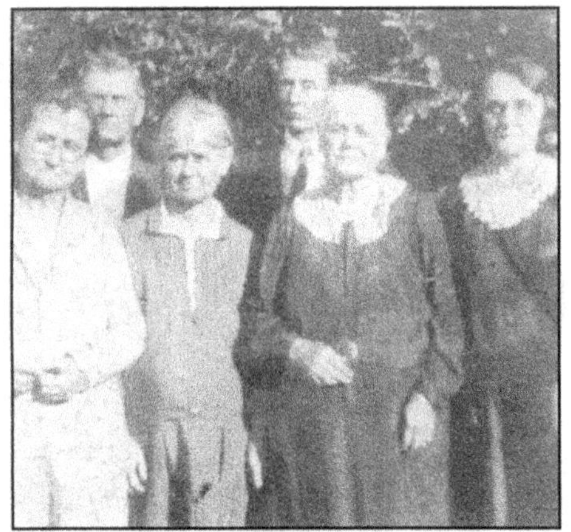
Ophelia (Floyd) Bush, Warren Webster Bush, Eudora "Dora" (Bush) Elliott, William P. Bush, Elizabeth "Lizzie" (Bush) Trice Scarbrough and Emma (McDaniel) Bush. Courtesy of Jane Gaulding.

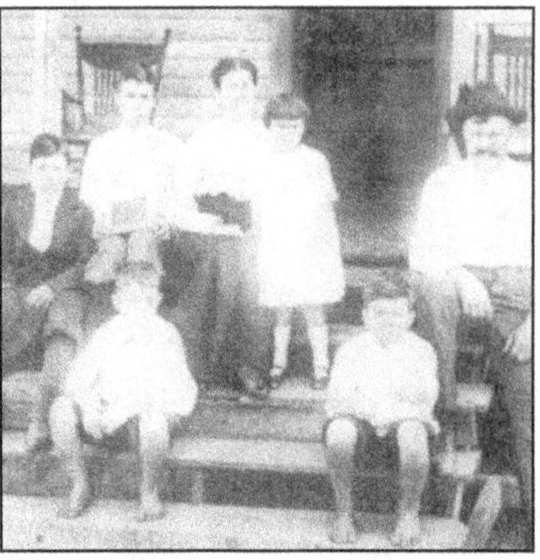
Trice Family: James Herbert Trice, Maude (Cooper) Trice, Olin, Curtis, Raymond, Emory and Evelyn. Courtesy of Jane Gaulding.

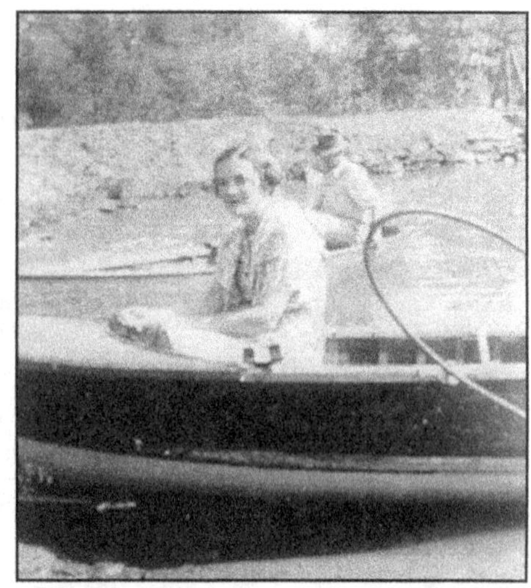
Sarah Margaret Howard. Courtesy of Jane Gaulding.

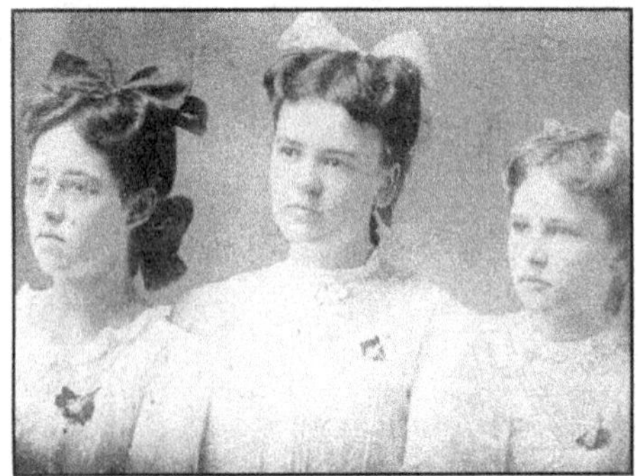
Alma Bush, Annie Lou Cannafax and Bessie Weaver. Courtesy of Jane Gaulding.

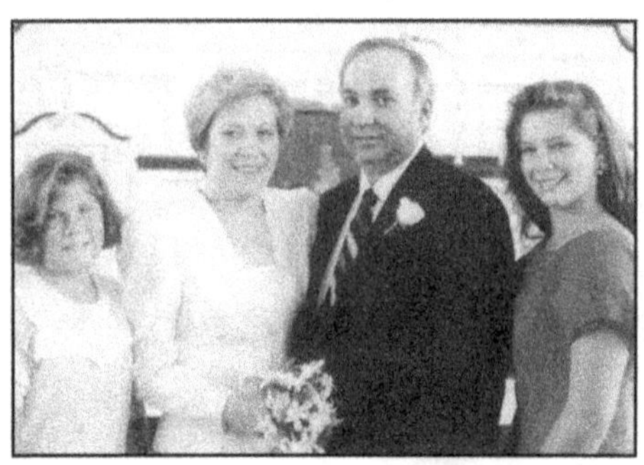
Charles Barker Gaulding, Deborah "Debbie" Sandison Hammontree Gaulding, Sandi Hammontree and Beth Hammontree, 1990. Courtesy of Jane Gaulding.

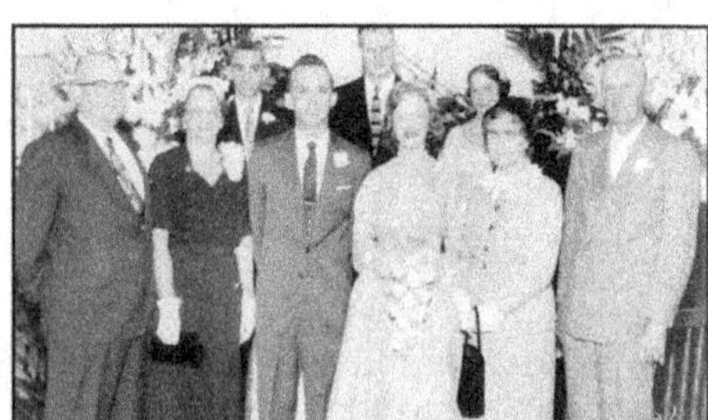
Wedding of Jimmy Gaulding and Jane Elliott, Oct. 23, 1956. Pictured left to right front row: John Ray, Vera, Jimmy Gaulding, Jane Elliott, Lula Elliot and Bill Elliott. Back row: Charles Gaulding, Rev. Charles Betts and Dora "Dodie" Hawkins. Courtesy of Jane Gaulding.

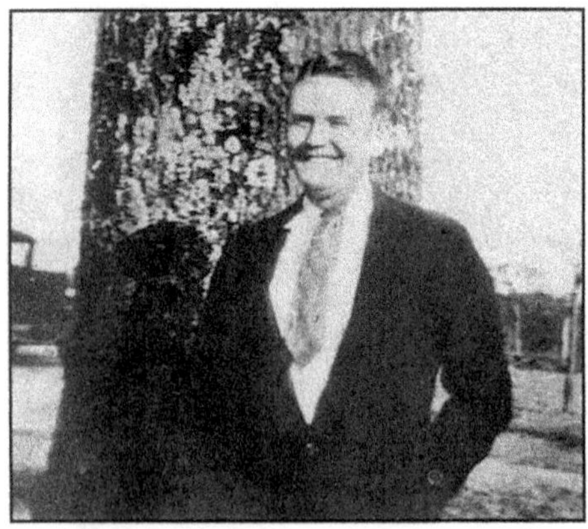
John Ray Gaulding (1903-1969). Courtesy of Jane Gaulding.

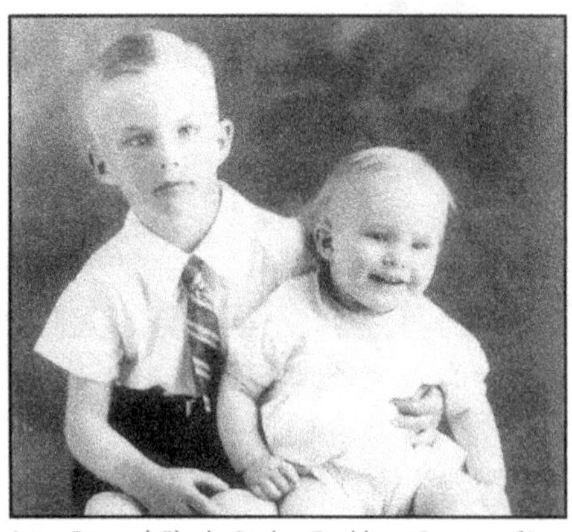
James Ray and Charles Barker Gaulding. Courtesy of Jane Gaulding.

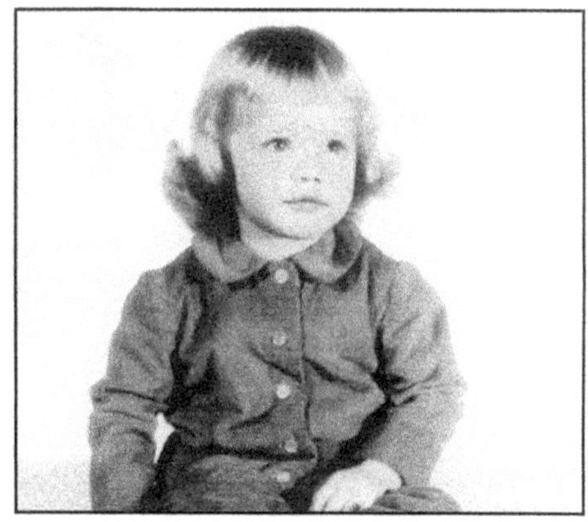
Melinda "Joy" Gaulding, born Dec. 27, 1957, picture taken in 1960. Courtesy of Jane Gaulding.

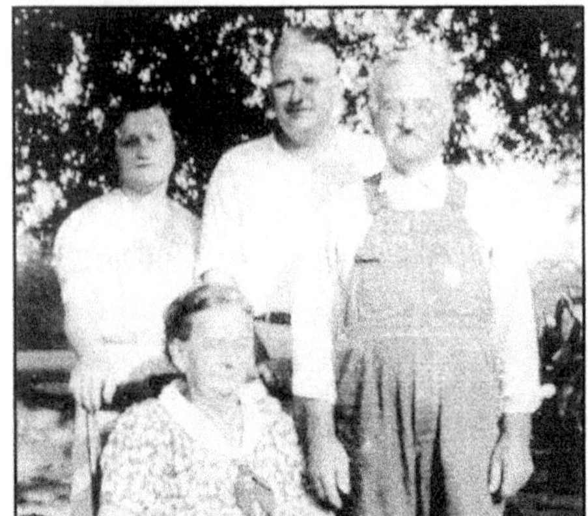
Madge, John Ray, Nettie Gaulding and Rhea Gaulding. Courtesy of Jane Gaulding.

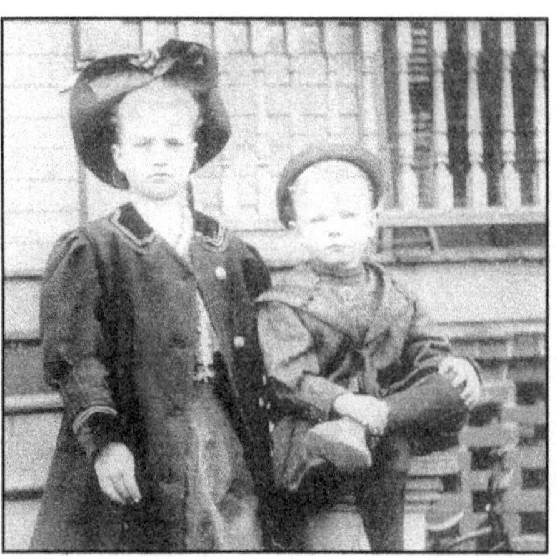
Madge and John Ray Gaulding. Courtesy of Jane Gaulding.

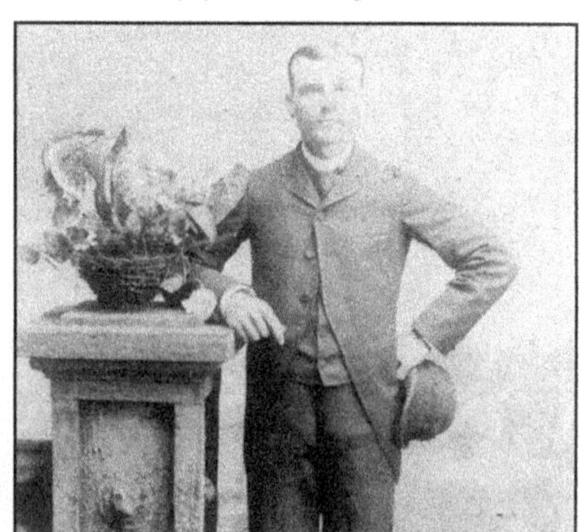
Elias Rhea Gaulding (1868-1948). Courtesy of Jane Gaulding.

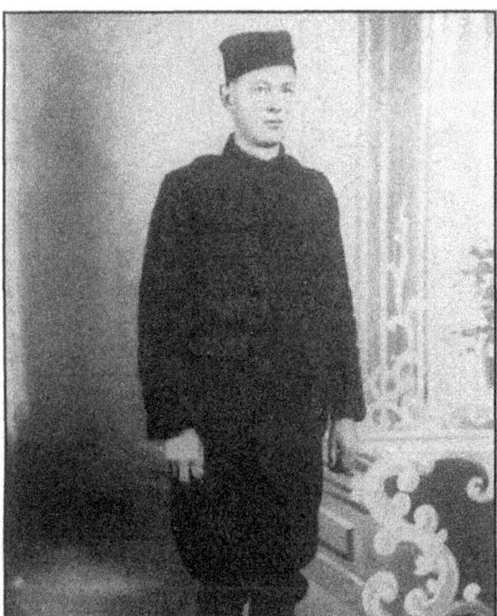

William Robert "Bill" Elliott (1893-1985). Courtesy of Jane Gaulding.

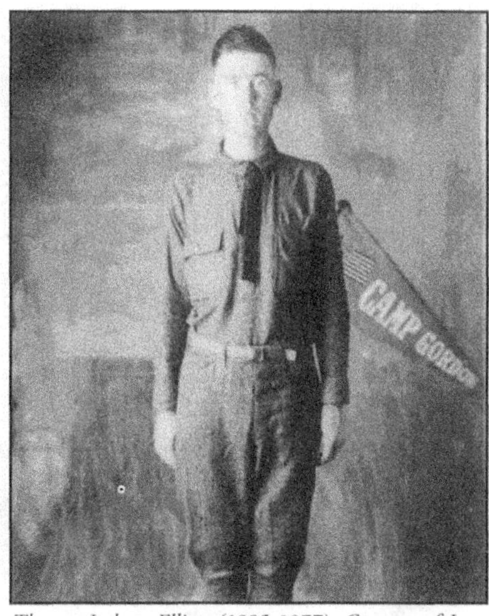

Thomas Jackson Elliott (1895-1977). Courtesy of Jane Gaulding.

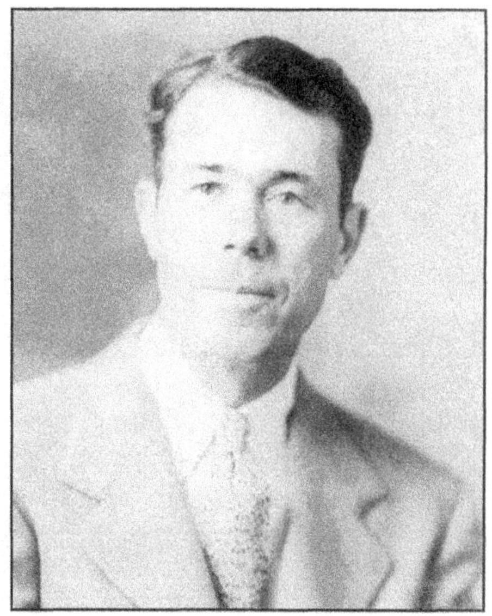

Douglas Boyd Elliott (1899-1996). Courtesy of Jane Gaulding.

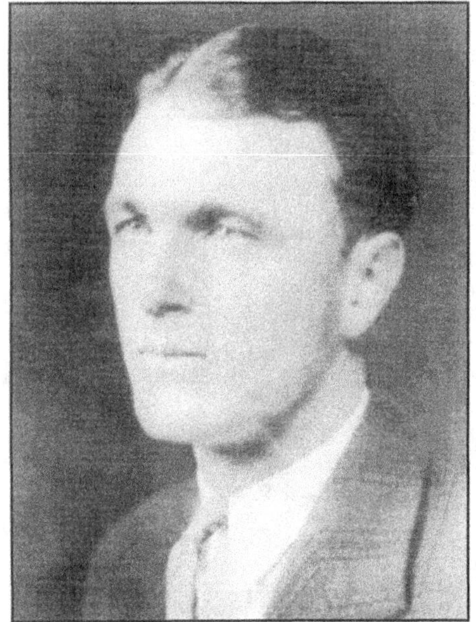

Warren Clark Elliott (1901-1969). Courtesy of Jane Gaulding.

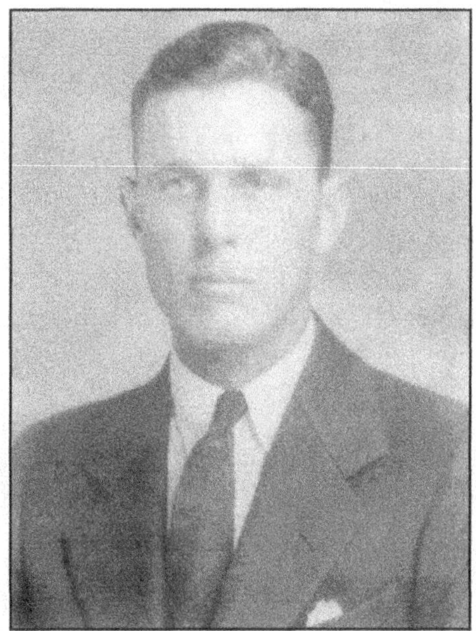

Jones Robins Elliott (1902-1961). Courtesy of Jane Gaulding.

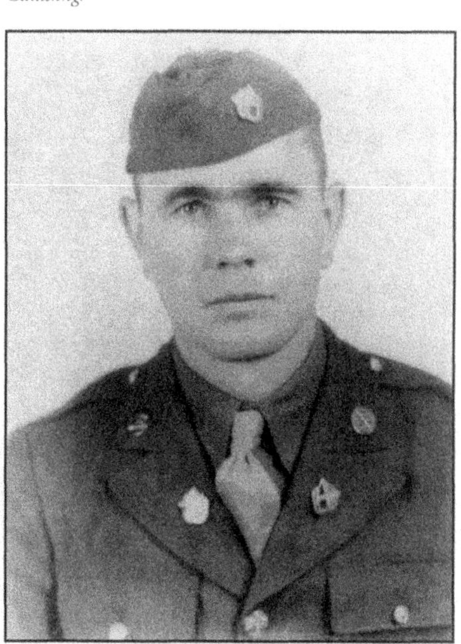

Jesse England "Bully" Elliott (1910-1992). Courtesy of Jane Gaulding.

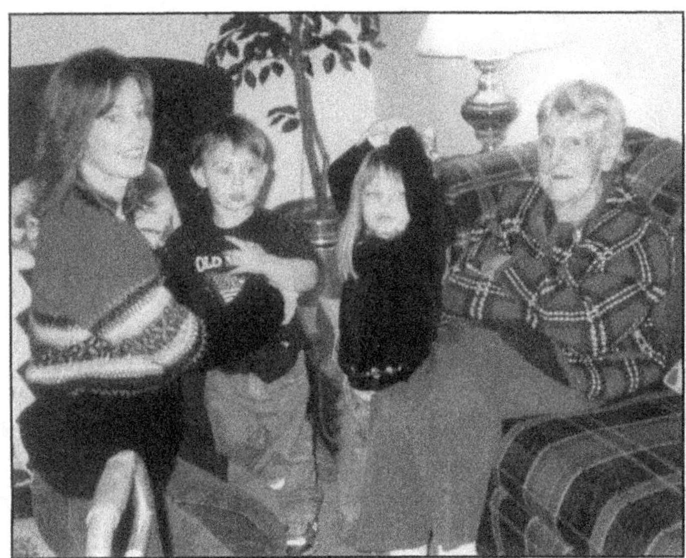

Mattie Lucy Elliott, Gay Osbolt, Zach Osbolt and Carlee Banks. Courtesy of Jane Gaulding.

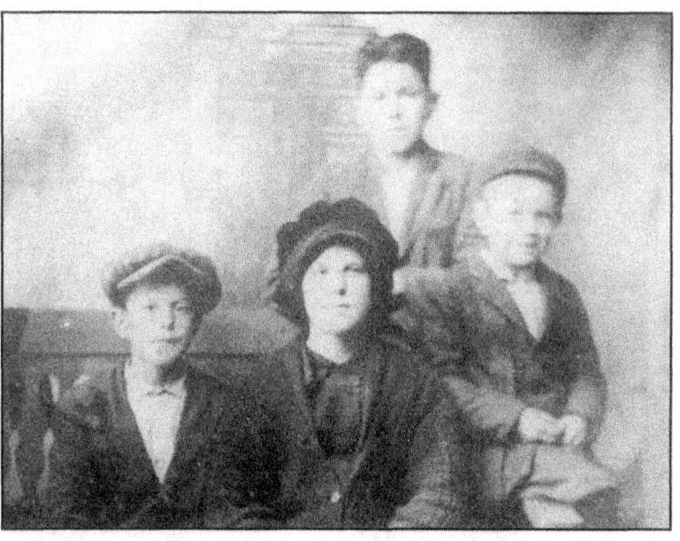

Four of the Elliott children around 1916-1917: Marion, Lucy, Jones and England "Bully" Elliott. Courtesy of Jane Gaulding.

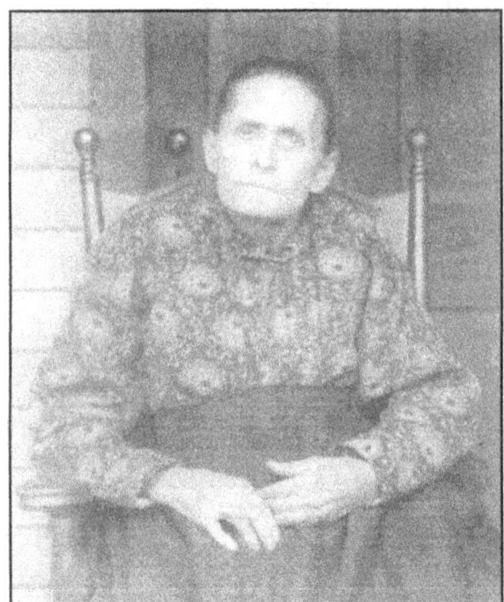
Judy Teressa (Capel) Barker (1842-1900). Courtesy of Jane Gaulding.

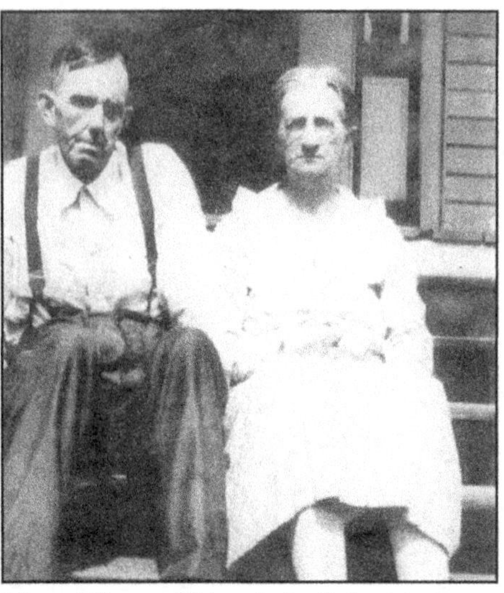
Thomas Jefferson and Roberta Jordan Barker sitting on steps of their home on Madden Bridge Rd. Molena, GA., circa 1930. Courtesy of Jane Gaulding.

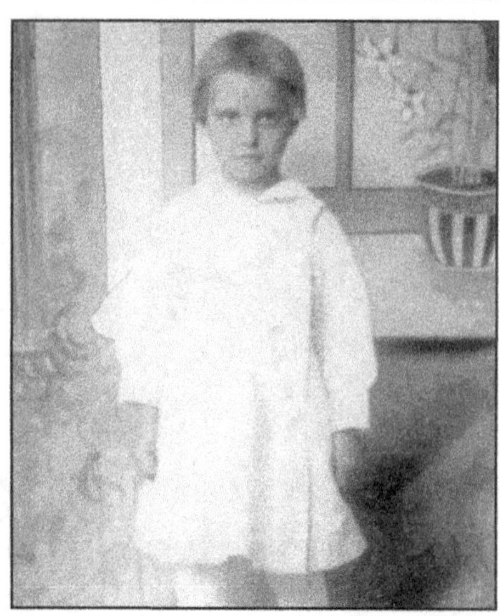
Vera Barker, born June 23, 1912. Courtesy of Jane Gaulding.

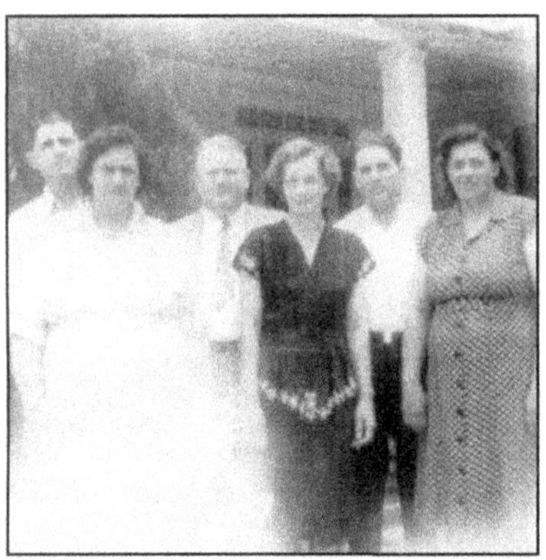
Roy Walton, Sara Walton, John Ray, Vera Barker Gaulding, Joel Eppinger and Mary Barker Eppinger, 1940's. Courtesy of Jane Gaulding.

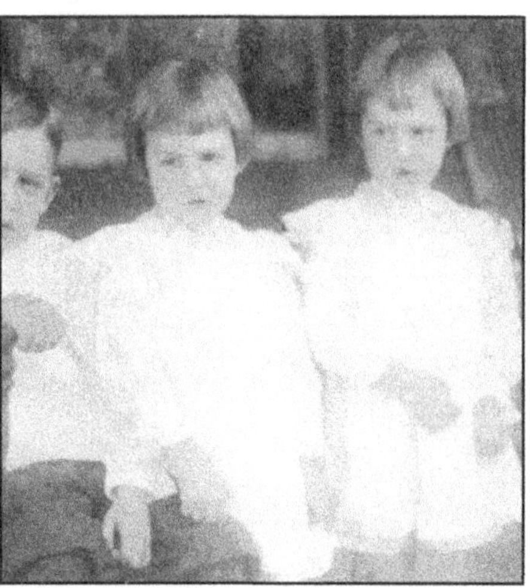
John Pope, Mary and Sara Barker. Courtesy of Jane Gaulding.

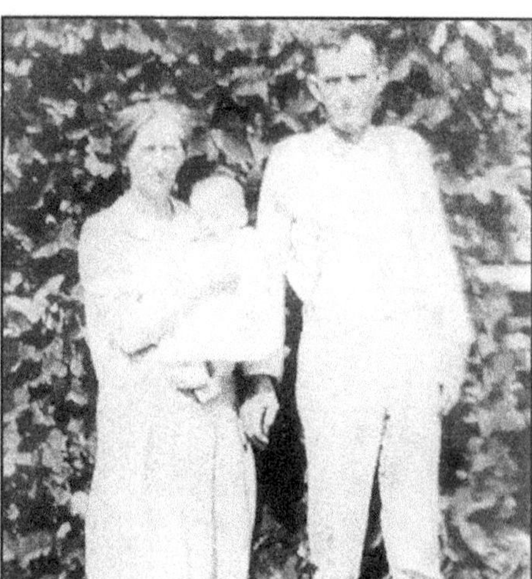
Thomas Jefferson, Roberta Barker and Willis Eppinger. Courtesy of Jane Gaulding.

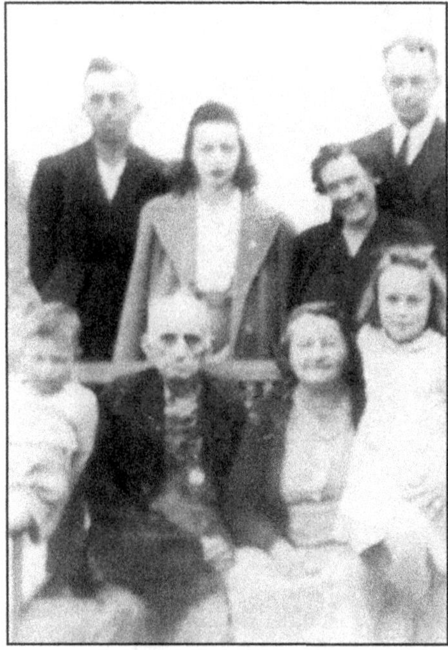
Henry T. (Pete) Barker family. Courtesy of Jane Gaulding.

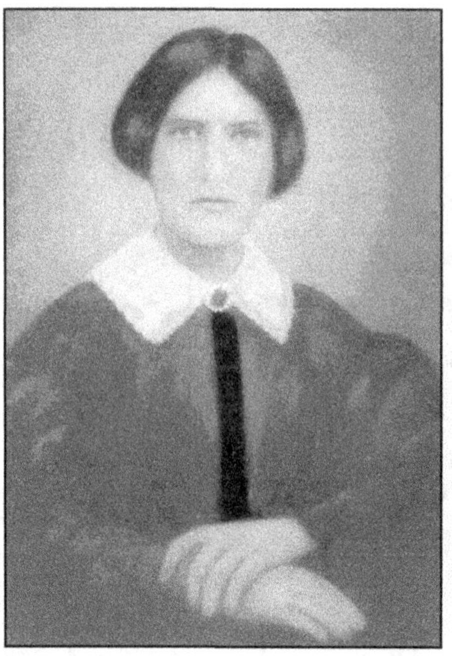
Ann Eliza Jordan. Courtesy of Jane Gaulding.

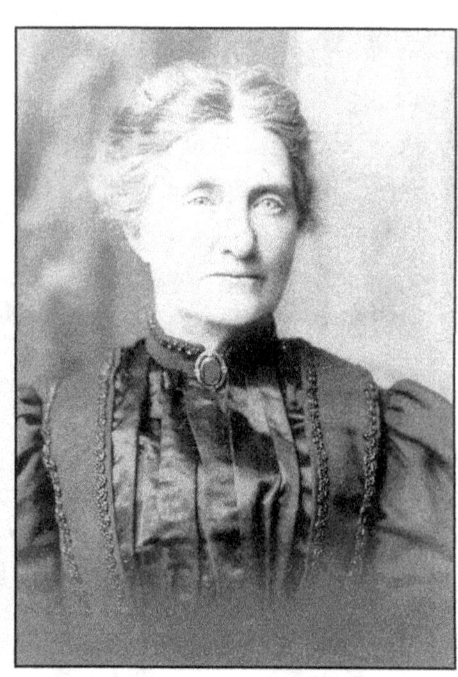
Sarah (Willis) Jordan. Courtesy of Jane Gaulding.

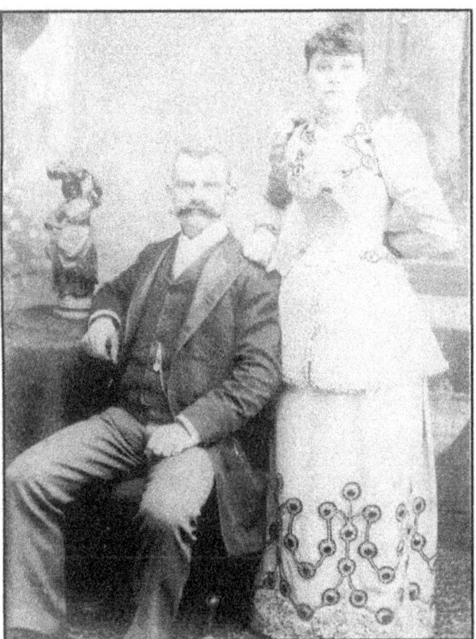
Charles and Cora Jordan. Courtesy of Jane Gaulding.

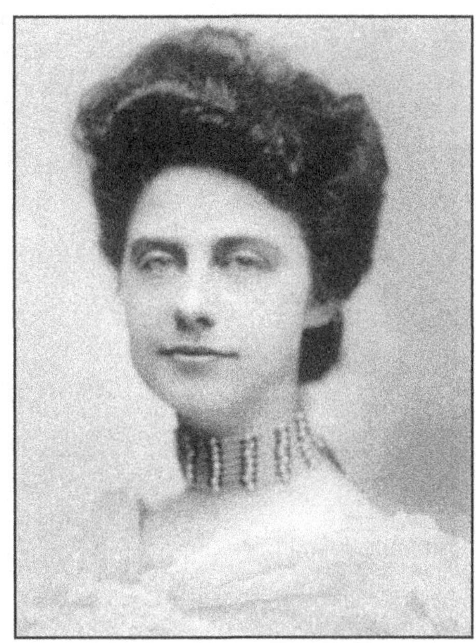
Ina Jordan. Courtesy of Jane Gaulding.

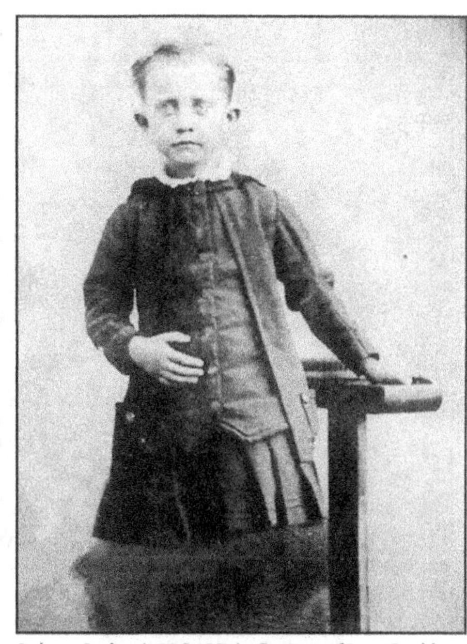
Roberta Jordan (1876-1971). Courtesy of Jane Gaulding.

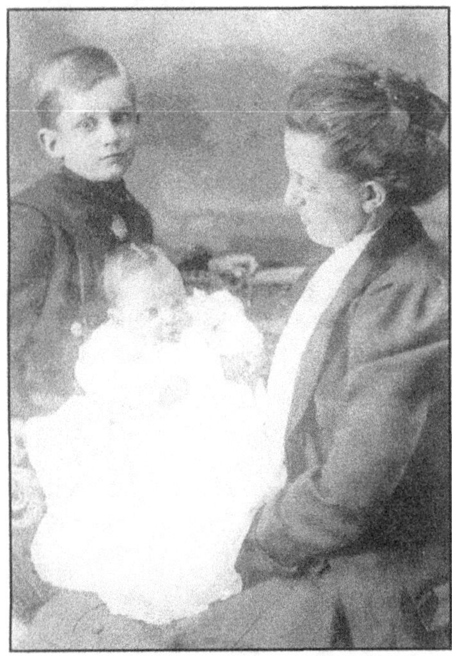
Jessie Dupree Jordan, Dupree Jordan and Kendall Jordan. Courtesy of Jane Gaulding.

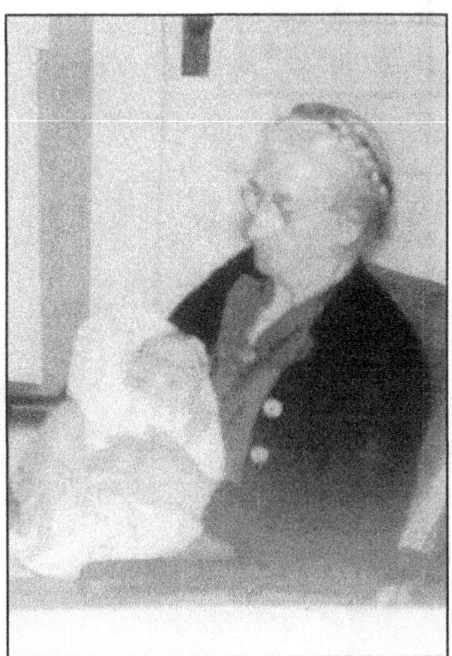
Roberta (Jordan) Barker and Melinda Joy Gaulding, 1958. Courtesy of Jane Gaulding.

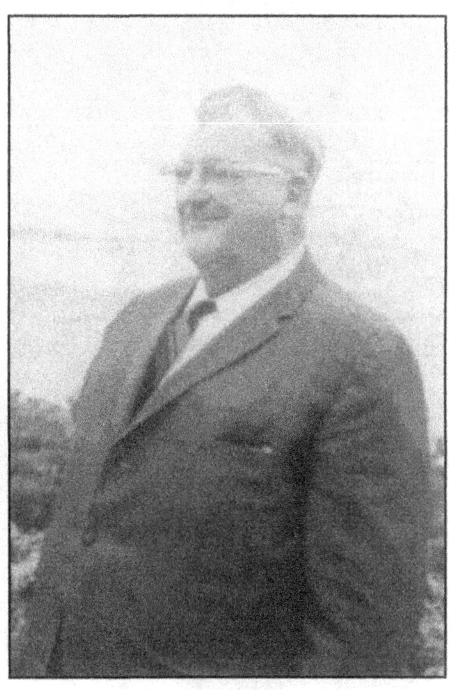
Wiley M. Jordan, Jr. Courtesy of Jane Gaulding.

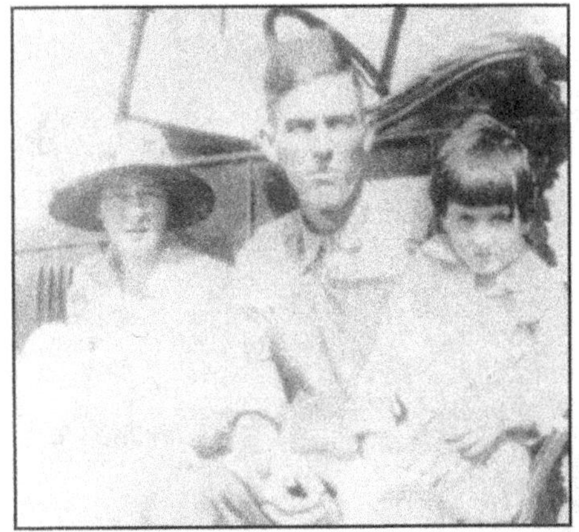
Lena Estelle McDaniel and Martha Jane Turner, circa 1922. Courtesy of Joann Fenley.

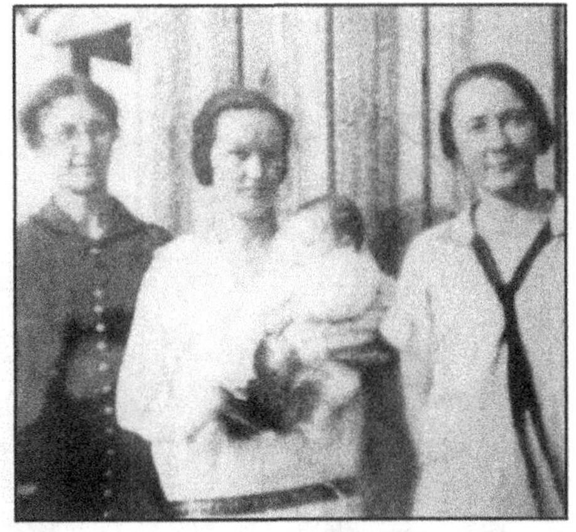
Martha Jane Turner, unknown and Lena Turner McDaniel. Courtesy of Joann Fenley.

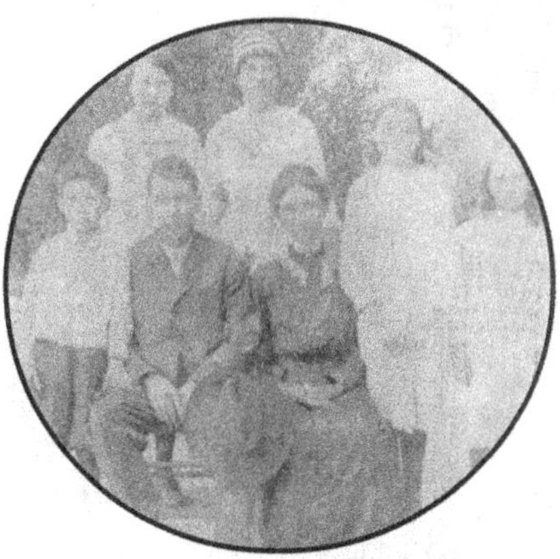
Martha Jane Ogletree, Oscar Turner, William Elmer Turner, Fannie Mae Turner, Rosa Inese Turner, Lena Estelle Turner and Desa Lendra Turner. Courtesy of Joann Fenley.

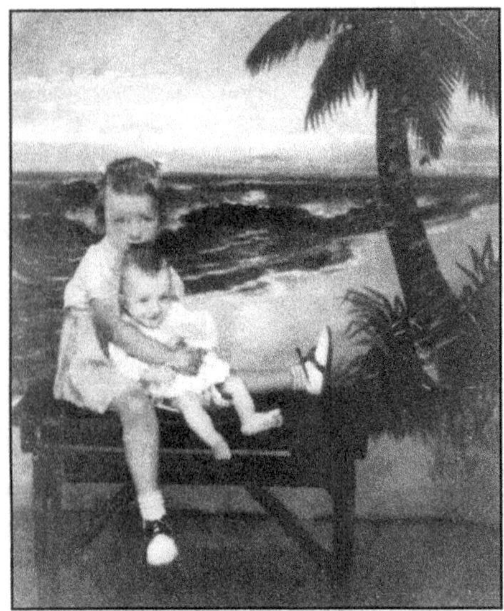

Annette Robbins and Harold Robbins, 1943. Courtesy of Joann Fenley.

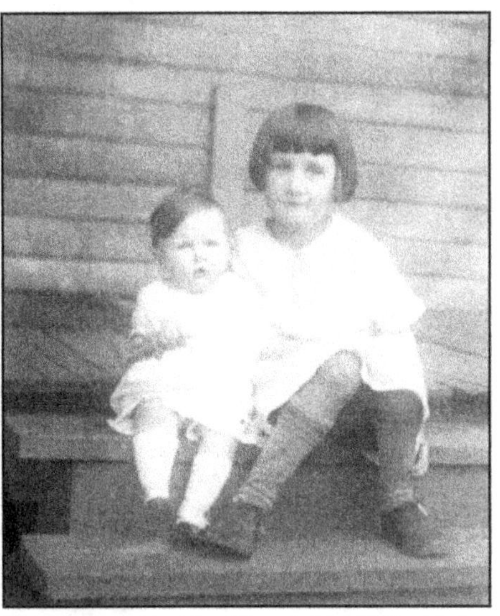

Daisy Estelle McDaniel and Dorothy Mae McDaniel, circa 1929. Courtesy of Joann Fenley.

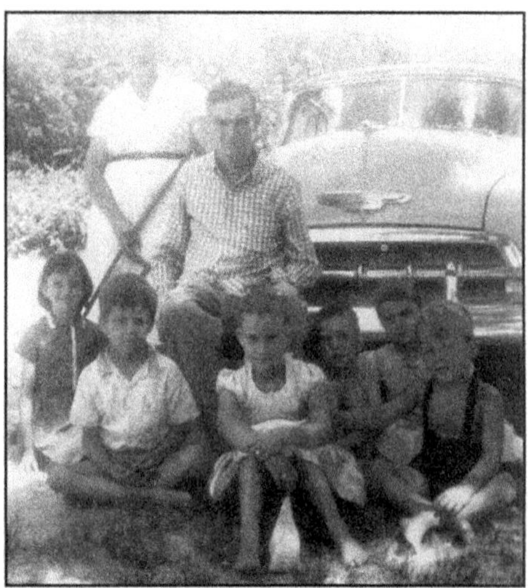

Fred Douglas McDaniel, Lena Estelle McDaniel, Martha Jane Turner, Winfred Turner, Darlene Norton, Danny Turner, Nadine Turner and David Norton. Courtesy of Joann Fenley.

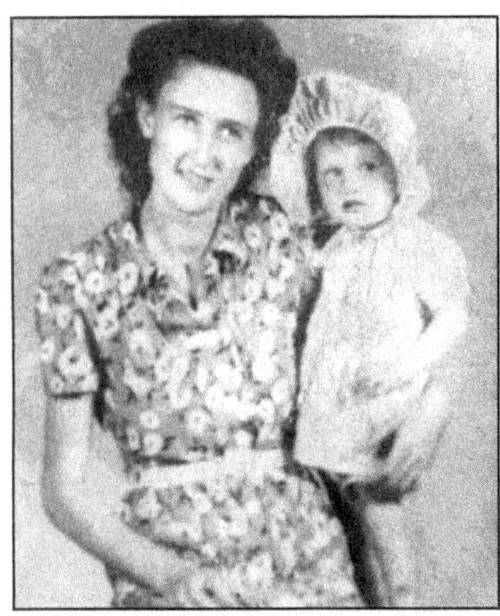

Estelle McDaniel Robbins and Betty Joann Robbins, circa 1946. Courtesy of Joann Fenley.

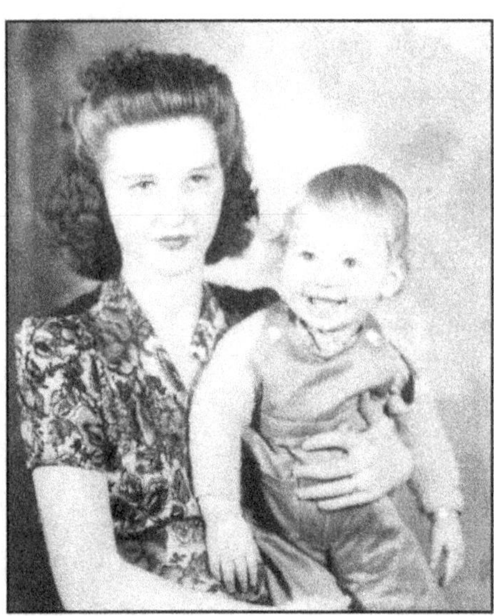

Dorothy Mae Norton and Donnie Norton, 1943. Courtesy of Joann Fenley.

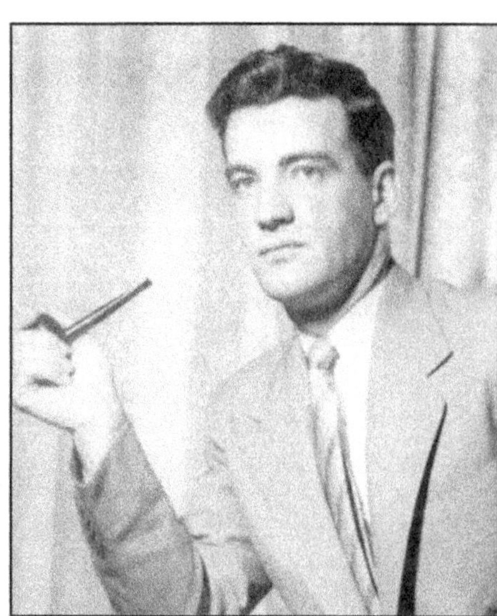

Jack Bishop and his pipe in the early 1940's. Courtesy of Bonnie Gardner.

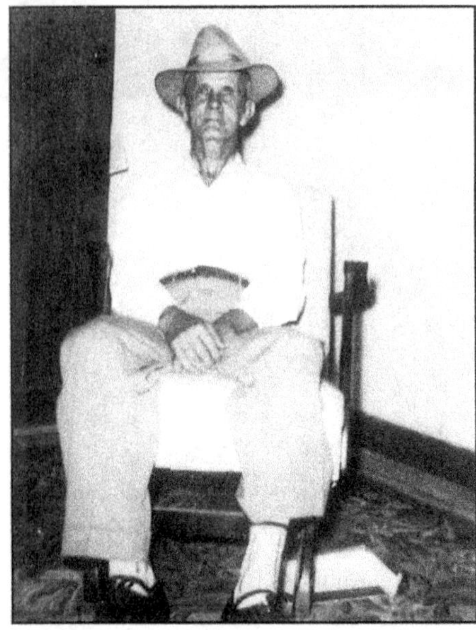

James W. Brooks. Courtesy of Bonnie Gardner.

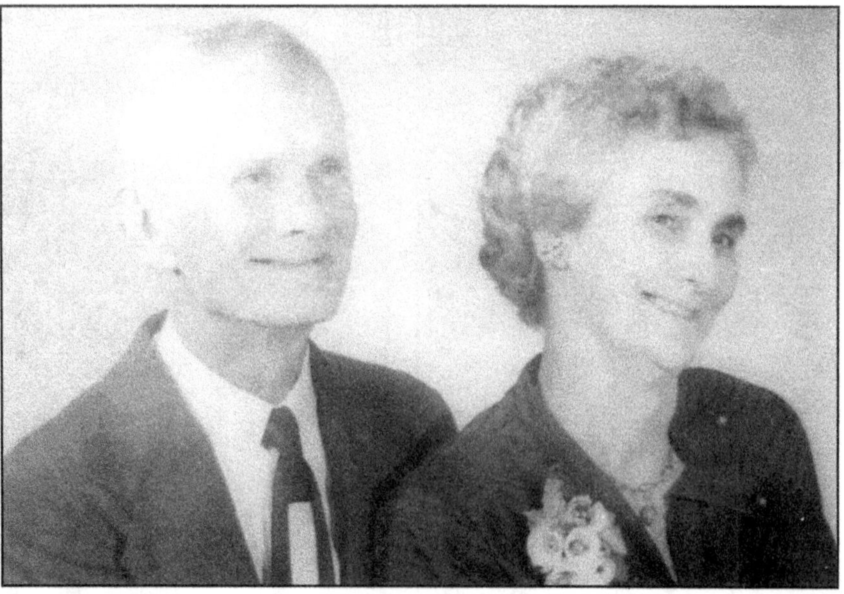

James W. and Dora (Rogers) Brooks. Courtesy of Bonnie Gardner.

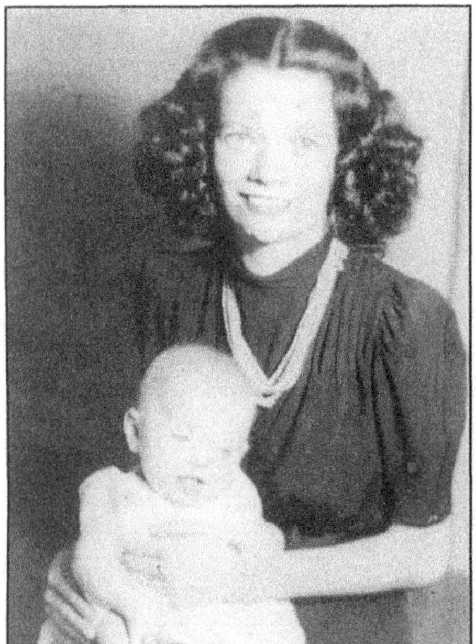

Pauline Brooks Bishop and her daughter, Bonnie Pauline Bishop. Courtesy of Bonnie Gardner.

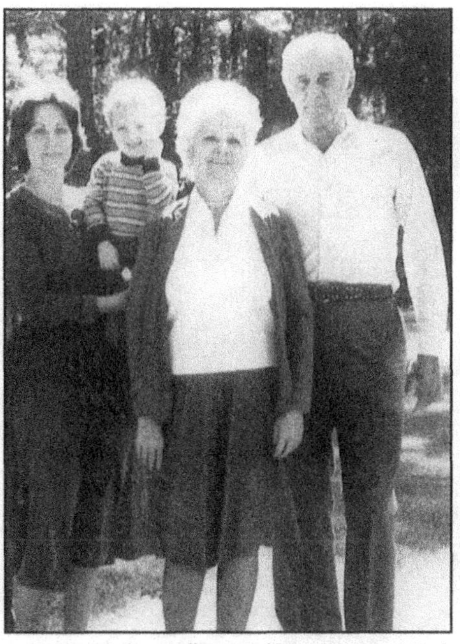

June Denise Bishop, William Maddox, Pauline and Hugh Bishop, 1983. Courtesy of Bonnie Gardner.

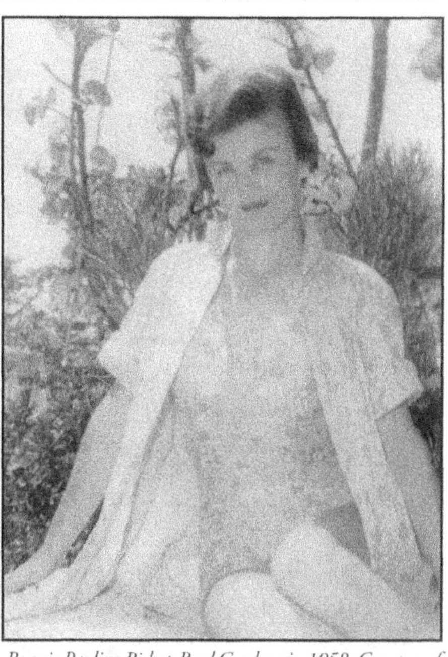

Bonnie Pauline Bishop Byrd Gardner in 1958. Courtesy of Bonnie Gardner.

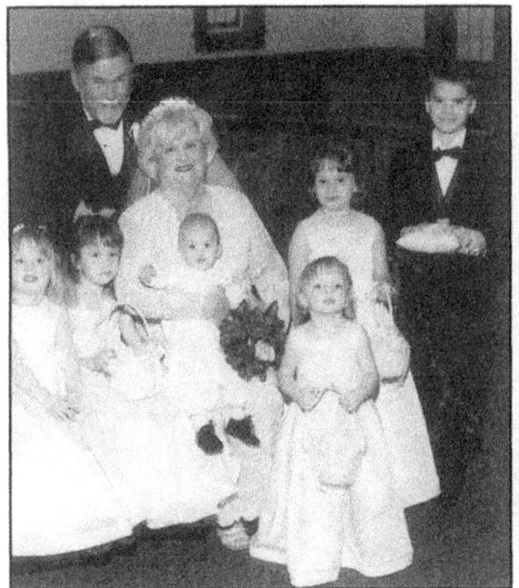

The wedding of Bill and Bonnie Gardner and their grandchildren, Leah Gardner, Savannah and McKenzie Byrd, Cailee Colegrove and Jeffrey and Walker Janney at Meansville Baptist Church. Courtesy of Bonnie Gardner.

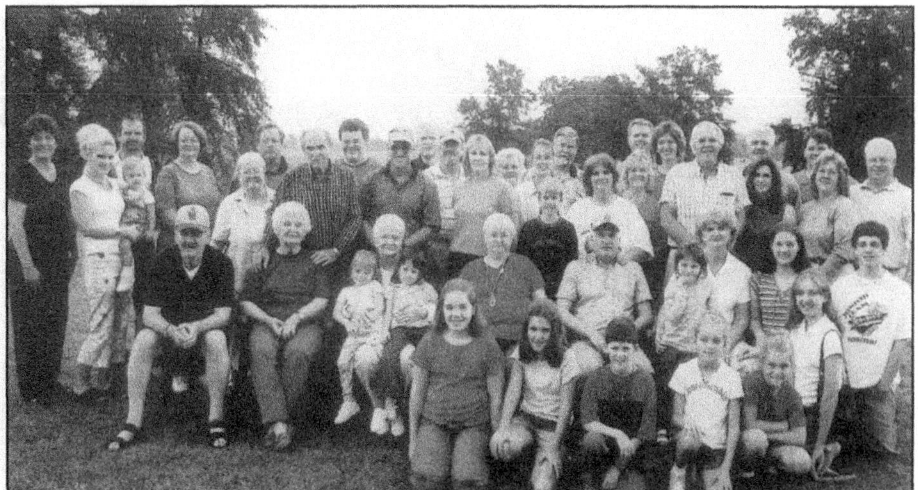

Bishop Family reunion in 2002 at the home of Jan (Bishop) and Billy Williams. Family members attending June, Pauline, Hugh Jr., Joan Chandler, Joel, Donald, Joan Boyd, Ellie, Jeannie, Daniel, Matthew Bishop, Ron Jr., April, Savannah, McKenzie Byrd, Rachel, Jeffrey, Walker Janney, Martha, John Radcliff, Jan, Billy, Greg, Jenny, Emily, Curt, Derek, Karen, Maggie, Betsy, Mollie, Chad Williams, Mike, Joan Wilson, Sylvia, Bradford Wright, Mary K. Price, Lynn H. Rogers, Charles W. Price, Judy B. Price, Paul, Kim, Allison and David Boggs. Courtesy of Bonnie Gardner.

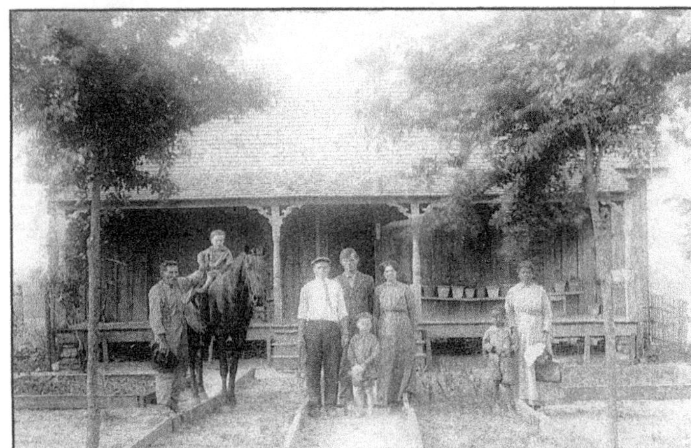

House on Capel farm where Clinton H. and Lizzie Mae started housekeeping in 1909. Pictured from left to right: Abner J. Capel, Clinton's father, A.J. on horse Dixie, George Clinton's half-brother, Lizzie Mae with son Bonnie and "Aunt" Catherine Hinds and her son Buck.

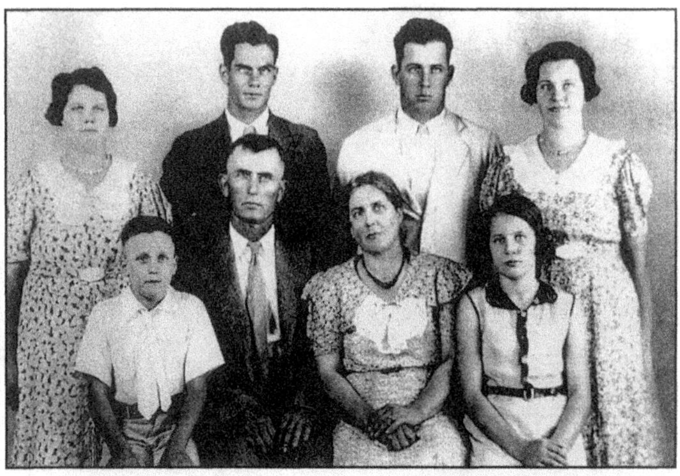

The Clinton H. Capel family: Homer L. Capel, Clinton H. Capel, Lizzie Mae Huckaby Capel, Landice Huckaby Capel, Elna Mae Capel, Bonnie Carl Capel, Abner J. Capel and Helen Capel, 1934. Courtesy of Elna Capel.

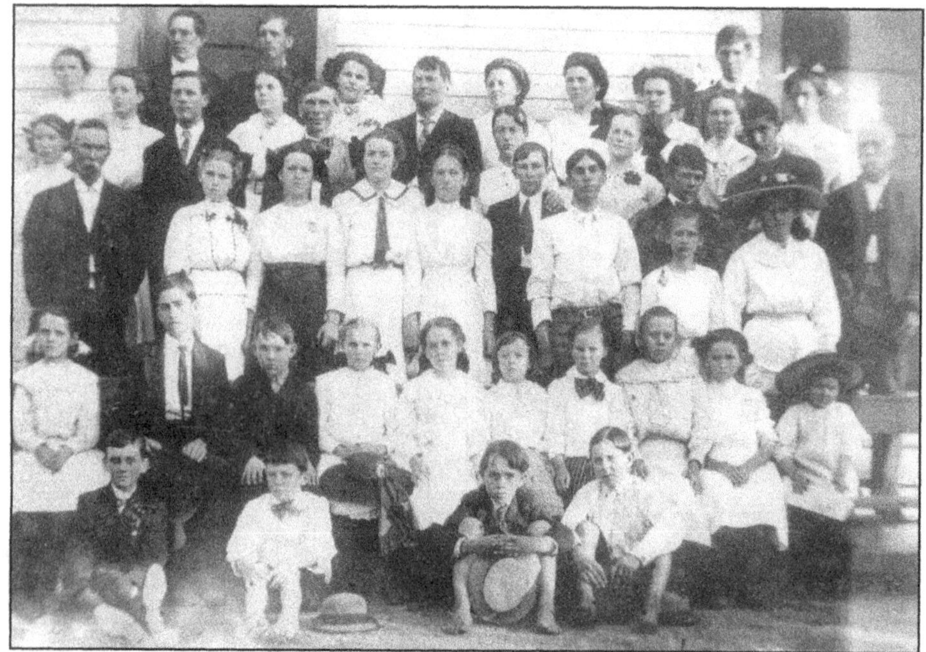

Mt. Gilead Baptist Church Singing School, 1910. Courtesy of Patsy Vaughn.

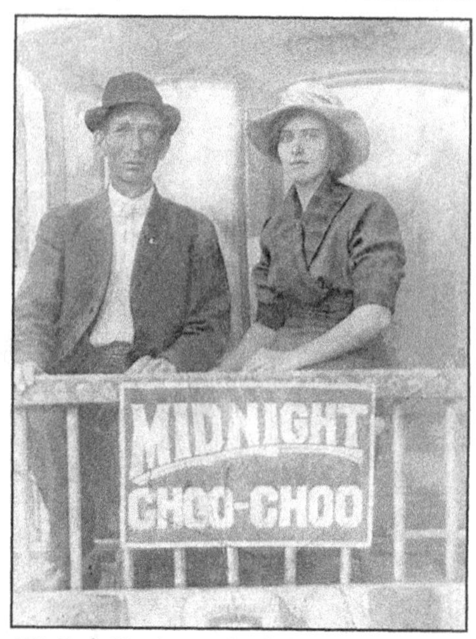

J.W. (Bud) Mangham and wife Essie Bankston on their wedding day in 1914 on the choo-choo at the fair grounds in Griffin. Courtesy of Rosalee King.

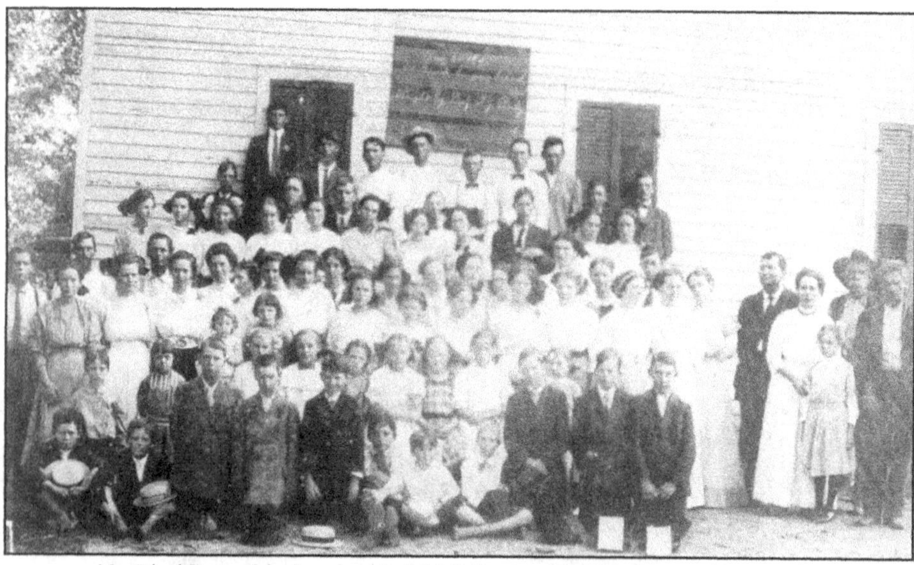

Mt. Gilead Singing School taught by Prof. S.J. Bailey, Aug. 21, 1911. Courtesy of Patsy Vaughn.

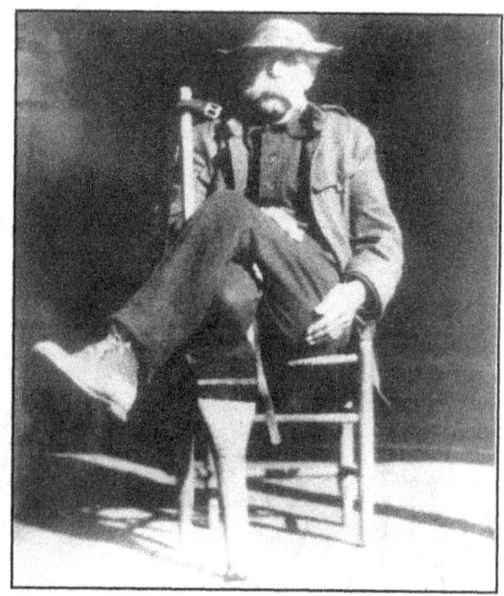

Mountain Hill Green (1840-1927), Baliff of the 2nd District of Pike Co. Courtesy of Patsy Vaughn.

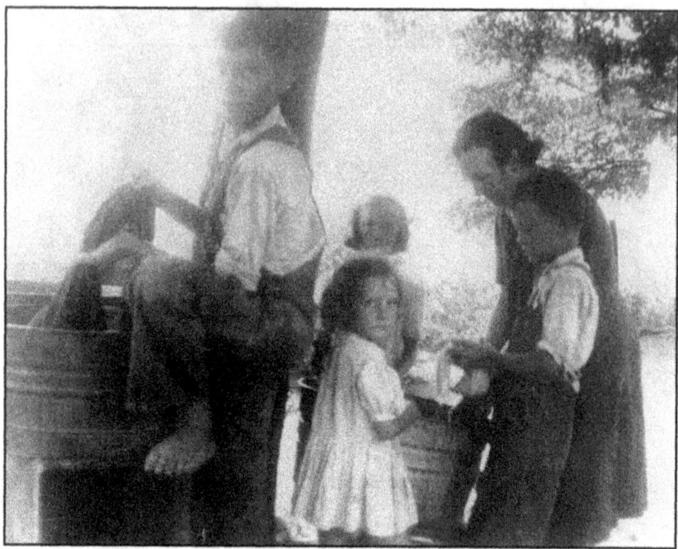

Ozella, Charlie, Winford, Molly and Hazel Vaughn. Courtesy of Patsy Vaughn.

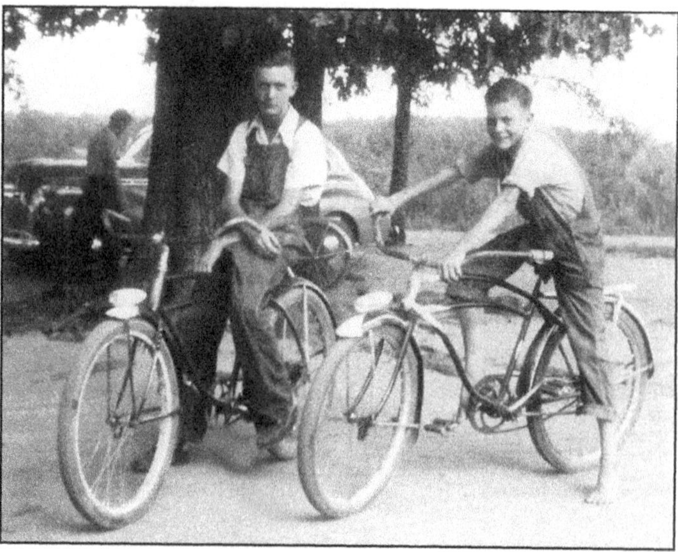

Junious Vaughn and Winford Vaughn. Courtesy of Patsy Vaughn.

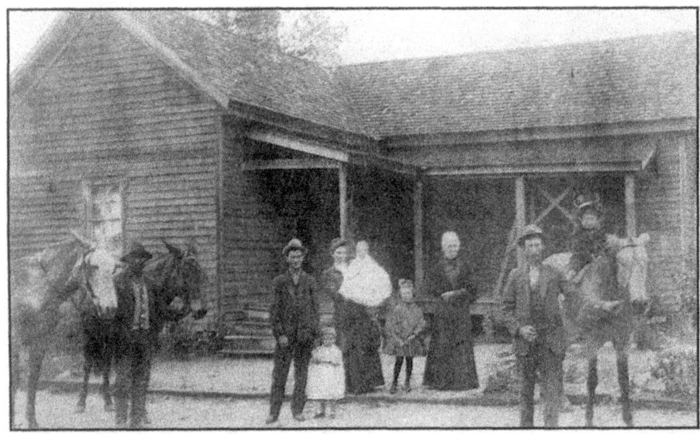

Emmett Richardson, Willie Lee Jimmerson, Martha, Anna, Robert, Erma, Martha Jane, Bud Mangham and Douglas Jimmerson at the home of William Decautur Mangham and family. The house still stands on Hwy 109 in Lifsey Springs and was remodeled and is owned by Parrish Swift and family. Courtesy of Rosalee King.

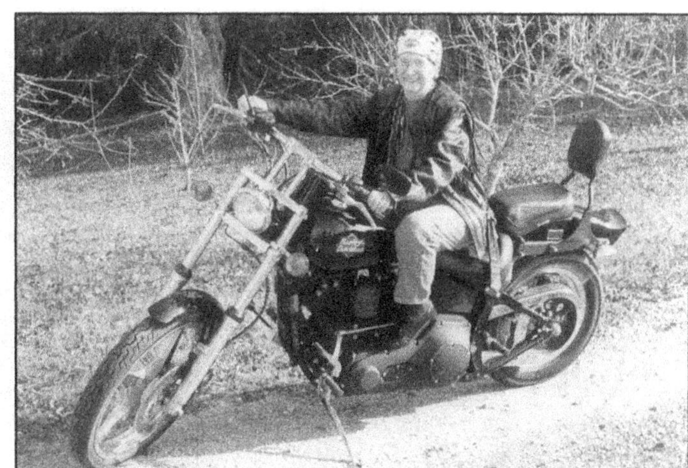

Rosalee King Pike County Journal Reporter/Columnist for Lifsey Springs since 1980. Courtesy of Rosalee King.

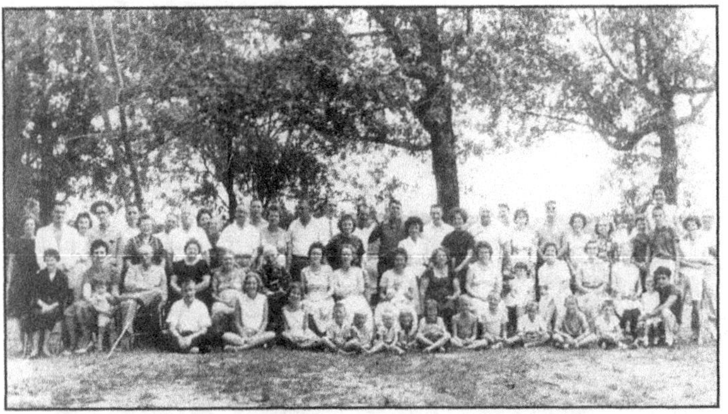

The Green-Shivers reunion. Courtesy of Patsy Vaughn.

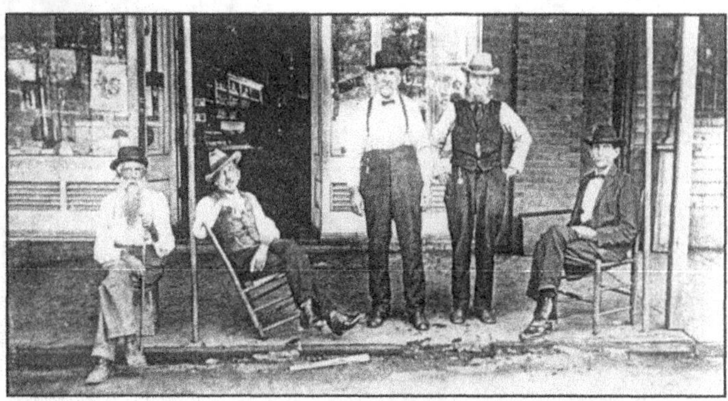

Patrick Shivers general store in Zebulon, Patrick is standing in the white shirt. Courtesy of Patsy Vaughn.

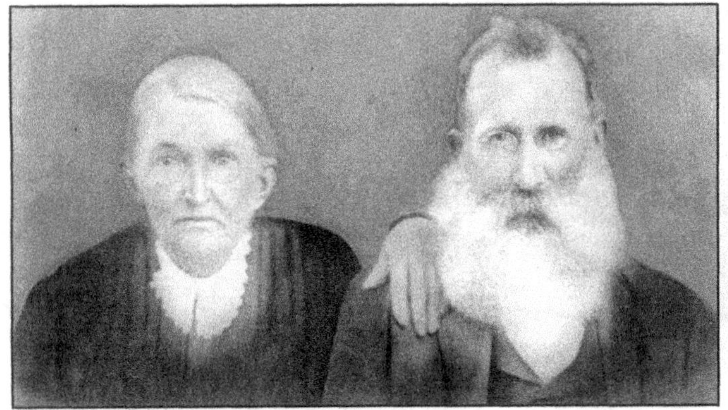

Carrie E. Newell King (1845-1919) and William Wesley King (1847-1924). Courtesy of Rosalee King.

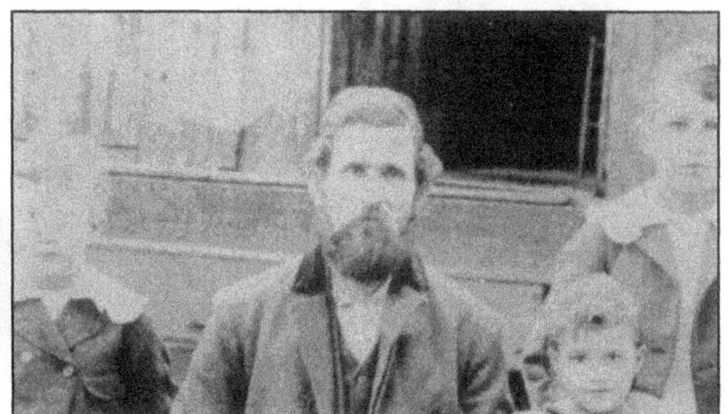

William Jefferson Shivers and Children, circa 1896. Courtesy of JBG.

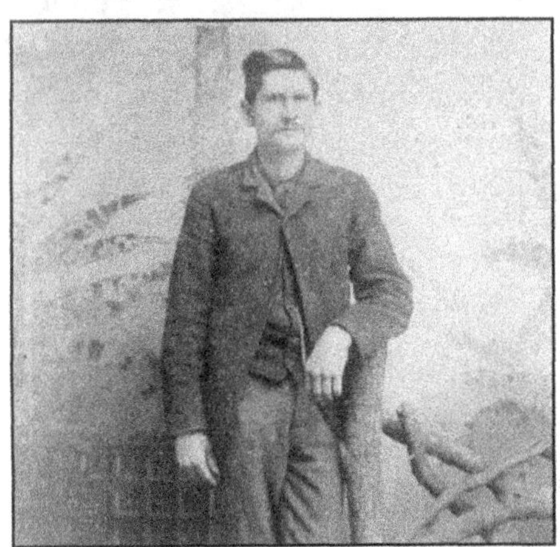

Milton Pitts. Courtesy of JBG.

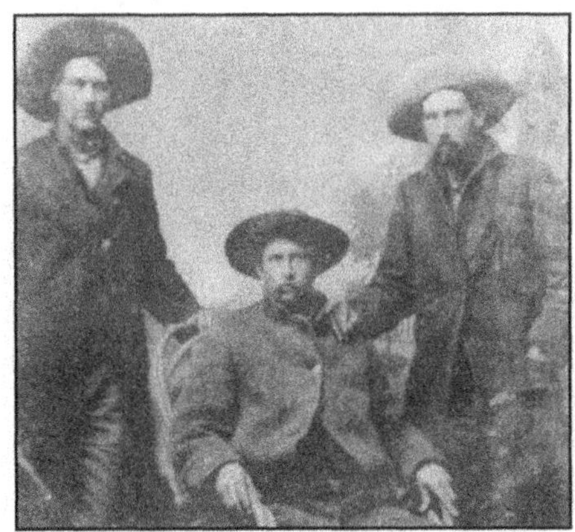

Pike County boys from around 1900 or before. Courtesy of JBG.

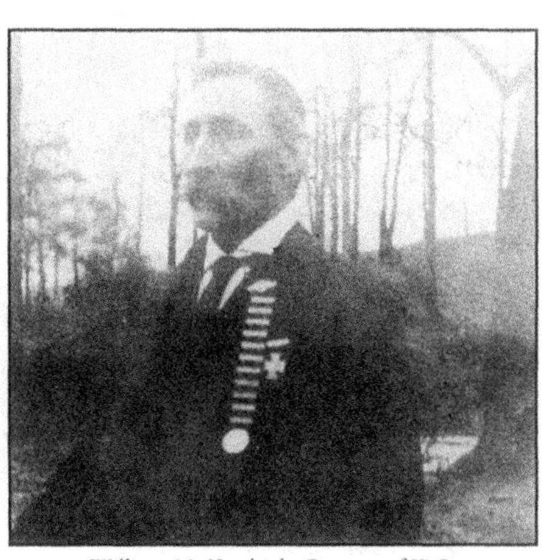

William M. Kendrick. Courtesy of JBG.

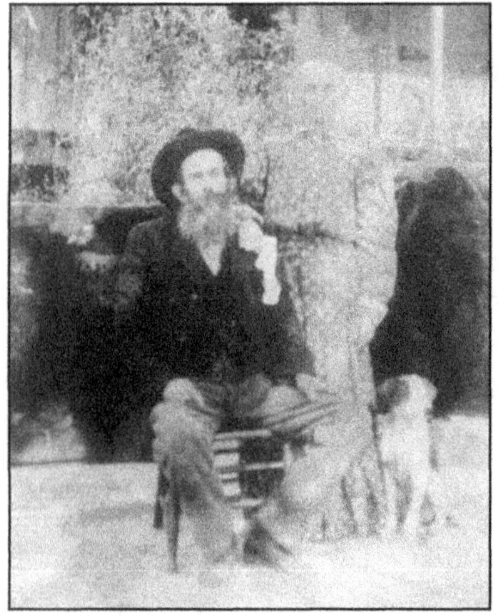
Milton Alexander Kendrick (1865-1924). Courtesy of JBG.

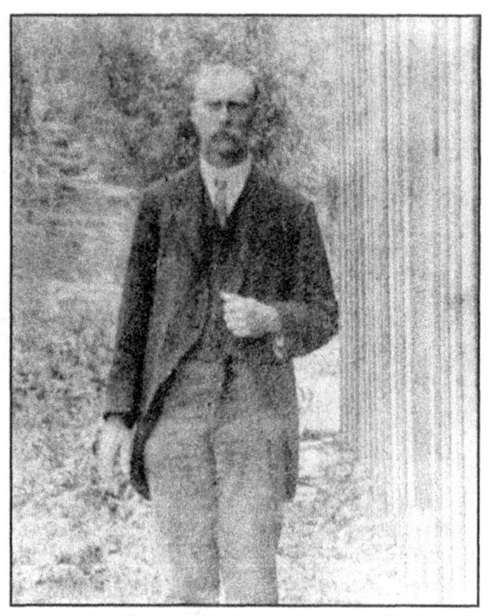
Union Green (1868-1938). Courtesy of JBG.

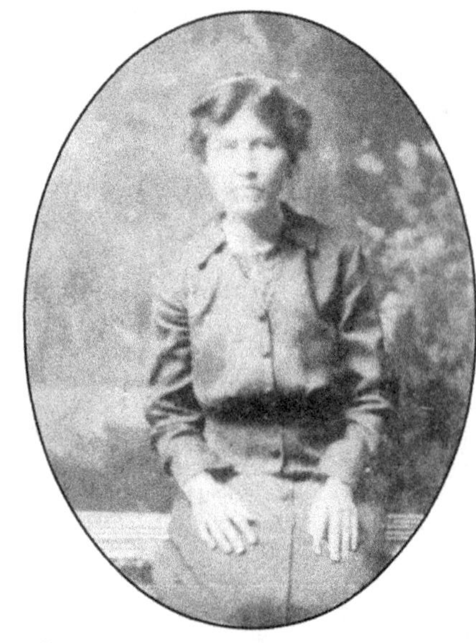
Leila Buchanan Green (1882-1961). Courtesy of JBG.

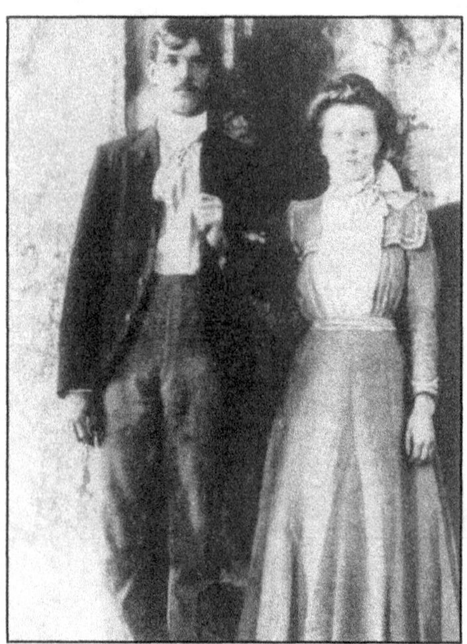
Joseph Shivers and Biddie May Green on their wedding day. Courtesy of JBG.

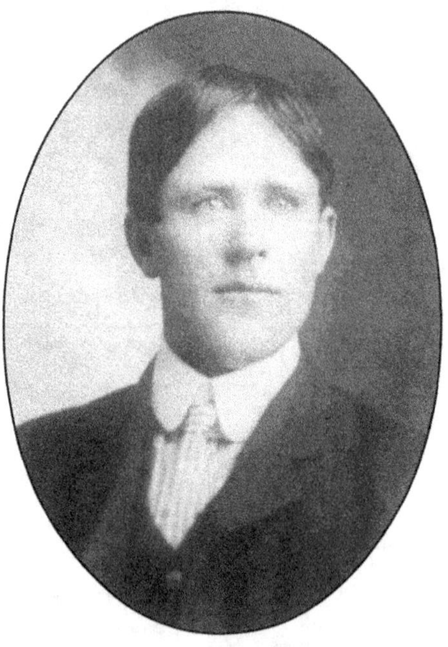
Cicero Green. Courtesy of JBG.

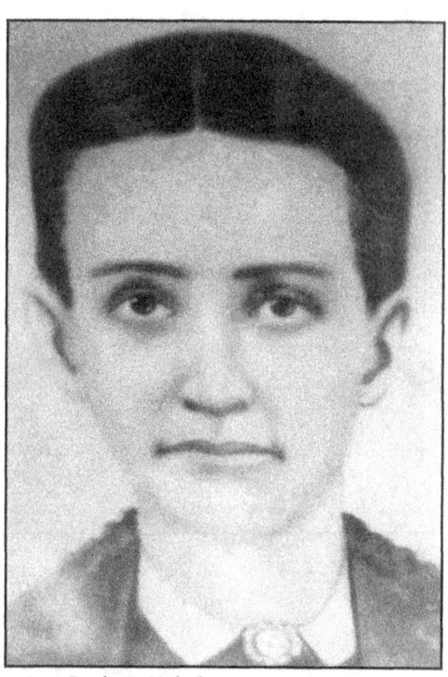
Partheria Kirk Green. Courtesy of JBG.

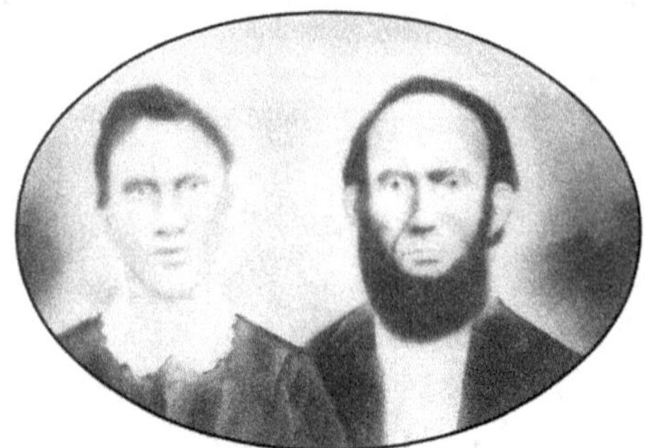
Jonah Green (1826-1891). Courtesy of JBG.

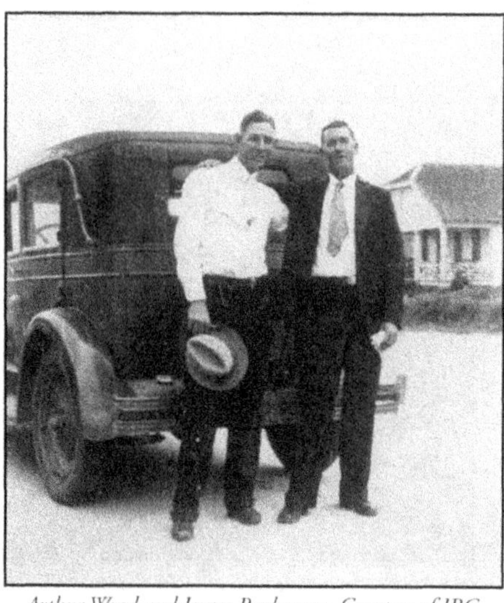
Arthur Wood and James Buchanan. Courtesy of JBG.

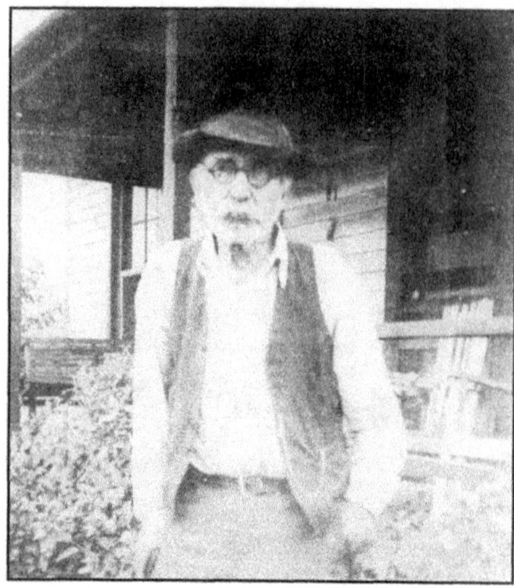
John Buchanan. Courtesy of JBG.

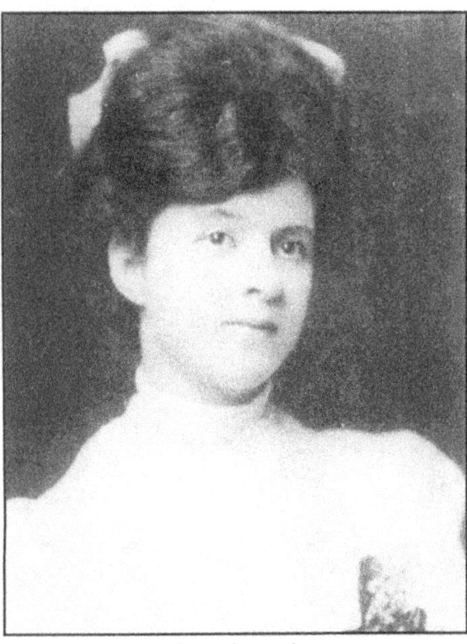
Alice Coker Sauley

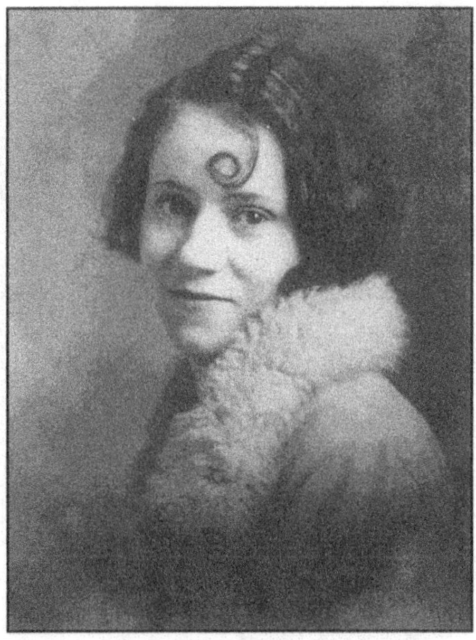
Amanda Estelle Tharpe, 1920's.

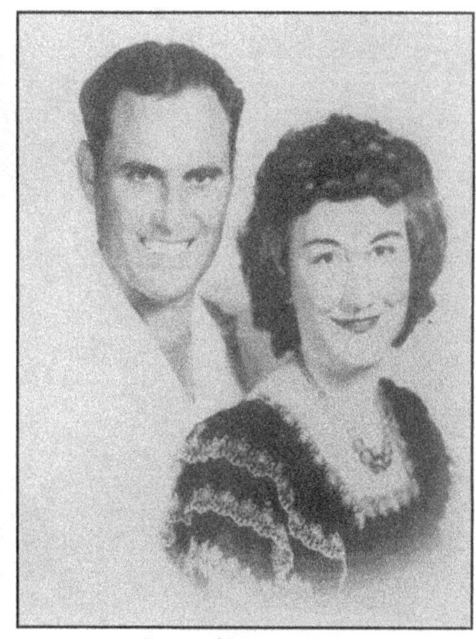
Drew and Margaret Payne

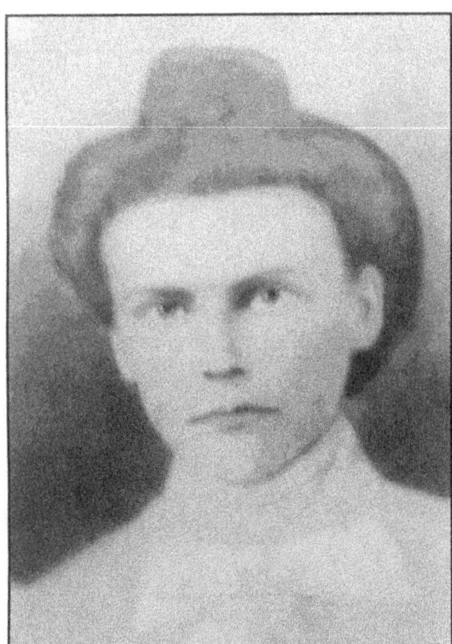
Loula Hamrick

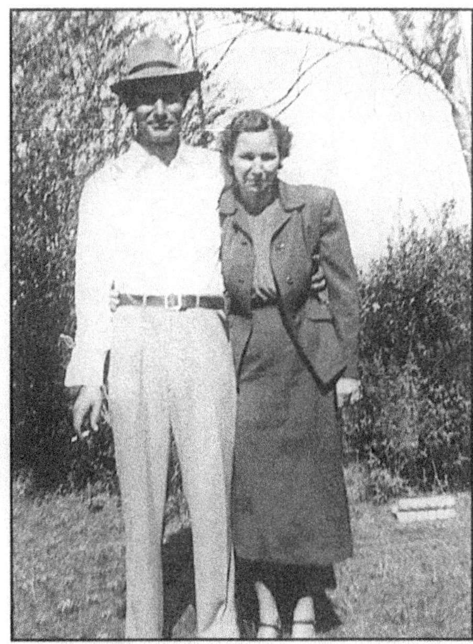
Horace Lemeul LaFayette Williams and wife Gladys Jones Williams. Courtesy of Lisa Jo Williams Kinser.

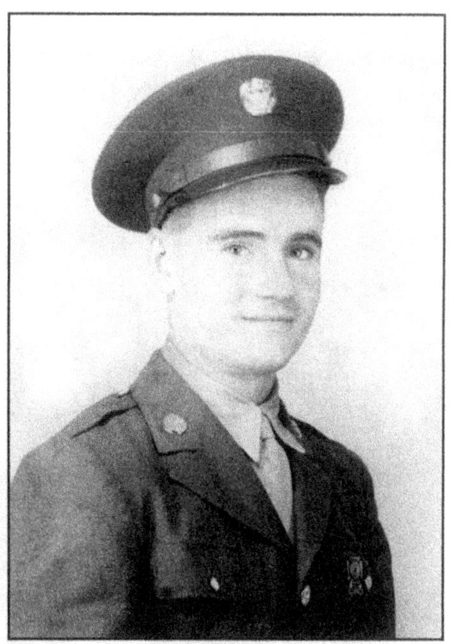
Harold Williams

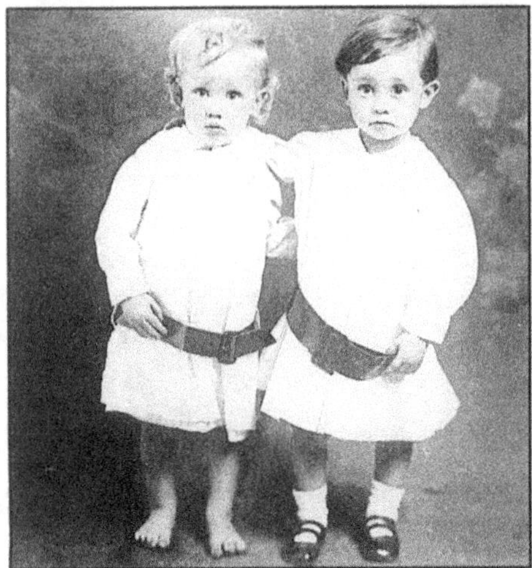
Horace Lemeul LaFayette Williams and his uncle "Tim" Olen Lemeul Crane. Courtesy of Lisa Jo Williams Kinser.

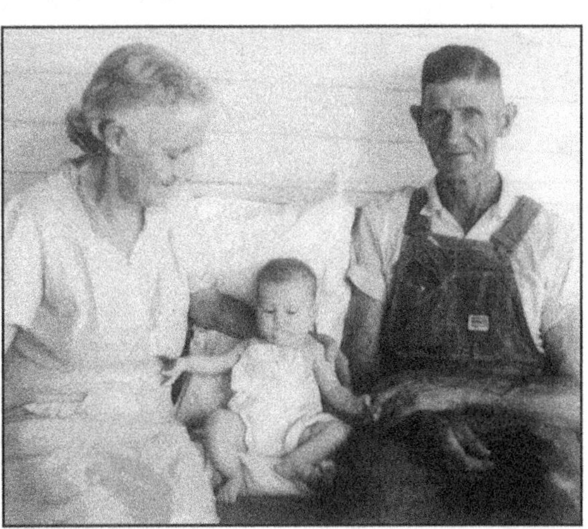
Luther Roscoe Williams, Myrtle Crane Williams with Lisa Jo Williams (center). Courtesy of Lisa Jo Williams Kinser.

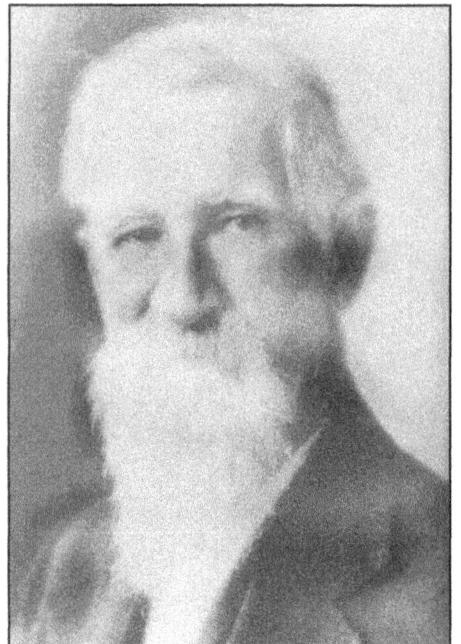

Parks Reno Coker

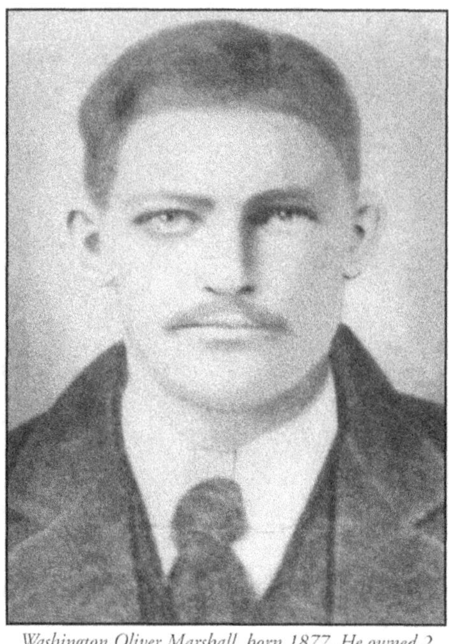

Washington Oliver Marshall, born 1877. He owned 2 lumber mills and a farm. Courtesy of John Henderson.

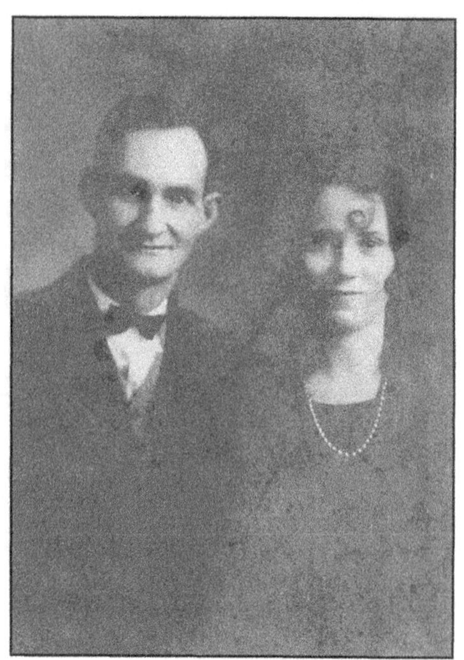

Amanda Estelle Tharpe and husband.

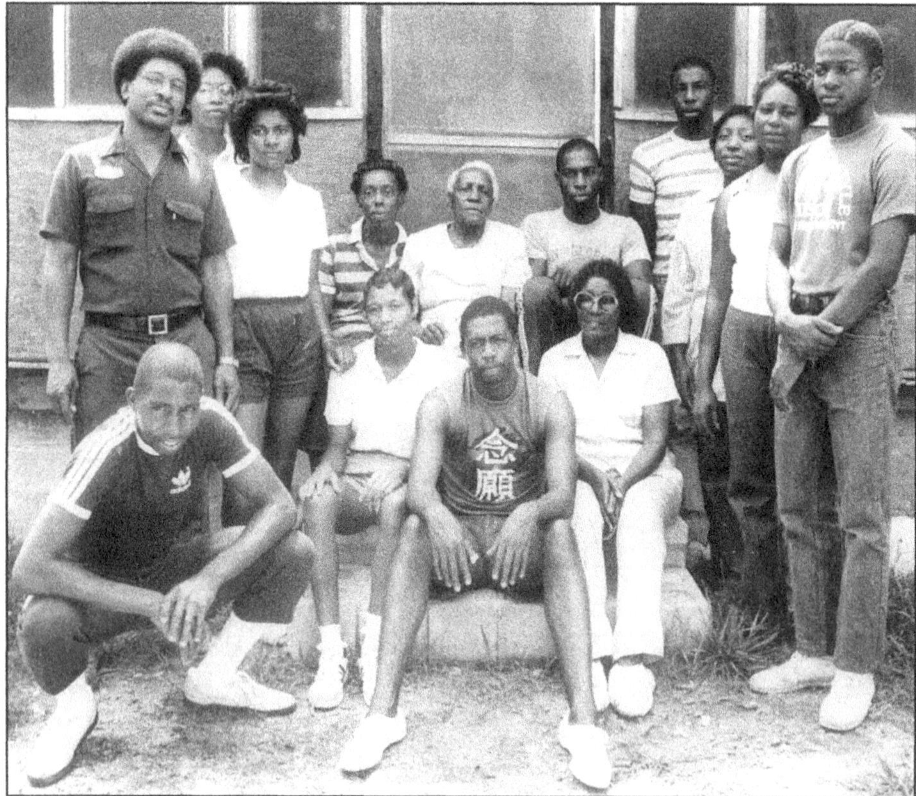

Midwife "Granny" Mary Reviere and her "children."

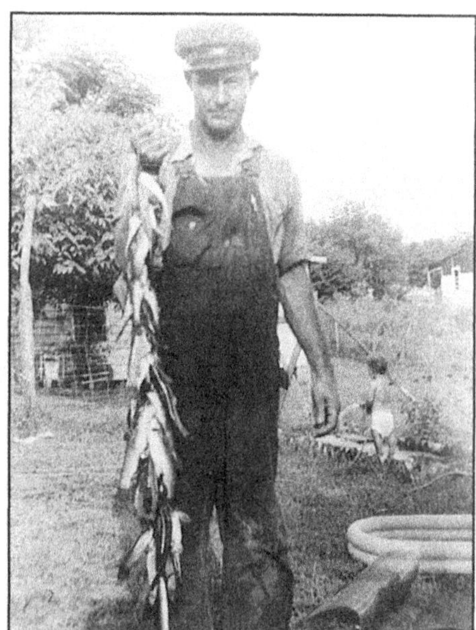

H.L. Williams with fish.

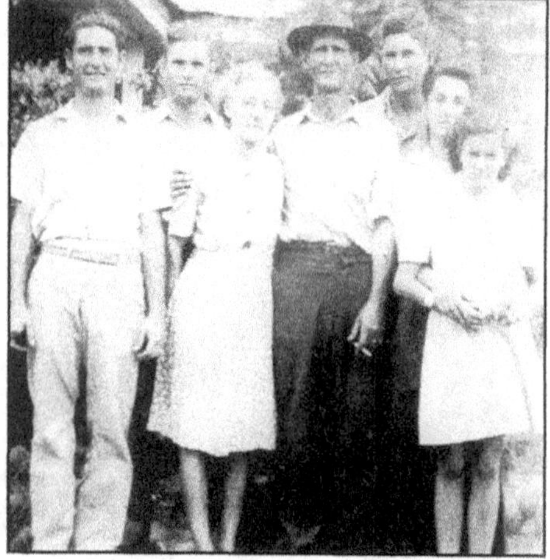

Children of Myrtle Crane Williams and Roscoe Williams. Left to right: Luther, Harold, Floyd, Naomi and Mary. Courtesy of Lisa Jo Williams Kinser.

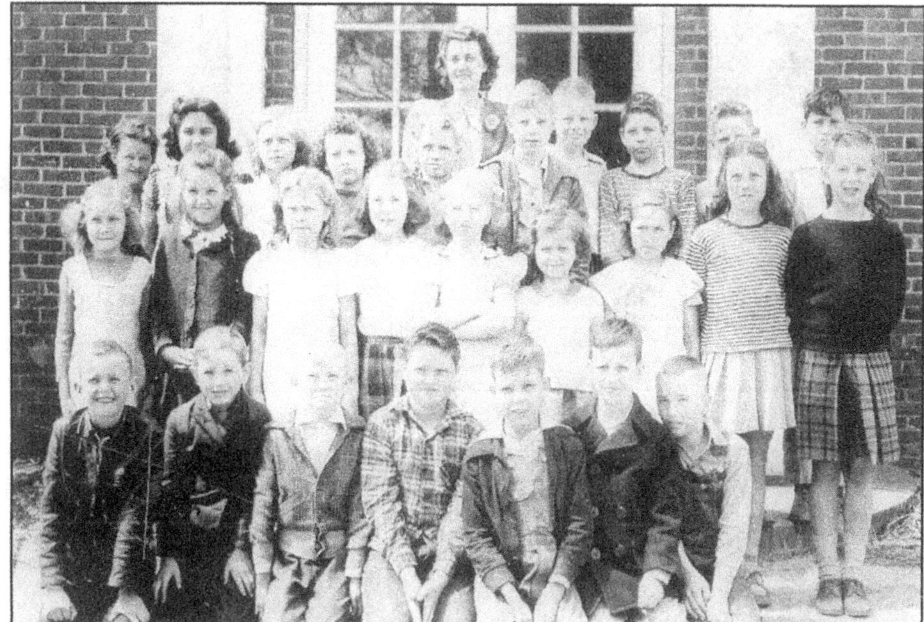

Zebulon Grammar School fourth grade class of 1946. 1st row: W.O. Smith, Carvel Williams, Johnny Minter, Buddy Gunnels, Wayne Shivers, ___ Lakey, Elmer King. 2nd row: Lucille Jones, Faye Sandefur, Mary Ann Reeves, Sue Elliott, Jane Elliott, Earline Jones, Ellen Manley, Carol Taylor, Elsa Sells. 3rd row: Phyllis Presley, unknown, Shirley Moss, Patricia Hawkins, J.C. Gill, unknown, unknown, Tommy Powers, unknown, Frank Glover. Teacher: Miss Barrett. Courtesy of Jane Gaulding.

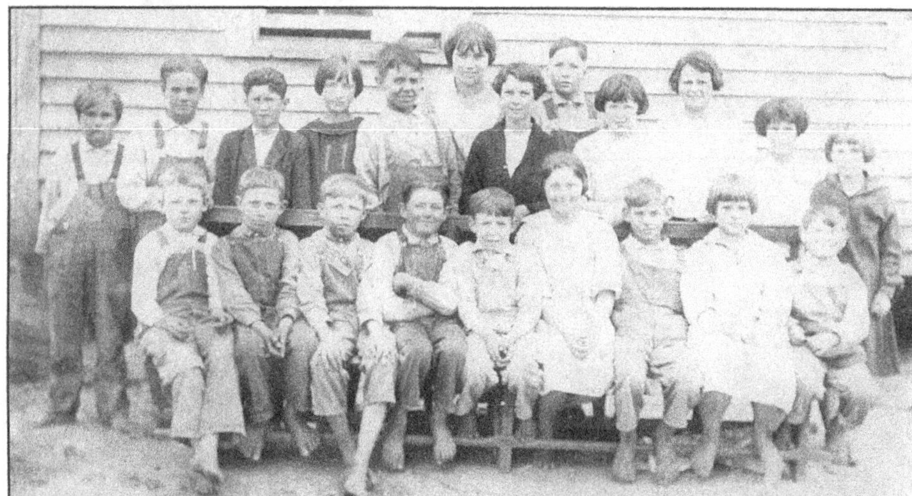

Students from New Hope School in Pike County. Teacher: Laura Mitchell, middle back row, Roger Brown to her immediate left (5th one over). Courtesy of Susan Brown Parham.

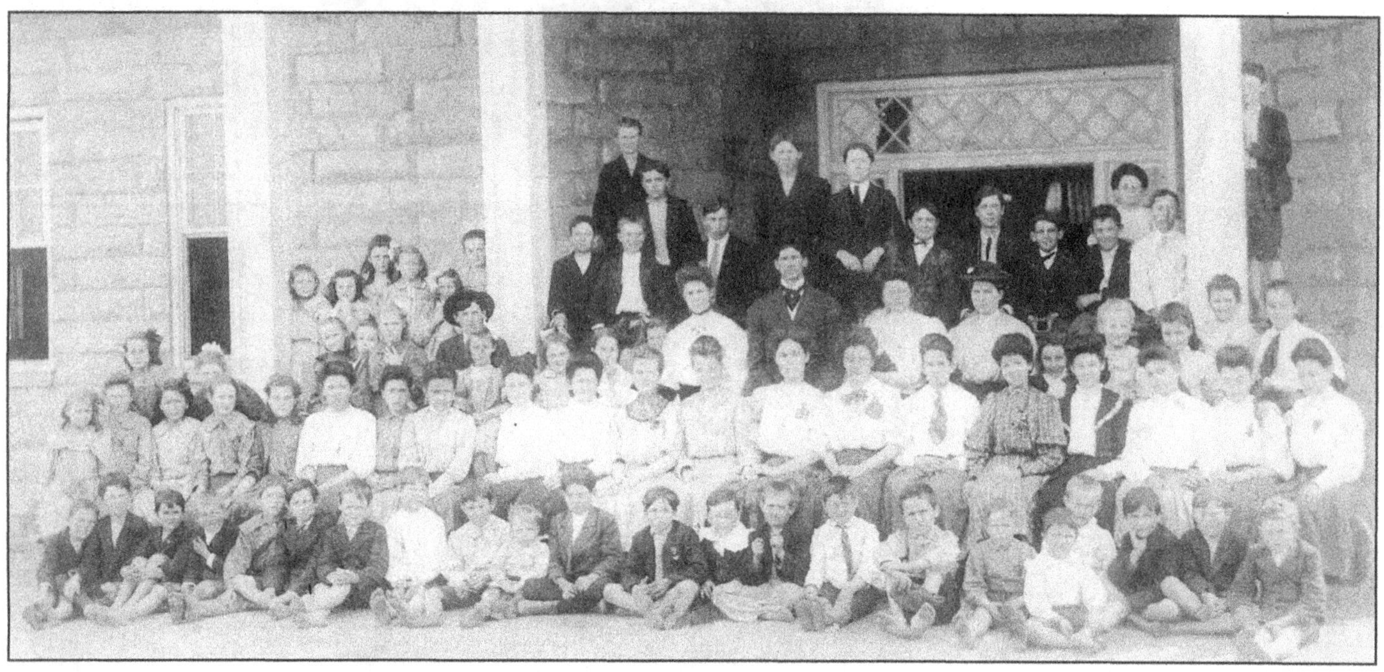

Students of Molena School, circa 1904. Courtesy of Robert F. Jones.

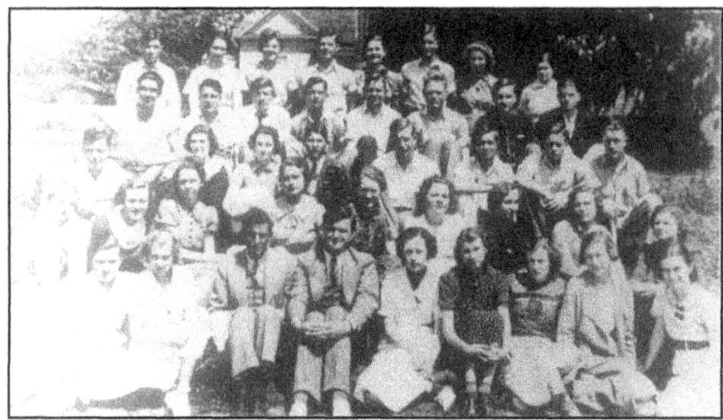

Zebulon High School class of 1937. Courtesy of Mrs. Clyde Gibson.

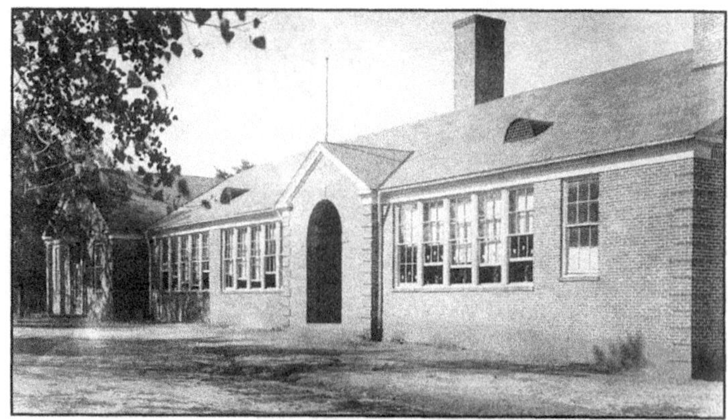

Zebulon Elementary School. Courtesy of Rachel McClelland.

Zebulon School, circa 1916. Courtesy of Joseph and Judith Reeves.

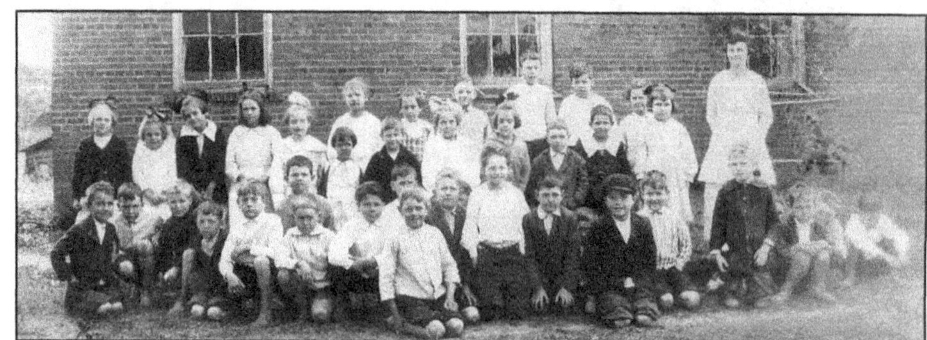

Zebulon High School class of 1938. Courtesy of Susan Brown Parham.

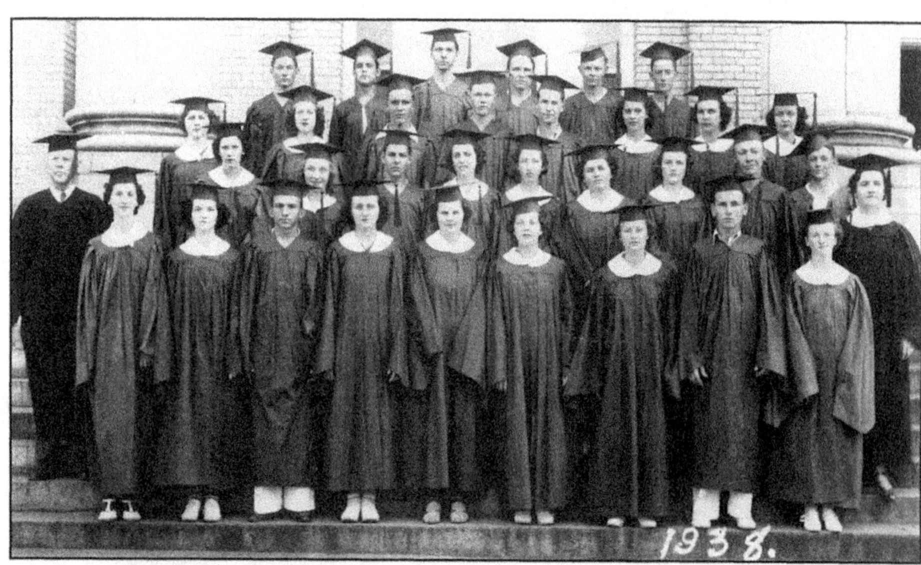

Zebulon High school students of the 1945-46 school year. 1st row, (seated, L-R): Vince Wilson, Billy Ballard, Clinton Davis, unknown, Junior Bush, unknown, Hoyt Williams. 2nd row: mostly unknown, far right–Donald Manley and Hanson Williams. 3rd row: (left side) Juanita Gunnels, (center) James Reeves, (right side) Doug Cochran. Back row: unknown, Marvin Littleton, unknown, Jack Ison, top right–Barton Elliott. Courtesy of Jane Gaulding.

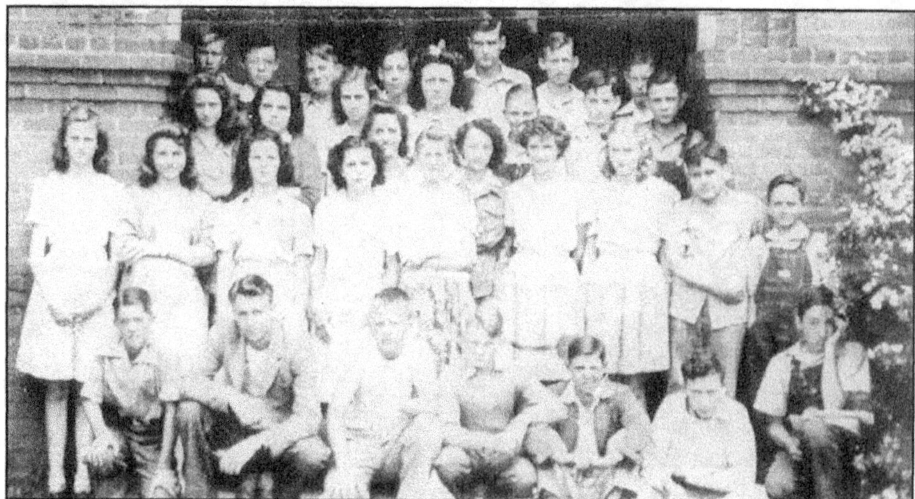

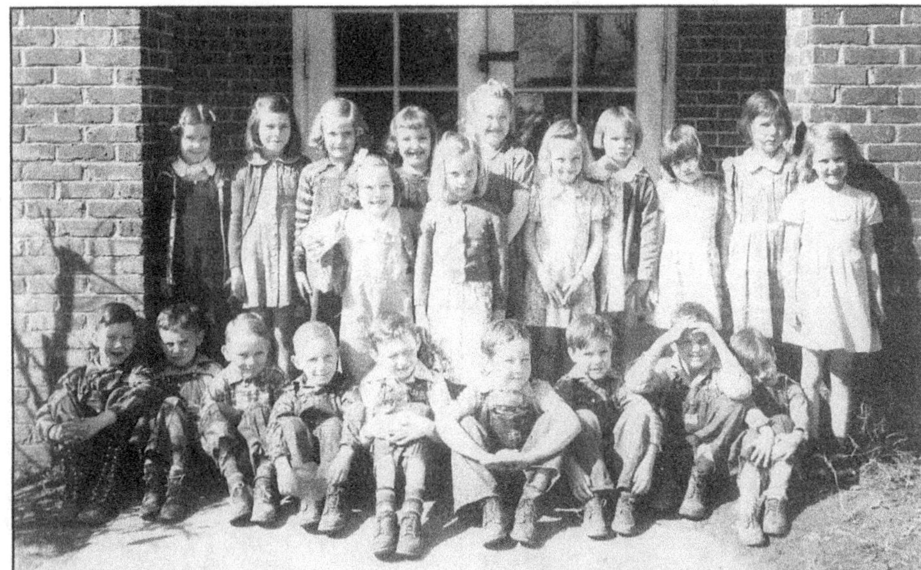

Miss Elizabeth Pilkenton's 1947-48 first grade class at Zebulon Elementary School. Courtesy of Fay Pilkenton.

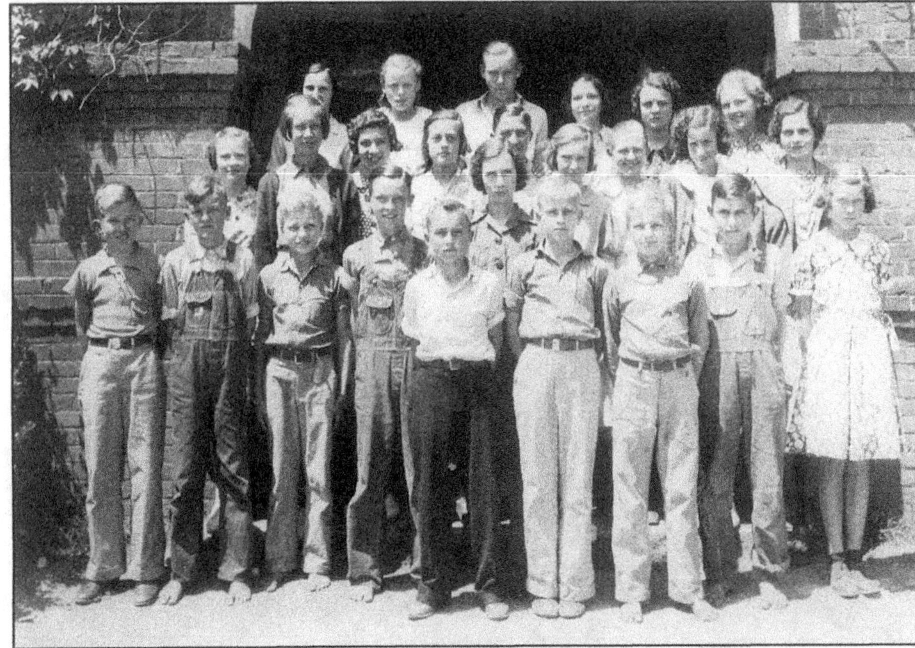

Zebulon School 7th grade class. Courtesy of Ophelia Shackelford.

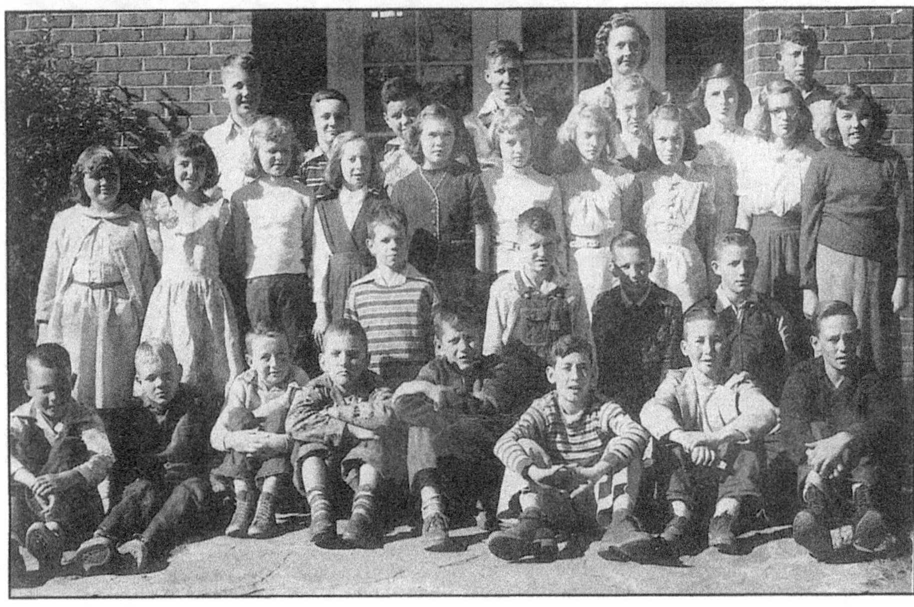

Zebulon Elementary School, 1947-48.

Zebulon High School 1951-52 ninth grade class. Front row: Earline Jones, Frances Johnston, Ellen Manley, Betsy Ross, Wylene Parks, Lucile Jones and Betty Sue Towery. Second row: Mr. R.E. Ballew, Patricia Hawkins, Ruth Bankston, Dale English, Earleen Goen, Faye Sandefur, Jane Elliott and Lee Willoughby. Third row: Ray Birdwell, Bobby Killingsworth, Warren Killingsworth and Julian Danielly. Courtesy of Jane Gaulding.

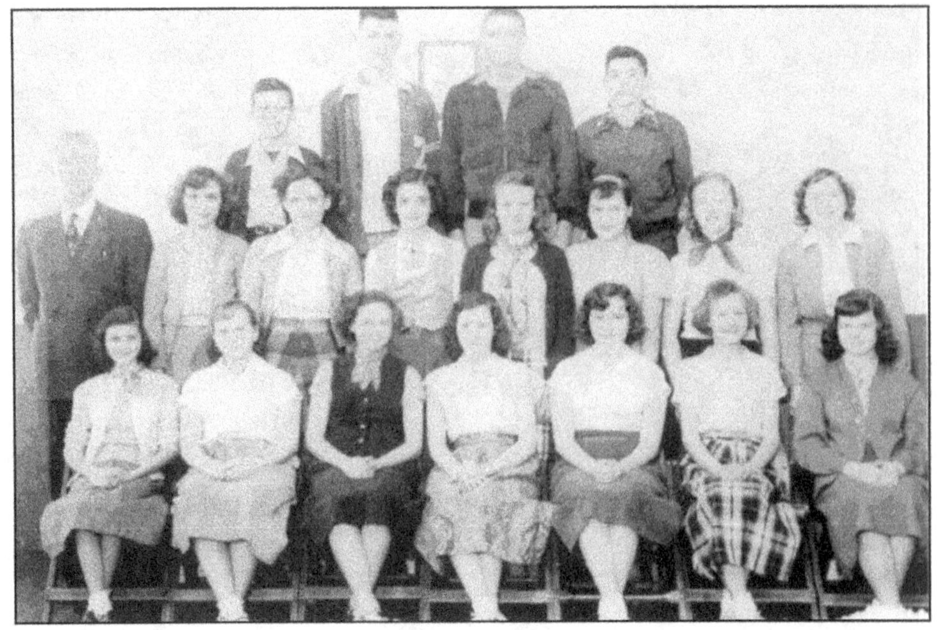

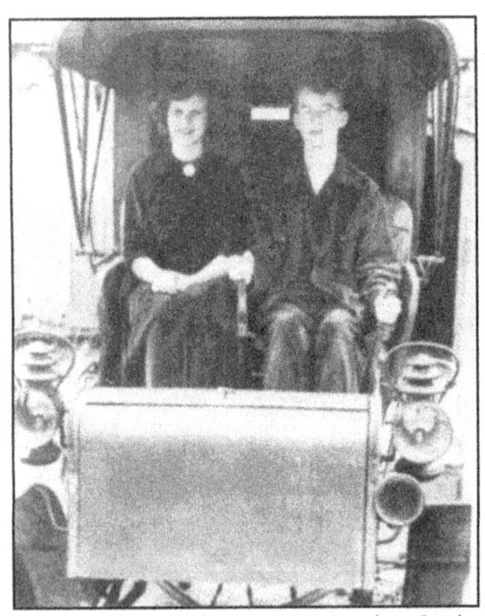

Zebulon High School, 1952 Most Popular: Carolyn McDougal and Sammie Baker. Courtesy of Jane Gaulding.

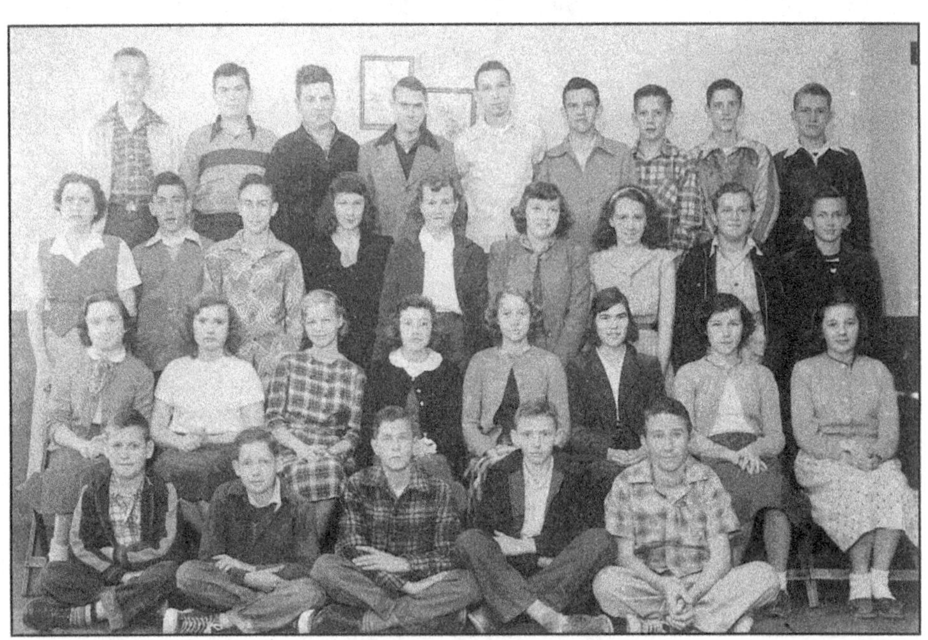

Zebulon High School, 1952.

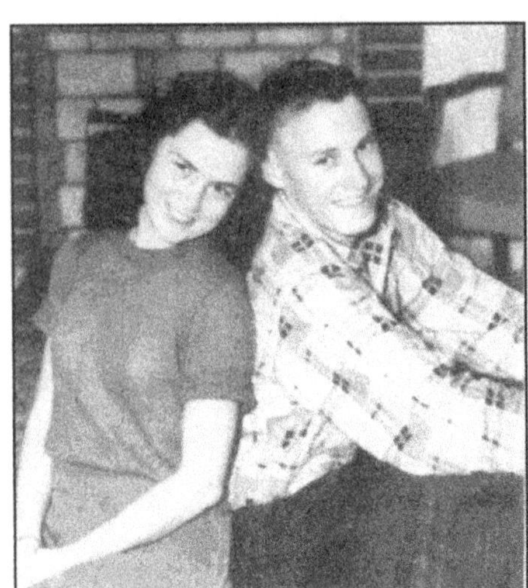

Zebulon High School, 1952 Cutest: Jeanette Stiles and Riley Shackelford. Courtesy of Jane Gaulding.

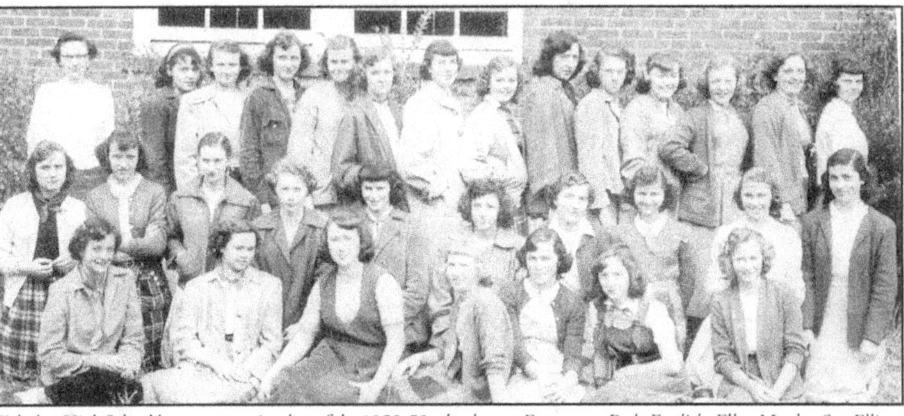

Zebulon High School home economics class of the 1952-53 school year. Front row: Dale English, Ellen Manley, Sue Elliott, Jackie King, Pearlie Ann Middlebrooks, Myrna Loy Cochran and Lucile Jones. Second row: Elaine Hawkins, Sara Holley, Allene Mann, Shirley Brannon, Katie Allen, Claudette Goldman, Lee Willoughby, Earline Jones, Mamie Malone and Louise Eubanks. Third row: Carolyn Whithurst, Faye Sandefur, Earlene Goen, Patricia Hawkins, Carolyn Gordy, Judy Johnson, Carol Taylor, Joyce Dukes, Elizabeth Smallwood, Martha Pitts, Phyllis McLeroy, Jane Elliott, Ruth Bankston and Betty Sue Towery. Courtesy of Jane Gaulding.

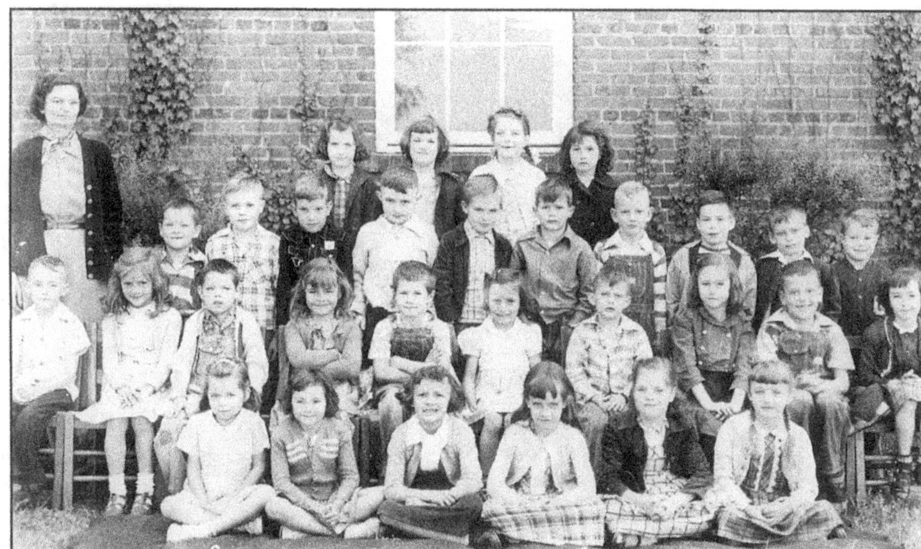

Miss Elizabeth Pilkenton's 1951 second grade class at Zebulon Elementary School. Courtesy of Fay Pilkenton.

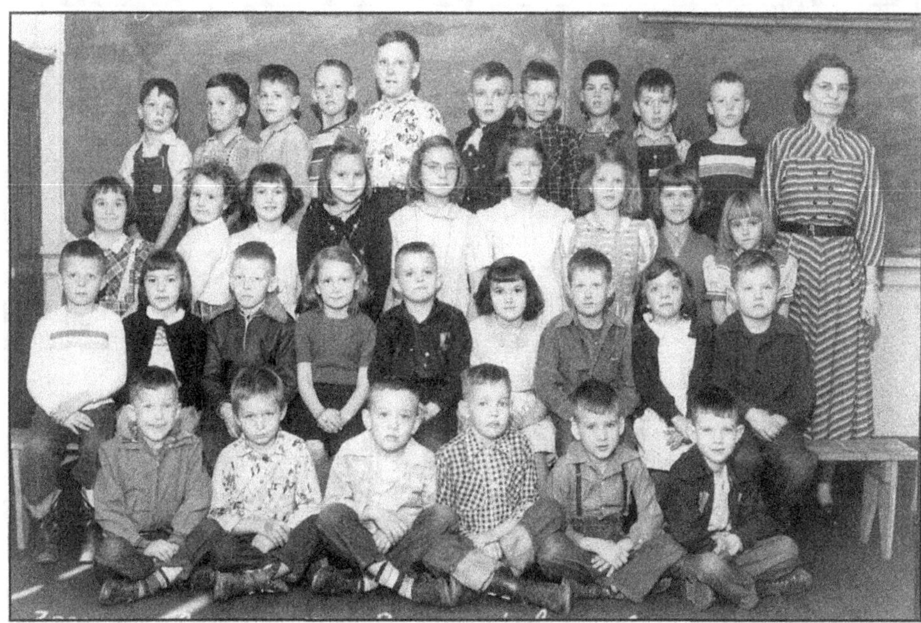

Miss Elizabeth Pilkenton's 1954 second grade class at Zebulon Elementary School. Courtesy of Fay Pilkenton.

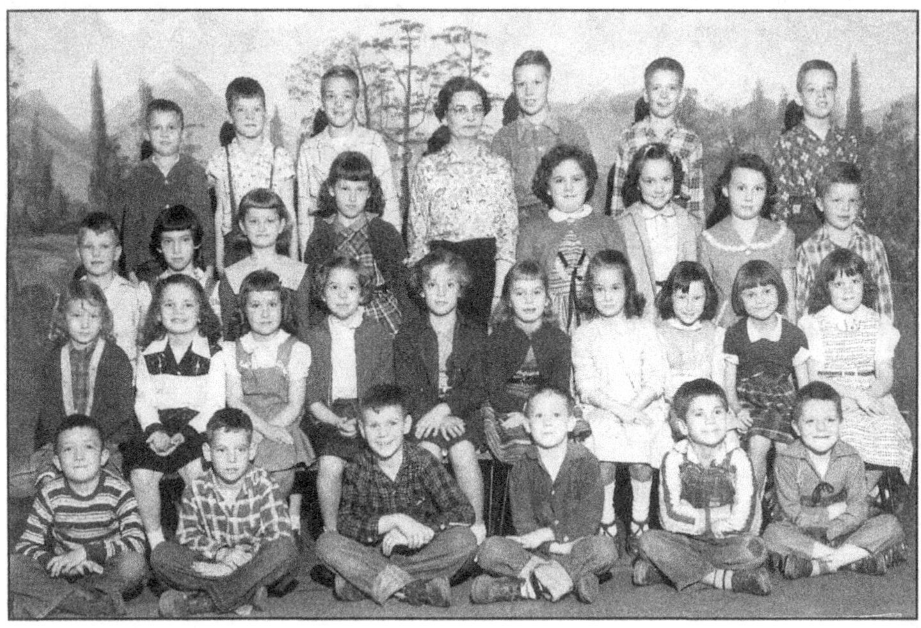

Miss Elizabeth Pilkenton's 1955-56 second grade class at Zebulon Elementary School. Courtesy of Fay Pilkenton.

Miss Elizabeth Pilkenton's 1952 second grade class at Zebulon Elementary School. Courtesy of Fay Pilkenton.

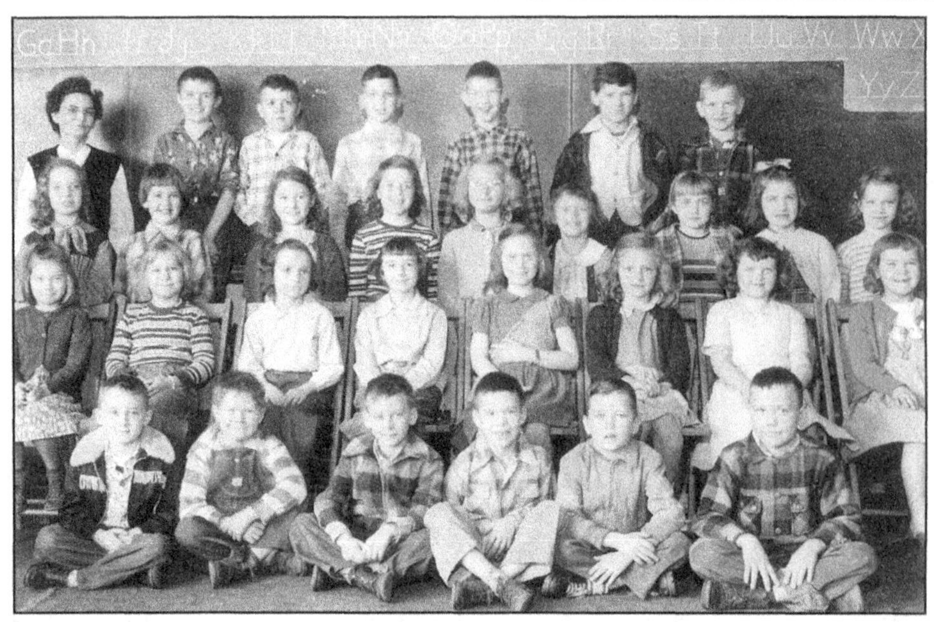

Zebulon High School Class of 1955. This was the last graduating class of Zebulon High. Front row: Eddie Brannon (Class Mascot), Dale English, Connie Rogers, Patricia Hawkins, Mary Ann Reeves, Shirley Brannon, Frances Johnston, Ellen Manley, Lee Willoughby, Judy Johnson and Joyce Smith (Class Mascot). Second row: Earlene Jones, Jane Elliott, Sylvia Bishop, Faye Sandefur, Betty Sue Towery, Madge Weatherly, Lucile Jones, Carol Taylor, Wylene Parks, Sue Elliott, Martha Pitts, Katie Allen and Mrs. Eva Peek (Teacher). Third row: Elmer King, Ray Johnston, Monroe Brown, Mr. Robert Bellew (Principal), Julian Danielly, Roy Littleton, Ray Birdwell, George Norris, Frank Glover, Warren Killingsworth, Buddy Gunnels, Wayne Shivers and Bobby Killingsworth. Courtesy of Jane Gaulding.

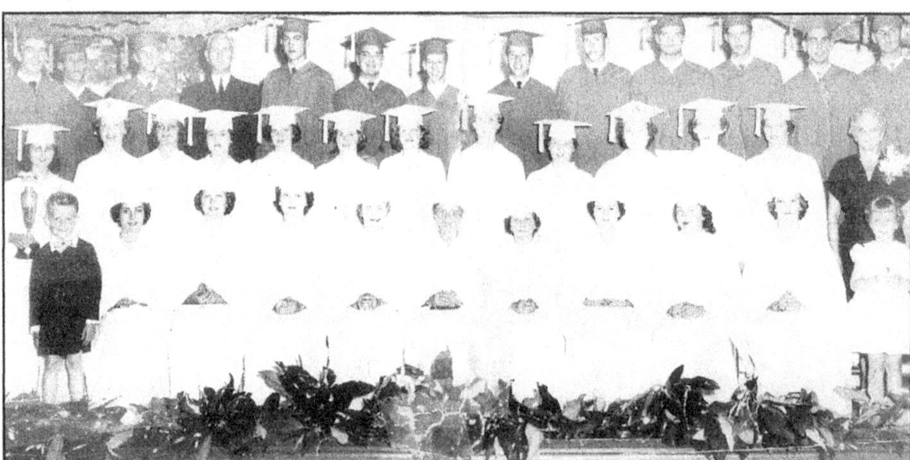

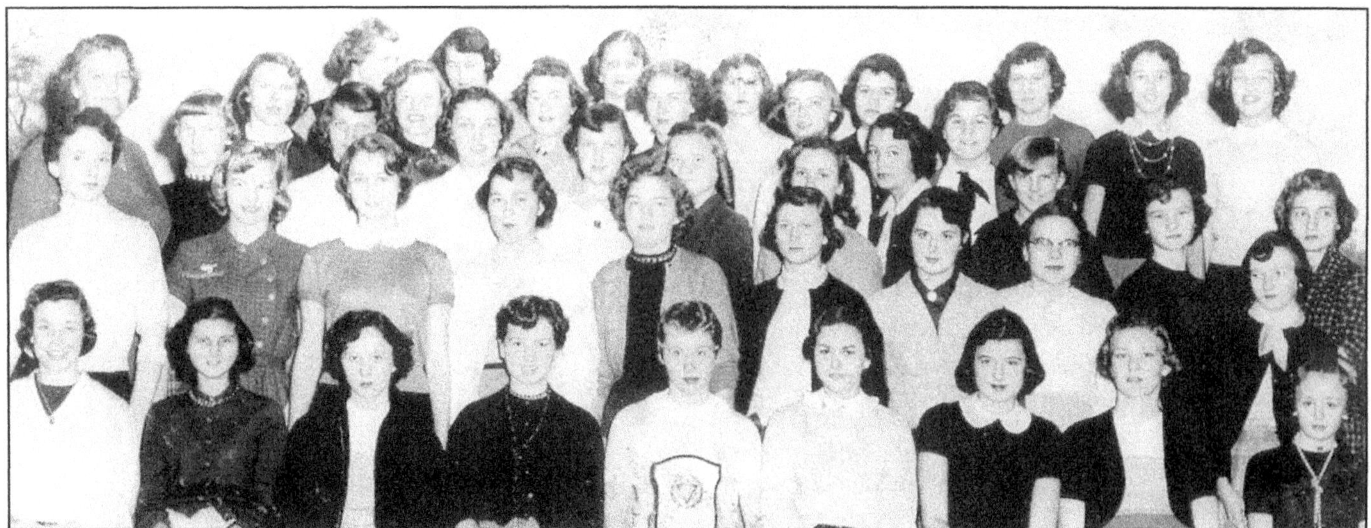

Zebulon High School TRI-HI-Y Club 1954-55. Front row: Carol Taylor, Earline Jones, Myrna Loy Cochran, Wylene Parks, Shirley Brannon, Ellen Manley, Mary Ann Sullivan, Judy Johnson and Brenda Ballard. Second row: Rachel Norris, Sue McKinley, Joanne Buffington, Pearlie Ann Middlebrooks, Lee Willoughby, Patsy Jones, Pat Brannon, Charlotte Murphy, Marie Dickens, Annie Bell Archer and Dale English. Third row: Lucille Means, Jackie King, Sylvia Bishop, Phyllis McLeroy, Betty Middlebrooks, Bobbie Jean Wilson, Elaine Hawkins, Sara Pilcher and Ramona Story. Fourth row: Connie Rogers, Jane Elliott, Sue Elliott, Martha Pitts, Dell Bottoms and Carol Garner. Fifth row: Gloria Taylor, Katie Allen, Martha Lee Means, Madge Weatherly, Faye Sandefur, Bernice Caraway, Donna McKinley and Lawanda McLeroy. Courtesy of Jane Gaulding.

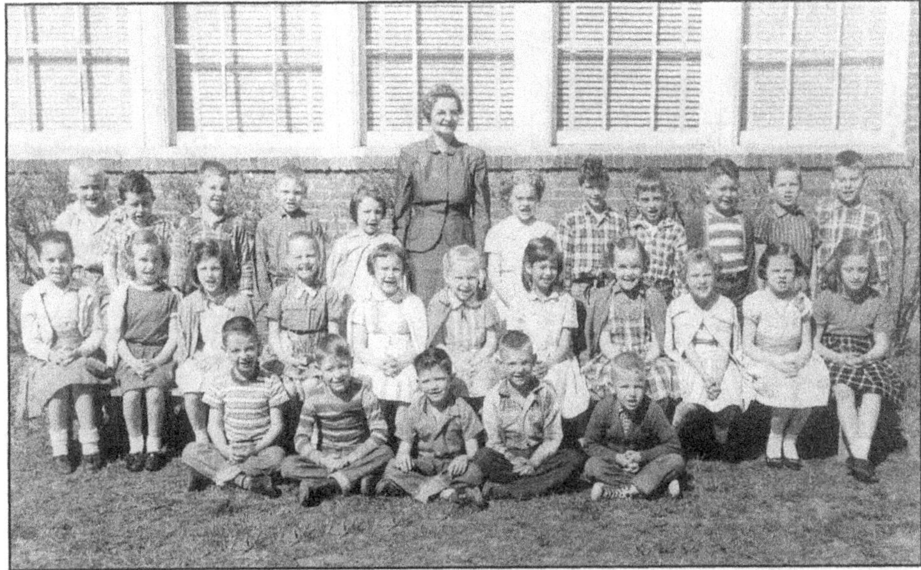

Miss Elizabeth Pilkenton's 1960 class at Zebulon Elementary. Courtesy of Fay Pilkenton.

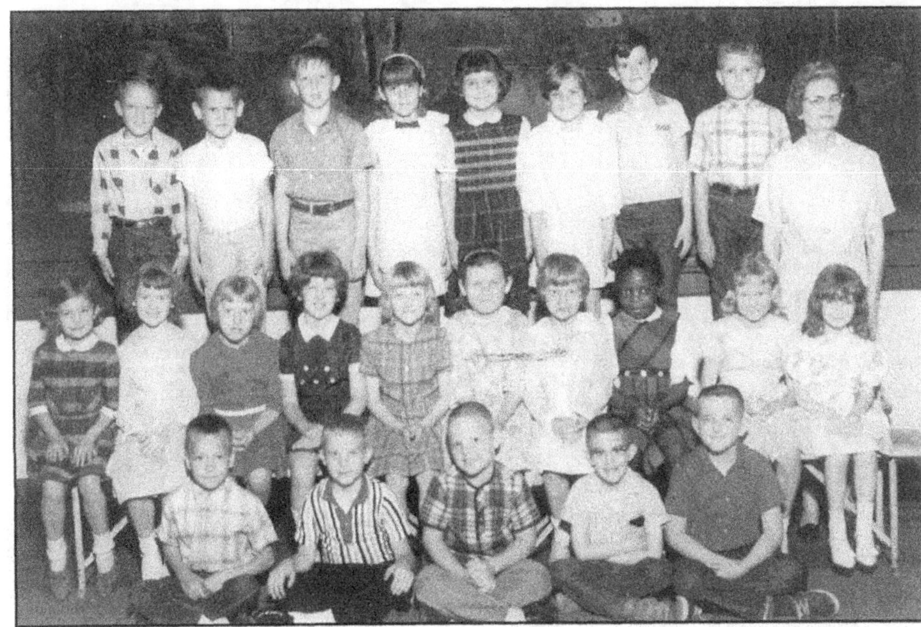

Zebulon School 1966-67 school year, Miss Pilkenton's second grade class. Courtesy of Dorothy Graham.

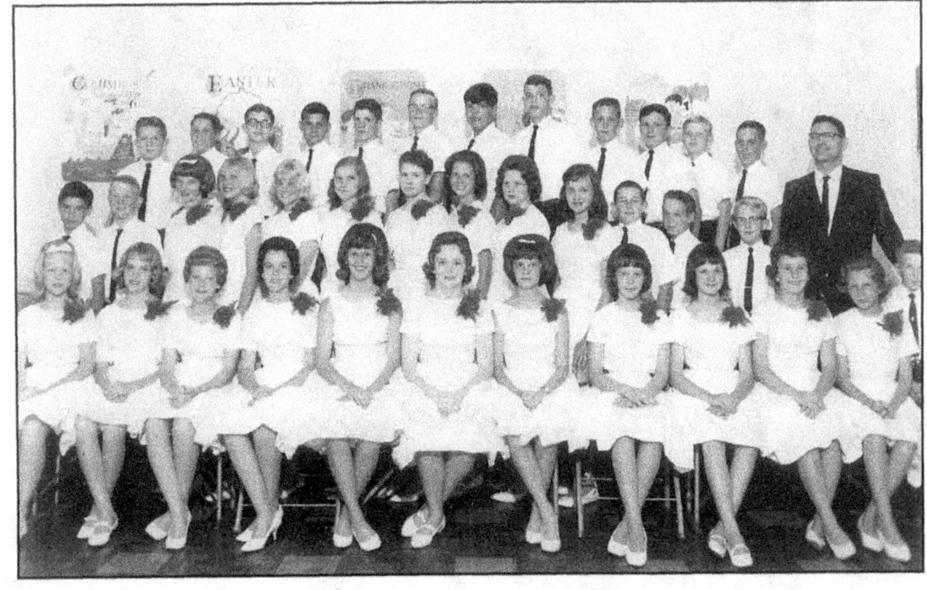

Zebulon Seventh Grade Graduation Class of 1965. Courtesy of Dorothy Graham.

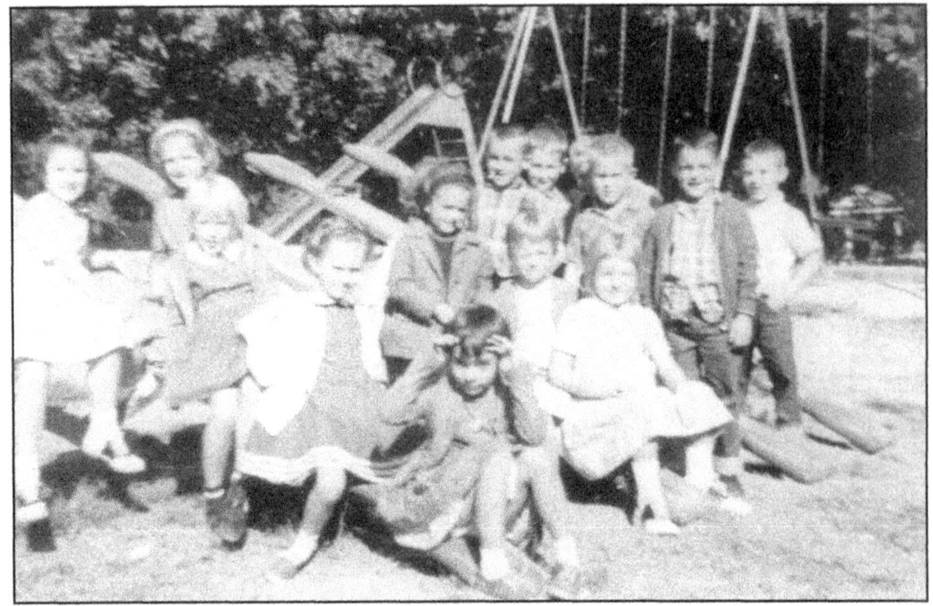

Old Zebulon elementary school 1963-64 first grade class. Courtesy of W.S. Rodgers.

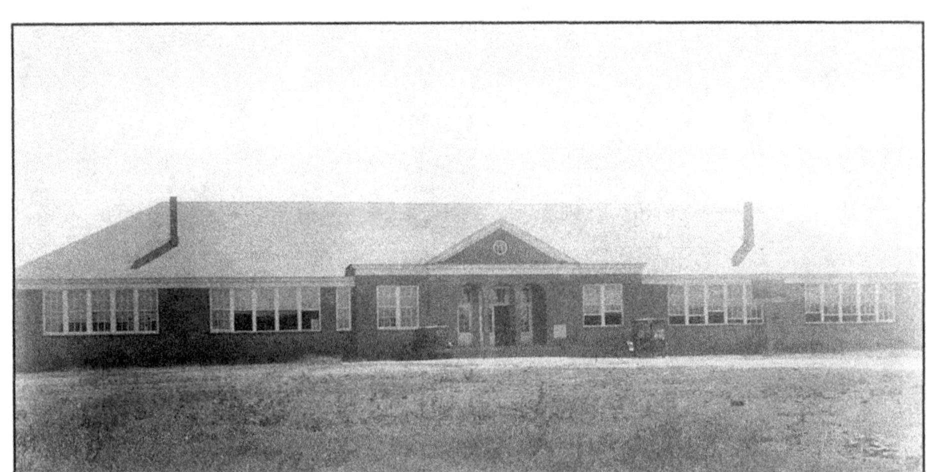

Molena School, built in 1915. It is now a nursing home. Courtesy of Rachel McClelland.

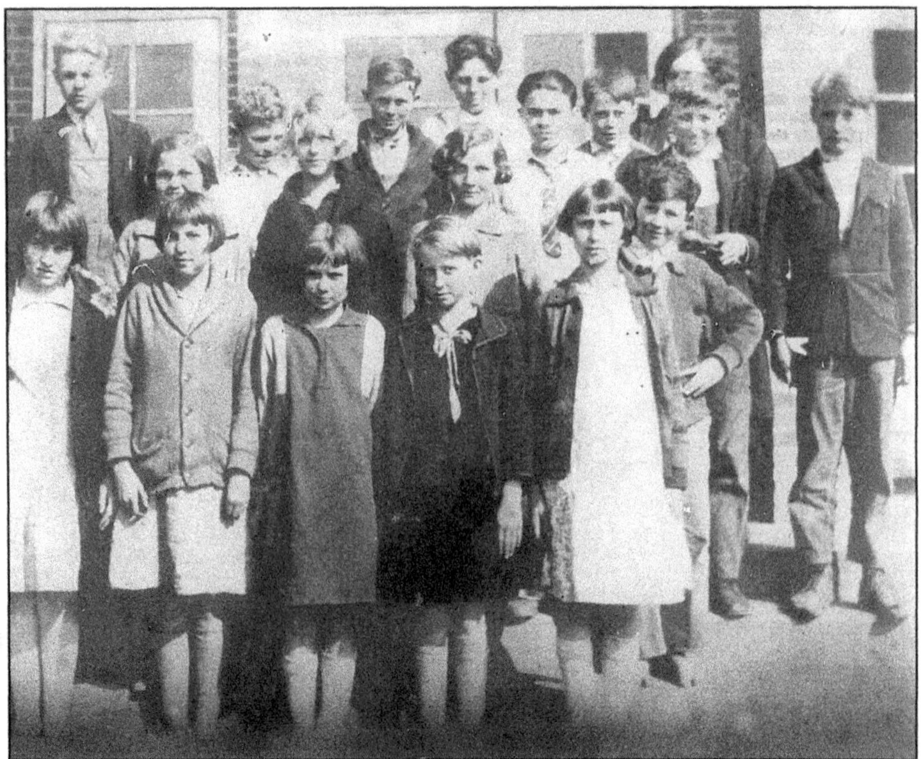

Molena High School 1927-28 8th grade class. 1st row, (L-R): Ezelle Davis, Doris Barber, Fay Pilkenton, Rubye Jones, Rebecca Reeves. Back rows: Ezra Cox, Hazel Brown, Leon Park, Jeanette Strikling, Mont Eppinger, Edna Kelley, Brooks Sartain-back of Edna, Carl Hill, James Griffin, Lowell Park, Linton Riggins-back of Lowell, Miss Ida Roberts, Teacher-back of Linton, Pruit Jones. Courtesy of Fay Pilkenton.

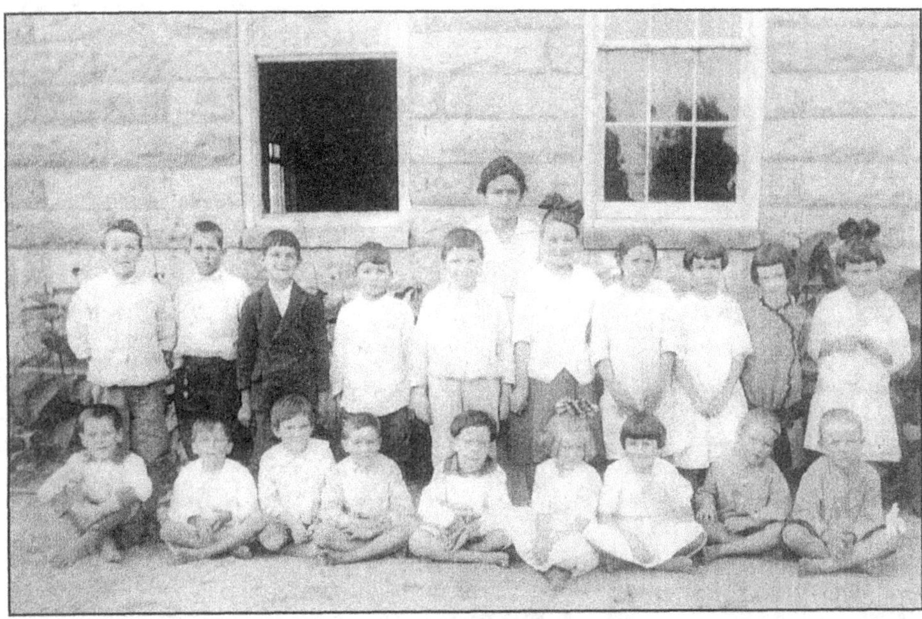

Students in front of Molena School, circa 1917 or 1918. Courtesy of Elna Capel.

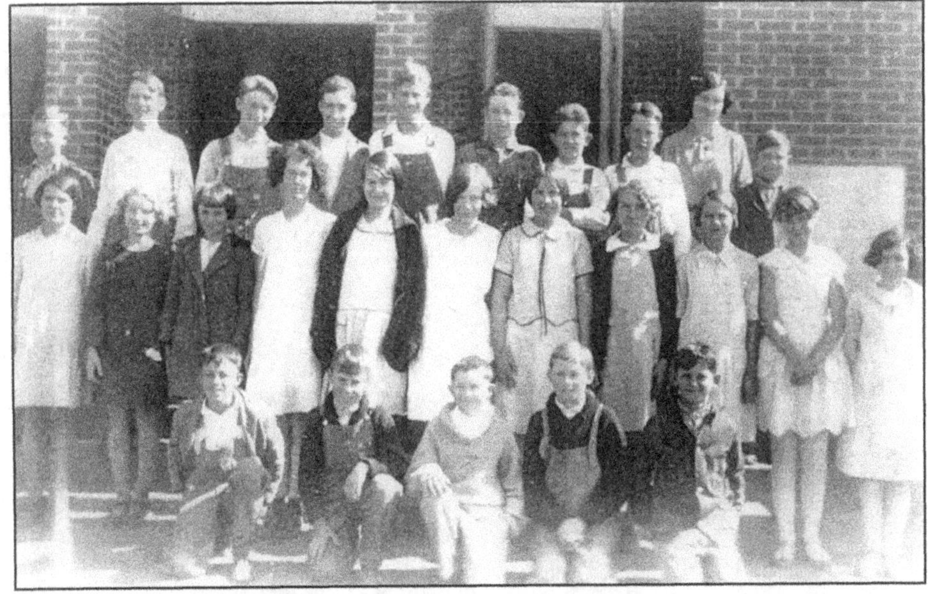

Molena School 6th and 7th grade students during the 1928-29 school year. Courtesy of Elna Capel.

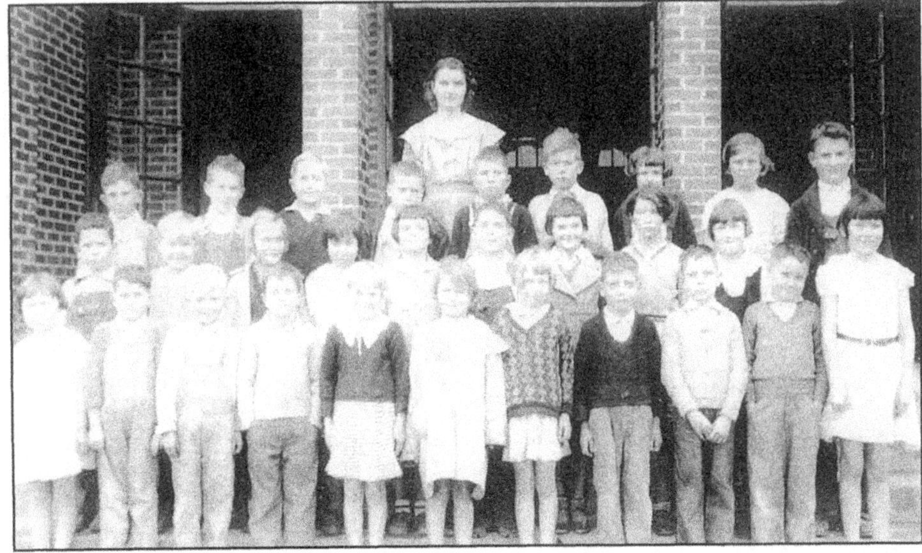

Molena School 2nd and 3rd grade students during the 1932-33 school year. Courtesy of Elna Capel.

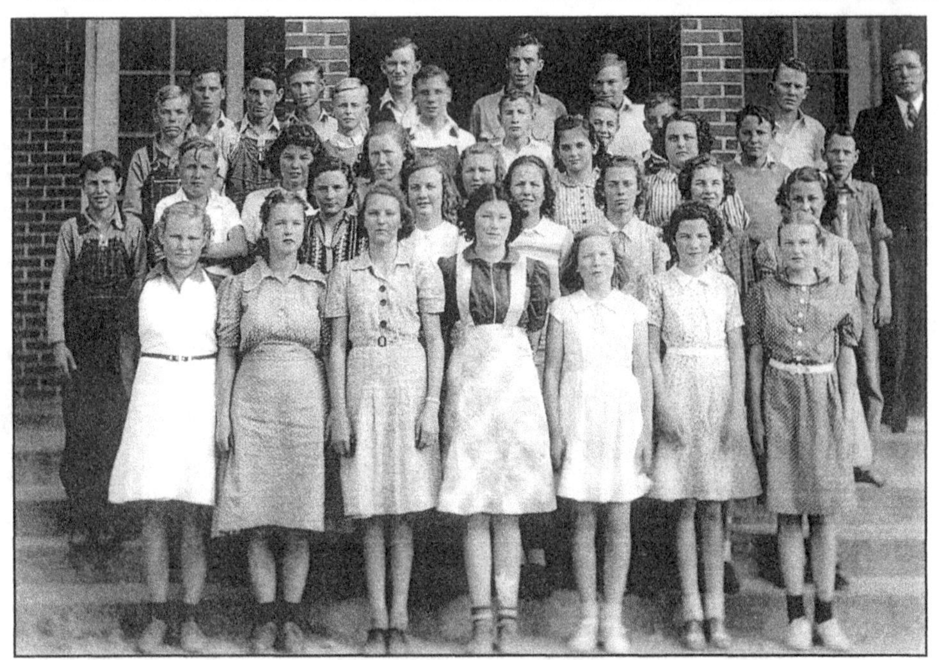

Grades 8 and 9 in 1939-40 at Molena High School. Courtesy of Elna Capel.

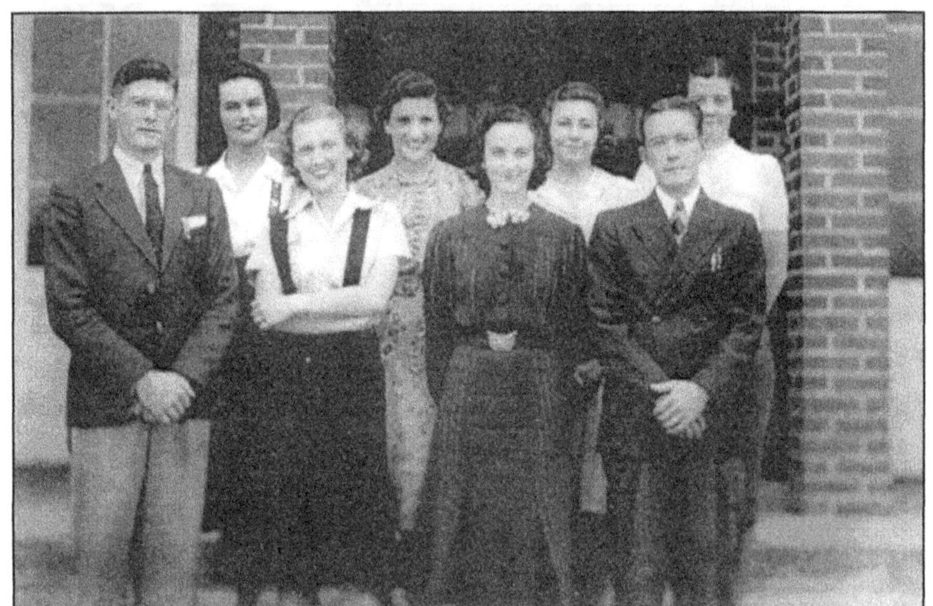

Faculty of Molena School 1939-40 school year. Front row: Marshall Elizen (Principal), Louise Hancock (7th Grade), Mary Wallace Quarels (6th Grade) and Therman Purcell (8th Grade, 9th Grade, Homeroom and Biology). Back row: Ernestine Woodson (10th Grade, Homeroom, English), Francine Neal (1st Grade), Ann McGarrah (4th and 5th Grades) and Annette Little (2nd and 3rd Grades). Courtesy of Elna Capel.

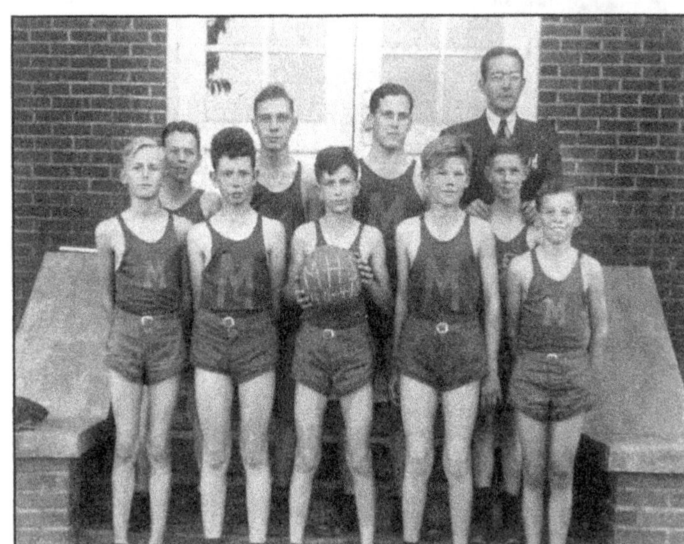

Basketball team of Molena High School in 1940. Courtesy of Geneva Sanders.

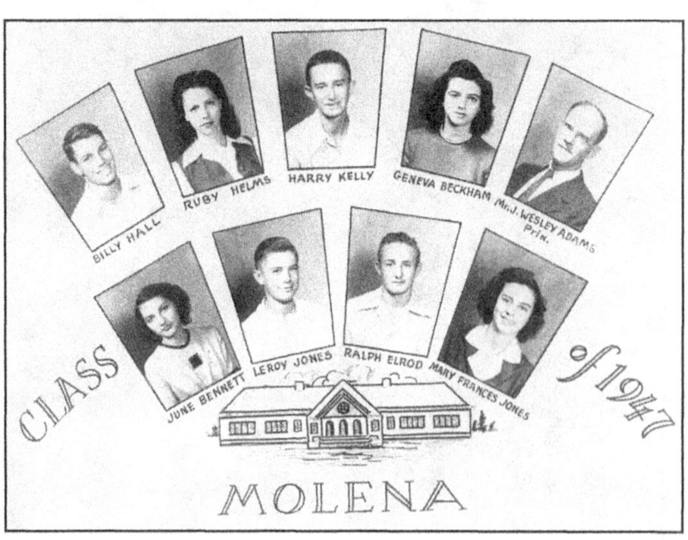

Last class at Molena High School before the school was moved to Concord. Courtesy of Geneva Sanders.

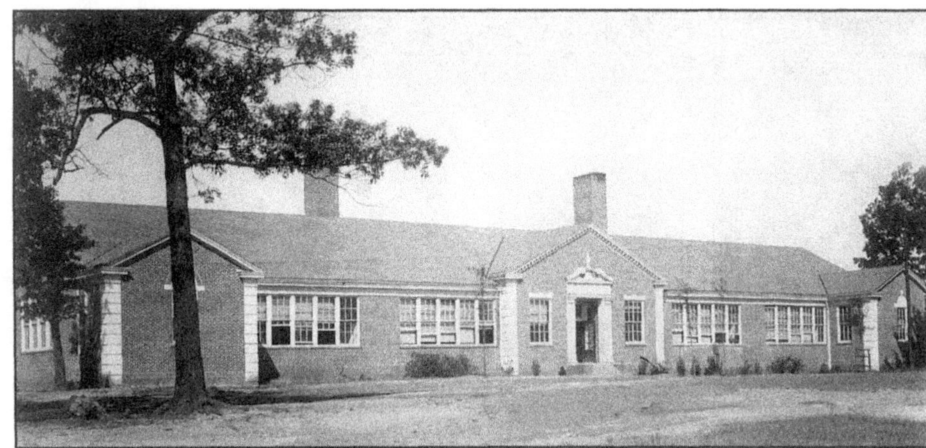

Concord School. Courtesy of Rachel McClelland.

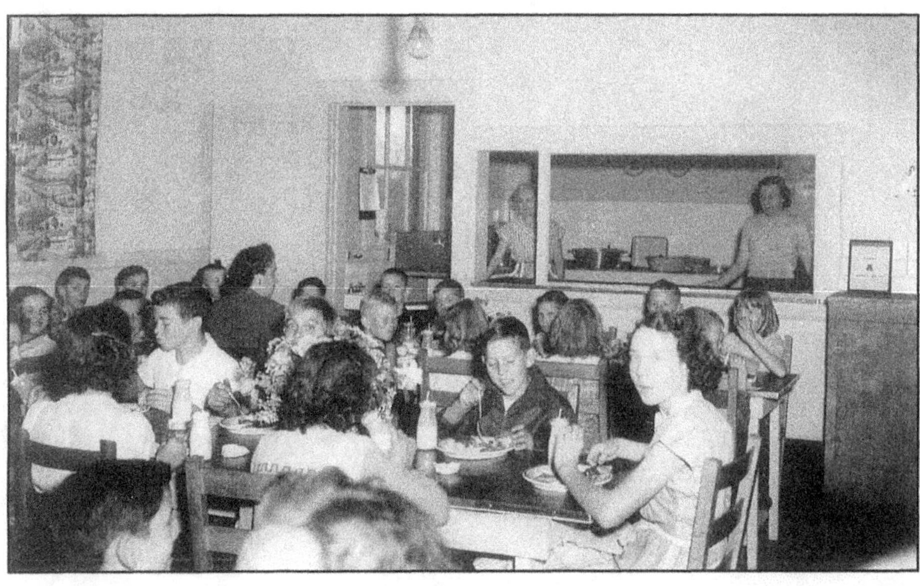

Concord School in the 1950's, Inez Crawford is on the left behind the counter. Courtesy of Barbara Dayhuff.

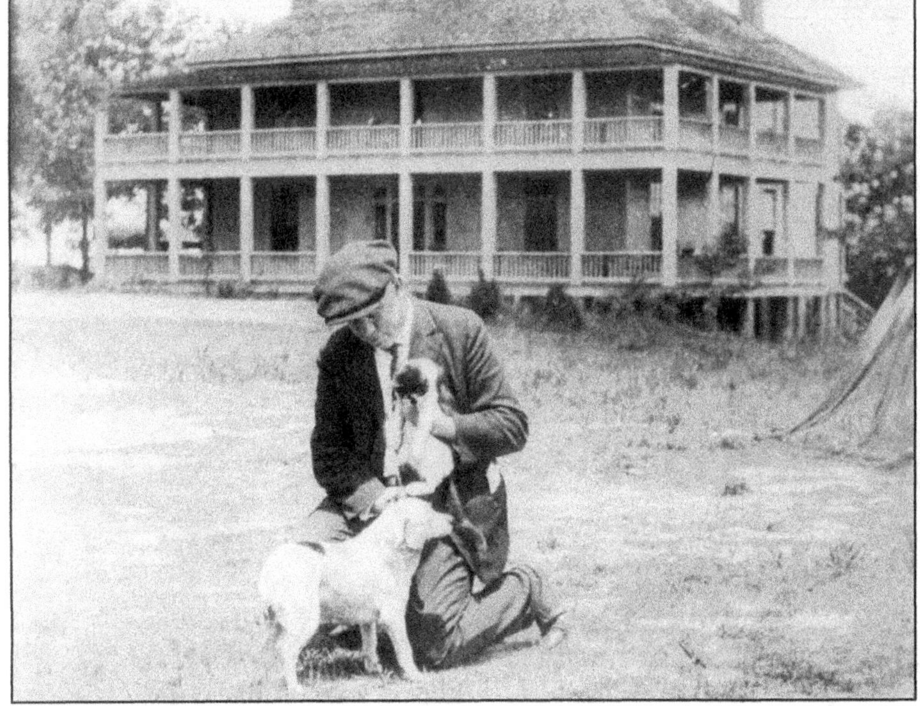

Supt. C.M. Carpenter and pets. Courtesy of Tom Morton and Ida Beckham.

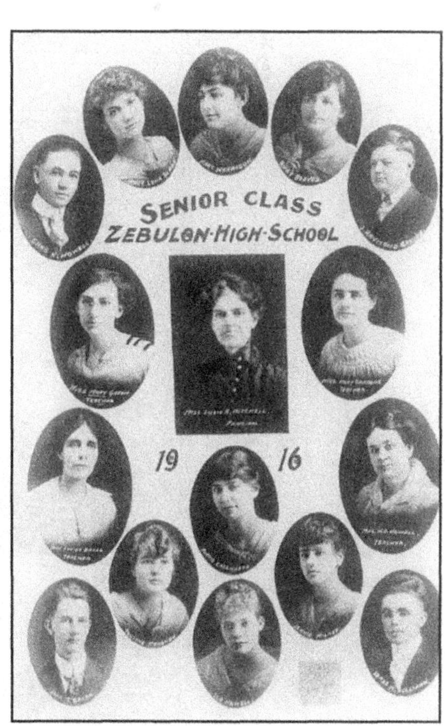

Zebulon High School 1916 senior class. Courtesy of Ida Beckham.

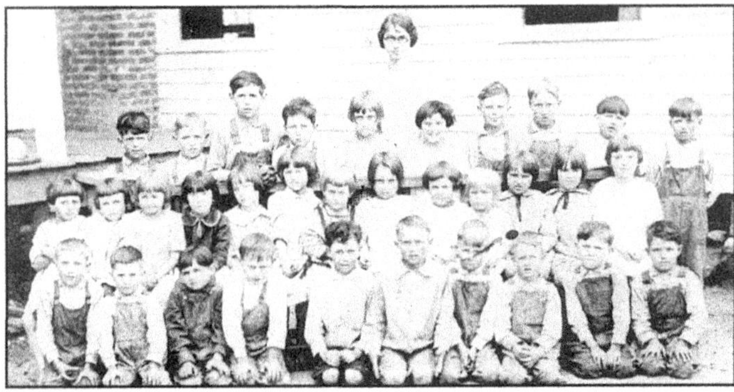

Mildred Brown's first grade class at New Hope School, 1921. Some of the children are: Alene Mullins, Ella Mae Cauthen, Claudia Brown, Bertha Smith, W.T. Buffington, James McCullough, Arvella Shivers, Lavenia Johnson and Mitchell Roan. All the children could not be identified. Courtesy of Wayne Foster.

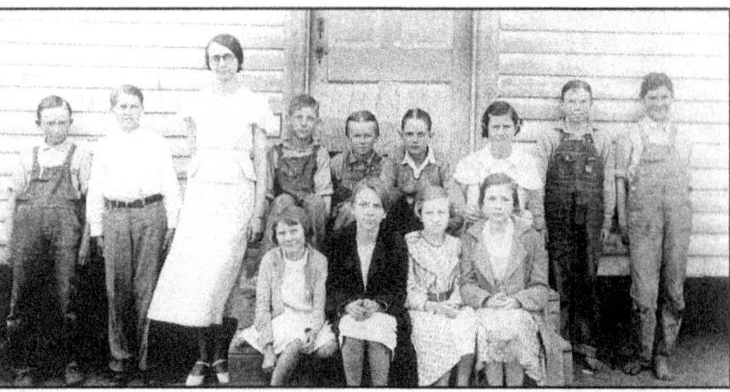

New Hope School, 1933-34 school year: Lamar Smith, Cecil McLean, Olene Caldwell (teacher), Carl Brown, Roland Ballard, James Perkins, Mildred McCullough, J.I. Harden, Luther Williams, Virginia Harden, Mary Perkins, Anice Harris and Ruth Cauthen. Courtesy of Wayne Foster.

Students from New Hope School in Pike County, circa 1927 or 1928. Courtesy of Susan Brown Parham.

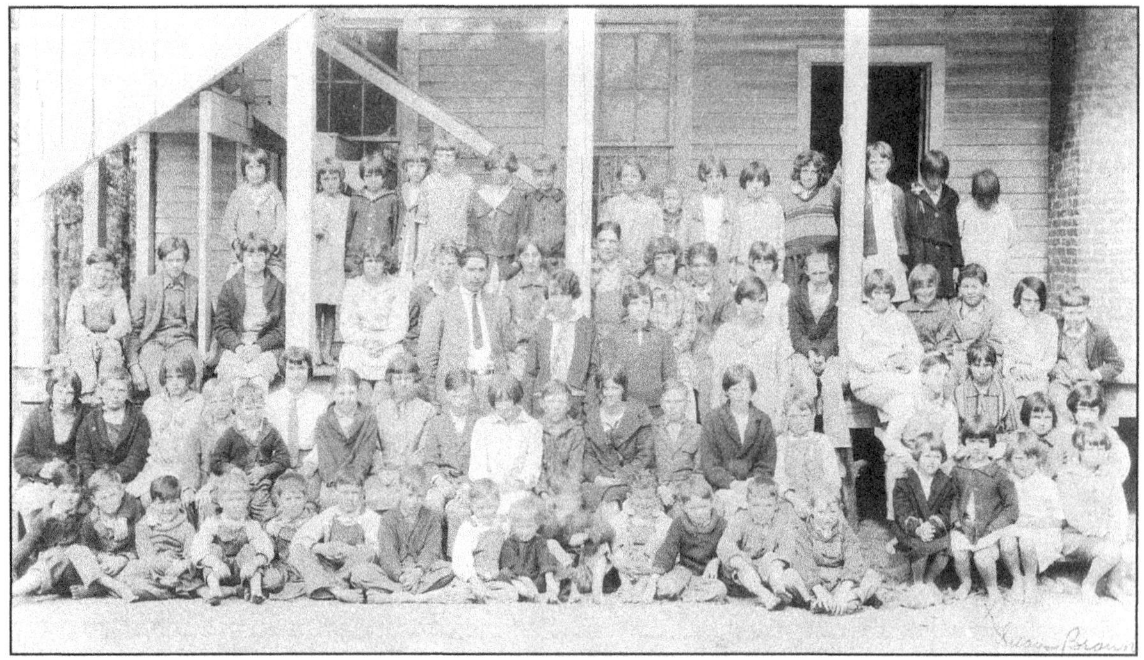

New Hope School class picture. Courtesy of Patsy Vaughn.

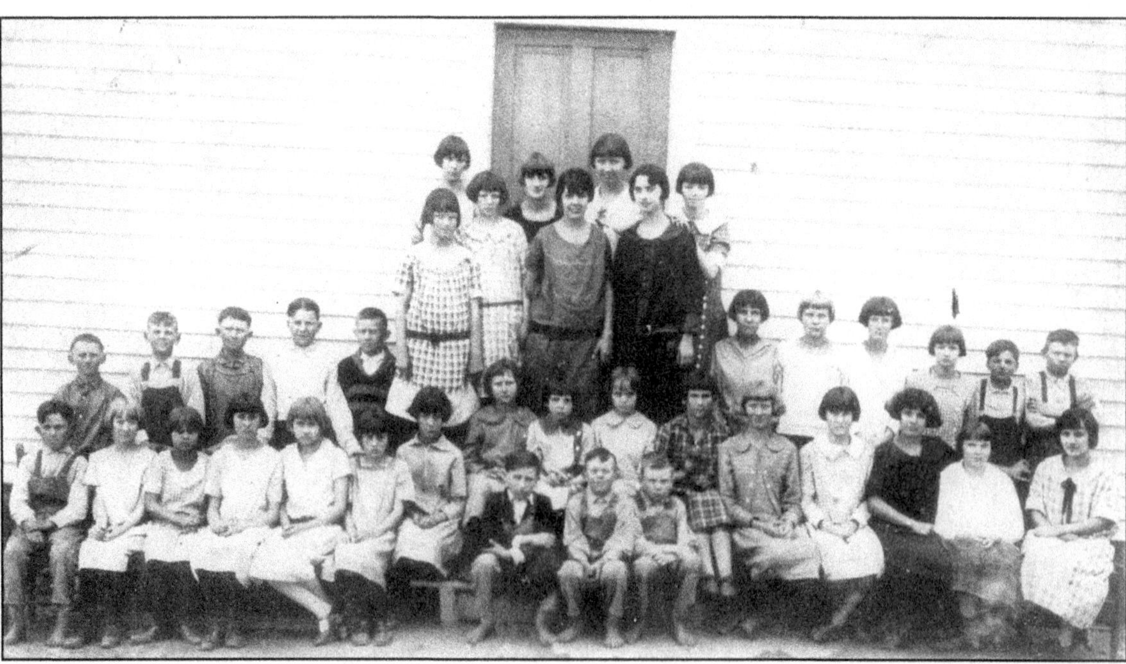

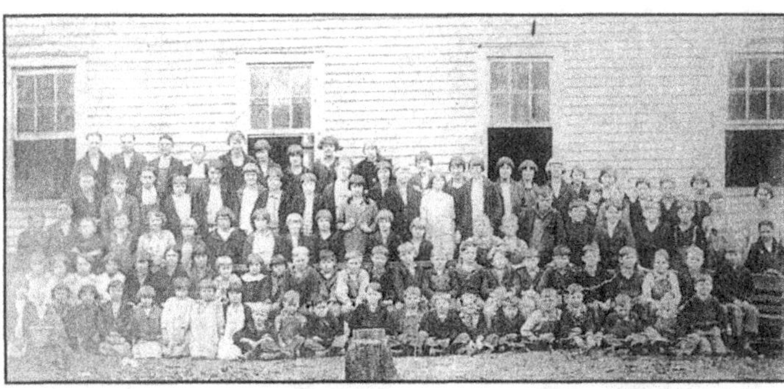

New Hope School students, circa 1923. Courtesy of Wayne Foster.

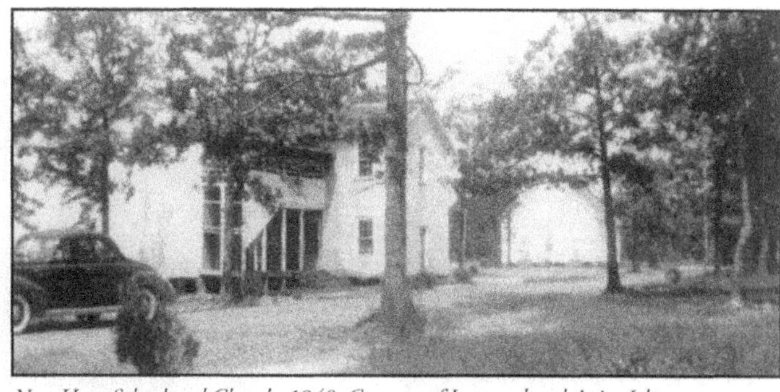

New Hope School and Church, 1940. Courtesy of Lynwood and Anita Johnson.

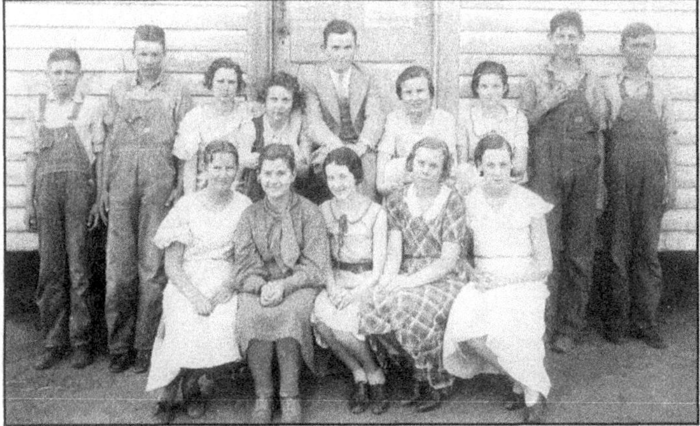

New Hope School in the 1930's: Hilton Harris, W.D. Cauthen, Frances McCullough, Elizabeth Perkins, Principal J.D. Roan, unknown student, Opal Roan, Charlie Brown, Gerald Ballard, Frances Glanton, Susan Brown, Mary Lena Ross, Inez Pitts and Lavania Harris. Courtesy of Wayne Foster.

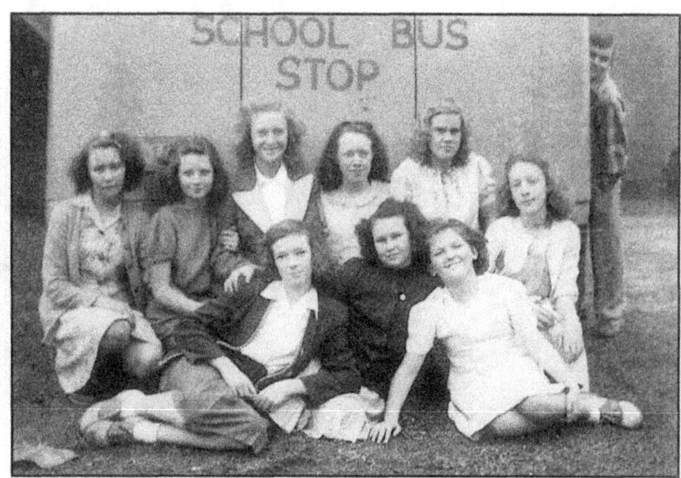

Williamson students waiting for the Zebulon High school bus in the late 1940's. Courtesy of William Ridley.

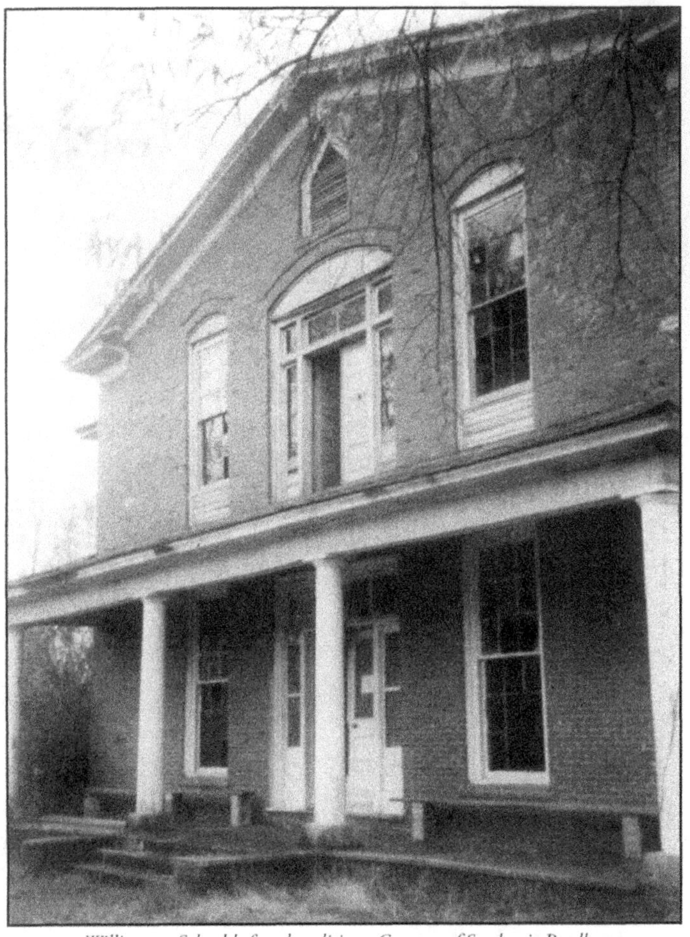

Williamson School before demolition. Courtesy of Stephanie Bradley.

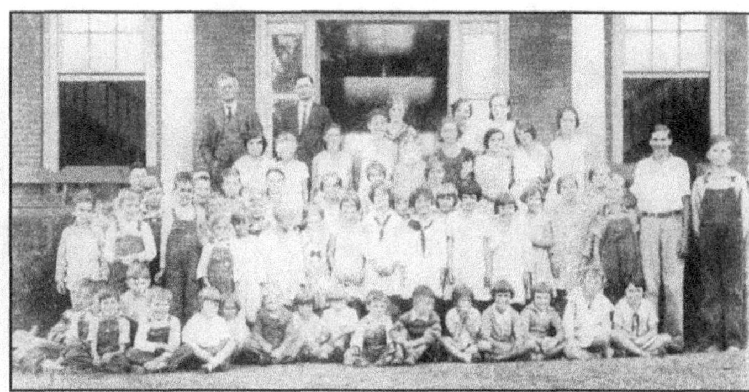

Williamson School students and staff, circa 1933. Courtesy of Joseph and Judith Reeves.

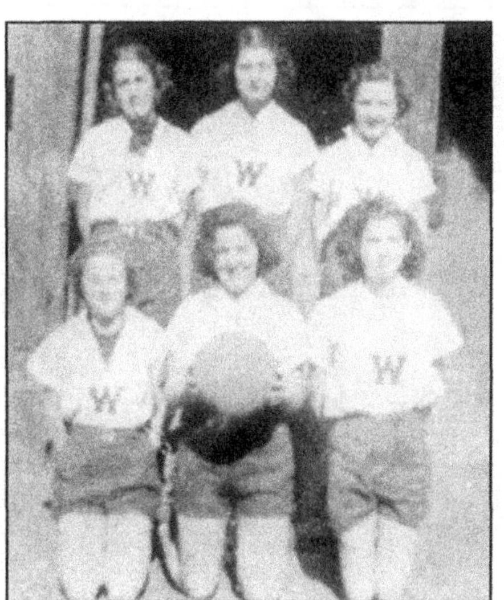

Girls basketball team from Williamson School, circa 1934. Back row: Elsie Terrell, Helen Hardy and Charlotte Pendley. Front row: Hazel Patton, Martha Pitts and Joy Jackson.

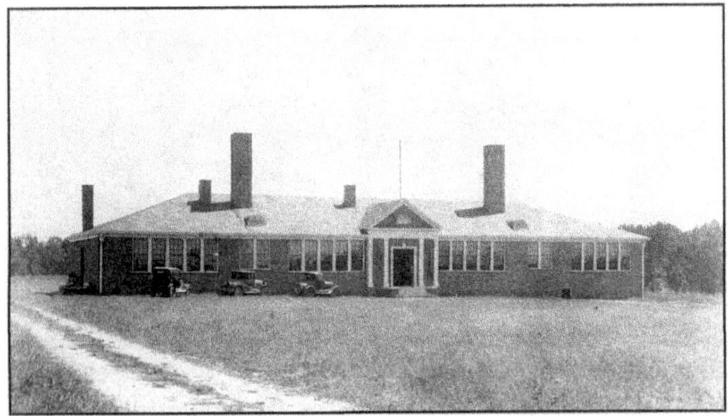

Meansville School. Courtesy of Rachel McClelland.

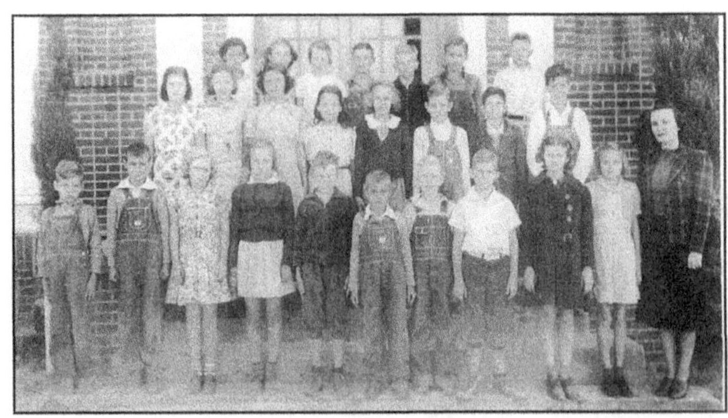

Meansville School Grades 5-6. Courtesy of Barbara Dayhuff.

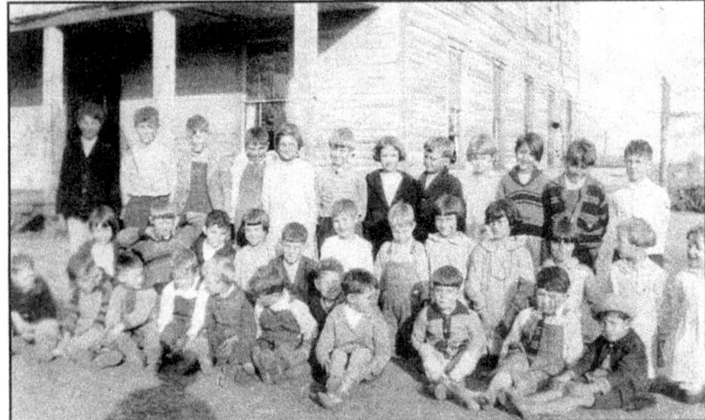

Meansville School students during the 1927-28 school year. Courtesy of Grace Ward.

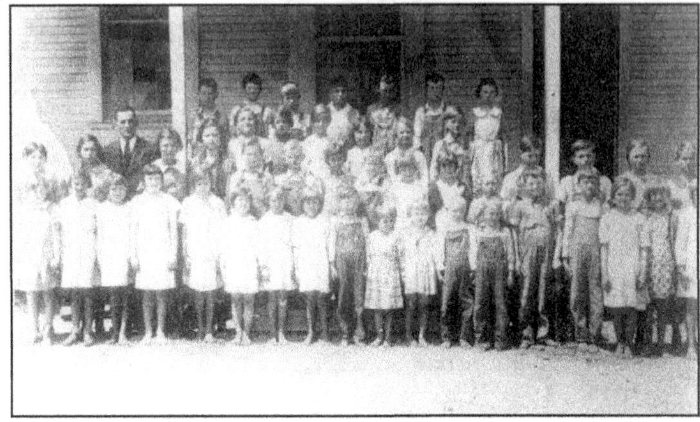

Lifsey Springs School, 1930. Courtesy of Virginia Brooks.

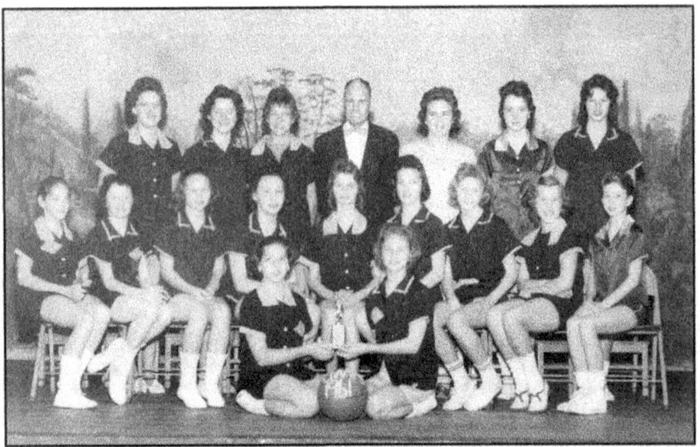

Class of 1961 basketball team. Courtesy of Dorothy Graham.

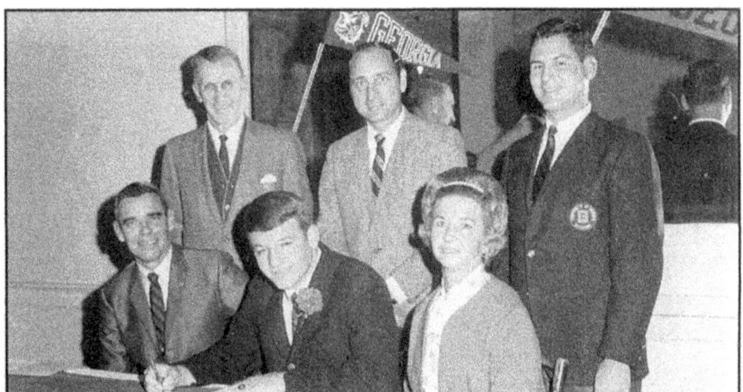

Charles Osbolt of Lifsey Springs signs a football scholarship with the University of Georgia at the Hotel Upson in Thomaston. Seated: John Osbolt, Charles Osbolt and Hazel Osbolt. Standing Jim Cavan, Vince Dooley (Head football coach UGA), Byrd Wigham (Assistant football coach UGA). Courtesy of Hazel Osbolt and Melissa Carraway.

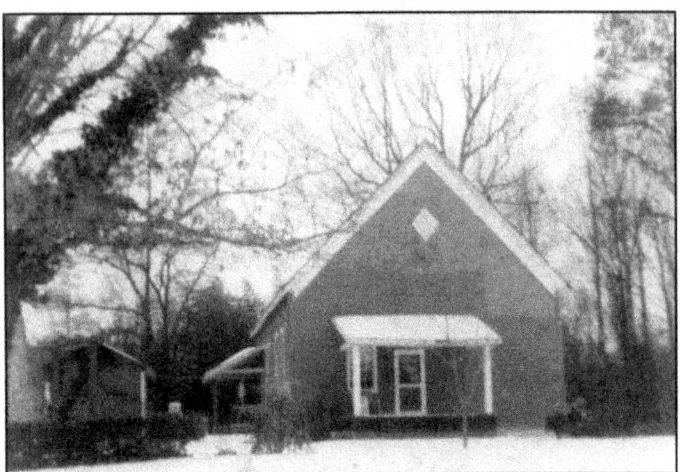

Lifsey Spring School house. Courtesy of Rosalee King.

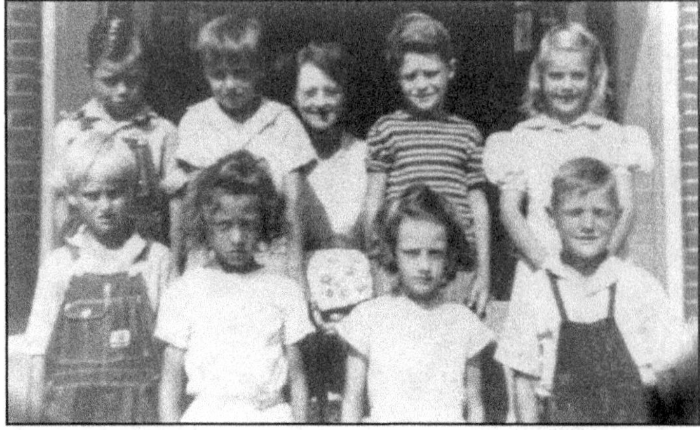

Hollonville School 1st grade picture 1945-46. Back row left to right: Alvin Quick, Bobby Kempson, Mrs. Mary Johnson, Eugene Blount and Barbara Pryor. Second row: Paul Garner, Betty Garner, Nancy Harrison and Bobby Turner. Courtesy of Barbara Martin.

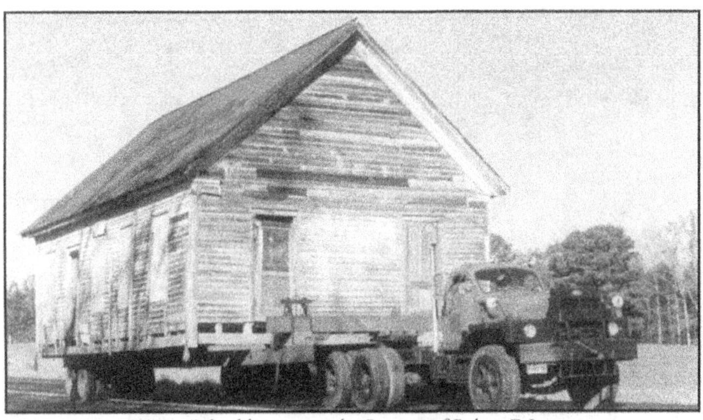

Union School being moved. Courtesy of Robert F. Jones.

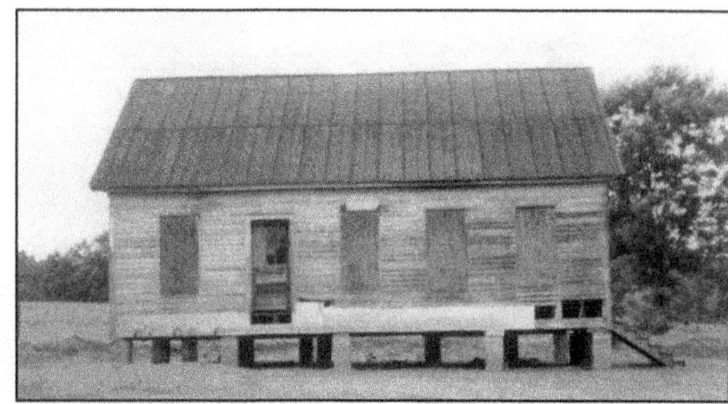

Old Union School, was located on Hwy 109 East of Molena, GA, it has been moved down the same road and is now located beside Jones Grocery store. Courtesy of Jane Gaulding.

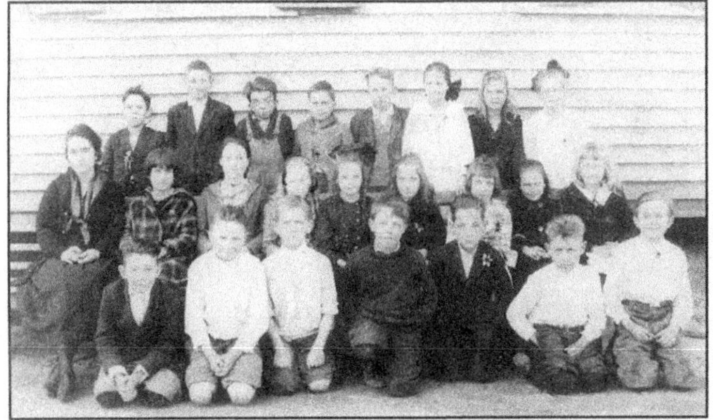

Pike County School 4th grade class, 1921. Courtesy of Tom Morton and Ida Beckham.

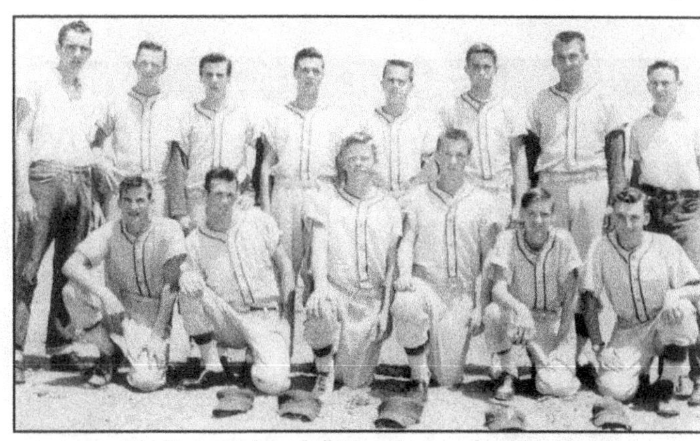

Pike County High Baseball Team. Courtesy of Jane Gaulding.

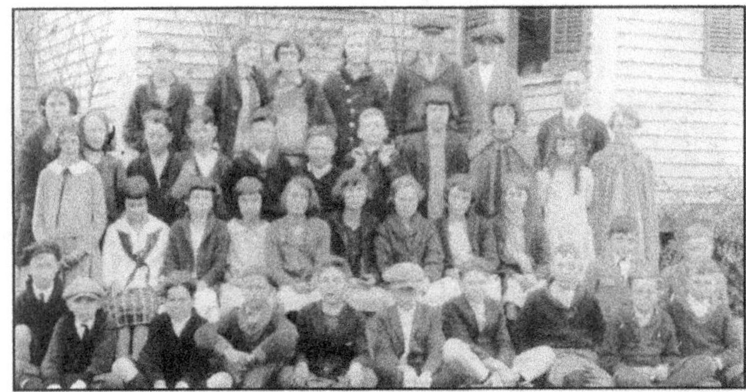

Mrs. Maude McClain's 6th and 7th grades classes of 1924. Courtesy of Tom Morton and Ida Beckham.

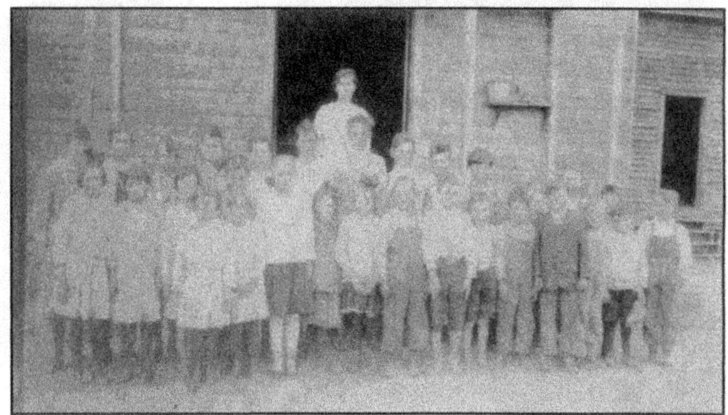

Flat Rock School

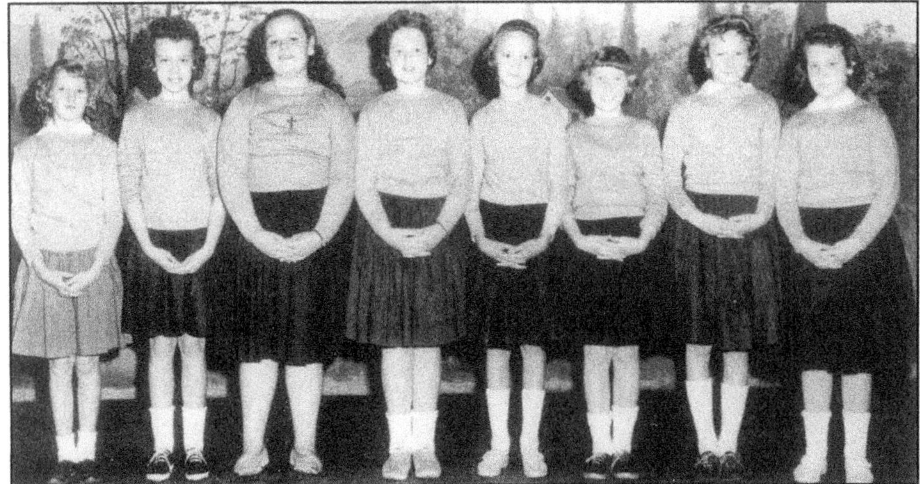

Cheerleaders for Pike County Elementary School: Jennie Brown, Sherrill Carter, Geraldine Durham, Rachel Hammock, Cathy Perkins, Jeannie Crump, Cathy Buffington and Patricia English, 1962 or 1963. Courtesy of Rachel Shaw.

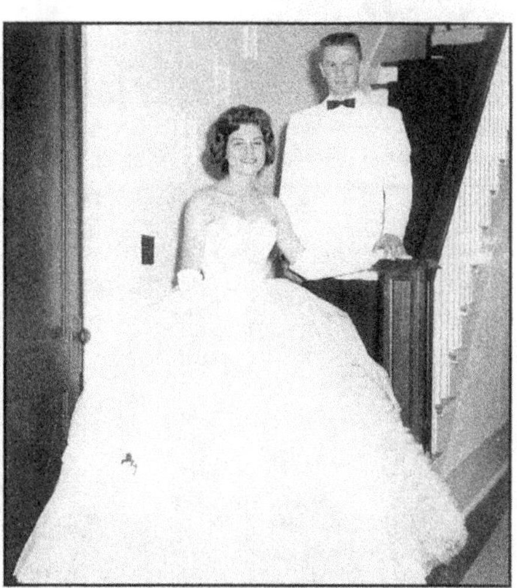

Cheryl Dunn and Jimmy Trice, voted "Best Looking" class of 1962, PCHS. Courtesy of Sylvia B. Wright.

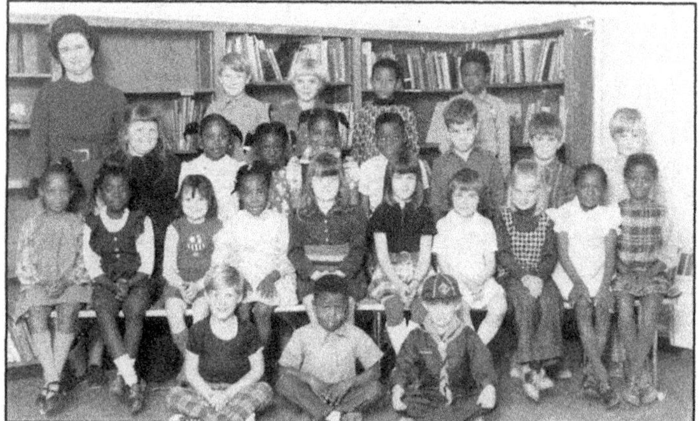

Pike County Primary School, Mrs. Watkins second grade class in 1974. Courtesy of Joann Fenley.

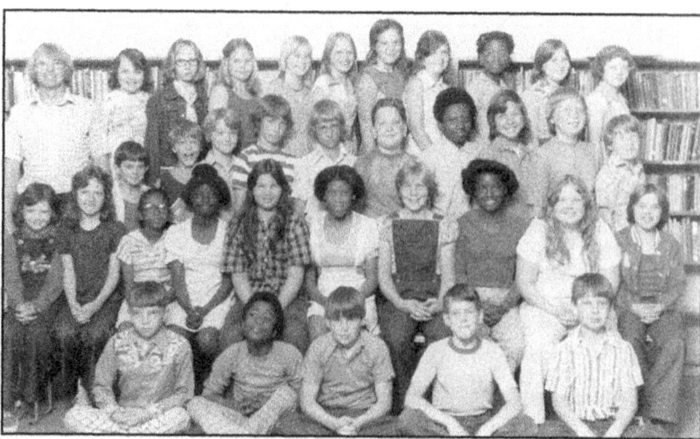

Mr. Campbell's 1976-77 fifth grade class at Pike County Elementary. Courtesy of Joann Fenley.

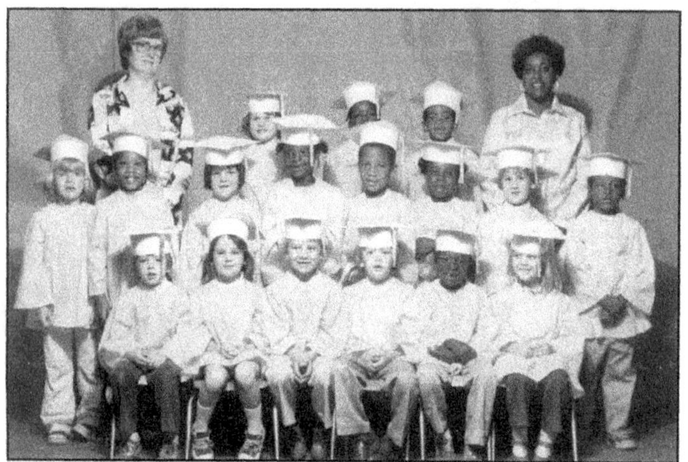

Mrs. Mays 1977-78 kindergarten class at Pike County Shool. Courtesy of Joann Fenley.

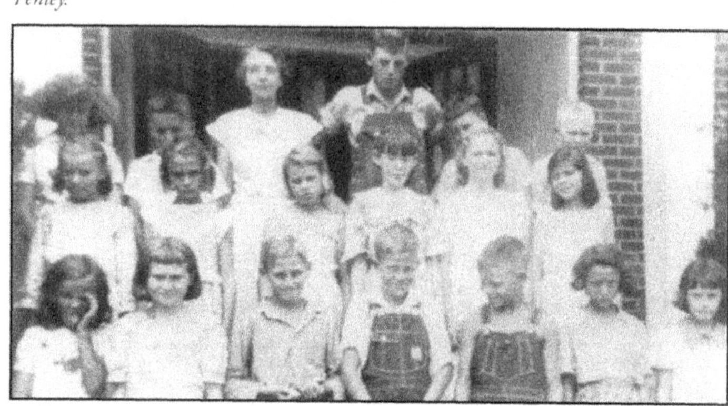

Back row: unknown, Bobby Kempson, Mrs. Ivee Adams, unknown, Wayne Pryor, Quincy Adams. Middle row: unknown, Emily Garner, Barbara Pryor, unknown, Carolyn Scott, Catherine McCullough, Front row: Frances McCard, Marie Scott, Paul Garner, unknown, Alvin Quick, Betty Garner, Nancy Harrison. Hollonville School, about 1949. Courtesy of Barbara Martin.

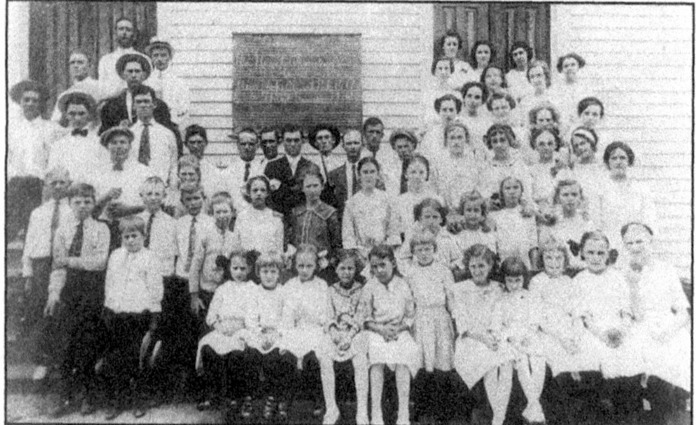

R.L. Hamil's Conservatory of Music. R.L. Hamil, Director, New Hope Church in Pike County Georgia, Third Session, 1914. Courtesy of Wayne Foster.

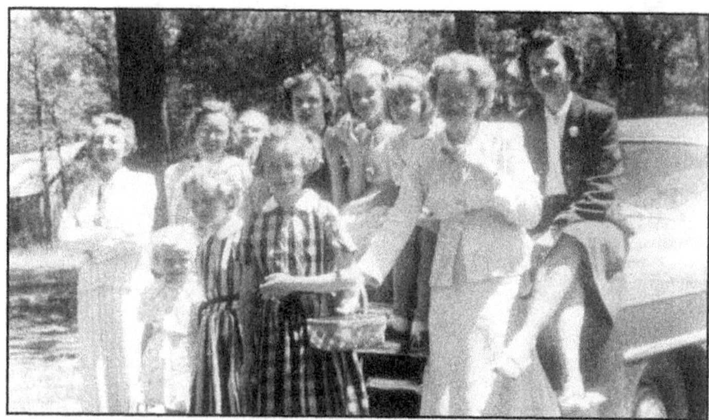

Easter Egg Hunt in 1954, front row: Ivie Adams, Ellen J. Lee, Sherry J. Reeves, Martha Johnson and Sara Smith. Back row: Elizabeth Johnson, Joe Gaulding, Jane Smith, Lorraine Herndon, Gail Hernden and Mary Gaulding. Courtesy of Virginia and Charles Oglesby.

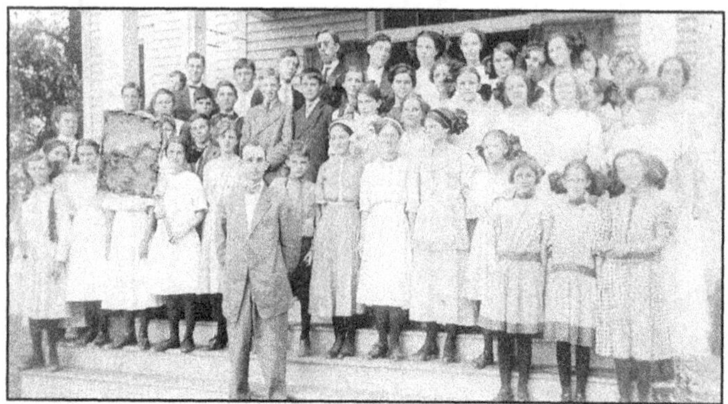

Donated by Ida Beckham.

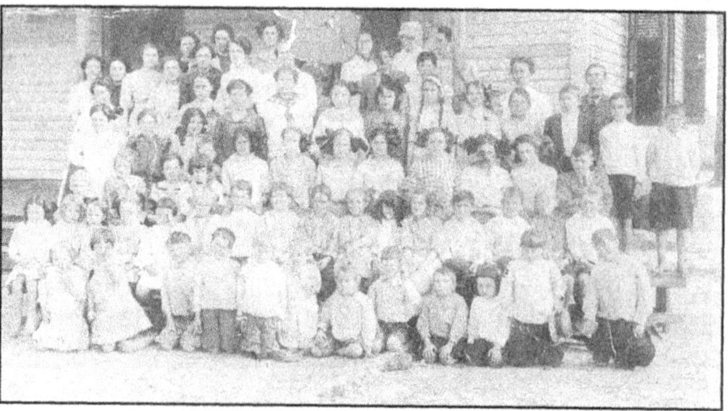

Donated by Ida Beckham.

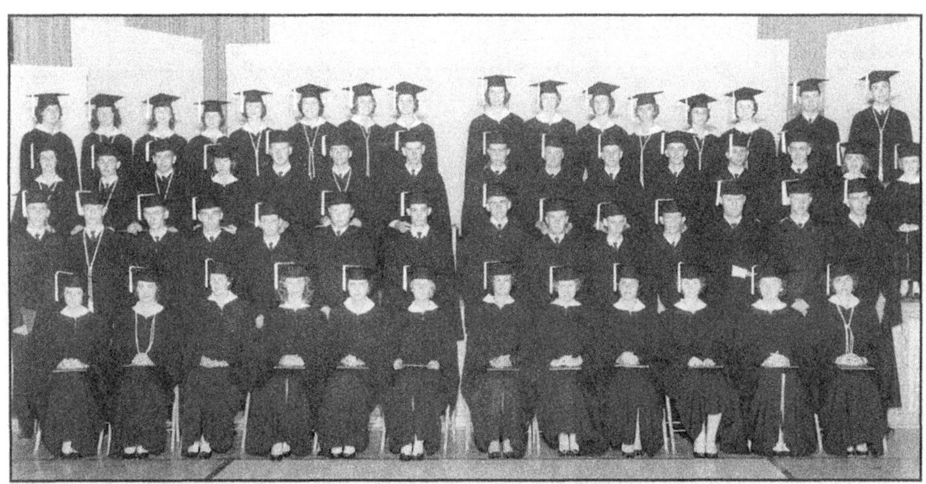

Pike County High School Senior Class graduation in 1962. Courtesy of Joann Fenley.

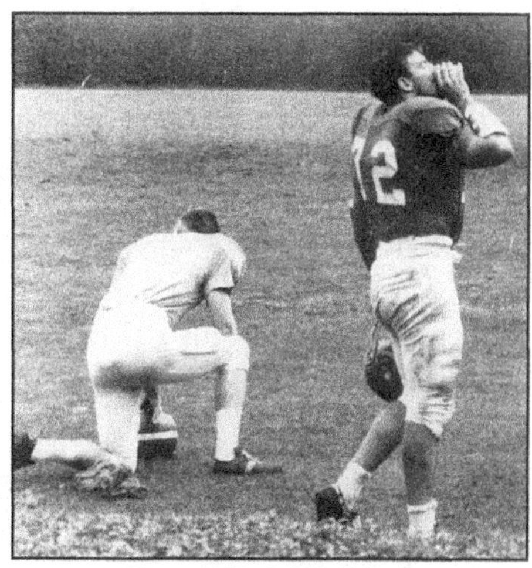

Courtesy of Rachel McClelland.

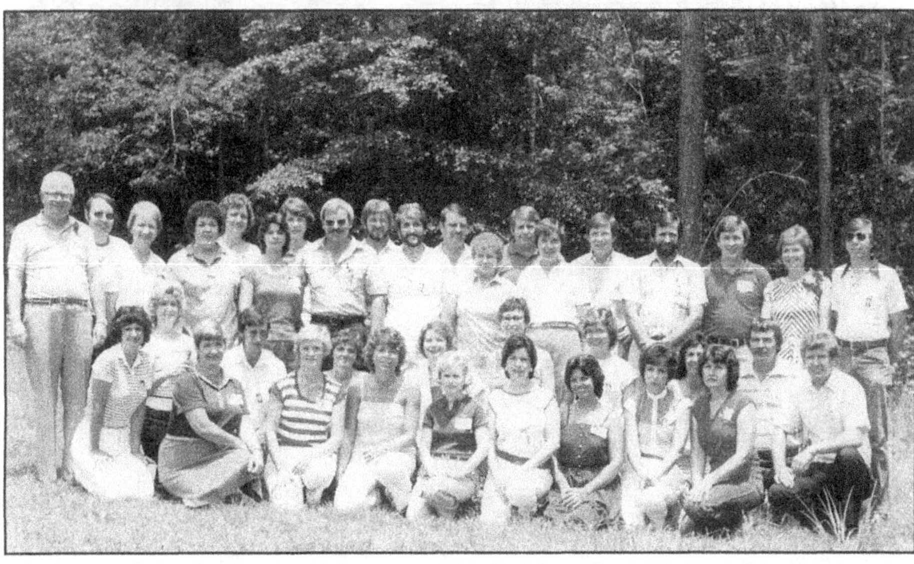

Pike County High class of 1962 at their 20th reunion in 1982. Top left, standing, is Pike County School Superintendent, Harold Daniel. Courtesy of Joann Fenley.

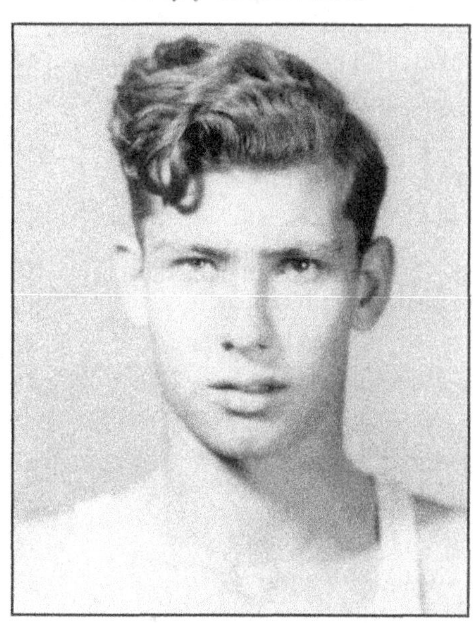

Ralph E. Bishop

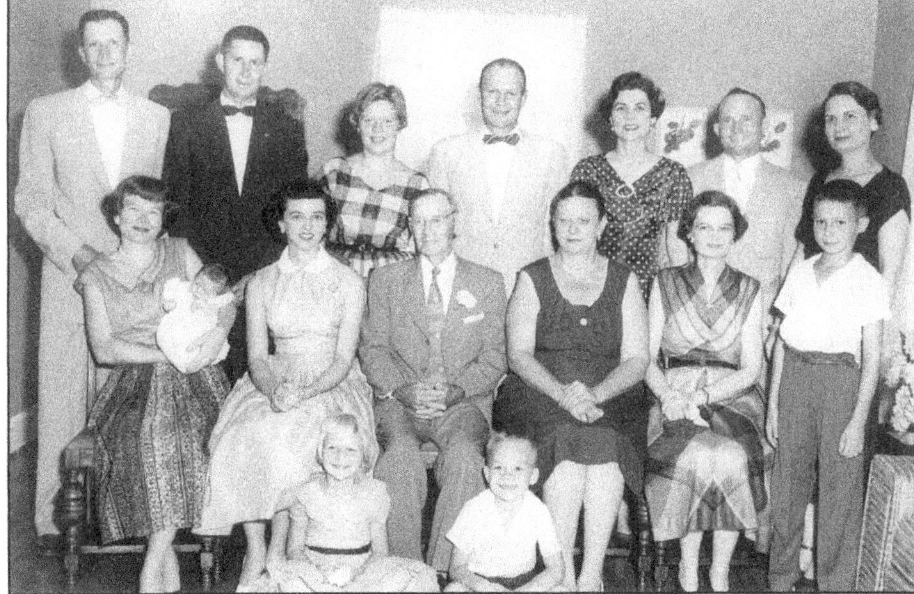

Celebration of John Thomas Pilkenton's 75th anniversary on August 21, 1955. Front row, L-R: Sara Beth Pilkenton Turner, Carl Presley, Jr. 2nd row: Margaret Story Pilkenton holding Jack (Bill) Pilkenton, Jr., Geneva Beckham Pilkenton, John Thomas Pilkenton, Lois Kersey Pilkenton, Elizabeth Pilkenton, John Thomas (Tommy) Pilkenton, II. Third row: Jack Pilkenton, Sr., Walter Carriker Pilkenton, Mary Ann Pilkenton King, Thomas Hewey Pilkenton, Nelle Pilkenton Presley, Carlton C. Presley, Sr., Fay Pilkenton. Courtesy of Fay Pilkenton.

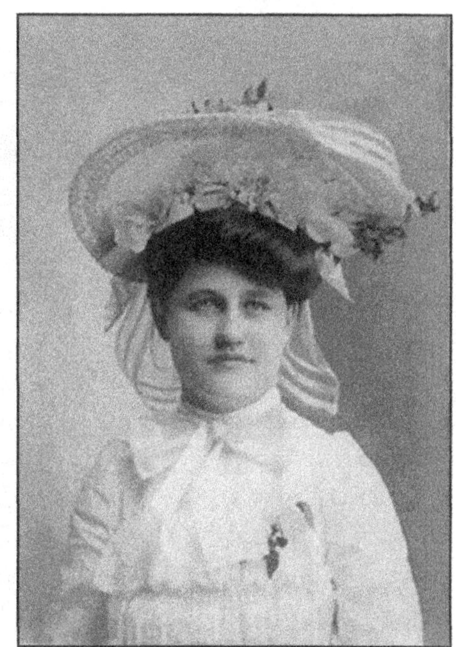

Virginia Williamson-McLeod
December 29, 1885 to January 22, 1970

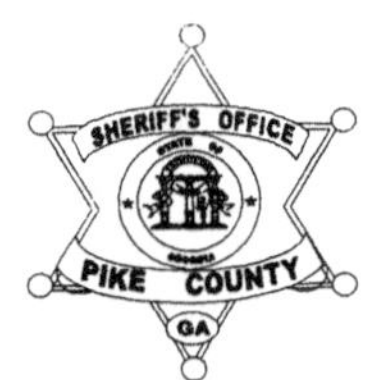

SHERIFFS OF PIKE COUNTY 1822 - 2004

W. Whatley	1822 - 1824
Burwell Orr	1824 - 1826
James R. Gray	1826 - 1828
J.P. Austin	1828 - 1836
J.R. (Uncle Dick) Culpepper	1836 - 1838
Burwell Orr	1838 - 1840
J.H. Shivers	1840 - 1842
Matthew Orr	1842 - 1844
J.H. Shivers	1844 - 1846
J.R. (Uncle Dick) Culpepper	1846 - 1848
Littleton Thornton	1848 - 1850
L.P. (Pike) Alexander	1850 - 1852
John Couch	1852 - 1854
Wiley W. Gresham	1854 - 1856
A.B. Vaughn	1856 - 1858
W.H. McLendon	1858 - 1865
W.D. Redding	1865 - 1877
William Barrett	1877 - 1879
W.P. Bussey	1879 - 1887
W.M. Howard	1887 - 1890
T.J. Slade	1890 - 1894
W.O. (Billie) Gwyn (Killed in the Line of Duty)	1894 - 1896
J.C. Slade	1896 - 1896
John H. Milner	1896 - 1907
M.G. Harrison	1907 - 1910
W.S. Slade	1910 - 1920
W.M. Marsh	1920 - 1925
Drewy Allen	1925 - 1929
Elmer M. Shackelford	1929 - 1933
John C. Bennett	1933 - 1945
Ira E. Davis	1945 - 1953
J. (Astor) Riggins	1953 - 1974
Ronald Copeland	1974 - 1976
Billy M. Riggins	1976 - 1993
James Gibson	1993 - 2001
Jimmy L. Thomas	2001 - present

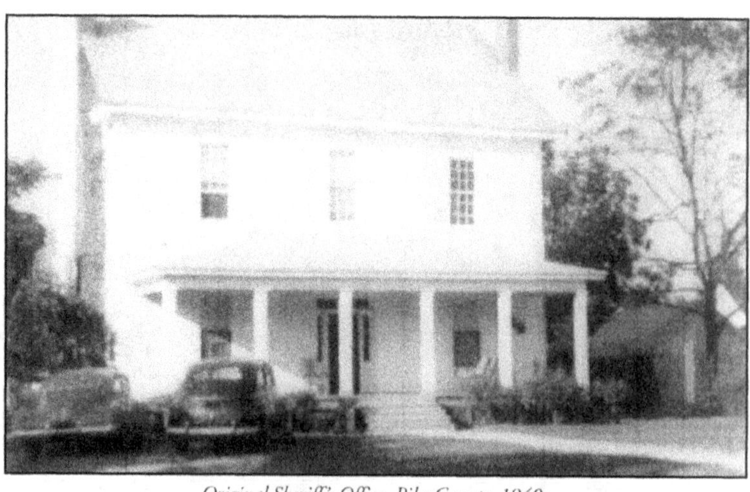

Original Sheriff's Office, Pike County, 1940s.

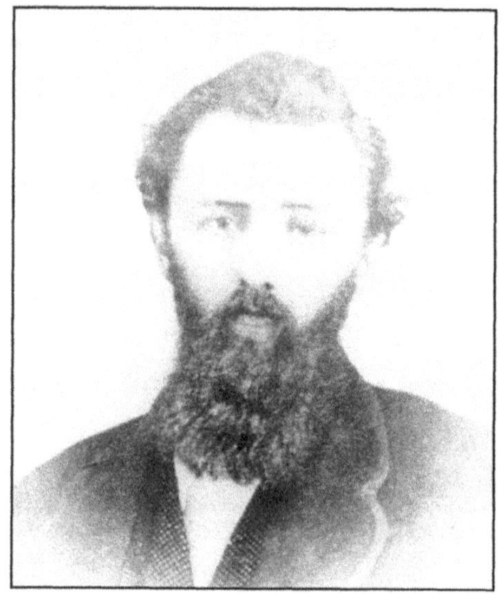

W.O. (Billy) Gwyn
1894 - 1896
Killed in the Line of Duty

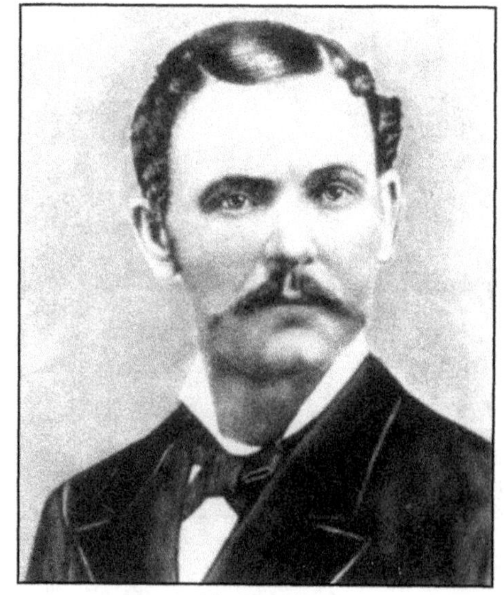

John H. Milner
1896 - 1907

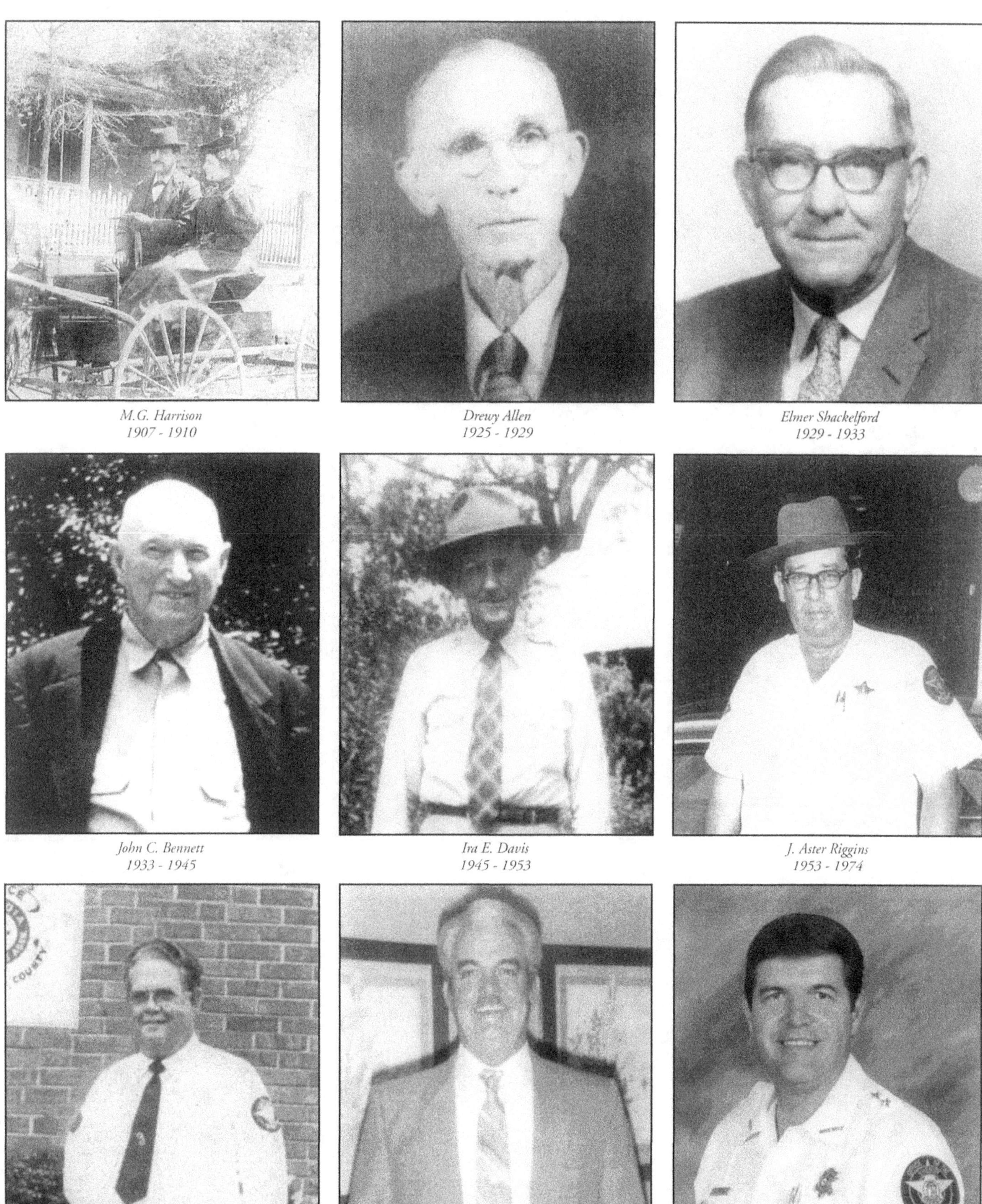

M.G. Harrison
1907 - 1910

Drewy Allen
1925 - 1929

Elmer Shackelford
1929 - 1933

John C. Bennett
1933 - 1945

Ira E. Davis
1945 - 1953

J. Aster Riggins
1953 - 1974

Billy M. Riggins
1976 - 1993

James Gibson
1993 - 2001

Jimmy L. Thomas
2001 - current

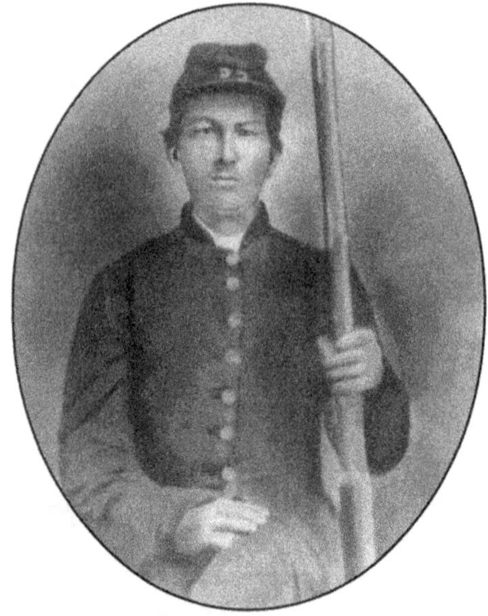

William Decatur Mangham in his Civil War uniform, he was born March 2, 1840 and died Nov. 1, 1874 of a heart attack. Courtesy of Rosalee King.

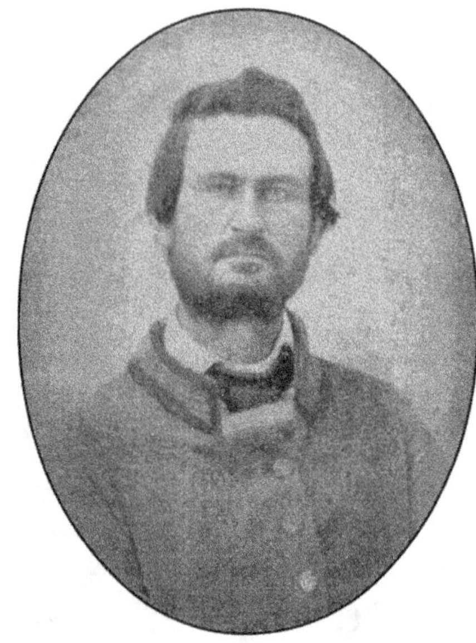

Jonathan James Milner in C.S.A. uniform father of Emmitt Milner. Courtesy of Tom Morton.

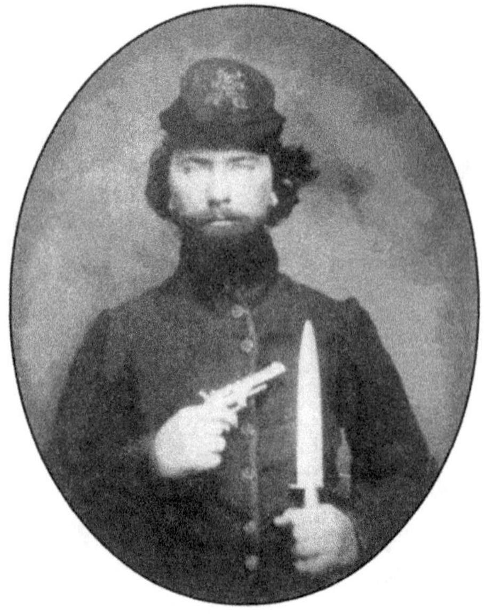

William P. Elliott, Confederate soldier from Pike County. Courtesy of James Adams.

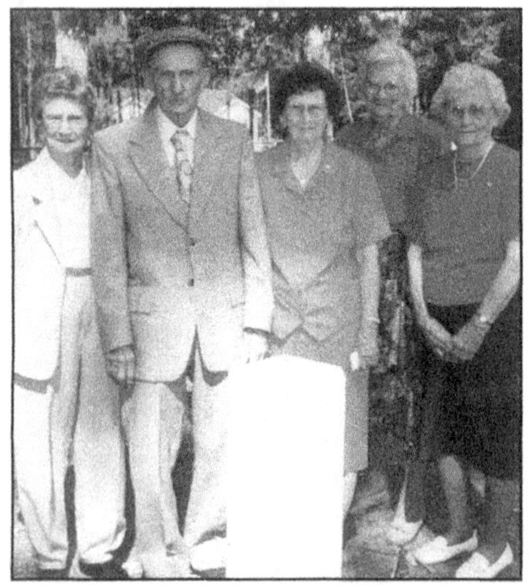

Rosalee King, W.D. Mangham, Virginia Brooks, Helen Mangham and Grace Ward in front of their grandfather's Civil War headstone in the cemetery where he is buried. Courtesy of Rosalee King.

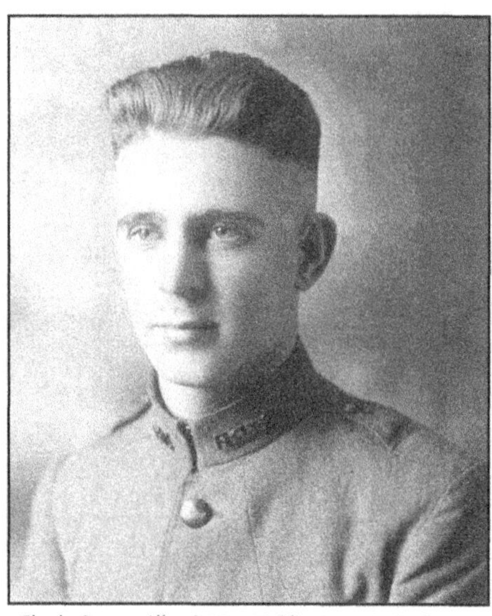

Charles Bryant Allen (1901-1964), circa 1915. Courtesy of Robert Allen.

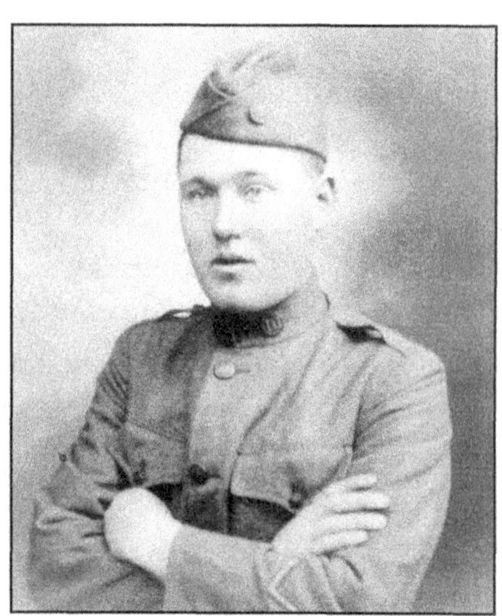

Thomas Jackson "Jack" Elliott (1895-1977), WWI – served in the Army and Navy. Courtesy of Jane Gaulding.

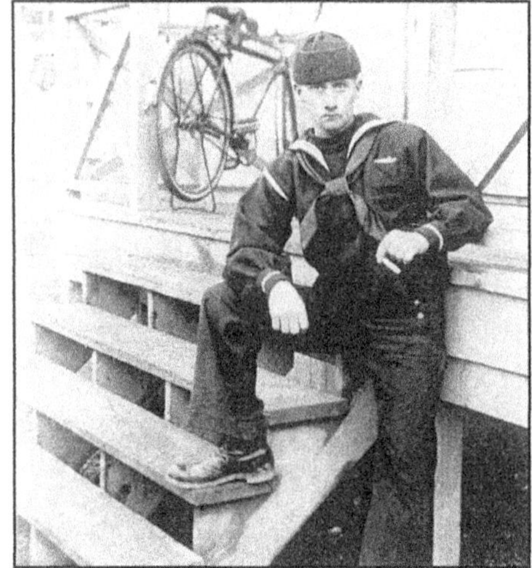

Marvin Foster, he joined the Navy in 1920, served on the USS Chewink, a submarine mine sweeper. He married Edna Peeples in 1926 and then died in a train-car accident in 1929 in Griffin. Courtesy of Wayne Foster.

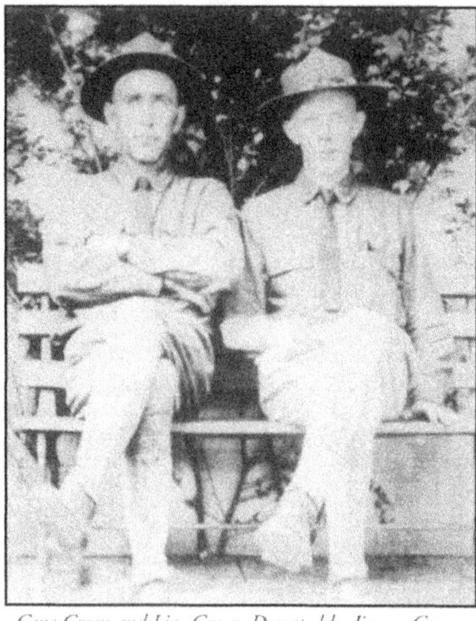

Gene Green and Lige Green. Donated by Jimmy Green.

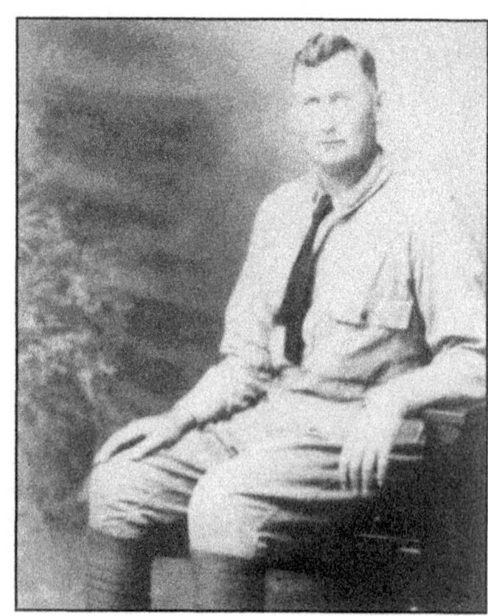

Newt Evans. Donated by Jimmy Green.

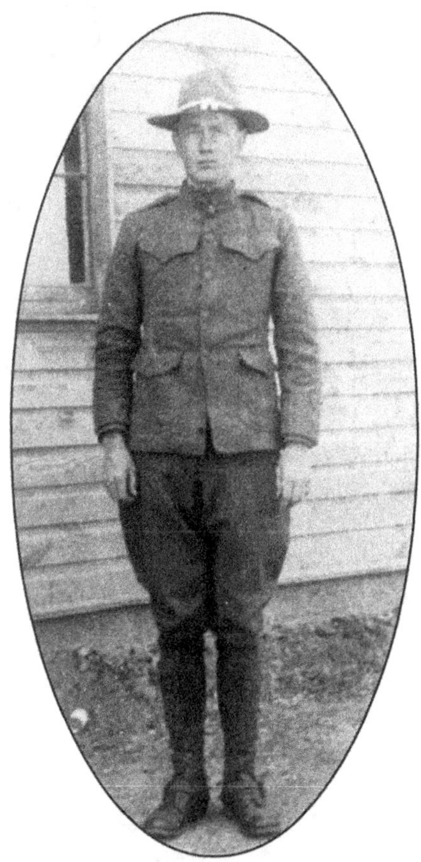

William Robert "Bill" Elliott (1893-1985). Courtesy of Jane Gaulding.

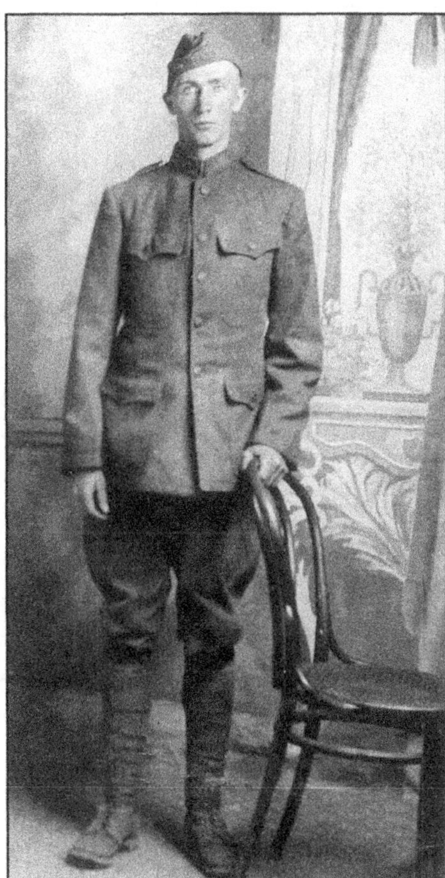

Charlie Clayton Vaughn. Courtesy of Patsy Vaughn.

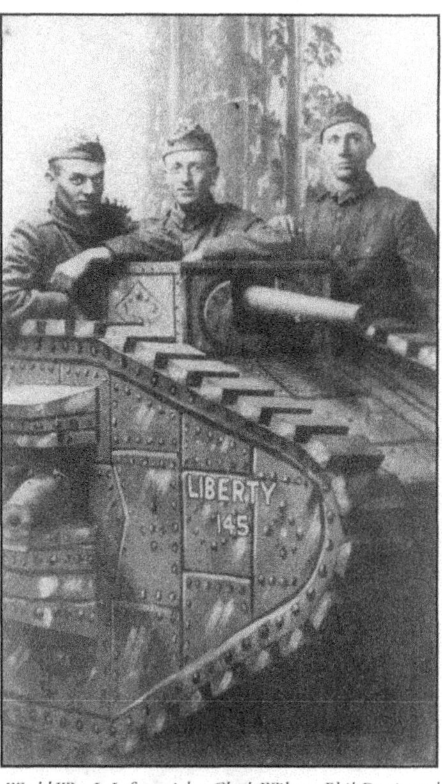

World War I. Left to right: Clark Wilson, Phil Davis and Charlie Vaughn. Courtesy of Patsy Vaughn.

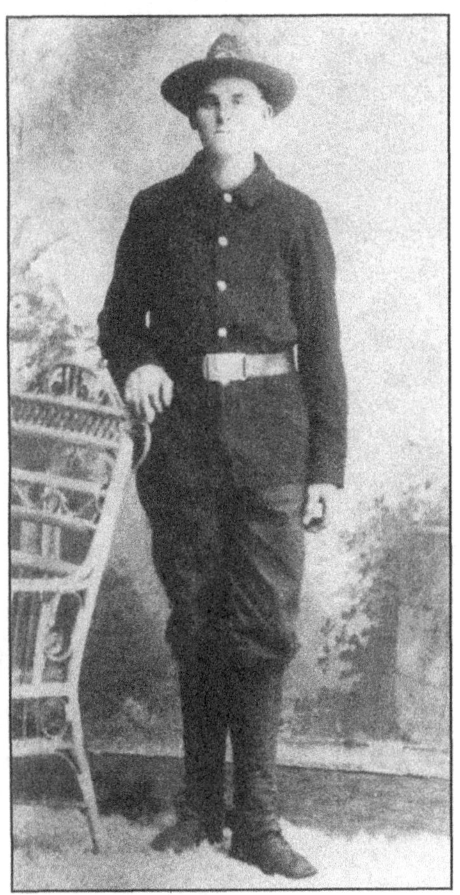

Oscar Williams. Donated by Jimmy Green.

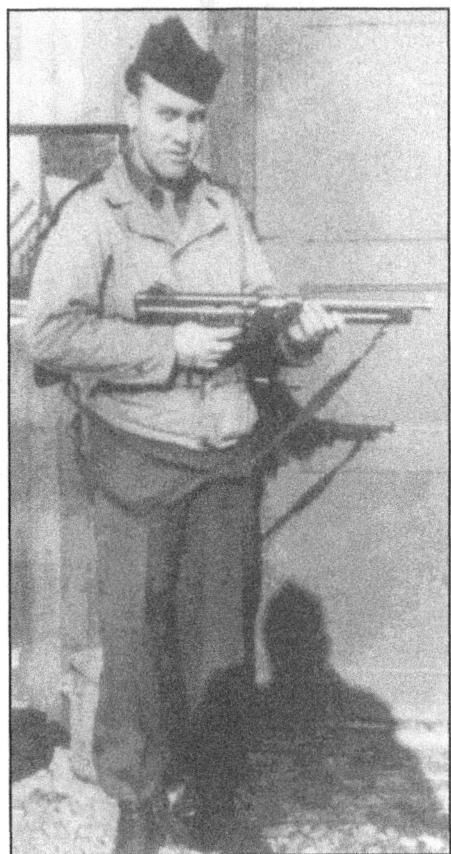

Buren Green (1922-1973). Courtesy of JBG.

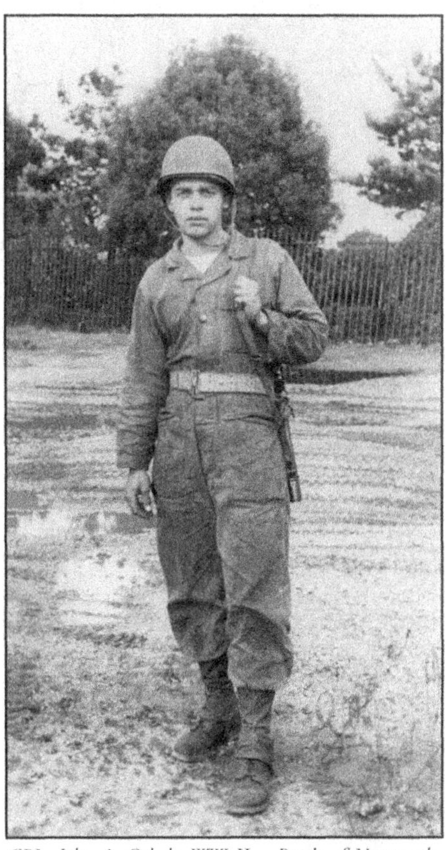

CPL. John A. Osbolt, WW II – Battle of Normandy. Courtesy of Hazel Osbolt and Melissa Carraway.

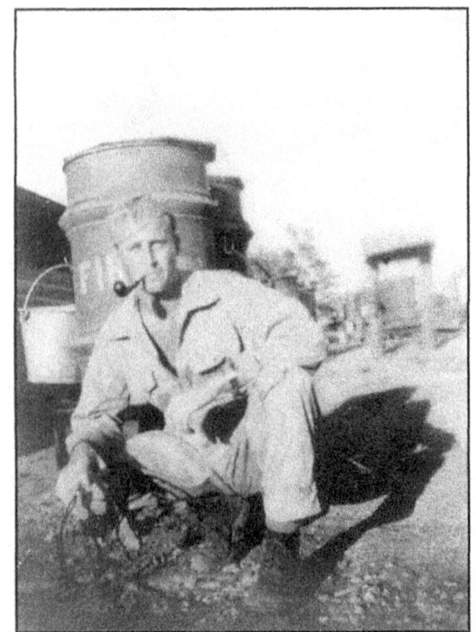
Robert S. Allen, Guam. Courtesy of Jeanette Adams.

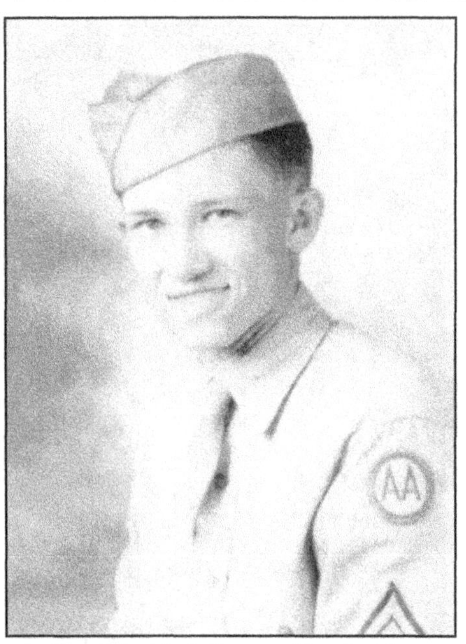
Albert Roland Bush. Courtesy of Jane Gaulding.

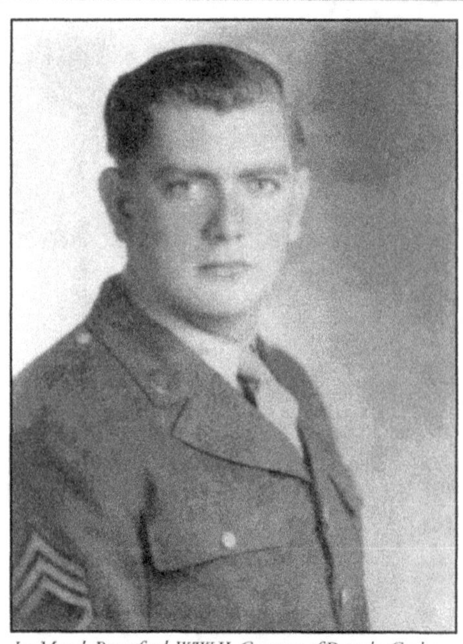
Joe Maroh Bransford, WW II. Courtesy of Dorothy Graham.

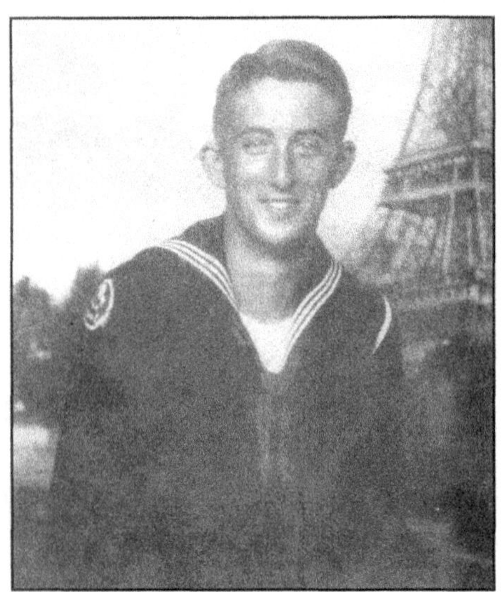
William Howard Smith, 1945. Courtesy of Dorothy Graham.

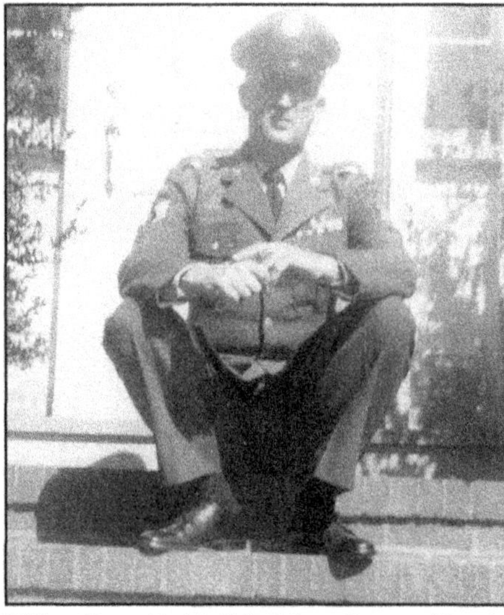
William Howard Smith, U.S. Airforce. Courtesy of Dorothy Graham.

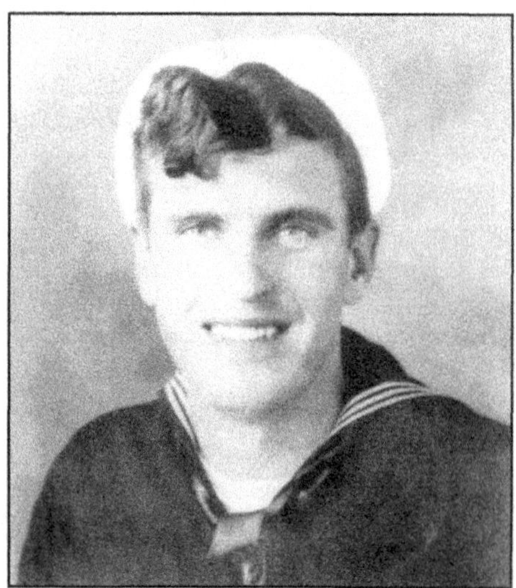
James Maron Graham served in US Navy from December 1943 to December 1945 during WWII. Courtesy of Dorothy Graham.

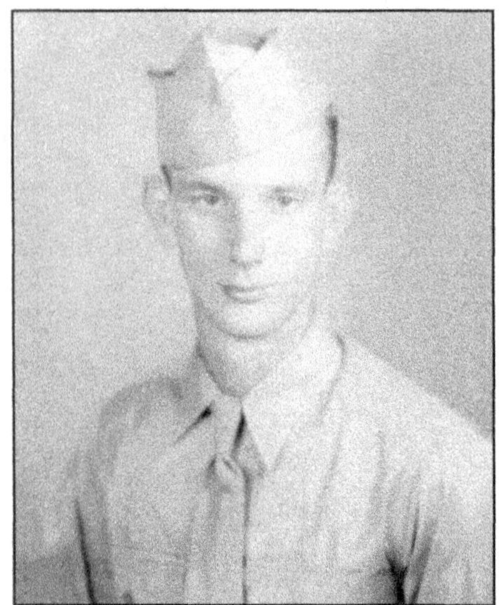
Bryant "Buddy" Casey. Courtesy of Jane Gaulding.

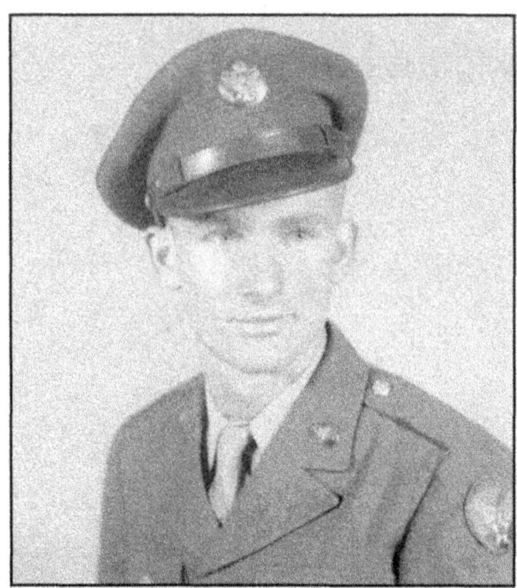
W.D. Mangham, 1942, namesake of Civil War veteran, William Decatur Mangham, shown on page 90. Courtesy of Virginia Brooks.

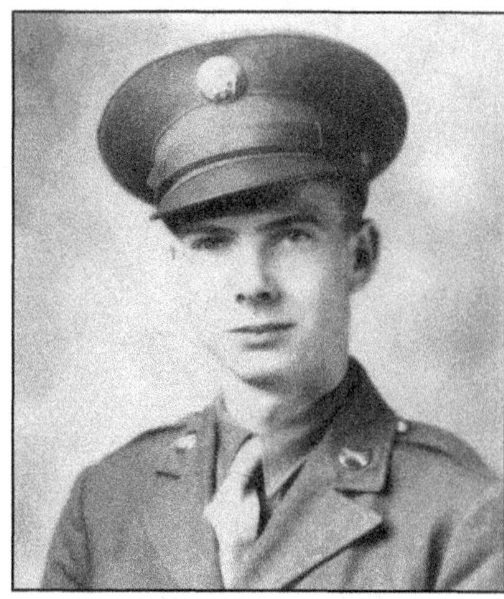
Alton Brooks, 1942, U.S. Army. Courtesy of Virginia Brooks.

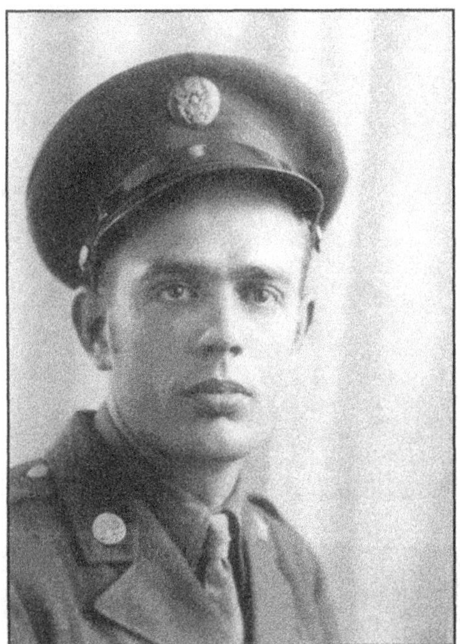

Willie Clyde Gibson, WW II. Courtesy of Mrs. Clyde Gibson.

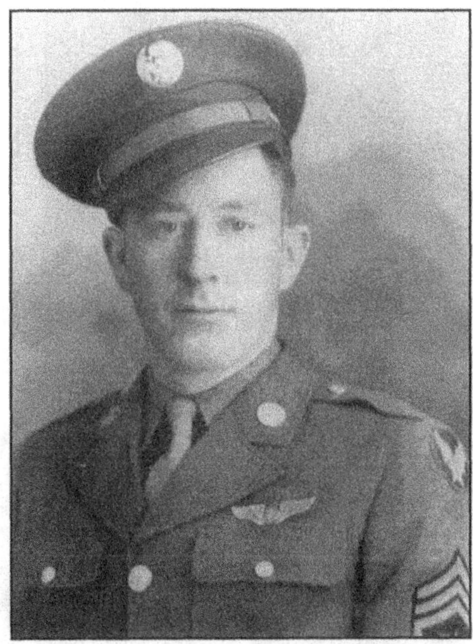

Staff Sgt. Kermit Q. Ward, WW II, 100th Bomber Group. Courtesy of Grace Ward.

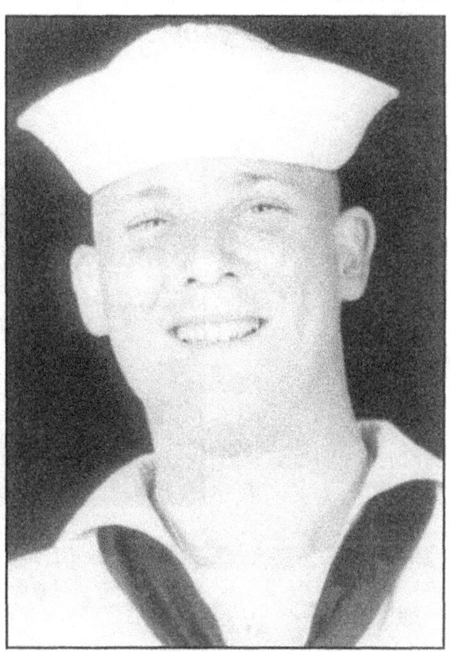

Douglas Claud Smith. Courtesy of Dorothy Graham.

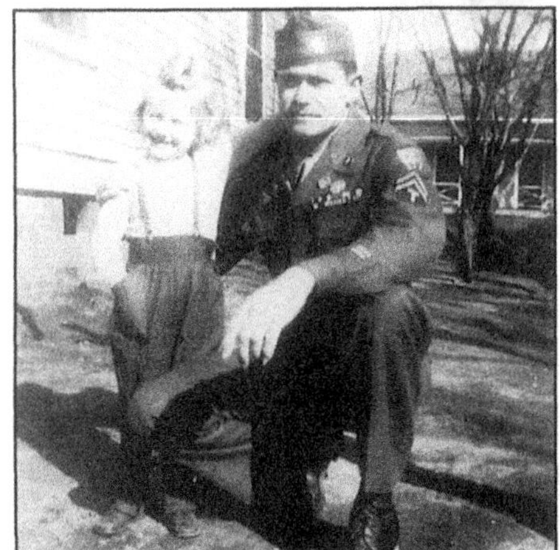

Leonard C. (Buddy) Flowers home on leave from World War II in the 1940's with his niece, Bonnie Bishop. Buddy served in the U.S. Army as a corpsman in France and Germany and was also at the Invasion of Normandy. Buddy received a Purple Heart. Courtesy of Bonnie Gardner.

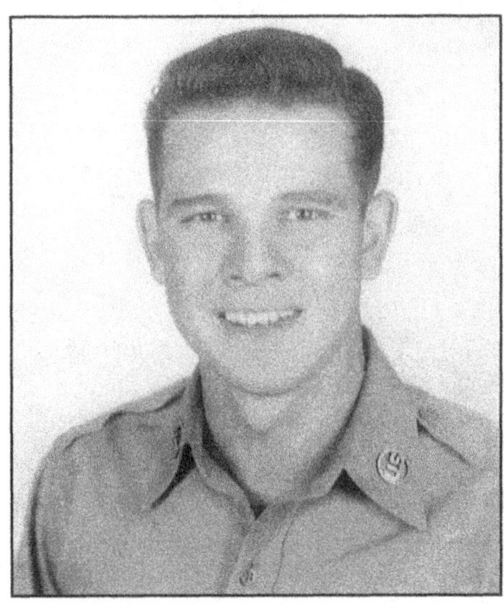

William Madison Maddox at his graduation from Pike County High School in 1998. Courtesy of Bonnie Gardner.

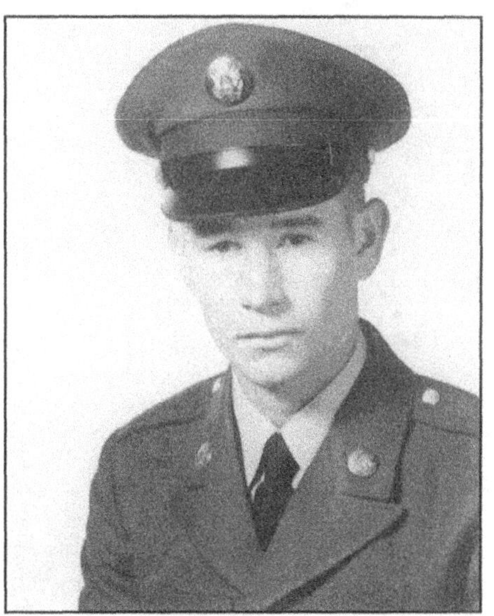

Jimmy Williams

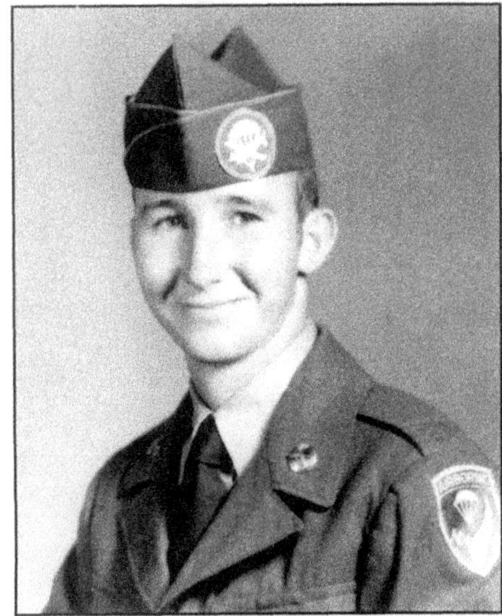

Joseph H. Williams

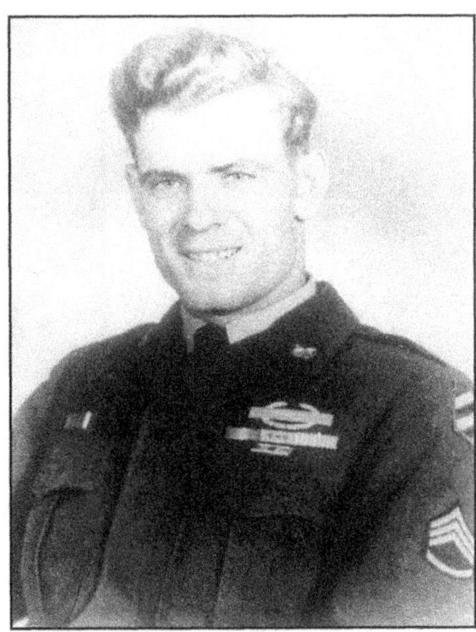

At left: James Shaw Jr. served in the US Army from october 23, 1952 through October 22, 1954, including 13 months and 13 days in the Korean Conflict. He was discharged with the rank of Sergeant, having earned a Korean Service Medal with two bronze stars, a United Nations Service Medal, a Good Conduct Medal and a National Defense Service Medal. Courtesy of Rachel Shaw.

Right: Dennis Brooks, 1968. Courtesy of Virginia Brooks.

Left: Bradford Wright, 1958. Courtesy of Sylvia B. Wright.

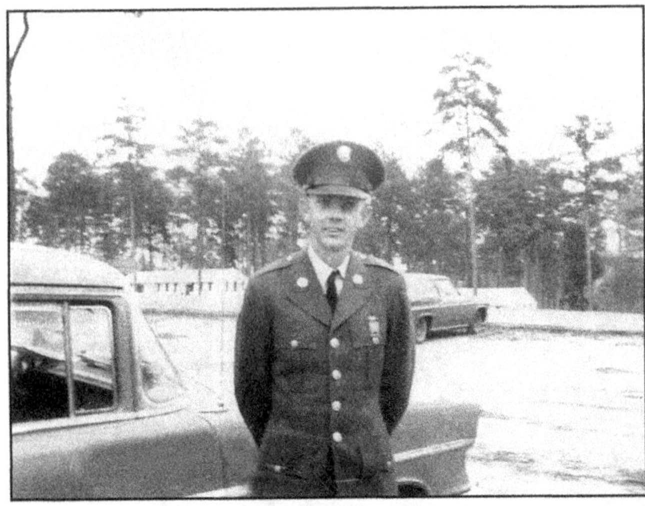

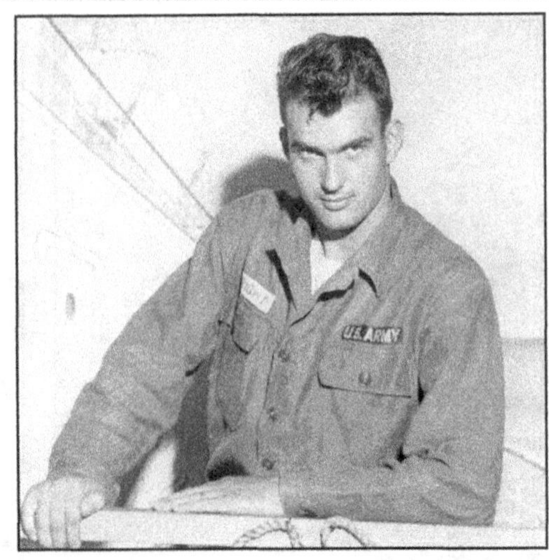

Three Pike County boys that were drafted and left for basic training at the same time. This was at the beginning of the Korean conflict. Left to right: James Floyd "Jim" Bush, Wilbur Collins Elliott and Milton "Chunk" Reeves. Thankfully they all returned safely. Courtesy of Jane Gaulding.

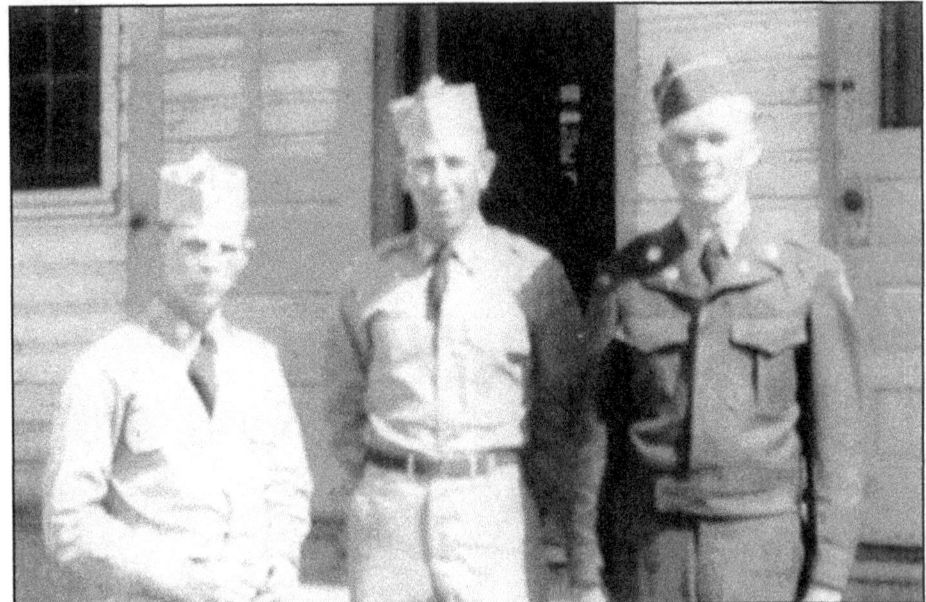

Harry Lamar Banks (1941-2002). U.S. Army, 82nd Airborne Vietnam. Courtesy of Jane Gaulding.

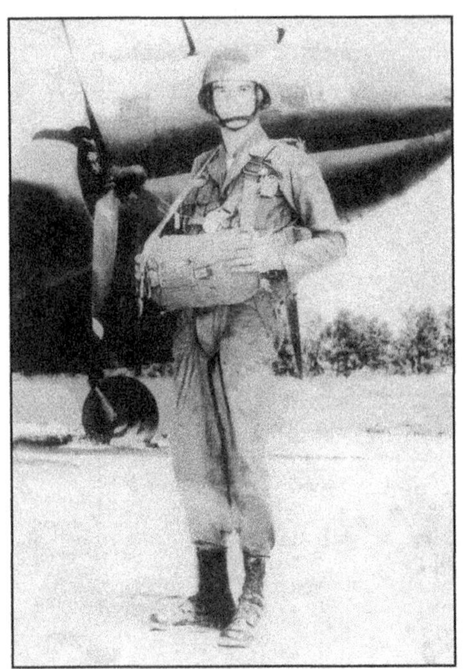

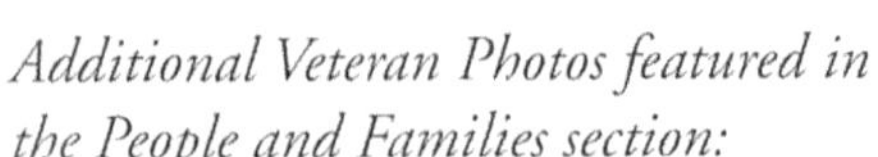

Additional Veteran Photos featured in the People and Families section:

In Memory of James Larry Childs, Sr.

Our Childs Lineage

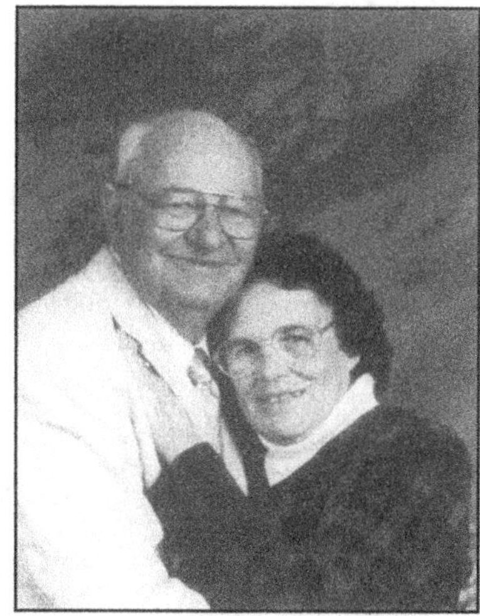

In Memory of James Larry Childs, Sr.

James and Elizabeth Childs were born about 1763, in Virginia. After their son Jeremiah's birth in 1801, they moved to Hancock County, Georgia. James is shown to have paid taxes in the Lewis precinct there in 1804 - 1805. James and Elizabeth's children were Jonathan Childs; Rebecca Ann Childs born Virginia, June 22, 1794, married William Hughes; Daniel Childs born 1795, Virginia; Jeremiah Childs born 1801, Virginia, married Catherine McLane; Joel Childs born 1804, Hancock County, Georgia, married Annie Cain of Washington County, daughter married Daniel Hall; Nancy Childs married David Allen of Wilkinson County. One daughter not accounted for.

In 1807 James had a successful land lottery draw for 202 acres in Wilkinson County, Georgia and then moved his family there. James sold some of his land September 27, 1816, and seven months later on April 1, 1817, his death was announced when some of his estate items were to be sold to satisfy debts against his estate.

Jeremiah married Catherine McLane (born Georgia 1799) on April 22, 1822 in Wilkinson County, Georgia. After their marriage, he moved to Monroe County. He purchased land in 1824 from David Allen, which is believed to be his brother-in-law. In 1830, he showed up in the Monroe County census with his mother, Elizabeth, as a member of the household. In 1840 and 1850 he was living in Upson County. At that time he had twelve children. They were living close to Fruit HIll on Log Town Road south of Yatesville during the 1850 census. Jeremiah moved to Meansville, Pike County about 1857 and lived there until his death after 1880.

Jeremiah and Catherine's children were: Hannah Jane Childs, born 1826, Monroe County, Georgia, married Jeremiah J. Hamrick who died about 1857 and after ten years Hannah Jane married James W. Brooks in 1866, Pike County, Georgia; Catherine Missouri Childs born May 15, 1827, died July 1872, married Isham J. Harrison born 1810, died February 10, 1886; Susan Malinda Childs born Jan. 9, 1829, died Feb. 23, 1915, married William Pinkery Jones, born Nov. 17, 1826, died Dec. 29, 1909; Nancy E. Childs born 1833, married Furney Jackson, 2nd marriage to Abel Ansley; James Childs, born about 1831; Jesse W. Childs, born about 1833; Rebecca A. Childs, born 1835, married Elisha J. Cox; Savannah P. Childs born about 1835; Luvina E. Childs, born about 1837, Upson County, Georgia; Samuel Childs, born 1840, Upson County, Georgia; Francis Caroline Childs, born about 1838, Upson County, GA; Hulda L. Childs born June 1839, died Jan. 8, 1922, married Henry Hagan born 1835 in Georgia, died Feb. 13, 1862; Daniel M. Childs born March 24, 1840, Upson County, Georgia, died Dec. 16, 1909, married Aug. 16, 1863 to Matilda Ann Brooks, born Oct. 27, 1842, died Dec. 9, 1919; One daughter is not accounted for born between 1822 - 1830.

Daniel M. Childs married Matilda Ann Brooks, who was the daughter of James and Reisia Mooday Brooks of Molena, Pike County. When Daniel and Matilda married in Pike County, they lived next door to her parents in Molena. They had four children: Ella Childs born 1868, died before 1900; Warren J. Childs born 1869, died before 1900; James Daniel Childs born March 27, 1869, died Aug. 28, 1922; Mary Francis Childs born 1870, married Fuller, is shown as a widow in 1900 living with her parents.

Ruth's parents were George Penleton Marshall born June 1858 and Amanda Carolina Calhoun born May 15, 1854 of Pike County.

James Daniel and Ruth Virginia Childs had four children: George Douglas Childs, born Aug. 16, 1897, died May 11, 1941, married Mattie Lois Salter; Blumma Basil Childs, born Sept. 17, 1898, died Nov. 11, 1968, married Linnie Mae Bevel; James Marvin Childs Sr., born Aug. 13, 1902, died Feb. 12, 1955, married mary Lelia Corbett; Willie Claude Childs born July 22. 1908. died April 3, 1965, married Julie Pauline Adams of Eufaula, Alabama. All James Daniel Childs children were born in Molena, Pike County, Georgia.

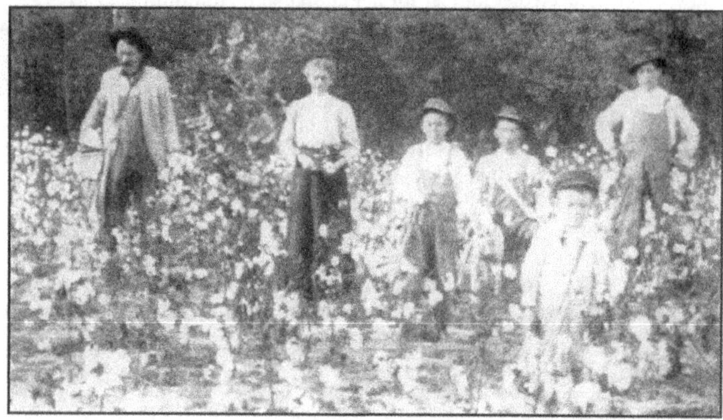

James Daniel Childs and his family in a cotton patch in Molena, Georgia. Ruth and Willie were at home when the man came to take the picutres. They got dressed and walked down to the cotton patch where the family was photographed. Pictured left to right are James Daniel, ruth virginia, James Marvin, George Douglas, Blumma Basil, and Willie Claude Childs is in the front.

Willie Claude and Julia Childs had five children: Julia Sylvilla Childs, Meredith Wilene Childs, James Larry Childs Sr., Sylvia Jeannette Childs, Ronnie Rae Childs.

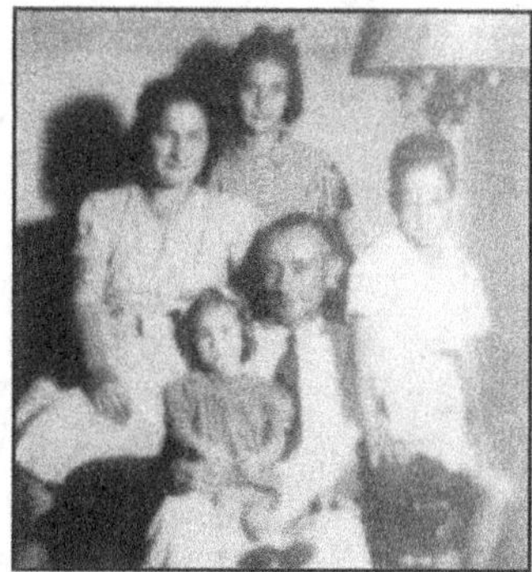

Grandparents Willie Claude Childs (adult sitting in chair), to the left, Julia Pauline Adams Childs; to her left, Meredith Wiline Childs; to her left James Larry Childs Sr. and in Grandfather's lap, Sylvia Jeanettte Childs. Ronnie Rae Childs was not born when this picture was taken.

The family genealogy work above is in memory of our father, James Larry Childs, Sr. and the love for our mother Shirley Ann (Brown) Childs, who started this lineage study. We love you. Larry, Sylvia, Susan, Cindy, Peggy and Chris Childs.

I would appreciate any information on any of the above family members or associated families. Write me at Larry Childs, 3611 Upper River Road, Macon, GA. 31211.

Tribute to Isiah and Pearl Jones

This tribute is dedicated to Pearl Lena Caldwell and the late Isiah Jones. Pearl and Isiah were both born in Pike County, Georgia.

Our parents were and continue to be our idols. They taught us the importance of church, family, and the Jones/Caldwell belief that through hard work anything is possible. They raised us to appreciate the importance of education. All of their children would graduate from high school and most would go on to obtain degrees in higher education. The family consists of lawyers, teachers, and just plain heroes. They raised a son who will forever be immortalized as the father who saved his daughter's life at the expense of his own. A son who has the distinction of being the only civilian to have a building named in his honor at Homestead Air Reserve Base, in Homestead, Florida, the Bernard Jones Civil Engineering Complex. They taught by example, my father singing the gospel as a member of The Sons of Daniel for over twenty years. My mother looking after her three sets of twins born in three years and three singles, as few mothers have. My mother would go on to become the first President of the Zeta Amicae of Zeta Phi Beta Sorority, Incorporated Auxiliaries, Homestead Florida Chapter, a leader on her job and a well respected volunteer for her church and community. "Miss Pearl", as she is affectionately called, has and continues to be a shining example of what is good about humanity. My father would die too young but would leave his legacy that hard work often leads to good things. These African-Americans of slave ancestry come from a long line of achievers.

THE ANCESTRY OF PEARL LENA CALDWELL
THE CALDWELL CLAN

Pearl Lena Caldwell, was born January 12, 1934, in Concord, Pike County, Georgia. She is one of eight children of the late Otis Bishop Caldwell and Lee Myrtis Harris. Growing up, my mother held me and my eight siblings spellbound with stories of her place of birth. Usually those stories were filled with tales of Rawhead and Bloodybone, Santa Claus Floorwalker, or some other apparition that appeared only in the middle of the night.

Pearl's father, Otis Bishop Caldwell, was born, April 24, 1900, in Neal, Pike County, Georgia and died on November 19, 1953 in Florida City, Florida. Otis Bishop Caldwell married Lee Mytis Harris on April 15, 1923. This union produced eight (8) children: Lois, Minnie Lee, Ida Mae, Peal Lena, Laura Geraldine, Ozella, Eria Marie, and Otis Bishop, all born in Pike County.

Her grandfather, John Horace Caldwell married Leila Nelson, also of Pike County, Georgia. John died on March 24, 1924. Their marriage produced eight (8) offspring. Mary Ann, James Walter, LeRoy, Otis Bishop, Irene, Benjamin Wesley, Hassie, and John Horace, Jr. Before John Caldwell died, he managed to put together a farming enterprise that consisted of over 100 acres. His obituary read as follows:

> **JOHN CALDWELL DIES AT HIS HOME NEAR NEAL**
> John Caldwell a well known and respected colored farmer died Sunday at his home near Neal and was buried at Neal on Tuesday. The deceased was a leader among his people in church and school work as well as an example to them as a successful farmer and land owner. He had by hard work and good management accumulated a good farm and other property. We have heard him say that there is no better place to live, and make a good living than right here in Pike County.

Her great-grandfather, Isom Caldwell, was born in Pike County, Georgia in April of 1823, he was the slave of a Dr. John J. Caldwell of Pike County, Georgia. Isom was one of the signatories to the deed which lead to the building of Bush Chappel African Methodist Episcopal Church in Concord, Georgia. A church which came in existence in 1867 and still stands today. Pearl's great-grandmother was Lucy Ann Madison, born in May of 1828. Nothing is known of the Madison line. Isom and Lucy Ann had fifteen (15) children: Andy, James, Anthony, Benjamin, Samuel, Ernest, Ennis, Henry, Sallie, Sousan, Edmond, John, Mat, Rance and Clarence.

THE NELSON CLAN

Leila Nelson was born August 14, 1873, in Pike County Georgia. She died on June 14, 1914. She was the daughter of James Nelson and Mary Ann. James Nelson was born in 1843, Mary Ann was born in 1845. This union produced nine (9) children, Chappel, Charles, Mack, William, Jimmy, Leila, Emmer, Ida, and Robert.

THE HARRIS/JACKSON CLAN

Lee Myrtis Harris was born February 21, 1901 in Meriwether County, Georgia, she died on Apirl 19, 1991, in Florida City, Florida. She was the only child of Minnie Bell Warner and Mansfield "Mank" Harris. Minnie Bell married James Jackson sometime between 1901 and 1906. This union produced seven (7) children: Mary, John Robert, Joe Taylor, Joseph Earl, Mozelle, Maggie Ruth and Melvin Curtis

Mansfield "Mank" Harris was born in May of 1865 in Meriwether County, Georgia, he died on September 27, 1933, in Concord, Georgia. Mank Harris was the son of Jesse Harris and Amanda Crowder. Jesse was born in October of 1843 and Amanda was born in May of 1845. This union of Jesse and Amanda produced eleven (11) children: Pompei, Mansfield, Charity, Allen, Nora, Lula, Grant, Greely, Unamed, Jesse and Ed.

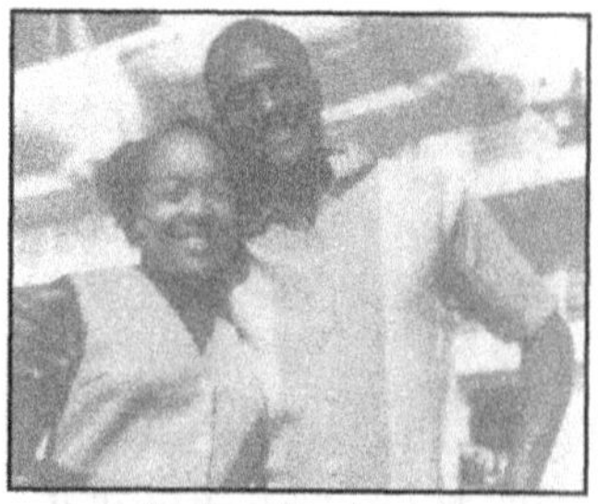

Isiah and Pearl Jones

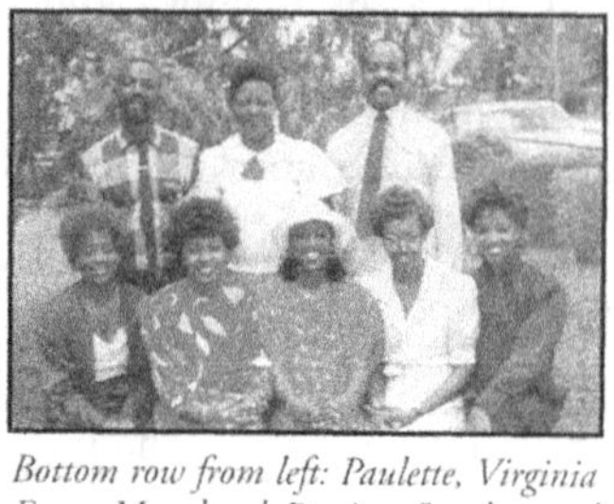

Bottom row from left: Paulette, Virginia Faye, Maryland Denise, Sandra and Brenda. Standing, from left: Bernard, Paulette and Andrew.

THE CROWDER CLAN

Amanda Crowder was born in May of 1845 she was the daughter of Ransom "Rance" Crowder and Mariah. Rance Crowder was born in 1825 and Mariah was born in 1820. This union produced four (4) children: Abe, Amanda, Harry and Howard.

THE WARNER CLAN

Minnie Bell Warner was born in 1885 in Meriwether County, Georgia. She was the daughter of Howard Warner and Myra. Howard Warner was born in March of 1845, Myra was born in April of 1848. This union produced eleven (11) children: Cicero, Lizzie, Mariah, Cindy, Madison, Julia, Rena, Hannah, Minnie Bell, Pearl and Glenn.

Howard Warner was the son of Jack Warner and Missouri. Jack Warner was born in 1828 and Missouri was born in 1830. This union produced six (6) children: Howard, William, Mansfield, Maryland, Lucinda, and Hudson.

THE ANCESTRY OF ISIAH JONES
THE JONES/STANLEY CLAN

Isiah Jones was born in Williamson, Pike County, Georgia on June 16, 1921. Isiah died on October 6, 1975 in Miami, Florida. Isiah was the only son of Andrew Jones and Willa May Walker. Nothing is known of the Jones branch of the family tree. Isiah had two siblings, James and Elizabeth Stanley. Elizabeth was born in May of 1925 in Griffin, Georgia and died in 1961 in Atlanta, Georgia.

THE WALKER CLAN

Willa May Walker was born on September 21, 1903. Willa May died on December 11, 1985, in Atlanta, Georgia. Willa May was the daughter of Sam Walker and Georgia Ann Pryor. Sam Walker was born in 1865 in Upsom County, Georgia and died on October 11, 1924 in Pike County, Georgia. Georgia Ann Pryor was born in 1867 in Pike County, Georgia and died on April 19, 1927 in Williamson, Pike County, Georgia. This union produced eight (8) children: Eddie Lewis, Daisy Mae, Glover, John Henry, Mattie Lou, Willa May, Marvin and Charles.

Sam Walker was the son of Cole Walker and Violet. Cole was born in 1824 and Violet was born in 1825. This union produced eight (8) children: Dock, Mark, Willie, Wesley, Eldora, Mansie, Sam and General Grant.

THE PRYOR CLAN

Georgia Ann Pryor was the only child of Thomas Pryor and Amanda Coggins. Thomas was born in March of 1824 in Jasper County, Georgia. Amanda was born in 1845 in Pike County, Georgia. Thomas Pryor married Suzanne in 1865. This union produced seven (7) children: Louisa, Ada, James O., Liza Ann, Emma, Thomas Jefferson and Jessie.

It is the rich legacy of these brave African-Americans that continues to nourish and encourage their descendants. The lessons taught to us by Isiah and Pearl were learned from many of the people who names appear in this our family tree. Those lessons they passed down to us. We can only hope to do as good a job with our offspring as they did for us in passing down those lessons of life. It was their sacrifices that blazed the path for those of us who have followed in their footsteps. We continue to do our best to make footsteps worthy enough for our descendants to follow.

SIGNED: THE OFFSPRING OF ISIAH JONES AND PEARL LENA CALDWELL

Sandra and Andrew, Pauline and Paulette,
Brenda and Bernard, Marilyn, Virginia and Randall.

Emmanuel Baptist Church

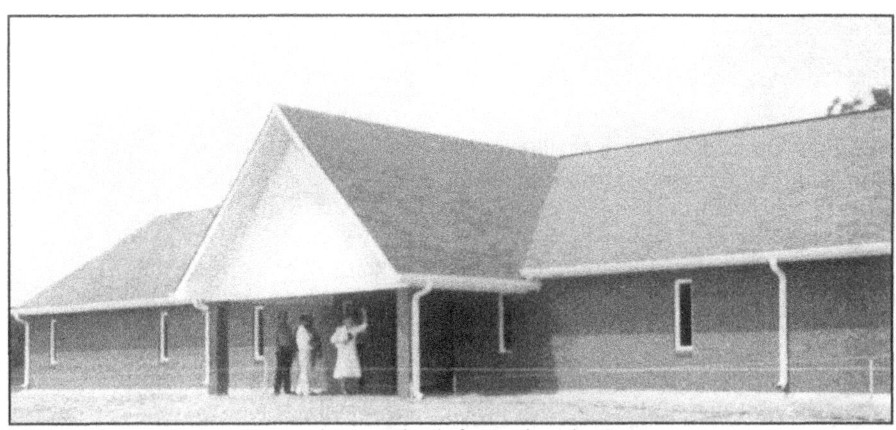

Emmanuel Baptist Church, first Sunday, July 24, 1988.

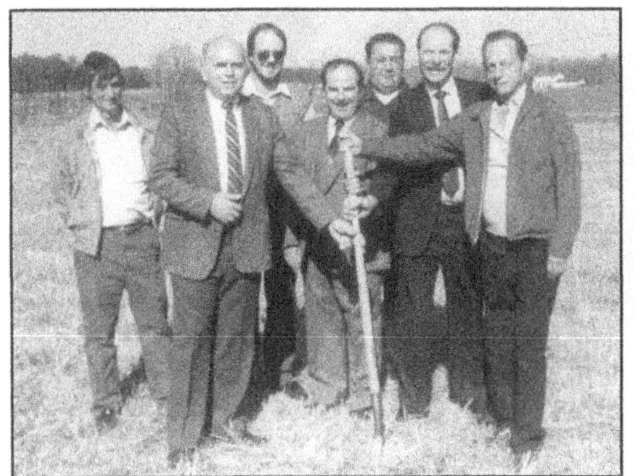

Ground Breaking, March 20, 1988. From left: Kenneth Ward, Richard Watkins, Steve Wiley, Rev. Gary Hately, C.W. Griffin, Richard Watkins, Arlie Ayers and Jack Hines.

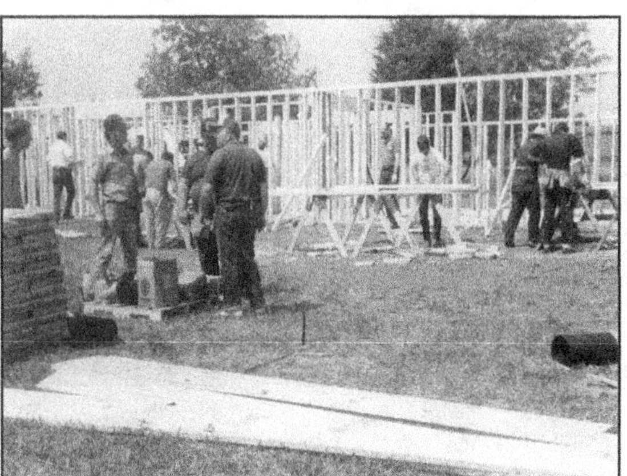

May 14, 1988, Flint River Associational men. Arlie Ayers, C.W. Griffin, Richard Watkins, Gary Hately (background).

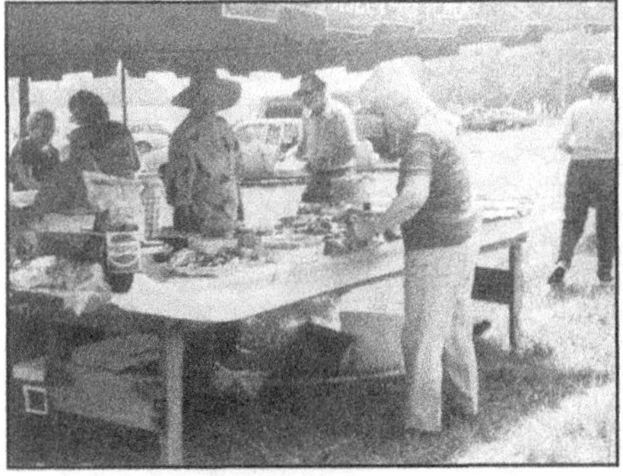

May 14, 1988. Lois Arrington, Cheryl Ward, Ellie Gibson, Louise Ward, Calvin Gibson, Eddie Lowery and Bobbie Watkins.

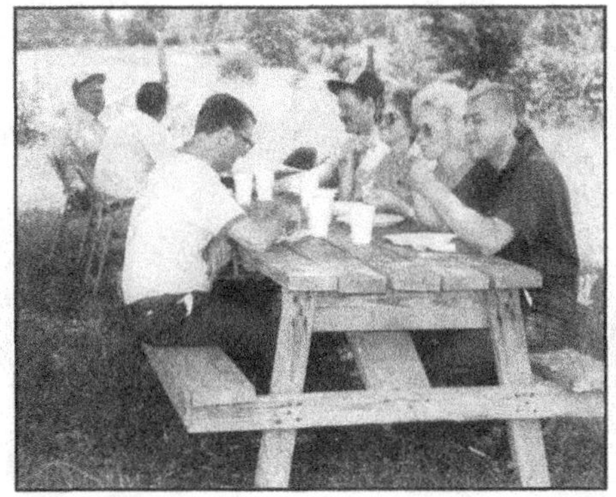

May 30, June 3, 1988, Alabama men and women, Emmanuel Baptist Church.

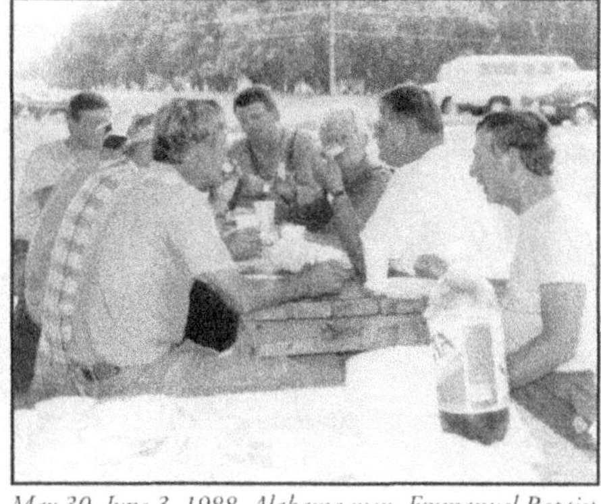

May 30, June 3, 1988, Alabama men, Emmanuel Baptist Church.

On October 18, 1987, thirty-three people agreed to form a new Church: "A Church Where Everybody is Somebody."

The first meeting was in the Chapel of Moody Funeral Home, Hwy 19, Zebulon, Georgia. Jewell Hammond played the organ. Arlie Ayers was the speaker. Officers elected were: Moderator, Richard Watkins; Deacons, C. W. Griffin, Arlie Ayers, Steve Wiley, Richard Watkins, Clerk, Cheryl Ward; Treasurer, Vivian Hilley; Pastor, Rev. Gary E. Hately.

The first service was held in the May Cox Chapel at The Georgia Baptist Children's Home and Family Ministries, Hwy 19, Meansville, Georgia, October 25, 1987. The church was constituted November 1, 1987, as Emmanuel Baptist Church, a member of the Flint River Baptist Association, with thirty-five charter Members.

On December 6, 1987, land was purchased from Cheryl A. Manders and Liz Manders Rawlins Hawkins. On March 20, 1988, ground was broken for the new church. The foundation was laid April 4, 1988. Fifty men from the Flint River Association, with the men of the church, raised the walls on May 14, 1988. The church ladies cooked and served the meals.

On May 30, 1988, sixteen men, two ladies and three teenagers from Moulton, Alabama, and the men of the church finished the inside. Emmanuel Baptist Church was dedicated on October 9, 1988. The speaker was Dr. Gene T. Bowman, Director of Missions at The Flint River Baptist Association.

God has truly blessed our church through the years.

On November 2, 2003, God sent us Dr. Preston B. (Bud) Gleaton and his wife Sharon Gleaton. Since November 2, 2003 our membership has increased by thirty members.

Pike County Lions Club

The Pike County Lions Club, chartered on March 4, 1946, is the largest service organization in Pike County. The old Zebulon Depot has been renovated and preserved by the Lions. The walls still display names written by people long ago. Railroad pictures and momentos donated by member, Past President Tom Morton and his wife, Sonya, have captured the original atmosphere. Each month he club meets on the first and third Mondays with a catered meal. There are now 35 members, whose support commitments include Lions Club International Foundation, Camp for the Blind in Waycross, Georgia, Children Eye Care Center at Emory, Lighthouse (glasses and surgery), Canine Companion for physically handicapped, Leader Dog for the blind, Recording for the Blind, Southeastern Guide Dogs for the blind and handicapped, and Children Support Program.

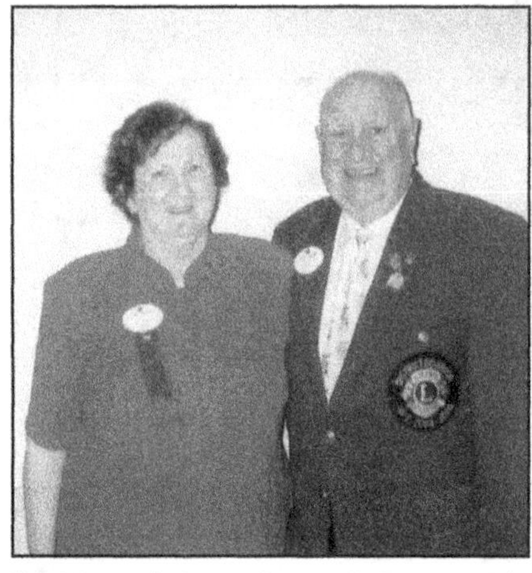

Tom Morton, the District Governor for District 18E for the Lions Club International and his wife, Sonya.

Community involvements include The Christian Outreach Center, Sight Program (glasses and hearing aides), Health Fair, AA Meetings at the Depot, High School Football Program, Holiday Baskets for the Elderly, and White Cane Day.

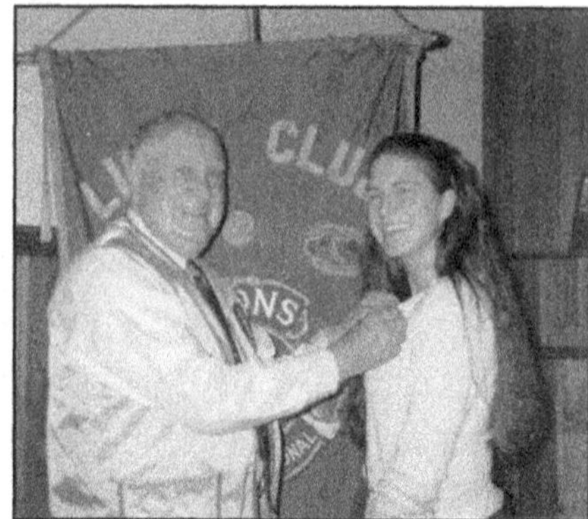

Tom Morton and Amanda Hollar.

Our club has provided three District Governors, Loretta Snowden and just-elected Tom Morton to serve 2004-05. Members take their turns serving the positions of the club. The officers for 2004-05 are President, Virginia Oglesby; First Vice-President, Ken Gran; Second Vice-President, Mary Jo Boswell; Third Vice-President, Don Snowden; Secretary, Loretta Snowden; Treasurer, Amanda Hollar; Lion Tamer, James Huckaby; Tail Twister, Charles Bentley; Two Year Directors, Bill Paris and Mike Oxford; One Year Directors, Richard Beckham and Sonya Morton; and Immediate Past-President, Tom Morton.

Our motto is: "We Serve."

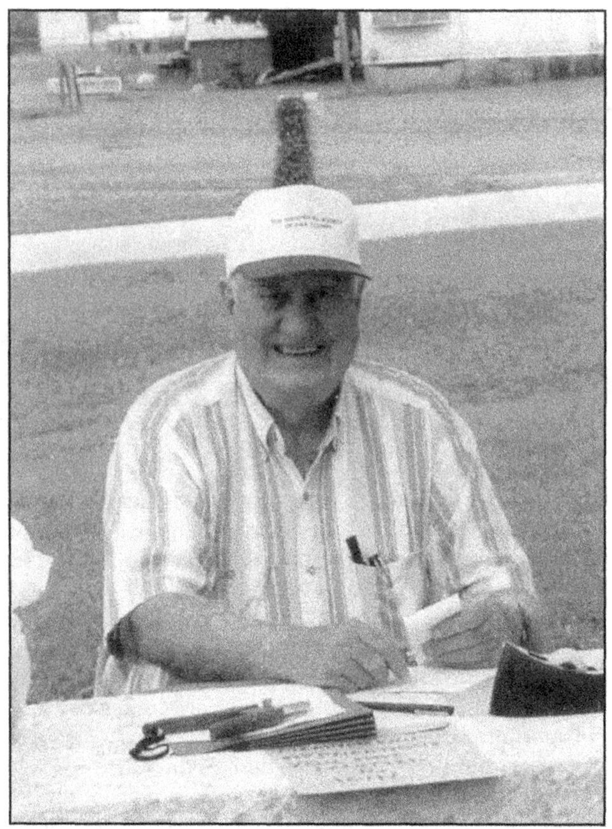

Tom Morton, President of the Pike County Historical Society, new member registration.

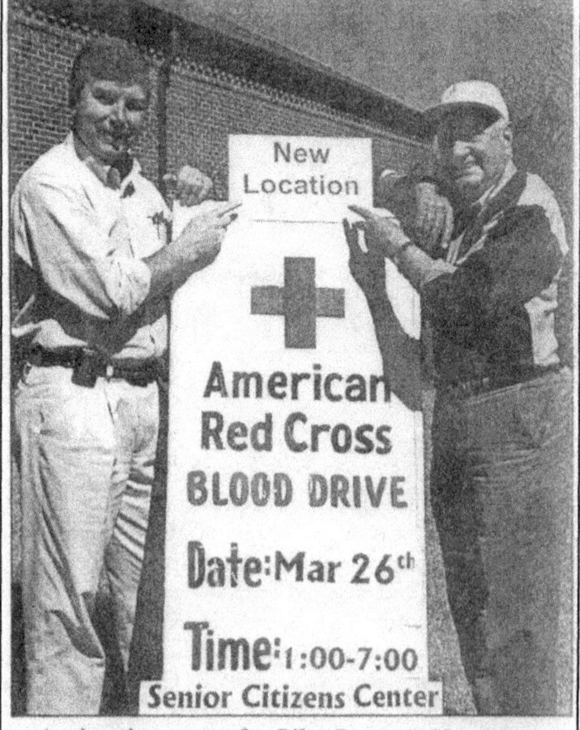

A win-win contest for Pike County's blood drive

Pike County Kiwanis Club president Wayne Lowrey, left, and Lion's Club president Tom Morton will lead their members to Monday's blood drive to be held at the Allie Bankston Edwards Senior Center. The two clubs are competing to have the most members donate blood.

Index

D

E

F

Y

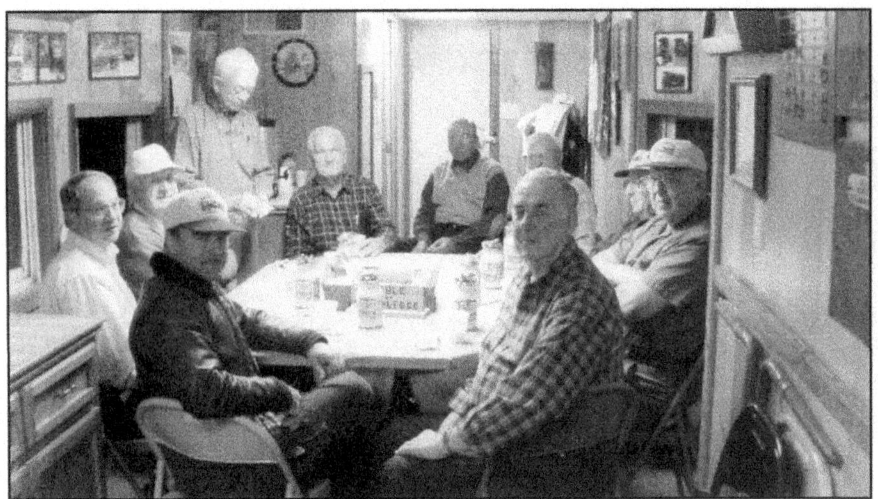

Members of the Williamson Caboose Club. Courtesy of Tom Morton.

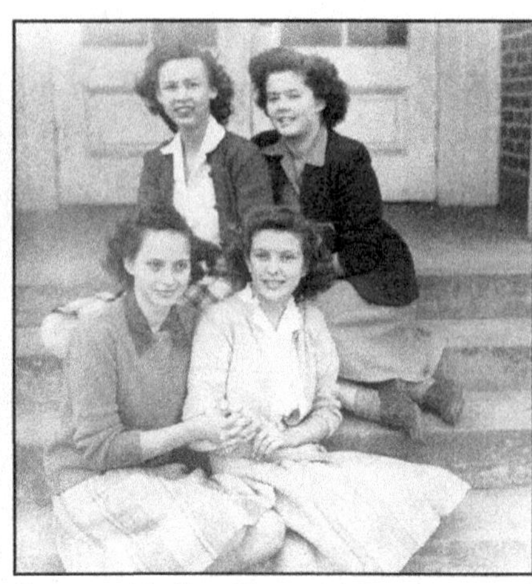

Top row: Madline Watts and Betty Crawford. Bottom row: Ann Willis and Betty Ann Strickland. Courtesy of Virginia and Charles Oglesby.

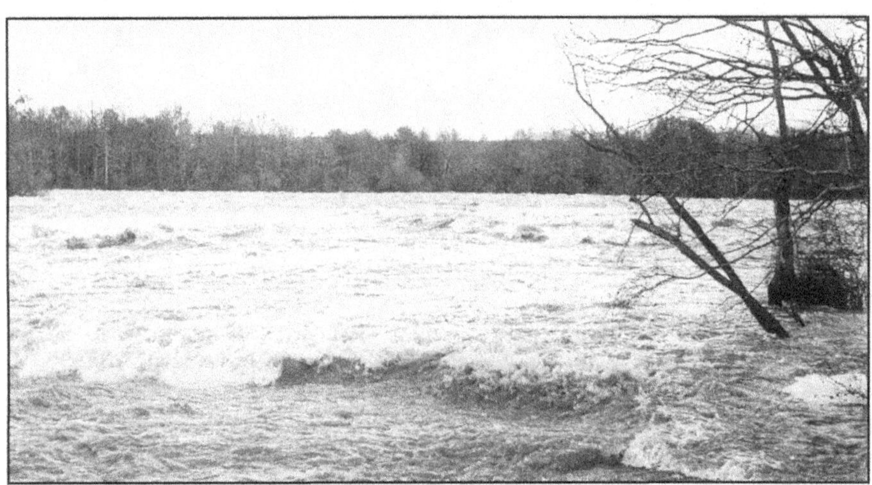

Flooding in Pike County. Courtesy of Rachel McClelland.

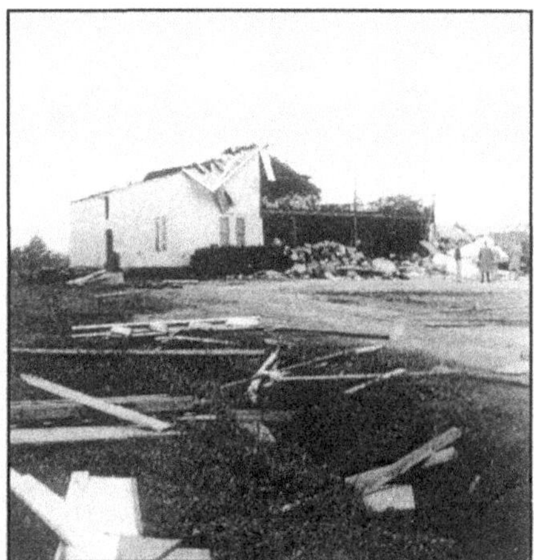

Storm aftermath in Zebulon, 1950. Courtesy of Joann Fenley.

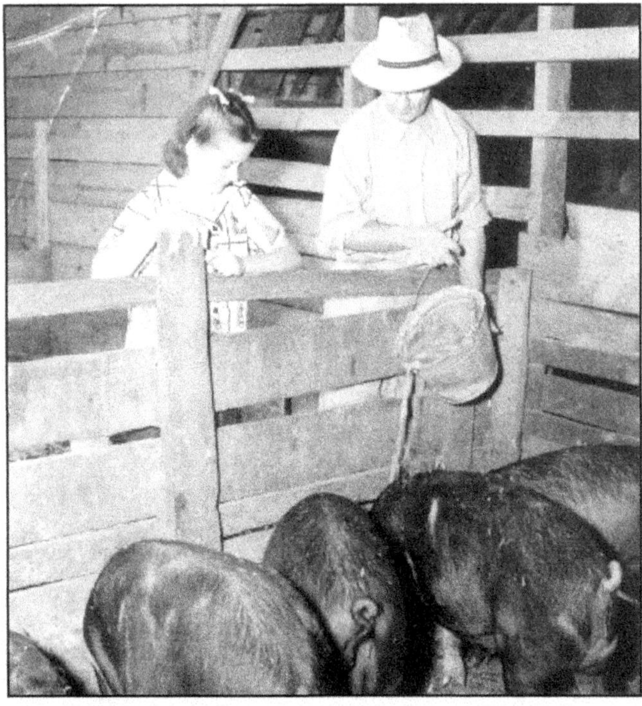

Willaminta Norris and father feed the hogs raised for food and market. Courtesy of Rachel McClelland.

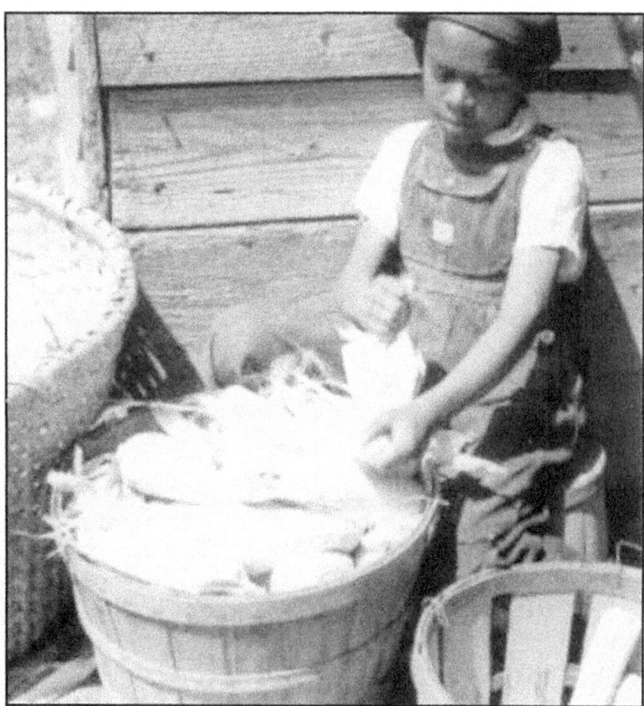

All farm and food preparation for both people and animals was accomplished manually. Courtesy of Rachel McClelland.

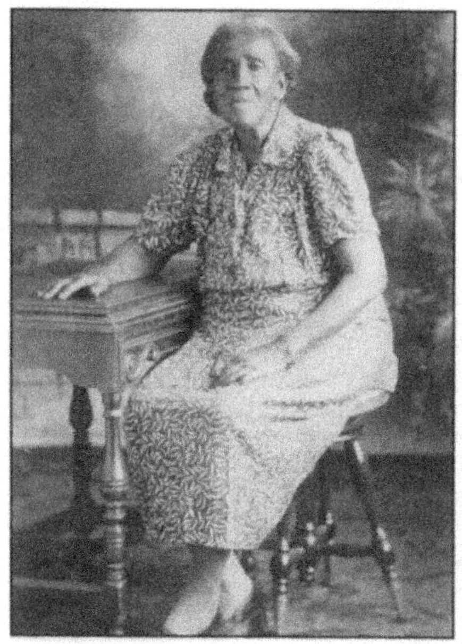

Emma Driver Reid (1852-1962). Courtesy of Fred Allen and Linda Dallas.

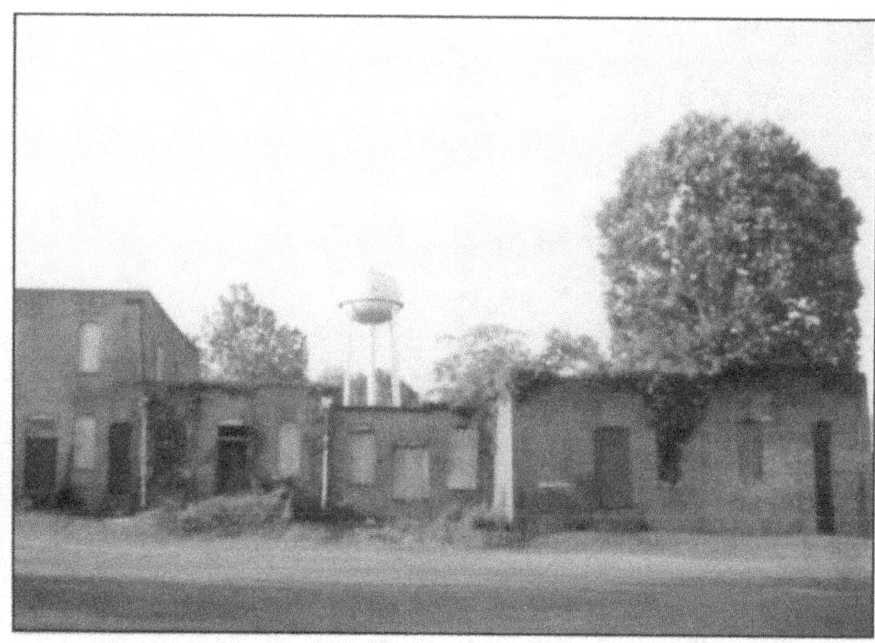

Back of Main Street in Molena, 1989. Courtesy of Stephanie Bradley.

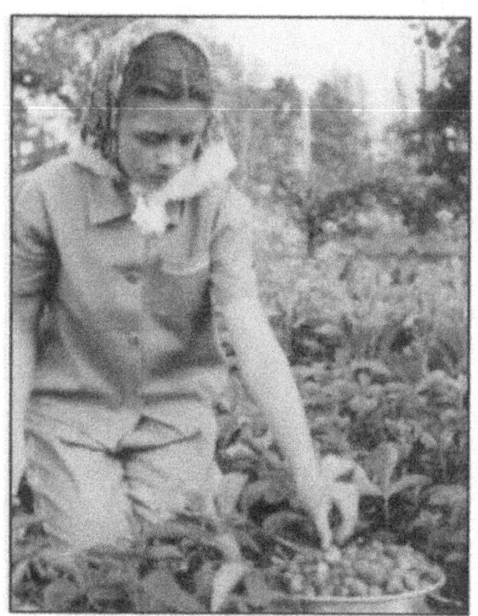

Williaminta Norris picks strawberries from the family garden. Courtesy of Rachel McClelland.

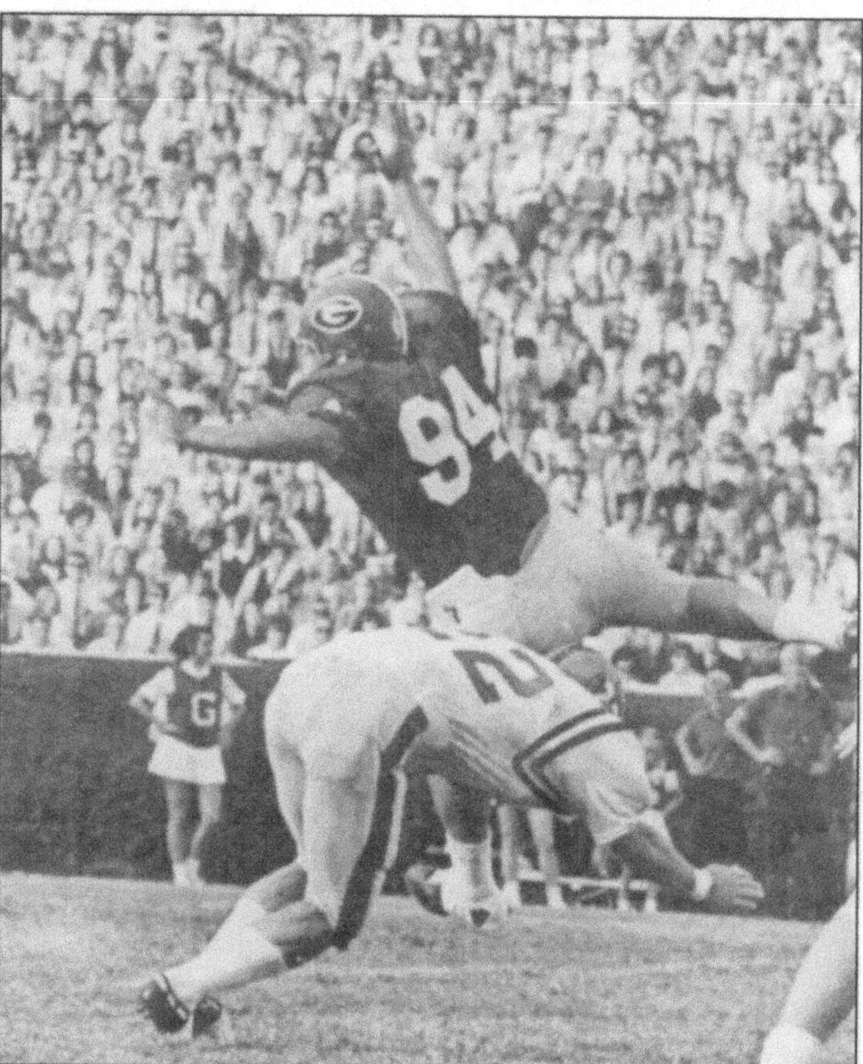

Terry Osbolt, Pike county resident, playing football for Georgia. Courtesy of Terry Osbolt.

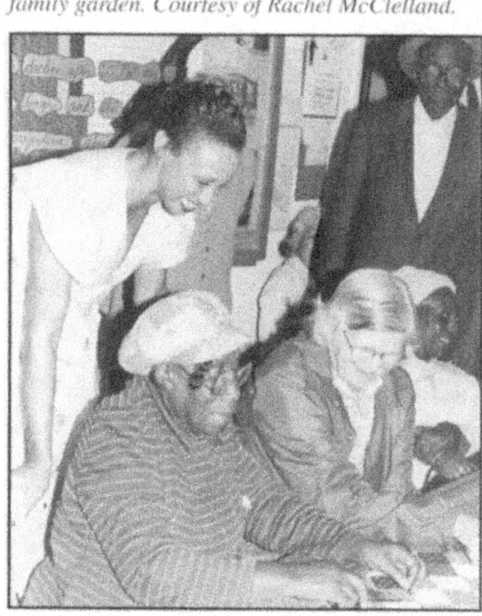

First senior citizens center on Griffin Street in Zebulon, GA. Courtesy of Rachel McClelland.

www.ingramcontent.com/pod-product-compliance
Lightning Source LLC
LaVergne TN
LVHW081252100826
845148LV00009B/1207

* 9 7 8 1 6 8 1 6 2 1 6 8 5 *